MW00995123

WHAT GOOD IS
GRAND STRATEGY?

WHAT GOOD IS GRAND STRATEGY?

POWER AND PURPOSE IN AMERICAN
STATECRAFT FROM HARRY S. TRUMAN
TO GEORGE W. BUSH

HAL BRANDS

CORNELL UNIVERSITY PRESS
Ithaca and London

For Emily, Henry, and Annabelle

First published 2014 by Cornell University Press

Printed in the United States of America

Library of Congress Cataloging-in-Publication Data

Brands, Hal, 1983– author.
    What good is grand strategy? : power and purpose in American statecraft from Harry S. Truman to George W. Bush / Hal Brands.
        pages cm
    Includes bibliographical references and index.
    ISBN 978-0-8014-5246-8 (cloth : alk. paper)
    1. United States—Foreign relations—20th century. 2. United States—Foreign relations—21st century   I. Title.
    E744.B6975 2014
    327.73009'04—dc23   2013027816

Cornell University Press strives to use environmentally responsible suppliers and materials to the fullest extent possible in the publishing of its books. Such materials include vegetable-based, low-VOC inks and acid-free papers that are recycled, totally chlorine-free, or partly composed of nonwood fibers. For further information, visit our website at www.cornellpress.cornell.edu.

Cloth printing   10 9 8 7 6 5 4 3 2 1

Contents

PREFACE

"Grand strategy" is very much in vogue these days. Since the end of the Cold War, politicians and pundits have consistently proclaimed the need for a new American grand strategy, and they have just as consistently flayed their opponents for failing to deliver one. Academics, journalists, and public figures have authored books and articles advocating particular grand strategies for the United States; publications like *Newsweek,* the *New York Times,* and the *Washington Post* carry pieces debating this subject. In 2008, the House Armed Services Committee even held hearings on the topic of "A New Grand Strategy for the United States." Grand strategy has become increasingly prominent on college campuses, too, with elite schools like Yale, Columbia, and Duke all developing programs on the issue. I myself have benefited from this interest: since 2010, I have co-taught Duke's course on American Grand Strategy.

But what exactly is "grand strategy"? Why is it so important and, it would seem, so elusive? Grand strategy, it turns out, is one of the most slippery and widely abused terms in the foreign policy lexicon. The concept is often invoked but less often defined, and those who do define the phrase do so in a variety of different, and often contradictory, ways. Expert observers also disagree on the question of whether grand strategy is a useful concept or simply a quixotic—even pernicious—pursuit. The result of all this is that discussions of grand strategy are often confused or superficial. Too frequently, they muddle or obscure more than they illuminate.

The purpose of this book is to grapple with the meaning, importance, and challenges of grand strategy—in other words, to provide a clearer understanding of what this much-discussed concept is all about. In the chapters that follow, I examine why grand strategy is both an essential and an extremely difficult undertaking, one that is central to effective foreign policy but often eludes even the most talented statesmen. I do so primarily through a historical lens, by analyzing the way in which the presidential administrations of Harry Truman, Richard Nixon and Gerald Ford, Ronald Reagan, and George W. Bush have approached grand strategy and the problems it entails. Drawing on the experiences of these administrations, I also offer suggestions for how current-day American leaders might think about grand strategy as an intellectual and geopolitical pursuit. In this sense, the book is a work of applied history: it aims not simply to study the past for its own sake, but to use history as a way of illuminating the promise and pitfalls of grand strategy as an endeavor.

Accordingly, the remainder of the book proceeds as follows. The introduction frames the inquiry by exploring what grand strategy is, and why it is simultaneously so important and so difficult to do. It raises a fundamental question at the heart of this project: Is grand strategy a worthy pursuit for foreign-policy officials, or is it simply a pipe dream that can never actually be realized? Chapters 1 through 4, which constitute the bulk of the book, constitute a historian's effort to answer this question. Each chapter analyzes the experience of a presidential administration that sought to devise and execute grand strategy at a key moment in modern U.S. foreign policy, and reflects on what these episodes can tell us about the problems and prospects of grand strategy writ large. The conclusion distills these insights and offers a set of guidelines for thinking about grand strategy going forward. For all its limitations, grand strategy is ultimately something that is worth doing—and worth doing well. The guidelines proposed in the conclusion represent a way of approaching that challenge in the crucial years ahead.

An unfortunate aspect of the academic enterprise is that a book's acknowledgments rarely do justice to the debts that authors accumulate along the way. This project is no exception. In completing this book, I have benefited from the assistance of individuals and institutions whose contributions can only insufficiently be acknowledged here. I could not have managed the research without the help of archivists from Washington, D.C., to Palo Alto, California, nor without the financial and intellectual support of the Sanford School of Public Policy at Duke University. Similarly, the Strategic Studies Institute at the Army War College sponsored my initial research on American grand strategy and provided an outlet for an early monograph on the subject; small portions of the introduction, chapters 1 and 2, and the conclusion were published in this monograph, *The Promise and Pitfalls of Grand Strategy* (Strategic Strategy Institute, Army War College, August 2012). At Cornell University Press, Michael McGandy shepherded the book through the publication process and offered incisive comments along the way.

I owe particular gratitude to those scholars whose comments and ideas have influenced—either intentionally or unintentionally—my thinking on the issues at hand. This process started some years ago, when I was fortunate enough to be a student in the Studies in Grand Strategy seminar at

Yale University, run by John Gaddis, Paul Kennedy, and Charles Hill. Subsequent conversations with Barton Bernstein, Adam Grissom, Dick Kohn, Josh Rovner, Jeremi Suri, Kevin Woods, and numerous others helped me develop my views on this subject (though I should add that they will probably disagree with some of the conclusions I have drawn). Williamson Murray, Frank Gavin, Jack Cann, Colin Dueck, and John Deni read all or parts of the manuscript and offered constructive criticism, and John Maurer of the Naval War College invited me to two conferences that helped shape my perspective on teaching and writing about grand strategy.

At Duke, Bruce Kuniholm and Bruce Jentleson were very generous with their time and insights, and my students in the American Grand Strategy seminar each fall often made me look at key issues in different ways. And since arriving at Duke, I have had the good fortune to teach that class in cooperation with Peter Feaver—my frequent intellectual sparring partner, and as good a mentor and friend as any young faculty member could hope for. Last but not least, there are Emily, Henry, and Annabelle—my wonderful family, to whom this book is dedicated.

ABBREVIATIONS AND ACRONYMS

ABM	antiballistic missile
APP	American Presidency Project
CENTCOM	U.S. Central Command
CIA	Central Intelligence Agency
CIA FOIA	CIA Freedom of Information Act Electronic Reading Room
CSCE	Conference on Security and Cooperation in Europe
CWH	*Cold War History*
CWIHP	Cold War International History Project
DDRS	Declassified Documents Reference System
DH	*Diplomatic History*
DOD FOIA	Department of Defense Freedom of Information Act Electronic Reading Room
DOSB	*Department of State Bulletin*
D&S	*Diplomacy & Statecraft*
ERP	European Recovery Program
ESF	Executive Secretariat File
FA	*Foreign Affairs*
FAOHC	Foreign Affairs Oral History Collection
FDCH	Federal Document Clearing House transcript
FNS	Federal News Service transcript
FRUS	*Foreign Relations of the United States* series
FRUS: SAR	*Soviet-American Relations: The Détente Years, 1969–1972*
GFKP	George F. Kennan Papers
GFL	Gerald Ford Presidential Library
HAK	Henry A. Kissinger
Hoover	Archive of Hoover Institution on War, Revolution, and Peace
HOS	Head of State File
HSTL	Harry S. Truman Presidential Library
ICBM	intercontinental ballistic missile
INF	intermediate-range nuclear forces
IRBM	intermediate-range ballistic missile

IS	*International Security*
JAH	*Journal of American History*
JCL	Jimmy Carter Presidential Library
JCS	Joint Chiefs of Staff
JCWS	*Journal of Cold War Studies*
LC	Library of Congress, Manuscript Division
MAD	mutual assured destruction
MemCon	memorandum of conversation
MFN	most favored nation
MIRV	multiple independently targeted reentry vehicle
NARA	National Archives and Records Administration II
NATO	North Atlantic Treaty Organization
NIC	National Intelligence Council
NIE	National Intelligence Estimate
NPM	Nixon Presidential Materials
NSA	National Security Archive
NSC	National Security Council
NSDD	National Security Decision Directive
NSPG	National Security Planning Group
NSS	*National Security Strategy*
NWC	National War College
NYT	*New York Times*
ORHA	Office for Reconstruction and Humanitarian Assistance
PPS	Policy Planning Staff
PPSP	*Policy Planning Staff Papers*
PSF	President's Secretary's Files
PSQ	*Political Science Quarterly*
RG	Record Group
RP	Donald Rumsfeld Papers
RRL	Ronald Reagan Presidential Library
RRRC	Ronald Reagan Radio Commentary
RRSC	Ronald Reagan Subject Collection
SALT	Strategic Arms Limitation Talks/Treaty
SDI	Strategic Defense Initiative
SF	Subject File
SLBM	submarine-launched ballistic missile
SMML	Seeley Mudd Manuscript Library
START	Strategic Arms Reduction Talks/Treaty
TelCon	telephone conversation
WMD	weapons of mass destruction

WP   *Washington Post*
WQ   *Washington Quarterly*
USAID   United States Agency for International Development

Introduction
The Meaning and Challenge of Grand Strategy

Grand strategy is the highest form of statecraft, but it can also be the most perplexing. Reduced to its essence, grand strategy is the intellectual architecture that lends structure to foreign policy; it is the logic that helps states navigate a complex and dangerous world. For precisely this reason, however, the making of grand strategy is invariably a daunting task. Devising a coherent, purposeful approach to international politics is hard enough, given the limits of human wisdom and the chaotic nature of global affairs. Implementing it can be harder still. Good grand strategy may be essential to effective statecraft, but in the eyes of some observers, it is so challenging as to be an illusion.

"The primary purpose of any theory," wrote Carl von Clausewitz, "is to clarify concepts and ideas that have become, as it were, confused and entangled. Not until terms and concepts have been defined can one hope to make any progress in examining the question clearly and simply and expect the reader to share one's views."[1] This maxim, offered by perhaps the greatest theorist of war, offers an appropriate point of departure for a book on grand strategy. Grand strategy is a notoriously slippery concept. The term is often invoked but less often defined; those who do define the phrase do so in many different ways. It is thus useful to begin this volume by explaining my own understanding of grand strategy, so as to clarify the analysis that follows.[2]

What is grand strategy? The term first came into common usage in English following World War I, and it was generally used to signify the integration of all forms of national power to achieve victory in war.[3] The concept grew out of the shortcomings of the traditional definition of "strategy," which was often construed rather narrowly, as the coordination of purely *military* blows to defeat an enemy. "Tactics," Clausewitz wrote, "is the art of using troops in battle; strategy is the art of using battles to win the war."[4] Yet across the expanse of human history, winning wars has required more than simply winning battles. Nations (or other combatant groups) must also isolate their enemies through diplomacy, generate the economic resources to prosecute the conflict, mobilize a political consensus in support of the war, and so on. During the 1920s, analysts like British army officer (and historian) J. F. C. Fuller thus began to employ the term "grand strategy" to describe the synchronizing of both military and nonmilitary activities to subdue an opponent. Grand strategy was "the national fabric upon which the war picture … is woven," he wrote; it entailed "directing all warlike resources towards the winning of the war."[5]

The concept of grand strategy subsequently gained wider currency during the 1940s and 1950s. This was in part because of World War II, the successful conduct of which required the Allies to coordinate diplomatic, economic, political, and military initiatives on a truly global scale. It was also due to the writings of prominent military theorists like Basil Liddell Hart and Edward Mead Earle. These writers disseminated the concept to a larger audience, and they substantially broadened its definition.

Earle, for his part, argued that the task of bringing together all aspects of national power to achieve an important objective was no less imperative in peacetime than in war.[6] Liddell Hart, by contrast, limited his definition of the term to periods of war. Yet he also added a crucial twist to the idea. He asserted that the purpose of grand strategy was not simply to turn all available capabilities toward achieving victory, but also to ensure that the resulting outlay of resources was worth the cost. Defeating an enemy was not an end in and of itself; it was simply the means of securing a better peace for the nation and its people. This distinction was hardly trivial, he believed, because the pursuit of military triumph could easily become so all-consuming that it would ultimately leave even the victorious nation weaker than it had been at the outset of the war. Accordingly, grand strategy "should not only combine the various instruments [of statecraft], but so regulate their use as to avoid damage to the future state of peace—for its security and prosperity." The essential purpose of grand strategy was to achieve equilibrium between means and ends: combining the former to achieve the latter, but also adjusting the latter so as to not to overtax the former. From the perspective of the grand strategist, Liddell Hart argued, a Pyrrhic victory was no victory at all.[7]

Since Liddell Hart's time, definitions of grand strategy have continued to multiply. They have also become more diverse. Most definitions of the term incorporate some version of Liddell Hart's insight that grand strategy involves synchronizing essential goals with limited resources. From here, though, they diverge considerably. Some analysts have extended the realm of grand strategy to encompass business, athletics, and other pursuits; others prefer a narrower concept that concentrates largely or even solely on military affairs. Some observers associate grand strategy with explicit "doctrines" and "national security strategies"; others contend that most grand strategies are more implicit and assumed than formally enunciated. Definitions of grand strategy are thus manifold, as are analyses that invoke the term without defining it.[8]

The fact that there are so many competing conceptions of grand strategy should probably tell us that the concept is subjective and ambiguous enough that it defies any singular definition. The best an analyst can do is offer a definition that is, in the strategic theorist Colin Gray's phrasing, "right enough." That is, the definition "does not have to meet any and every objection, but it must highlight the core of its subject and it must not mislead."[9]

In this book, I define grand strategy as the intellectual architecture that gives form and structure to foreign policy. Leaders who are doing grand strategy are not just reacting to events or handling them on a case-by-case basis. Rather, a grand strategy is a purposeful and coherent set of ideas about what a nation seeks to accomplish in the world, and how it should go about doing so. Grand strategy requires a clear understanding of the nature of the international environment, a country's highest goals and interests within that environment, the primary threats to those goals and interests, and the ways that finite resources can be used to deal with competing challenges and opportunities. From this intellectual calculus flows policy, the various concrete initiatives—diplomacy, the use of force, and others—through which states interact with foreign governments and peoples. At its best, then, a grand strategy represents an integrated scheme of interests, threats, resources, and policies. It is the conceptual framework that helps nations determine where they want to go and how they ought to get there; it is the *theory, or logic, that guides leaders seeking security in a complex and insecure world.*[10]

For the sake of clarity, several aspects of this definition bear further elaboration. The first is that grand strategy is not any one aspect of foreign policy, nor is it foreign policy as a whole. Foreign policy is the sum total of a government's interactions with the outside world, and it is expressed through initiatives ranging from diplomacy to foreign aid to humanitarian relief to the use of military force. Grand strategy, in contrast, is the conceptual logic that ensures that such instruments are employed in ways that maximize the benefits for a nation's core interests. Grand strategy inevitably shapes a nation's foreign policy—and thus its military policy, its diplomacy, and other subsidiary components of foreign policy—but the concepts are not one and the same.

Second, grand strategy provides the crucial link between short-term actions and medium- and long-term goals. As noted above, grand strategy should originate not from mere reactions to day-to-day events, but from a judgment of those enduring interests and priorities that transcend any single crisis or controversy. As Dean Acheson once put it, the task of the grand strategist is "to look ahead, not into the distant future, but beyond the vision of the operating officers caught in the smoke and crises of current battle; far enough ahead to see the emerging form of things to come and outline what should be done to meet or anticipate them."[11] Yet as Acheson's comment implies, grand strategy is not just about setting medium- and long-term goals, but also about determining how to achieve those goals via the day-to-day conduct of foreign policy. In other words, grand strategy involves figuring out how to align today's initiatives with tomorrow's desired end-state—how to get from where one is to where one ultimately wants to be.

Third, as Liddell Hart argued several decades ago, grand strategy is obsessed with the relationship between means and ends, objectives and capabilities. Power is inherently multidimensional: it stems not only from a nation's military might, but also from its economic strength, internal cohesion, ideological appeal, and a variety of other factors. Accordingly, grand strategy involves combining all aspects of national power so as to defeat enemies and accomplish important objectives. Yet nations, even—especially—great powers, exist in a world of limited resources, where capabilities are never sufficient to exploit all opportunities and confront all threats. In these circumstances, grand strategy also requires ruthless prioritization. Leaders must determine which interests are truly vital, which threats and opportunities are most urgent, and they must deploy their resources accordingly. Grand strategy is therefore a discipline of trade-offs: it requires using the full extent of national power when essential matters are at stake, but it also involves conserving and protecting the sources of that power. Means must be integrated to serve great ends, but ends must be selectively defined so as to preserve a nation's means.[12]

Fourth, grand strategy is as much a process as it is any single principle. When Americans think of grand strategy, they often think of terms like "containment," the organizing principle that guided U.S. policy for decades.

But as John Lewis Gaddis has pointed out, containment was not a single, forty-five-year grand strategy but rather a string of several distinct grand strategies that took varying approaches to the overriding problem of taming Soviet power. As circumstances changed and new problems arose, American grand strategy evolved as well.[13]

Such is the case with grand strategy in general. Grand strategy occurs in a world where almost nothing sits still, so the calculations underlying grand strategy must inevitably shift as well. The overall goal of a grand strategy may remain constant, but its various subcomponents—decisions on how best to allocate resources, for instance—should come in for reassessment from time to time. In this sense, grand strategy requires not just a capacity for systematic thinking, but also flexibility and an ability to adapt.

This imperative is particularly relevant in light of a fifth point, which is that grand strategy is an inherently interactive endeavor. Clausewitz wrote that war is not "the action of a living force upon a lifeless mass ... but always the collision of two living forces." Likewise, grand strategy deals with an international system that is characterized by competition and dynamic interaction. States have to contend with living, thinking rivals that seek to control events and have their way, as well as allies and other actors that are wont to pursue interests all their own. Hence, grand strategy both influences and is influenced by the behavior of others. Any competent grand strategist will try to shape his country's interactions in the most advantageous way possible, but his choices will unavoidably be affected by the fact that adversaries as well as allies are trying to do exactly the same thing. This interactive quality adds considerably to the messiness of grand strategy, and to the difficulty of getting it right.[14]

Sixth, its often competitive nature notwithstanding, grand strategy operates no less in peacetime than wartime. There is certainly a case to be made that the logic of statecraft during war differs from that during peace.[15] Similarly, the need for strategic coherence is most painfully evident in war, when threats are most severe, interests most imperiled, and resources most obviously stretched. Yet the key premises of grand strategy—that states must link long-term interests to short- and medium-term policies, that they must prioritize among competing threats and often-contradictory goals, that they must recognize and exploit the multidimensional nature of power—apply no less to the realm of peace than the realm of war. Indeed, it is frequently the effectiveness of a nation's grand strategy in peacetime that determines how well prepared it will be to meet the challenge of war.

A seventh point has to do with the issue of whether grand strategy must be formally enunciated and defined to qualify as such. The answer, in a word, is no. While grand strategy certainly requires a purposeful approach to policy, it does not necessarily have to be formalized, detailed, or labeled as grand strategy in official speeches and documents. After all, the very concept of "grand strategy" is a relatively recent one, and the notion that states should explicitly articulate their grand strategies— whether in public or in private—arose more recently still.[16] (Even in the present era, there are plenty of good reasons why strategy-conscious governments might *not* want to so forthrightly declare their essential objectives and methods.) More broadly, while some leaders do deliberately set out to construct, piece by piece, a logical chain running from interests to threats to policies, statecraft is often made in a more iterative or idiosyncratic manner. That being the case, the real criterion for grand strategy is not whether there exists a single document fully outlining that grand strategy from the outset; it is whether there exists a coherent body of thought and action geared toward the accomplishment of important long-term aims.

In fact, even when a country's leaders decline to lay out a formal grand strategy, they engage in grand strategic decision making nonetheless. All countries must make trade-offs between competing interests and priorities. All leaders—consciously or unconsciously, on the basis of reasoned analysis, pure ideology or intuition, or something in between—make judgments about which goals are most important, which threats most deserving of attention, and how resources should be deployed to meet them. These sort of grand strategic choices are inherent in the process of governing, and so the real question is how intelligently a country's leaders will make them.[17] Or as Trotsky might have put it, you may not be interested in grand strategy, but grand strategy is interested in you.[18]

But if all states thus have to grapple with grand strategic challenges, not all of them do so in particularly effective fashion. The history of international affairs is replete with examples of leaders who have fallen short in this regard—those who confused core with secondary interests, pursued contradictory strategic ideas and principles, failed to ration resources or combine them synergistically, or fundamentally misjudged the effects of action or inaction. "Those who have developed successful grand strategies in the past have been much the exception," writes historian Williamson Murray. "Wars begun with little or no thought of their consequences, assumptions unchallenged in the face of harsh reality, the possibility of second- or third-order effects casually dismissed with the shrug of a shoulder, and idle ignorance substituted for serious consideration have bedeviled the actions of statesmen and generals over the course of recorded history."[19] This brings us to two additional points about grand strategy: that it is essential to effective statecraft, but also immensely challenging to pull off.

Why is grand strategy so important? To devotees of the concept, the relationship between grand strategy and good policy often seems self-evident. For those not so well acquainted with, or less enamored of the idea, the relevance of grand strategy can seem no less nebulous than its definition. Contrary to what is often assumed, this latter group does not consist merely of naïfs and pacifists. The idea that there is an overriding logic that governs all aspects of statecraft has come in for criticism among hardened soldiers and politicians as well. "In the case of tactical victory, strategy submits," argued the Prussian chief of staff Helmuth von Moltke the Elder—better simply to worry about winning the battle than to obsess about the relationship between that battle and larger political ends.[20] Few modern statesmen have derided grand strategy so bluntly, but many—including at least one recent U.S. president—have echoed this criticism in one way or another.[21]

Notwithstanding these objections, a coherent grand strategy is fundamental to competent statecraft, for several reasons. The first has to do with the inevitable gap between resources and interests. When it comes to foreign policy, there is never enough of anything to go around. Money, troops, intelligence assets, time, and other finite resources are always insufficient to neutralize every threat and exploit every opportunity. Nor are great powers exempt from this dilemma. Expanding interests come with new opportunities and new threats, and even the most powerful countries the modern world has ever seen—the British Empire at its peak, the United States in the wake of World War II—frequently struggled to meet the multitude of demands imposed on them. Overstretch is a constant peril. States that try to do too much will limit their ability to do any one thing well, they will leave themselves vulnerable to the actions of clever adversaries, and they will deplete the economic power that gave them influence in the first place. The prioritizing function of grand strategy is thus essential. If statesmen are to avoid strategic exhaustion, exposure, and eventual national decline, they must maintain a firm conception of core interests and deploy their resources accordingly.[22]

Second, even if great powers can avoid this resource dilemma, the diversity of their interests risks exposing them to distraction and confusion. Great powers—superpowers especially—often have interests in nearly every region of the world, and find themselves dealing with dozens of foreign policy issues from day to day. Even if it were possible to address all of these issues case by case, the various solutions would inevitably come into conflict with one another. For governments lacking a clear view of core goals and priorities, there is thus a danger that policy will wander according to the crisis or fashion of the moment. Statecraft will go in multiple, contradictory directions; leaders will succumb to "theateritis"—the tendency to neglect the broader geopolitical significance of a given problem.[23] A coherent grand strategy, by contrast, offers what one scholar calls a "conceptual center of gravity," an ability to keep fundamental interests squarely in view in dealing with a range of complex and competing demands.[24] If military strategy is what guides the use of mass violence, then grand strategy is what guides and imparts order to an expansive foreign policy.[25]

These first two points are closely related to a third, which is that grand strategy provides statesmen with the "heuristic power" needed to address the day-to-day demands of global diplomacy.[26] The nature of foreign policy is that it confronts statesmen with challenges for which they have not adequately prepared, and which in some cases they have not even considered. In many cases, these challenges must be addressed in days or hours rather than weeks or months—in other words, there is no opportunity for prolonged reflection on all aspects of the matter. "The tragic aspect of policy-making," remarked Henry Kissinger in 1970, "is that when your scope for action is greatest, the knowledge on which you can base this action is always at a minimum. When your knowledge is greatest, the scope for action has often disappeared."[27] No grand strategy can provide leaders with ready-made solutions to these crises, but performing the intellectual tasks involved in doing grand strategy—defining and prioritizing goals and threats, understanding the extent and limits of a state's capabilities—can provide statesmen with the basic conceptual backdrop against which to formulate an appropriate response. In this sense, the function of grand strategy approximates what Clausewitz wrote about the uses of theory in war:

> Theory cannot equip the mind with formulas for solving problems, nor can it mark the narrow path on which the sole solution is supposed to lie by planting a hedge of principles on either side. But it can give the mind insight into the great mass of phenomena and of their relationships, then leave it free to rise into the higher realms of action. There the mind can use its innate talents to capacity, combining them all so as to seize on what is *right* and *true* as though this were a single idea formed by their concentrated pressure—as though it were a response to the immediate challenge rather than a product of thought.[28]

Fourth, grand strategy is crucial because of the competitive nature of international politics. If the world were entirely peaceful and cooperative, nations would not have much need for grand strategy. But this is not the case, and nations—particularly great powers—have enemies that seek to engage them in dangerous and disruptive ways. Grand strategy cannot allow countries to transcend such challenges, but it can permit them to deal more purposefully with the threats they face. A well-designed grand strategy can help a country leverage its own strengths while exploiting an opponent's weaknesses, and it can provide the sustained focus that is necessary to succeed in medium- and long-term rivalries. Not all grand strategies have to be centered on a single, defining competition, but when such a competition exists, an effective grand strategy becomes all the more valuable.

Fifth, and perhaps most important, grand strategy is crucial because it is so difficult to compensate for flaws and shortcomings therein. Effective statecraft is not just a product of competent grand strategy: it requires efficient execution by the soldiers and diplomats who occupy the lower levels of foreign policy as well. That said, states with a well-crafted grand strategy may be able to overcome mistakes in the daily conduct of military or diplomatic policy, while those with a fundamentally deficient grand strategy will be hard pressed to preserve their core interests over the long term. If statecraft flows from misperceptions of fundamental interests or flawed calculations of what a state's resources will allow, or if diplomacy and military force are allowed to proceed without guidance from these higher-level assessments, even brilliant tactical performance may ultimately be for naught.[29]

A prominent example of this phenomenon is Wilhelmine Germany. Before and during World War I, Germany pursued a number of policies that made sense in narrow tactical or operational terms, but that neglected larger grand strategic considerations and eventually proved ruinous to the higher interests of the state. The construction of a fleet of blue-water battleships reconciled domestic factions and made Germany a leading sea power, but also ensured the enmity of the one nation—Great Britain—whose naval expenditures Berlin could not hope to match.[30] The effort to force a decisive battle in the west at the outset of World War I was designed to meet the challenge of a two-front conflict with France and Russia, but by requiring German troops to violate Belgian neutrality it ensured that a wavering Great Britain would enter the struggle as well. The decision to resume unrestricted submarine warfare in early 1917 was meant to resolve this dilemma by starving Britain into submission, but it was also virtually certain to bring the United States into the conflict. In each case, the imperatives of prudent grand strategy—the need to minimize rather than maximize the number of one's enemies, the need to ensure that weapons acquisition and military strategy conformed to the larger purposes of the state—ceded pride of place to lower-level considerations. The consequences were ultimately disastrous.[31]

The Kaiser's Germany may be the most commonly invoked example of the perils of a flawed grand strategy, but it is hardly the only one. In the 1970s, Kremlin officials were so intoxicated with their recent run of successes vis-à-vis the United States that they lost sight of the rapidly approaching limits of Soviet power. The result was a series of initiatives—the deployment of SS-20 missiles to threaten Western Europe, the invasion of Afghanistan, and others—that invited overstretch and provoked the United States into a high-tech military buildup that the Soviet economy was poorly positioned to match.[32] Nor was the United States immune to the consequences of grand strategic failure during the Cold War. Washington's misadventure in Vietnam is often attributed to flawed military doctrine and tactics, but it resulted, first and foremost, from the fundamental grand strategic miscalculation that America's vital interests were served by engaging in a prolonged, large-scale conflict in a country of minimal geopolitical significance.

What all this indicates is that while grand strategy is not the only determinant of successful policy, it is a highly important one. Where grand strategy has been flawed or neglected, statecraft has frequently been ineffective or even counterproductive. Yet if a coherent grand strategy is essential to good policy, devising and deploying such a grand strategy can be exceedingly hard to do.

In many ways, the challenge of grand strategy flows directly from its meaning. As defined in this book, grand strategy is an inherently difficult endeavor that will test the abilities of even the capacious leader. It requires a holistic view of interests, threats, and resources, as well as an understanding of the multidimensional yet finite nature of power. It demands the ability to make sense of a multitude of complicated and confusing international events, and an awareness of how a country's responses to these events may complement or contradict one another. It necessitates the vision to link today's policies to a country's highest and most enduring interests, and the willingness to make hard decisions about priorities and trade-offs. In sum, grand strategy is not just a struggle to defeat one enemy or another; it is also a contest against the complexity, disorder, and distraction that inevitably clutter the global scene. Accordingly, it requires a supple mind that can reconcile multiple, often competing demands; it also requires a farseeing mind that can deal with the crisis or contingency at hand while simultaneously looking beyond it. Grand strategy is thus bound to be an exacting task, one that is full of potential pitfalls.

Indeed, if grand strategy is an important pursuit, it can also be a dangerous one. Grand strategy has been referred to as an ecological discipline, in that it calls for a holistic perspective on world affairs. Yet it is also a reductionist discipline, because it impels leaders to impose a sense of order on a stubbornly complex international environment. Officials who are doing grand strategy do not view world events purely on their own terms; they interpret these events through the prism of the priorities they have set and the chief threats they perceive. As a result, a full understanding of the richness of any particular issue becomes less important than an intuitive grasp of its implications for a nation's core international mission.

This tendency is unavoidable and even necessary: decision makers with limited time and intellectual capacity must have some way of rendering the global scene more legible to themselves and the domestic audience. Yet this approach can also be distinctly pernicious, because the world is just too messy to be reduced to any single theory. There is a fine line between clarity and dogmatism, between a useful heuristic and a distorting myopia. In fact, as U.S. officials often found during the Cold War, too intense a focus on any particular principle, enemy, or strategy can easily lock a country into inflexible interpretations of events that are actually complicated and idiosyncratic. This tension between coherence and rigidity is a constant in the making of grand strategy, and it is a dynamic that is present in even the best of circumstances.[33]

Unfortunately, grand strategy is rarely made in the best of circumstances. Rather, it must be forged by officials who operate under significant constraints and pressures, and who are prone to the same cognitive fallibilities that plague all humans. Like all people, statesmen operate in a world of bounded rather than perfect rationality.[34] Their decisions are shaped by the limits of their own intelligence, as well as by the potent mixture of values, experience, emotions, and ideology that makes up a person's worldview. Moreover, they make these choices in a chaotic and uncertain environment, where crucial information is often unknown or unknowable, where conditions can change rapidly and unexpectedly, where foes and spoilers lurk at every turn, and where there is rarely enough time for sustained reflection on all the relevant issues.[35] "The greater our involvement in the world, the more the railroad train which always seems to be coming down the track toward you is likely to hit you," Kissinger once remarked. "And while the chance that the train will hit you is growing enormously, your ability to deal thoughtfully with issues is of course declining."[36] Ideally, a good grand strategy will prepare policy makers to deal with these challenges. It may be just as likely, however, that events will require existing concepts to be reexamined, if not junked altogether.

Simply devising a coherent grand strategy is thus challenging enough for most policy makers. Unfortunately, conception is only half the battle. "The best ideas in the world are of no benefit unless they are carried out," explained Harry Truman: even a flawless plan can be bankrupted by failures of implementation.[37] This is particularly true of the subject at hand, as there are numerous stumbling blocks to the enactment of a successful grand strategy.

One such obstacle is the bureaucratic system through which policy must be executed. Grand strategy may, in some cases, be conceived by a small group of high-level officials, or even by a single official, but implementation flows downward and outward, through the agencies that are responsible for the daily workings of foreign policy. This fact has often been a source of grief to grand strategists, for while bureaucracies are designed to provide expertise and routinization—both of which can be quite helpful to statecraft—they can also be ponderous, resistant to change, and hostile to policies that seem detrimental to their organizational interests. As a result, what is desired by a policy maker and what is implemented by the bureaucracy can be two different things. Conflict *between* different bureaucracies can similarly hinder the execution of policy. Finally, even if the bureaucracy seeks to implement a leader's policy faithfully, the process of transmission between the high-level officials who craft a grand strategic concept and the diplomats, soldiers, and other lower-level individuals who carry it out brings with it the risk of distortion. "Even if we had the most excellent conceptual foundation for an American foreign policy and the greatest mastery of diplomatic method in our external relations," George Kennan once argued, "I feel we would still find ourselves seriously hampered ... by the cumbersomeness of our governmental machinery."[38]

Then there is the nature of the U.S. political system. Contrary to what is sometimes thought, it is far too simplistic to see democracy solely as an impediment to purposeful statecraft. Walter Russell Mead has compellingly argued that democracy is good for the long-term health of foreign policy, because it provides mechanisms for aggregating interests and correcting flawed concepts.[39] Similarly, democracy and grand strategy must always go together in the American system, for the simple reason that the highest purpose of the latter should be the preservation of the former.

But even so, the push and pull of democratic politics is very much a mixed blessing when it comes to grand strategy. The diversity of a large nation like the United States can make it difficult to identify a single "national interest."[40] And even if such an interest is defined, the routine features of democratic rule—partisan wrangling, legislative-executive discord, the state of public opinion—can throw the entire process off kilter. Democratic governance may reward statesmen for placing acceptability above effectiveness, and it may punish them for making more enlightened choices. Likewise, it may prevent leaders from attaining the resources or the freedom of action that they need, or undermine the unity of effort and steadiness of purpose that good grand strategy requires. To the extent that a successful grand strategy involves tactics like secrecy and surprise, it may prove even more challenging to execute in a system that appropriately prizes openness and transparency. None of this is to say that authoritarian regimes necessarily do grand strategy any better than democracies, but it is to note that democratic politics can introduce a variety of confounding variables into statecraft.[41]

This is particularly the case because grand strategy and democratic politics often operate according to very different time horizons. Grand strategy generally requires a degree of constancy, because important international objectives can usually only be achieved over a fairly significant period of time. Yet the American political system is driven by two- and four-year election cycles, and by a news cycle that is far less patient than that. Consequently, there are built-in temptations to privilege the immediate over the long-range, and to avoid—or waver in implementing—those policies that might come at a near-term electoral cost. To be sure, the popular thing can also be the geopolitically prudent thing, and so the dictates of good policy and good politics are not always at odds. But when they are, this problem of clashing time horizons can make responsible grand strategy all the harder to sustain.

Internal obstacles aside, grand strategy must also be implemented in the same tumultuous global environment in which it is formulated. Rarely do events conform to the expectations of even experts on international affairs. More commonly, implementation of policy will be buffeted by a range of surprising and unwelcome developments. A country's actions can be frustrated by those of its enemies or even its allies; they can also produce blowback in the form of unpredicted (and perhaps unpredictable) third- or fourth-order reactions. In these circumstances, there is almost never a straight line from theory to reality. Clausewitzian friction is a constant; what the Prussian officer wrote about war is no less applicable to grand strategy:

> Everything in war is very simple, but the simplest thing is difficult. The difficulties accumulate and end by producing a kind of friction that is inconceivable unless one has experienced war.... Countless minor incidents—the kind you can never really foresee—combine to lower the general level of performance, so that one always falls far short of the intended goal.[42]

At best, then, the doing of grand strategy is a highly daunting task that requires flexibility, resilience, and a capacity for adaptation. The end point of a grand strategy may remain constant, but the route between here and there will have to be adjusted as resistance accumulates, adversaries react, and new threats and opportunities arise. Doing grand strategy is therefore an iterative process, one that involves processing feedback and correcting course in consequence. As such, it places a premium not just on a willingness to look ahead, but on the judgment and wisdom needed to determine whether perseverance, adaptation, or some mixture of the two constitutes the proper route forward.

Yet this is undeniably a tall order—so tall, in fact, that any number of observers have questioned whether consistent, purposeful grand strategy is even possible. "The greatest masters of statecraft," wrote British historian A. J. P. Taylor, "are those who do not know what they are doing."[43] Looking more specifically at the United States, Edward Luttwak—no opponent of the idea of grand strategy—argued that the American people and their leaders were incapable of practicing it. "The record of recent years," he wrote of the post-Vietnam period, "shows quite conclusively that there was no true desire for the discipline and consistency of a grand strategy."[44] Likewise, Walter McDougall has asked whether the federal government can "plan, coordinate, and execute grand strategy with sufficient competence to secure the nation and defend its vital interests."[45] In his book on U.S. policy toward the Persian Gulf, political scientist Steve Yetiv answers this question in the negative. He argues that the U.S. approach to the region has long reflected no overriding grand strategic concept. It has stemmed, rather, from unavoidably ad hoc reactions to unexpected events. "Randomness all too often parades as design," he writes. "It may become a historical truism that great powers start with grand ideas but end up with a high dose of reality. Alas, they may strike up notions of grand strategy and get struck down by the caprice endemic in the human condition."[46]

This type of lament is not the peculiar province of scholars and other "outsiders." It can also be found in some unexpected places, even at the highest levels of government. In the late 1970s, Carter administration officials responsible for just one aspect of grand strategy—policy toward Latin America—concluded that the complexities of that region precluded the application of any grand design. "The best overall policy may be a non-policy," argued Deputy Secretary of State Warren Christopher.[47] Looking at the world more broadly, Secretary of State Cyrus Vance came to the same conclusion. "Policy is baloney," he said—better to simply deal with events case by case.[48]

In recent decades, this sentiment has even been present in the Oval Office. In the early 1990s, President Bill Clinton explicitly rejected the notion that grand strategy was a useful concept. Clinton, recalls adviser Strobe Talbott, had been reading biographies of Roosevelt and Truman that convinced him that neither had grand strategies for how to exert American leadership against the global threats posed by Hitler and Stalin. Rather, they had "powerful instincts about what had to be done, and they just made it up as they went along." Strategic coherence, he said, was largely imposed after the fact by scholars, memoirists and "the chattering classes."[49]

In Clinton's eyes, grand strategy was not simply difficult; it was altogether an illusion.

Was Clinton correct? Is it reasonable to expect American leaders to design and implement a successful grand strategy amid the crosscurrents generated by bureaucratic wrangling, domestic politics, and world affairs? Or is the task so difficult as to be quixotic or even counterproductive? Put another way, is grand strategy a helpful concept, and a good grand strategy the goal to which responsible leaders should aspire? Or, as Clinton believed, is grand strategy simply a pipe dream?

The remainder of this book seeks to answer these questions by analyzing the statecraft of four presidential administrations of the post–World War II period: those of Harry Truman during the early Cold War, Richard Nixon and Gerald Ford two decades later,[50] Ronald Reagan during the 1980s, and George W. Bush in the years following the terrorist attacks of September 11, 2001. Each of these administrations governed at a key inflection point in modern American foreign policy; each, in its own way, made a determined effort to do grand strategy. By understanding the ways that these presidents and their advisers approached this challenge, and evaluating the successes and failures that followed, we can gain a greater appreciation not only of their own qualities as leaders, but also of the problems and prospects of grand strategy writ large.

Any selection of case studies poses problems of inclusion and omission, and this book is no different. Scholars interested in American grand strategy might easily point to other cases that deserve analysis—the administrations of Dwight Eisenhower and Franklin Roosevelt in the twentieth century, for instance, or the statecraft of John Quincy Adams or Abraham Lincoln in the nineteenth. In this book, however, I have chosen to focus on cases from the post–World War II period: the era in which U.S. foreign policy became fully and consistently global in scope, and in which the foreign policy, defense, and intelligence bureaucracies began to take on something approximating their current size and form. More importantly, I have opted to take an illustrative rather than an exhaustive look at the problem under consideration. There is just no way to write a modestly sized book that examines all postwar American presidents who sought to do grand strategy, so it is necessary to focus on a few administrations that did so at important moments in the history of this period. The cases I selected are not the only ones that meet these criteria, but as I think the chapters that follow show, they arguably meet them as well as any others. And in any event, while focusing on a small number of administrations that grappled with grand strategy may not provide conclusive answers to the questions posed above, it should be sufficient to support an informed analysis of the subject.

There is, of course, a limit to what the past can teach us about meeting the challenges of the present and future, and historical analogies or "lessons" can mislead as much as they inform. The point of this work is therefore not to argue that successful grand strategies can be ripped from their historical context, or to use the past as a way of strip-mining answers to contemporary policy problems. Instead, the purpose of this project is simultaneously broader and less ambitious: it is to use these cases as a way of asking what type of challenges the leader concerned with grand strategy is likely to encounter, to gain a general sense of how well grand strategy equips leaders for meeting the dilemmas of foreign policy, and thereby to offer some tentative thoughts on the utility of grand strategy as a pursuit for American officials. The starting point for that inquiry is a look at the statecraft of the Truman administration as it addressed the dangers and opportunities of the early Cold War.

CHAPTER 1

The Golden Age Revisited

The Truman Administration and the Evolution of Containment

The Truman years are often thought of as the golden age of American grand strategy, a time when farseeing officials laid down lasting policies for containing Soviet power and stabilizing the global order. Dean Acheson famously titled his account of these years *Present at the Creation,* while Clark Clifford, another of Truman's advisers, later opined that "we saved Europe and we saved the world."[1] Since the end of the Cold War, pundits and policy makers have similarly described the Truman era as a time of unmatched grand strategic vision and innovation, and invoked it as a model for present-day foreign policy. The search for a new grand strategy in the early 1990s was commonly referred to as the "Kennan sweepstakes"; calls for a concept as clear and enduring as containment have been ubiquitous ever sense. "The Truman team's strategy marked the golden age of U.S. foreign policy," wrote former Council on Foreign Relations president Leslie Gelb in 2009, "as glorious in our history as the founding fathers' creation of the Constitution."[2]

This chapter revisits Truman-era grand strategy, examining the relationship between planning and policy, goals and tactics, and means and ends during the early Cold War. As this analysis makes clear, the Truman years were certainly a time of great purpose and accomplishment. As the Cold War unfolded, Truman and his advisers grasped that containment represented a desirable middle ground between appeasement and war, that containing

Soviet power meant maintaining a favorable geopolitical balance, and that maintaining that balance primarily meant securing and rehabilitating the key industrial regions of Western Europe and Northeast Asia. The administration placed these insights at the heart of its grand strategy, and gradually translated them into the specific policies—the Marshall Plan and the North Atlantic Treaty Organization (NATO), the revival of Japan and West Germany, the eventual buildup of Western military strength during the Korean War—that harnessed America's great power in the service of these worthy ends. By the time the administration left office in 1953, it had largely stabilized the Western world and created "situations of strength" that would redound to American benefit for years to come. This, as Melvyn Leffler has argued, was Truman's chief grand strategic legacy, and it is one that is eminently worthy of admiration.[3]

Yet the "golden age" tag can also be misleading, for it obscures just how messy and vexatious a process Truman-era grand strategy could be. Containment was not a program that took shape all at once; it was a concept that had to be developed, refined, and adjusted amid a seemingly ceaseless flow of events. Although the administration's basic goals and geographical priorities remained largely constant from 1947–48 onward, its tactics evolved considerably as the period went on. "Any policy must rest on principles," Kennan himself acknowledged, "but its application must be in a constant state of flux."[4] And while Truman's team was generally successful in blending tactical flexibility with strategic vision, the evolution of containment nonetheless occasioned a number of potent dilemmas—about the appropriate level of military spending, the proper extent of U.S. commitments, the relationship between rhetoric and policy, and other issues—that the administration was never able to resolve. In the end, the Truman era testified not just to the possibilities of grand strategy, but to the inherent complexity and limits as well.

The basic grand strategic problem of the Cold War flowed directly from the hot war that preceded it. World War II transformed America's geopolitical position. The United States emerged from that conflict with half of the world's manufacturing capacity and an economy roughly five times larger than its nearest competitors. The U.S. military position was no less commanding. America accounted for nearly *three-quarters* of world military spending in 1945, and it alone possessed the atomic bomb, an air force with global striking power, and a navy that outclassed all of its peers combined. In 1941, Henry Luce had predicted the dawning of an "American Century," but even he could not have foretold the extent of American power at the end of World War II.[5]

In other ways, however, the war left a deeply unsettling legacy. The attack on Pearl Harbor in 1941 had demonstrated that enemies could reach across the oceans to strike the United States at home, and advances in airpower and missile technology raised the prospect of even more devastating attacks in the future. More broadly, the entire experience of the 1930s and 1940s seemed to show that aggressive authoritarian regimes had to be confronted before it was too late, and that global economic health and peace were inextricably intertwined. It would not be enough, then, to safeguard the Western Hemisphere once the war was done; the United States would henceforth have to define its security in global terms. "We are now concerned with the peace of the entire world," said Army Chief of Staff George Marshall.[6]

During and after World War II, American officials were therefore determined to put the nation's power to good use. The Roosevelt and Truman administrations worked to create an open, liberal economic order that could prevent another slide into depression and war, and an international organization—the United Nations—that might be used to confront aggressors. More unilaterally, military planners emphasized the need for assured access to vital raw materials and resources, and for an enlarged "strategic frontier" composed of military bases from which American forces could project power and interdict approaching enemies. Above all, they argued that the United States must prevent any unfriendly country from dominating the Eurasian landmass. This vast area contained immense economic and industrial capabilities, and if any rival controlled these assets, it could generate military power that might render the American homeland insecure. In any future conflict, wrote military officials in 1947, "We must have the support of some of the countries of the Old World unless our military strength is to be overshadowed by that of our enemies."[7]

This was an expansive conception of America's postwar interests. The problem, however, was that World War II also occasioned just those developments that seemed likely to imperil this vision. The war left much of Europe and Asia devastated militarily, economically, and politically, shattering the international balance of power and raising the specter of upheaval and even revolution from France to China and beyond. The conflict virtually bankrupted Great Britain, leaving it unable to play its traditional role as global stabilizer. Additionally, World War II undermined the colonial order throughout the developing regions, setting off waves of nationalist ferment and radicalism in points from the Korean peninsula to the Middle East. The world was faced with "social *disintegration,* political *disintegration,* the loss of faith by people in leaders who have led them in the past, and a great deal of economic *disintegration,*" warned Acting Secretary of State Dean Acheson in 1945.[8]

Looming amid this instability was the Soviet Union, a brutal tyranny with a sharp ideological hostility to the West. World War II had already brought the Red Army deep into Europe and parts of the Middle East and Asia as well, and the postwar upheaval threatened to carry Soviet influence—ideological, political, perhaps even military—much farther still. "Russia will emerge from the present conflict as by far the strongest nation in Europe and Asia—strong enough, if the United States should stand aside, to dominate Europe and at the same time to establish her hegemony over Asia," predicted the Office of Strategic Services in April 1945.[9] Whether Joseph Stalin harbored such grandiose ambitions remained uncertain, but what was clear was that the natural geopolitical barriers to Soviet expansionism had largely been destroyed. Having just faced one totalitarian challenge to the international system, the United States and the Western world now had to reckon with the possibility of another.

Wartime planning notwithstanding, this challenge was not one for which American officials were especially well prepared. As noted above, U.S. military officials had certainly given a great deal of thought to the *general* requirements of postwar security. Yet the top levels of the Roosevelt administration—notably the president himself—had not developed any systematic approach to a possible competition with the Soviet Union *specifically*. In reality, many of Roosevelt's wartime policies were more likely to undercut such a program than advance it. The president was more concerned about the evils of colonialism than the probable advance of communism, and he often worried that London and Paris—not Moscow—would pose the greatest obstacles to a harmonious international system. Nor did Roosevelt have a meaningful plan for filling the power vacuum that was sure to emerge in Europe. He was willing to leave Germany economically prostrate, and he resisted British requests for a postwar strategic commitment to the continent. For all the virtues of Roosevelt's wartime leadership, his preparation for postwar diplomacy remained remarkably superficial.[10]

This shortcoming might not have been so problematic had Washington and Moscow managed to sustain a productive relationship after the fighting ended. Roosevelt had staked his wartime diplomacy on the premise that Stalin could be integrated into a peaceful world community, and Harry Truman—his occasionally confrontational rhetoric aside—initially believed the same thing. To be sure, Truman and his aides hardly overlooked U.S. interests, and in mid- and late 1945 they sought to make Stalin more pliable through the use of sticks—such as the power implicit in the atomic monopoly—as well as carrots like the promise of a postwar loan. Yet the assumption remained that superpower cooperation was possible. Stalin, Truman remarked, "was a fine man who wanted to do the right thing."[11]

By early 1946, however, Truman's views had changed. In the months prior, Stalin had installed subservient governments in parts of Eastern Europe, pushed for territorial concessions from Turkey, and sought Kremlin trustee-ships over former Italian colonies in the Mediterranean. Soviet troops lin-gered in Iran and Manchuria, raising fears that Stalin desired these territories as well. U.S. officials interpreted these actions as threats to the open global order they envisioned, and as troubling precedents in a world where there were few natural checks on Kremlin power. For their part, the Soviets felt threatened by America's massive economic and military power, and by its objections to what Stalin saw as Moscow's legitimate security requirements. When all this was added to the inevitable ideological tensions, the result was a series of bilateral disputes and a downward spiral in the relationship. "Unless Russia is faced with an iron first and strong language another war is in the making," Truman wrote in January 1946. "I do not think we should play compromise any longer."[12]

The incipient Cold War mind-set was best expressed in George Kennan's "Long Telegram" from Moscow in February. The Soviets, Kennan argued, were incapable of long-term cooperation with the West. Driven by traditional Russian insecurity, Marxist-Leninist ideology, and the need to legitimize ruthless repression at home, they viewed the outside world as implacably hostile and were determined to "seek security only in patient but deadly struggle for total destruction of rival power." "We have here," he wrote, "a political force committed fanatically to the belief that with U.S. there can be no permanent *modus vivendi,* that it is desirable and necessary that the internal harmony of our society be disrupted, our traditional way of life be destroyed, the international authority of our state be broken, if Soviet power is to be secure." Moscow would work ceaselessly to subvert and enfeeble the capital-ist world; the only answer was an equally determined response. Soviet power was "impervious to logic of reason," Kennan wrote, but "highly sensitive to logic of force. For this reason it can easily withdraw—and usually does when strong resistance is encountered at any point."[13]

Kennan's Long Telegram, and his subsequent "X Article," were immensely influential documents. They helped define American views of the Soviet threat, and they laid out the intellectual premises for a strong but measured response. The Kremlin was determined to destroy its rivals and achieve a dominant world position, Kennan argued, but it was in no hurry to do so. Badly weakened by the war, and conscious of America's superior overall power, the Soviets would retreat when met with determined resistance. Out-right military conflict could therefore be avoided; it should be possible to check Soviet advances through "a policy of firm containment, designed to confront the Russians with unalterable counter-force at every point where they show signs of encroaching upon the interests of a peaceful and stable world." Over the long term, such a policy would do more than just stymie the threat. It would weaken the Soviet system, discredit its leaders and dogma, and thereby bring about "either the breakup or the gradual mellowing of Soviet power."[14]

Scholars still debate whether Kennan's writings adequately captured the complexities of the Soviet worldview, but there is little question that his analysis contained real geopolitical insight. Kennan was fully attuned to the frailties of the Soviet system, particularly its economic backwardness and its nonconsensual, totalitarian nature. He understood that the United States was the stronger party in the unfolding strategic competition, and that if it acted wisely it could eventually turn Moscow's own weaknesses against it. Above all, he saw that there was no need for rash or precipitate action, and that a combination of patience, prudence, and firmness would be crucial in the years ahead. Here, in very broad terms, were the central intellectual tenets of U.S. policy over the next four decades. As Henry Kissinger later put it, Kennan "came as close to authoring the diplomatic doctrine of his era as any diplomat in our history."[15]

As the Cold War began, however, that doctrine remained gauzy in the extreme. Kennan's famous writings were intended mainly as an explanation of Soviet behavior and a general call to action. They set forth no detailed policy recommendations, and were beyond vague when it came to key strategic issues like priorities, methods, and limits. In the X Article, Kennan actually argued that the United States must respond equally to Soviet thrusts *everywhere,* but he himself was soon acknowledging that this was infeasible. Kennan's "predictions and warnings could not have been better," Acheson later recalled, but his practical recommendations "were of no help." Containment, as Kennan initially expressed it, was more of an aspiration than a strategy.[16]

There was also a strategy deficit in the broader scheme of U.S. policy. As superpower tensions increased in 1946–47, Truman undertook a flurry of initiatives aimed at restraining the further spread—actual or merely potential—of Soviet influence. The administration insisted that Moscow withdraw its troops from northern Iran, and Truman sent U.S. naval forces to the Eastern Mediterranean after Stalin sought to intimidate Turkey into making concessions in the Dardanelles. "We must decide that we shall resist with all means at our disposal," State Department officials insisted. In Western Europe, Truman dispatched food and economic aid to check rising political radicalism, and U.S. occupation authorities worked to revive coal production and commerce in western Germany. In the Far East, U.S. troops remained in Korea to prevent Soviet influence from spreading to the southern part of the peninsula, and Washington provided large amounts of military, economic, and logistical assistance to Chiang Kai-shek's Chinese government in its struggle against Mao Zedong's Communists. American officials had not totally given up on a decent relationship with Stalin, but they were nonetheless resolved to hold the line.[17]

This trend reached a culmination in early 1947, after financial stringencies forced Great Britain to terminate assistance to Greece and Turkey. The former country was grappling with a Communist-led insurgency; the latter was sitting anxiously in the shadow of Soviet power. Determined to hold these key positions along the Mediterranean rim, Truman pledged to fill the void with $400 million in emergency military and economic aid. He framed the issue in universalistic terms, telling Congress that "nearly every nation must choose between alternative ways of life," and declaring that the United States would henceforth "support free peoples who are resisting attempted subjugation by armed minorities or by outside pressures." A failure to act would open up the Middle East and perhaps Western Europe to Soviet pressures, he warned. "If we falter in our leadership, we may endanger the peace of the world—and we shall certainly endanger the welfare of this Nation."[18]

Truman had good reason for speaking in such dramatic tones. He was worried about securing the support of a fiscally conservative, Republican-led Congress, and he intended to signal—to audiences both at home and abroad—that the United States would not retreat from the challenge before it. "This was America's answer to the surge of expansion of Communist tyranny," he later wrote. "It had to be clear of hesitation or double talk."[19]

The speech proved to be a highly effective use of presidential rhetoric, but it also underscored that Truman's policies did not yet add up to a coherent Cold War grand strategy. The administration was piling up obligations around the globe in 1946–47, but it was doing so just as political pressures and fears of inflation led Truman to slash U.S. military expenditures. With overall military strength having fallen from twelve million Americans under arms in 1945 to fewer than two million in 1947, it looked like the services might not be able to carry out existing occupation duties in Europe in the Far East, let alone meet additional contingencies. Even in the absence of war, shrinking military resources might undercut diplomacy vis-à-vis Moscow. And while deficit-conscious Republicans had supported aid to Greece and Turkey, they were expected to resist additional calls for large-scale foreign assistance. Expansive rhetoric aside, the United States clearly lacked the resources to support "free peoples" everywhere. "We were spread from hell to breakfast," one official later recalled. "All around the world."[20]

Bureaucratic disorganization compounded the problem. Grand strategy requires unity of effort and long-range planning, but neither of these virtues was in abundance. The National Security Act would not be passed until mid-1947, meaning that there was no unified defense establishment to take charge of military planning, and no National Security Council to coordinate policy. Interservice rivalry was ubiquitous, with the various branches of the armed forces warring to protect their own prerogatives. The State Department was also a mess, its effectiveness undermined by low morale and the dominance of geographically focused regional bureaus with no institutional incentive or mandate to consider the wider scheme of American diplomacy. The department, Undersecretary Acheson believed, was afflicted with "the sin of ad hocery [sic]," and policy had become reactive in consequence. Truman himself sometimes seemed overwhelmed. The president had a strong sense of where he wanted to go and was generally quite decisive on specific issues, but he struggled to achieve harmony within the administration or translate broad principles into a coherent strategic program. Secretary of the Navy (and later Secretary of Defense) James Forrestal summed up the situation in April 1947: "There has been a notable lack of any central planning on American policy."[21]

As the superpower struggle took shape, strategic thinking was lagging behind events. Containment had emerged as the lodestar, the basic organizing principle, of U.S. diplomacy. Yet if one thinks of grand strategy not simply as a goal or a doctrine, but as a realistic plan for getting from here to there with the resources available, then American statecraft remained lacking. In the coming years, the Truman administration would gradually develop its Cold War grand strategy; events, in turn, would continually test and reshape that design.

The grand strategy that started to emerge in 1947–48 was shaped by both design and improvisation. It reflected design in the sense that Truman moved, in early 1947, to bring greater structure to policy. "This is only the beginning," he said in March; with crises looming almost everywhere, priorities and planning would be essential.[22] To this end, Truman named Marshall, the "organizer of victory" in World War II, as his new secretary of state, and endowed him with broad latitude in conducting foreign policy. Marshall promptly created a Policy Planning Staff (PPS) charged with developing "long-term programs for the achievement of U.S. foreign policy objectives," and tapped Kennan as its head. Kennan had spent the year prior putting flesh on containment in lectures at the National War College. If U.S. diplomacy was to succeed, he believed, Washington would need "a pattern of grand strategy no less concrete and no less consistent than that which governs our actions during war."[23]

The same imperative was being felt throughout the executive branch. In April, the Joint Chiefs of Staff (JCS) conducted a major study to determine priorities in allocating military assistance and resources more broadly.[24] The passage of the National Security Act three months later led to the creation of the Central Intelligence Agency (CIA) and National Security Council (NSC), as well as a unified National Military Establishment (later the Department of Defense) with Forrestal as its head. Foreign policy could not be conducted "in swiftly changing moods," Forrestal believed; the United States must "advance on a solid front and not on a jagged and spasmodic line."[25] Forrestal's appointment did not end service rivalries, nor did the new administrative arrangements eliminate bureaucratic conflict. On the whole, though, they did provide somewhat greater orderliness to policy making as the decade went on.

It was well that they did, for the pressure of events frequently seemed relentless in the late 1940s, and crucial decisions often had to be made on little warning. Just weeks after taking charge at the PPS, Kennan was already lamenting the difficulties of planning policy in this environment:

> The complexity of these things is so staggering that sometimes it seems to me that the only way we could ever hope to solve them would be if we could persuade the world to stand still for six months while we sit down and think it over. And even then I bet it would be five months and 28 days before we would get down to the drafting stage. But life does not stand still, and the resulting confusion is terrific.[26]

Grand strategy could not, in these circumstances, be formulated through quiet, a priori reflection. It would have to be forged amid the heat of crisis and in real time.

The first such crisis to break was in Western Europe. Throughout the region, harsh winter weather had exacerbated the profound devastation caused by the war, raising the prospect of starvation, chaos, and revolution by the spring of 1947. As Winston Churchill put it, the center of Western civilization had become "a rubble heap, a charnel house, a breeding ground for pestilence and hate." As in many cases during the late 1940s, the Soviets had done little to create this situation, but with well-organized—and increasingly popular—Communist parties waiting in the wings, they were positioned to benefit from it. If the radical Left took power in Western Europe, via legal or extralegal means, then Moscow might gain effective political control of the region without a shot being fired.[27]

The U.S. response was the Marshall Plan, one of the single most important initiatives of the postwar era. The primary purpose of the plan (known formally as the European Recovery Program, or ERP) was to use a massive jolt of financial and technological assistance—ultimately some $13 billion—to restore self-confidence, kick-start recovery, and combat the exhaustion and desperation that might lead to Communist triumphs. In the short term, the United States needed to be "on the offensive instead of the defensive, to convince the European peoples that we mean business, to serve as a catalyst for their hope and confidence," Kennan argued in his definitive PPS paper on the subject. Over the longer term, U.S. assistance should be used to break bottlenecks, rebuild productive capacity and infrastructure, and encourage regional integration. The aim was to use Washington's overwhelming economic power "to combat not communism, but the economic maladjustment which makes European society vulnerable" to communism.[28]

The three western zones of Germany, then occupied by the United States, Great Britain, and France, were crucial in this regard. In one sense, the revival of the German economy—especially coal production—was a prerequisite for reviving Western Europe writ large. No less important, ameliorating the appalling economic conditions in western Germany was imperative if the Germans were to be convinced that their long-term fortunes lay with Western Europe rather than the Soviets and their satellites to the east. U.S. officials expected that the Western occupation would end someday; once it did, hungry and disillusioned Germans might decide to cast their lot with Moscow in return for access to East-bloc markets and the reunification of their divided country. Then, warned Kennan, "we would really have to watch our step, because then there would have come into existence an aggregate of economic and military industrial power which ought to make every one of us sit up and take notice, damn fast."[29] From 1947 onward, the stabilization and rehabilitation of western Germany would be central to the Marshall Plan and American policy as a whole.

As U.S. officials readily acknowledged, the Marshall Plan was in many ways an ad hoc reaction to a fast-developing crisis. The initial preparation of ERP was nothing if not harried: Kennan, drawing on the ideas of numerous other officials, pulled together its basic outlines in just three weeks. "The best answer we can give today," he told Marshall, "is perhaps more useful than a more thoroughly considered study one or two months hence."[30] The ERP would remain a work in progress long after Marshall's famous speech at Harvard in June 1947, with U.S. and European officials laboring to turn the basic concept into a workable aid program. Only in the fall of 1947 was a formal proposal ready for congressional consideration; an interim aid package was approved at year's end, with the main appropriation coming in early 1948.

Yet if the Marshall Plan reflected the sort of improvisation that is inevitable in foreign policy, it also flowed from several key concepts that were coalescing in the administration. The first was that the United States had to focus its attention on securing and stabilizing the key industrial areas of Eurasia. "Our resources are not unlimited," said Truman in September 1947. "We must apply them where they can serve the most effectively to bring production, freedom, and confidence back to the world." Given its immense industrial potential, Western Europe—and particularly western Germany—came at the top of the list, as the unprecedented size of the Marshall Plan indicated. Western Europe was, in Truman's words, "the decisive theater ... the only power complex sufficiently strong, combined with the U.S., to decisively redress the world power balance and the only one which, if seized by the USSR, might render her almost impregnable." Japan, then under U.S. occupation, ranked second; by 1947–48, American officials regarded Japanese rehabilitation as a core strategic priority. "Any world balance of power means first and foremost a balance on the Eurasian land mass," noted Kennan. "That balance is unthinkable as long as Germany and Japan remain power vacuums."[31]

None of this meant that the Truman administration was willing to ignore other areas of the globe, for U.S. planners emphasized the need for bases, raw materials, markets, and lines of communication in locales from Latin America to the Middle East to the western Pacific.[32] The idea was simply that the vital industrial centers—Western Europe especially—would have first call on finite resources and attention. By focusing primarily on these areas, the United States could maintain a favorable balance of power in Eurasia—and thus globally—without courting the exhaustion that a less discriminating approach would surely invite. The goal, wrote Kennan, was not "to hold equally everywhere," but to "hold in enough places, and in sufficiently strategic places, to accomplish our general purpose." The United States, Marshall agreed, must avert "dispersal of our forces when concentration appears to be the wisest cause especially in view of our present limitations."[33]

This issue of priorities was closely related to a second key concept, which was that money, not arms, represented the primary tool for promoting geopolitical stability. While U.S. officials were painfully cognizant that the Kremlin enjoyed a major conventional military edge at virtually every point in Eurasia, they did not expect Moscow to opt for war anytime soon. The Soviets lacked strong naval and air forces, and they had suffered horrendously in the last global conflict. Moscow would certainly work to intimidate and subvert its rivals, usually by using indigenous Communist parties as proxies, but in the end it would remain cautious to avoid a war it was not yet prepared to wage. "The USSR is unlikely to resort to open military aggression in present circumstances," CIA analysts wrote in late 1947. "Its policy is to avoid war, to build up its war potential, and to extend its influence and control by political, economic, and psychological methods."[34]

The upshot was that the United States had a window of opportunity in which it could use its own chief strategic advantages—namely, its wealth—to address the economic and political weaknesses underlying the Communist threat. Military assistance would undoubtedly be required in select cases, and the maintenance of dominant naval and air power would help deter Soviet aggression. On the whole, though, Washington should focus on providing the economic and technological assistance that would foster longer-term stability. "The United States had everything which the world needed to restore it to normal and the Russians had nothing—neither capital nor goods nor food," Forrestal remarked. Provided that Washington retained superior overall power, it could therefore emphasize reconstruction and tolerate a severe disparity in land power. Forrestal put it squarely: "As long as we can outproduce the world, can control the sea and can strike inland with the atomic bomb, we can assume certain risks otherwise unacceptable. The years before any possible power can achieve the capability effectively to attack us with weapons of mass destruction are our years of opportunity."[35]

This stress on economic aid, in turn, touched on a third and final concept, one that was more important at the time than is often remembered today. This was the idea that the purpose of American engagement now should be to reduce American burdens later. In 1947–48, no responsible official doubted that Washington would have to make extraordinary exertions to stabilize a fragile global order. "The reins of world leadership are fast slipping from Britain's competent but now very weak hands," noted Undersecretary of State Will Clayton; only if the United States seized those reins could peace be preserved.[36] There was also a strong sense, however, that long-term stability would best be served by a system in which other powers were once again capable of resisting Soviet pressures *without* much American assistance. "It should be a cardinal point of our policy to see that other elements of independent power are developed on the Eurasian landmass as rapidly as possible, in order to take off our shoulders some of the burden of 'bipolarity,'" wrote Kennan in October 1947. Bipolarity was unsustainable, he repeated in November: the United States should aim "to stiffen local forces of resistance, wherever we can, and to see first whether they cannot do the work."[37]

This notion of revitalizing friendly but independent centers of power was central to the Marshall Plan. American officials fully expected that a non-communist Western Europe would incline toward Washington politically

and economically. But they did not initially see ERP as prelude to a permanent U.S. security presence in Western Europe, much less as the forerunner
to a formal military alliance. The purpose, rather, was to use a temporary
infusion of resources to restore European vigor and strength, encourage integration, and thereby allow that region to pull together and withstand Communist pressures without engendering a lasting transatlantic dependence.
"The idea," commented Marshall Plan administrator Paul Hoffman, "is to
get Europe on its feet and off our backs."[38] John Hickerson, the influential
head of the State Department's European desk, elaborated on this point in
early 1948, saying he

> had envisaged the creation of a third force which was not merely the
> extension of U.S. influence but a real European organization strong
> enough to say "no" both to the Soviet Union and to the United States,
> if our actions should seem so to require. We would be willing to take
> our chance in dealing with any such organization of freedom-loving
> nations confident that we could settle any differences with them.

Marshall and other high officials often said similar things. The United States
would eventually create an informal empire of sorts in Western Europe, but
this was not what American policy makers initially had in mind.[39]

In fact, if the "third force" concept now seems rather quaint, at the time it
was a natural fit with the key ideas shaping U.S. policy. As late as the beginning
of 1948, few American policy makers would have accepted the argument that
the United States should assume more-or-less permanent responsibility for
the security and well-being of far-flung regions like Western Europe. Such an
arrangement would impose a significant, long-term strain on U.S. resources,
and it would presumably trample on local desires for autonomy and influence.
It would represent a sharp break with American diplomatic heritage, while
also saddling Washington with responsibilities for which planners like Kennan
thought it singularly ill-suited. He was skeptical, he told a National War College audience, of "the ability of any country so conceived and so organized as
our own to handle successfully for any length of time the problems of great
peoples other than our own."[40] The third-force arrangement, by contrast,
would allow the United States to strengthen Western Europe against Soviet
influence without incurring these longer-term costs and obligations. For a
country still seeking an economical approach to containment, the third-force
concept made eminently good sense.

Kennan drew the basic ideas underlying U.S. policy together in PPS 13,
a strategic overview prepared for Marshall in November 1947. "The danger
of war is vastly exaggerated in many quarters," he began. The task for the

United States was to proceed, energetically but selectively, in reinvigorating those areas of the noncommunist world that were most vital to American security. "It is urgently necessary for us to restore something of the balance of power in Europe and Asia by strengthening local forces of independence and getting them to assume part of our burden," he wrote. The main U.S. effort should come in Europe and Japan; more peripheral areas, such as Korea and China, would probably have to be downgraded or perhaps even abandoned. Marshall quickly endorsed the conclusions of the paper, telling Truman and others that "the objective of our policy from this point on would be the restoration of balance of power in both Europe and Asia and that all actions would be viewed in the light of this objective."[41]

The implications of this approach became apparent as the administration turned its attention to the Far East in late 1947 and early 1948. By late 1947, the Chinese civil war had turned sharply against Chiang, and the JCS recommended a major program of military and economic assistance to forestall a Communist victory. Kennan disagreed. The collapse of Chiang's regime would "not be a catastrophe," he argued, because China was too underdeveloped to matter much to the global balance of power, because the Nationalist government was too incompetent to save, absent direct military intervention, and because Moscow could not necessarily dominate a Communist-run China in any event. Marshall concurred, and persuaded Truman to begin what was envisioned as a gradual disengagement from the conflict. American aid continued so as to avoid incensing Chiang's Republican allies in the United States, but at reduced rates that constituted only a small fraction of what was initially sent to Europe via ERP. "We cannot afford, economically or militarily, to take over the continued failures of the present Chinese Government to the dissipation of our strength in more vital regions," Marshall explained to the Senate Foreign Relations Committee.[42]

As the administration pivoted away from Chiang, it also shifted policy toward Japan. So far, the U.S. occupation had focused mainly on breaking the power of the ruling elite, and the country remained economically and politically precarious as a result. By late 1947 and early 1948, however, State Department officials—led, again, by Kennan—were insisting that the punitive aspects of the occupation should be ended, that Washington should "dispense with bromides about democratization," and that primary emphasis should be placed on achieving "maximum *stability* of Japanese society, in order that Japan may best be able to stand on her own feet when the protecting hand is withdrawn." A strong Japan had earlier been a counterweight to Russian expansion, Kennan argued, and it must become "again an important force in the Far East." Reparations, controls on industry, and major social reforms were soon phased out; financial and trade assistance, repression of the Japanese Communists, and a focus on political stasis and economic growth were ushered in. For the next twenty-five years, Japan would be the keystone of U.S. policy in the Far East.[43]

Between early 1947 and early 1948, the Truman administration thus began to transform containment from a lofty but vague idea into a more fully developed grand strategy. The administration was now operating with a clear sense of priorities, a firm understanding of America's competitive advantages vis-à-vis Moscow, and a determination to derive maximum utility from finite resources. In accordance with these guiding precepts, the United States would focus its efforts on the key geostrategic regions of Eurasia; it would emphasize economic reconstruction; and it would revive "local forces of independence" that could eventually relieve the strain on American capabilities. These initiatives were the keys to containing Soviet power, fostering a stable and prosperous noncommunist world, and perhaps, eventually, doing even more. If Washington stymied Soviet advances where it mattered most, Kennan predicted, then "I think you might see a general crumbling of Russian influence and prestige which would carry beyond those countries themselves, beyond the satellite countries, and into the heart of the Soviet Union itself."[44]

The virtues of this approach would become apparent with time. Historians generally agree that ERP played a key role in breaking bottlenecks, stabilizing trade, encouraging regional integration, and catalyzing the recovery that took hold in the late 1940s and 1950s. In Japan, the results were similar. While the "reverse course" (the shift from a punitive policy to one of rehabilitation) did not itself bring about prosperity, it ended the harshest aspects of the occupation and constituted the indispensable first step toward decades of growth and stability. In both cases, the concentrated application of economic power allowed the United States to leverage the strengths of devastated but still-vibrant societies, laying the foundations for long-term security at key points along the Eurasian periphery.[45]

The administration's approach also helped ensure the survival of an internationalist consensus at home. Truman and his advisers continually worried during the late 1940s that Americans would shun the expensive commitments required to check Soviet power. Americans wanted a "firm foreign policy," Forrestal warned, but they also wanted "high wages, low prices for manufactured goods, reduced taxes, a balanced budget, [and] debt reduction." In this context, emphasizing economic reconstruction hardly ended domestic controversy over the Truman Doctrine, Marshall Plan, and other early initiatives. Yet the decision to avoid the much *higher* costs associated with a major rearmament program lessened the chances of a political blow-up that might have grounded Truman's internationalism before it ever truly took flight. In this sense, a key advantage of the administration's grand strategy was that it minimized the pain—economic and thus political—of American globalism in the crucial early period of the Cold War.[46]

Things did not seem so rosy at the time, however, because in late 1947 and early 1948 the geopolitical situation remained highly tenuous. The Marshall Plan would eventually help put Western Europe on the road to recovery, but in the short term it touched off a new set of crises. Launching ERP had required Western European leaders to take several potentially dangerous steps. They had to evict Communists from their governments; in Italy and France, the Left responded with strikes and riots that shook the domestic order. More disconcerting still, the economic logic of ERP required the revival of western Germany—but for many Europeans, this step uncovered the psychological scars left by two world wars. French diplomats were particularly concerned at "the possibility that Germany might once again dominate Europe, if not militarily, then economically." Anxieties ran high, essential economic reforms stalled, and the future of the continent looked very ominous.[47]

These developments threw Truman's emerging grand strategy into doubt. By late 1947, American officials were acutely concerned by the possibility of western Germany slipping into chaos and perhaps the Soviet orbit. At the London conference of foreign ministers beginning in December, U.S. diplomats pushed for financial reforms, fusion of the three Western zones of occupation, increased industrial production in the Ruhr and Rhine valleys, and the formation of a provisional government. If western Germany were to become stable and prosperous, the State Department argued, it would have to be treated as a "political and economic unit." "The question fundamentally of all of this," said Undersecretary of State Robert Lovett, "is whether or not Western Germany becomes a Russian satellite, or Germany as a whole becomes a Russian satellite." Yet preventing this outcome required French cooperation, and fears of a resurgent Germany ensured that this cooperation remained halting at best.[48]

The sense of crisis in Europe—and in U.S. policy—was further exacerbated by the Soviet reaction to the Marshall Plan. American officials had not seen ERP solely as a means of thwarting Communist inroads in Western Europe. By offering economic aid to Eastern Europe as well, they had also hoped to strain Moscow's relations with the satellites.[49] The ploy worked roughly as intended, but in doing so it elicited an alarming Soviet response. Stalin refused to sit by and allow the Marshall Plan to proceed; instead, he mounted his own campaign to disrupt American policy. Intending to derail ERP, he encouraged the disorders in France and Italy. Determined to solidify his control of Eastern Europe, he brutally cracked down on dissent in the region. The climax came in February 1948, when the Czech Communists staged a coup d'état that snuffed out democratic rule in that country. It was a terrifying precedent for Western European governments that were struggling to deal with their own Communists and painfully aware of their susceptibility to Soviet coercion. There was a "real possibility," Marshall acknowledged, that developments in Czechoslovakia "would stimulate and encourage Communist action in Western European countries, particularly in Italy."[50]

The course of events in Europe in late 1947 and early 1948 demonstrated one of the key reasons why early Cold War grand strategy could be so difficult to do. As the centerpiece of its emerging grand strategy, the Truman administration had crafted a sensible, forward-thinking program for the reconstruction of Europe, one that was rooted in a firm understanding of America's core geopolitical strengths. But that program could not be implemented in a vacuum; rather, it interacted potently with the European security environment, causing second-order consequences that created new problems for U.S. policy makers. The Marshall Plan sparked anxieties and domestic disruptions in the very countries the United States sought to rebuild, and it provoked a disturbing Soviet response that threatened to undermine regional stability and security even further. Before long, these developments would illustrate the need for new measures to redeem those U.S. investments already made. In the meantime, they showed that Washington was dealing with a very fluid international situation in which action-reaction dynamics caused dilemmas all their own.

As the situation in Europe deteriorated, the Truman administration initially relied on stopgap measures to hold the line. In December 1947, Congress approved emergency aid for Italy, France, and Austria, meant to tide those countries over until the full ERP legislation could be considered. The administration also redoubled its commitment to Greece after the fighting flared in that nation, increasing military aid and eventually dispatching a 450-man advisory group to oversee the counterinsurgency. And in Italy during late 1947 and early 1948, Washington used a raft of covert and psychological tools to marginalize the strident Communist opposition. Truman issued a firm statement that the United States would not tolerate a Communist coup, and he ordered additional military forces to the Eastern Mediterranean as a warning to the Left. Following the Czech coup, the CIA covertly initiated a financial and propaganda offensive in support of

Italy's anticommunist Christian Democrats, while American diplomats made clear that Marshall Plan aid would be withheld if the Communist Party triumphed in upcoming elections.[51]

These measures helped the Christian Democrats win decisively in the April vote. Yet any sense of relief was fleeting, because Stalin launched the Berlin blockade in June. As U.S. officials understood, this maneuver was really an act of desperation. Stalin had been stung by the recent defection of Tito's Yugoslavia from the Soviet bloc, and he feared—correctly—that the revival of western Germany was in the offing. The Kremlin dictator needed a victory, and he sought to gain one by squeezing the Western powers out of Berlin. Truman responded prudently and effectively with the Berlin airlift, which kept the western part of the city alive for the next eleven months, but the tension was nonetheless palpable. Even though U.S. intelligence analysts thought that the Soviets did not want a military showdown, events could easily spiral out of control. "I have a terrible feeling . . . that we are very close to war," Truman wrote. The Europeans were even more alarmed, for if war did break out, their countries would be at the mercy of invading Soviet armies. The Europeans, Marshall told Forrestal and the JCS, were "'completely out of their skin, and sitting on their nerves,' and hope must be recreated in them very soon."[52]

What all this indicated was that the administration's grand strategy remained incomplete. American officials had initially hoped that the Marshall Plan would stabilize Western Europe, and with it, the global balance of power. The trouble was that the success of the plan hinged on the Europeans' willingness to take bold and potentially dangerous steps, and that willingness hinged on a sense of security that was evaporating by the moment. By mid-1948, it had therefore become apparent that leaders in France and elsewhere had little desire to be made into an autonomous European "third force" that would someday have to face Moscow alone. What they wanted were stronger guarantees against the various threats they confronted in the here and now—the threat from their own Communists, from the potential resurgence of German power, from the looming Soviet menace to the east. The Europeans certainly needed "economic revival," State Department official Philip Jessup acknowledged, but they also needed "the feeling of security and hope without which a man can't put his heart into his work." The Marshall Plan provided for the former but not for the latter; something more would be necessary to fulfill American aims.[53]

This was the genesis of the major security commitments that would come to define U.S. policy toward Western Europe. By late 1947, British, French, and Benelux officials were making plans for a collective defense pact, and they pushed insistently for U.S. support of the initiative. Marshall assented, and in 1948–49 the administration went further still. Largely at the behest of its European partners, Washington committed to a major military assistance program for the region and began shipping matériel to France and Italy. Even more significantly, the administration agreed to full U.S. participation in a transatlantic military alliance, the North Atlantic Treaty Organization,[54] and pledged to defend Western Europe at the Rhine in case of war. The alliance, Truman declared, represented "a shield against aggression and the fear of aggression"; the United States had officially and explicitly made Europe's security problems its own. With this commitment in place, Washington and its new allies were able to proceed to the formation of a unified West German state in 1949, and from there—albeit gradually and with difficulty—to the arrangements through which German industrial strength would be harnessed to serve the needs of broader regional recovery.[55]

NATO thus became the cornerstone of U.S. policy in Europe. The alliance, remarked State Department counselor Charles Bohlen, was "the very logical development of almost everything that has happened since the end of the war." In one sense, this was true enough. NATO was firmly rooted in the belief that the United States should do whatever necessary to secure Western Europe, and the alliance was seen by its creators as being fully consonant with the overriding goal of economic recovery. Truman and his advisers did not expect an unprovoked Soviet attack on Western Europe, and they sent no additional U.S. troops to the region in 1948–49. The point of NATO, in their eyes, was not to make Western Europe an impregnable military bastion (for this was impossible, given resource constraints), but simply to offer the ironclad, long-term security commitment that would revive local confidence and enable the Europeans to push ahead with economic reconstruction, political stabilization, and the rehabilitation of Germany. The goal, as Bohlen put it, was to "instill that sense of security in the people which they felt so essential if recovery was to go forward."[56]

In the long run, of course, NATO succeeded brilliantly in this task. It provided the institutional framework that bound the United States to its key geopolitical partners, and it offered the reassurance that those partners so badly craved. By doing so, it answered the twin strategic problems posed by the Soviet threat and the rebirth of German power, and it addressed the dilemmas that the third-force concept and the Marshall Plan had left unresolved. For decades, NATO served as a pillar of stability and cooperation in the world's crucial strategic theater, and its founding constituted a signal achievement of Truman's presidency.

Yet precisely because the alliance ultimately became so effective, it is easy to forget that its creation also reflected a significant—even revolutionary—shift in the *modalities* of American policy. U.S. officials had not initially planned on forging a peacetime, transatlantic military alliance that would represent a break with more than 150 years of American diplomatic tradition; the initiative for the pact came from Western Europe. Nor had they originally thought of creating what was essentially a semipermanent U.S. protectorate in that region; the idea had been to foster a more autonomous grouping that could stand on its own.[57] What NATO showed, then, was a flexibility of *methods* within a continuity of *aims*—once events demonstrated that the Marshall Plan would not suffice to secure Western Europe, the Truman administration took on a new responsibility that it had not intended beforehand. It had become evident, as one official concisely put it in 1948, that "neither ERP nor military support ... can achieve success without the other."[58] Amid the pressures of crisis and the actions of friends and enemies alike, grand strategy had to adapt if it were to keep pace with events.

If the *nature* of the U.S. commitment to Europe was shifting, it was the *scope* of the American commitment to Asia that was in flux in the late 1940s. Throughout this period, it was an article of faith that Washington had to be ruthless in setting geographical priorities, in avoiding, as Marshall believed, "the dispersion of our money and material." This went especially for Asia, which was a secondary theater in the Cold War, and where Japan was the only major industrial center. It followed that the United States should be very wary of overcommitting itself in the region, particularly on the underdeveloped and conflict-ridden Asian mainland. "We must observe great restraint in our attitude toward the Far Eastern areas," noted Kennan in early 1948. The key was to determine "what parts of the Pacific and Far Eastern world are absolutely vital to our security" and deemphasize the rest.[59]

This logic had informed the decision to pivot away from Chiang in 1947–48, and it soon resurfaced in the "defensive perimeter" concept adopted by the administration in 1948–49 (and publicized by Acheson in his ill-starred speech to the National Press Club in January 1950). The idea was that the United States could protect its essential interests in Asia without holding any positions on the mainland, so long as it controlled the offshore island chain encompassing the Aleutians, Japan, Okinawa, and the Philippines. In wartime, these bases—which were already securely within Washington's sphere of influence—would allow the United States to dominate the maritime approaches to Japan, the real strategic prize in the region. Control of the poverty-stricken and infrastructure-poor mainland, by contrast, would not afford Moscow any decisive advantages. Ideally, then, the United States could hold aloof from costly entanglements in Asia proper, and focus on retaining more stable and defensible positions offshore. "While we would endeavor to influence events on the mainland of Asia in ways favorable to our security," wrote Kennan in 1948, "we would not regard any mainland areas as vital to us."[60]

The defensive perimeter was closely related to a second concept that gained traction in 1948–49, the idea of driving a "wedge" between Stalin and Mao. Even as U.S. officials accepted that a Communist victory in China was probably inevitable, they believed that a Sino-Soviet alliance was not. State Department advisers like Kennan and John Paton Davies pointed out that Mao was a nationalist as well as a Communist, and with Tito's example in mind, they predicted that he and his fellow Chinese would chafe at Stalin's compulsion to dominate the international Communist movement. If the United States could craft a nuanced, carrot-and-stick policy that exacerbated these strains and drew Beijing toward the West, it could prevent Moscow from reaping the geopolitical fruits of Mao's victory. This, in turn, would reduce pressures on the U.S. position in Asia, further limiting the need for major exertions in the area. The goal, said Acheson (who replaced Marshall as secretary of state in early 1949), should be to play "for a split."[61]

In theory, the defensive perimeter and the wedge strategy represented efficient, interlocking approaches to managing U.S. interests in East Asia. In practice, neither concept ever got very far. Consider the case of the wedge strategy. In retrospect, one of the key problems with the wedge was that Mao simply refused to behave as American policy makers hoped and expected he would. It is now clear that the Chinese leader was never as receptive to U.S. overtures, or as hostile to Soviet influence, as proponents of the wedge had thought. On the basis of both experience and ideology, Mao believed that Truman would not tolerate a Communist government in China, and he viewed Moscow and Beijing as partners in spreading the revolutionary gospel. By 1948–49, he actually feared that the United States might intervene militarily—perhaps with nuclear weapons—in China, and he was convinced that the revolution must "lean" toward Stalin for support. Chinese negotiators soon agreed to a "division of labor" with the Kremlin in promoting revolution abroad, and following the Communists' triumph in October 1949, Mao pushed strongly for a bilateral defense and coopera-tion pact with Moscow. It was not the sort of behavior that Kennan and Davies had anticipated.[62]

Even had Mao been more pliable, the wedge strategy still would not have worked. Preventing a Sino-Soviet alignment would have required a policy of great subtlety, coherence, and flexibility, one that laid ideological antagonisms aside and offered Mao real incentives—diplomatic recognition, economic

aid—for cooperation with the West. And because this policy presumably
would have required time to change Mao's preferences, it would also have
required considerable patience on the part of U.S. officials.

In the Cold War climate of 1948–49, however, such a policy proved
impossible to implement. Part of the problem had to do with Truman and
Acheson themselves. While both men accepted the basic logic of the wedge
strategy, both men also had trouble reconciling their geopolitical instincts
with their visceral anticommunism. Acheson referred to Mao's forces as
"hatchet men," while Truman called them "bandits" and warned that "we
can't be in a position of making a deal with a communist regime." The president was outraged by the treatment that Americans suffered in areas overrun
by Communist troops, and he increasingly came to view Sino-American
relations through a moral lens as time went on. Needless to say, these issues
impinged upon the prospects for nonideological diplomacy toward Mao and
his followers.[63]

Patience was also hard to come by. While the wedge strategy seemed to
represent the best long-term approach to splitting Moscow and Beijing, it
did nothing to relieve the growing near-term strain on the U.S. position in
East Asia. Nor did it hold much benefit for an administration that had to
deal with immediate political problems in addition to longer-range strategic
imperatives. By 1949, a vocal "Taiwan lobby" was already criticizing Truman
for not doing more to support Chiang, and it would undoubtedly savage
any attempt at accommodation with Mao. In these circumstances, the likely
time horizon for the wedge strategy stretched far beyond what the domestic
political climate would allow.

In consequence, the wedge "strategy" was never translated into a workable program of action, and U.S. policy toward China remained incoherent
in the extreme. Acheson occasionally spoke of recognizing Mao's regime
once the dust from the civil war settled, but he also lent encouragement to
anticommunist resistance fighters in western China. He hoped to promote
Chinese independence of Moscow, but his frustration at Mao's policies led
him to deride the Chinese leader as a Kremlin puppet. "The Communist
leaders," Acheson wrote in the administration's "White Paper" on China
in mid-1949, "have foresworn their Chinese heritage and have publicly
announced their subservience to a foreign power." Most damaging of all,
Truman and Acheson continued the policy of limited assistance to Chiang's
forces (now regrouping on Taiwan), even as those forces blockaded Chinese
ports and used U.S.-supplied planes to bomb Chinese cities. These actions
only exacerbated Mao's insecurities, and the administration ended up encouraging just the Sino-Soviet partnership it had hoped to avert.[64]

Meanwhile, the defensive perimeter concept was also proving problematic. That concept was based on the idea that it was possible to draw a clear line between vital and peripheral interests. In reality, however, the line could be very blurry. A key strategic dilemma of the Cold War was that Third World areas could actually be quite central (or at least seem quite central) to the prosperity and security of the First World. The Middle East, for instance, had none of the concentrated industrial power that made Japan and Western Europe so important. But it did have airfields and lines of communication that would be essential in wartime, and resources without which the developed economies could not function. "The Marshall Plan for Europe," noted Forrestal, "could not succeed without access to the Middle East oil." As a result, U.S. planners came to see the entire area from Morocco to Iran as vital to American interests in the late 1940s, even as they counted on the British (and, to a lesser extent, the French) to bear primary responsibility for stability in the area.[65]

The same core-periphery dynamics were present in the Far East, particularly Southeast Asia. That region, wrote Kennan, was "at best of secondary significance," but to leave it at that was a "gross over-simplification." Reviving Western Europe and Japan—the latter particularly—meant finding markets for their exports and raw materials for their industries, and Southeast Asia loomed large as a source of both. The region possessed large quantities of tin, rubber, and other resources, and it provided much of the rice imported by Japanese consumers. If Tokyo lost access to areas like French Indochina in addition to China and Manchuria, the CIA warned in May 1948, "the ensuing economic distress, with its attendant political instability, might force Japan to align itself with the U.S.S.R."[66]

In Indochina particularly, the result of this conclusion was as logical as it would ultimately be tragic. American officials understood that backing a French colonial war in Indochina might well mean heading "blindly down a dead-end alley, expending our limited resources . . . in a fight that would be hopeless."[67] Yet because French support was central to the success of NATO, and because even Kennan's PPS was listing Southeast Asia as "a vital segment on the line of containment," the administration concluded that there was no choice but to help Paris suppress the Communist-led Vietminh insurgents. In 1949, Acheson decided to recognize the pliant monarchy installed by the French in Saigon; military aid for the counterinsurgency soon followed. He hoped, without great optimism, that Paris would make the political reforms necessary to co-opt nationalist sentiment in Indochina. But Acheson also understood that he could not compel the French to do as he wished, and he accepted that he was bound to support his ally's policies regardless.

"Unavoidably, the United States is, together with France, committed in Indochina," concluded a State Department working group.[68]

Nor could the United States disengage from Korea, another marginal mainland outpost. Virtually no one in Washington believed that South Korea constituted a core U.S. security interest. The occupation troops stationed there were sorely needed elsewhere, as was the aid money being spent to keep the southern economy afloat. Within the administration in 1947–48, there was thus a strong inclination to withdraw "as soon as possible with the minimum of bad effects."[69]

The last part of that formulation proved crucial, however. In 1948–49, South Korea was facing an internal rebellion, cross-border skirmishes with the North, and continued economic instability. It would undoubtedly collapse without U.S. assistance, allowing Moscow and its North Korean allies to control the entire peninsula. The material consequences of this development would not be devastating, but the psychological effect might be. South Korea was, after all, largely an American creation. If Washington pulled out and the country fell apart, an NSC study predicted, it would "be interpreted as a betrayal by the U.S. of its friends and allies in the Far East and might well lead to a fundamental realignment of forces in favor of the Soviet Union throughout that part of the world." American troops did come out of Korea in 1949, but the administration continued to support the Syngman Rhee government with economic and military aid. To abandon South Korea, said Acheson, would be "the most utter defeatism and utter madness in our interests in Asia."[70]

The blurring of the defensive perimeter was compounded by events in China in 1949. As the Nationalist regime crumbled, Truman and Acheson sought to keep clear of the fighting, and they refused to commit U.S. military forces to the defense of Chiang's last bastion, Taiwan.[71] They also concluded, however, that the United States could retreat no farther in Asia. The advent of a Communist government in Beijing would give impetus to radical forces in Southeast Asia, isolate Japan and South Korea, and exact a toll on U.S. prestige. It would infuriate pro-Chiang observers in Washington, who were already damning the administration for not backing him to the hilt. In short, accepting a setback in China made it imperative to avoid another defeat elsewhere. It was "a fundamental decision of American policy," wrote Acheson in July 1949, "that the United States does not intend to permit further extension of Communist domination on the Continent of Asia or in the Southeast Asia area."[72] When Congress subsequently appropriated $75 million for use in the "area around China," the administration employed the funds to shore up anticommunist forces in Indochina, Thailand, and elsewhere in Southeast Asia.[73] Priorities were still important, but holding the line had become imperative.

By the time Acheson gave his Press Club speech in early 1950, the defensive perimeter strategy was already turning into something messier and more ambitious. To be sure, the United States would have to fall back to the offshore islands if global war broke out, and Acheson steadfastly refused to pledge U.S. forces to the defense of Taiwan, South Korea, or Indochina in the event of local hostilities.[74] Yet the administration had resolved that the loss of additional mainland areas would be disastrous to U.S. interests, and it had committed to helping pro-Western forces survive in the region. So far, the amounts expended were minimal relative to other American responsibilities. Given the instability at work in much of East Asia, however, these initial outlays represented mere down payments on far larger obligations to come.

Events in Asia during the late 1940s thus demonstrated that the implementation of policy could be far more difficult than the conception. They also showed that in Europe and Asia alike, there was an evolving—and expanding—quality to U.S. grand strategy. Throughout this period, the Truman administration sincerely desired to economize by adhering to a firm scheme of priorities and bounding both the scope and nature of its exposure abroad. Yet responsibilities had a tendency to snowball; in an unstable and threatening international environment, one commitment could easily lead to another. In Western Europe, this process led to the formation of NATO and, ultimately, a great deal of security for the United States and its allies. In turbulent and conflict-plagued Asia—particularly Indochina and Korea—the outcome would be just the overextension the administration had hoped to avoid.

As Truman's second term unfolded, American policy makers viewed the world with both confidence and anxiety. The Marshall Plan, the Berlin airlift, and the creation of NATO were gradually stabilizing Western Europe, while Tito's defection from the Soviet bloc in 1948 had thrown Stalin on the defensive. The West was now consolidating a "secure power base," Truman told the NATO foreign ministers in April 1949. From here it would be possible to combat "the social and economic pressures on which Communism thrives," and even "to create active counterpressure to undermine the base of Soviet power itself."[75] By mid-1949, these counterpressures were already under way. The administration was providing economic assistance to Tito to bolster his regime against Soviet intimidation, while also deploying covert action, propaganda, and other limited efforts to undermine Kremlin rule in Eastern Europe. "The time is now ripe for us to place greater emphasis on the offensive," Kennan wrote.[76]

Yet amid this guarded optimism, there was also cause for alarm. The situation in Asia was deteriorating, and around the world, expanding U.S. commitments were once again straining the relationship between means and ends. Washington had pledged to hold Europe at the Rhine, for instance, but the conventional capabilities to do so simply did not exist. The alliance, in Acheson's phrasing, was being "held together with string, chewing gum, and safety pins."[77] More broadly, the United States was now moving energetically to combat Soviet influence on a variety of fronts, but it lacked the military capacity to make good on these commitments if hostilities should occur. "The trouble," Marshall had told Truman as early as February 1948, "was that we are playing with fire while we have nothing with which to put it out."[78]

Truman and his advisers still took some comfort in the atomic monopoly, and they doubted that Stalin wanted war anytime soon. Yet fighting could easily erupt if a diplomatic crisis spun out of control, and if it did, the U.S. position would be dire. During the late 1940s, the United States had nowhere near the four hundred atomic bombs that Pentagon planners thought necessary to cripple Moscow's war-making capacity, much less the detailed intelligence or the strategic airpower capabilities necessary to put all existing bombs on target. One classified report issued in 1949 predicted that an all-out U.S. nuclear assault would kill 2.7 million people and inflict a 30–40 percent reduction of Soviet industrial capacity, but it would not, "per se, bring about capitulation, destroy the roots of Communism, or critically weaken the power of Soviet leadership to dominate the people."[79]

Even more troubling, what atomic capabilities did exist offered no answer to the problem of Soviet tanks sweeping through Europe and the Middle East in the first weeks of a conflict. Air Force intelligence assessments estimated that Soviet forces could reach the English Channel and the Pyrenees within ten days, while also inhibiting the United States from using its crucial airfields in the Middle East. Truman summed up the basic problem in 1949: "We have the atomic bomb; but we must recognize the present limitations of our strategic methods for delivering it, and the vast problem of subduing a sprawling empire stretching from Kamchatka to the Skagerrak with this weapon, to say nothing of the problem of using it against our occupied Western European allies."[80] As long as it retained a nuclear monopoly, the United States would probably win a war with Moscow in the end, but it would be a drawn-out affair that would devastate many of the areas Washington meant to defend.

Even if war did not come, State Department officials recognized that a sense of military impotence vis-à-vis Moscow could undercut morale among U.S. allies. "If the shadow of the Soviet armed strength remains too formidable, in comparison with ours," warned Kennan, it could have a "para-lyzing effect on the will to resist." This was no abstract concern in 1949–50. The West Germans were particularly aware of their vulnerability, and if not given some reassurance that they could actually be protected in time of war, they might feel forced to seek accommodation with the Soviets instead. "We must offer security to Germany," Acheson believed.[81]

These dilemmas ensured that the late 1940s were a time of fierce battles over the military budget. Truman insisted on minimal outlays, fearing that anything more would cause inflation, harm the economy, and tarnish the image of the Democratic Party. "He is determined not to spend more than we take in in taxes," wrote Forrestal. "He is a hard-money man if I ever saw one."[82] With the help of Forrestal and his successor, Louis Johnson, Truman managed to keep spending from reaching more than a modest $14.2 billion during the late 1940s. Still, neither military nor civilian officials could ignore the stark deficiencies in preparedness. Writing for the JCS, Admiral William Leahy warned that "it is essential to our national security to bring our military strength to a level commensurate with the distinct possibility of global war." Even Acheson, as devoted a subordinate as the president ever had, later acknowledged that "Mr. Truman's period of retrenchment in 1948 and 1949 ... put means out of relation with ends."[83]

The political foundations of grand strategy were also becoming shaky. Between 1947 and mid-1949, the Truman administration had enjoyed remarkable bipartisan support for its major policy initiatives. That support owed partially to the administration's courtship of leading Republicans like Senator Arthur Vandenberg, and no less to its use of highly ideological and even Manichean rhetoric to market the Truman Doctrine, the Marshall Plan, and NATO. "The only way we can sell the public on our new policy," wrote one official, "is by emphasizing the necessity of holding the line: communism vs. democracy should be the major theme."[84] Such rhetoric served its immediate purpose, but it also limited the administration's flexibility down the road. As one scholar has noted, "hyperbolic, apocalyptic, and brazenly anti-Communist" themes "became woven into the cultural milieu, largely to the dismay of American policymakers."[85] In this charged atmosphere, distinctions between vital and non-vital interests were all the more difficult to make, and a setback anywhere—no matter how peripheral the location—could easily be politically damaging to the administration. With the Republicans determined to find an issue with which to avenge their defeat in the 1948 presidential election, this latter danger loomed even larger.

It was amid these growing pressures that the United States absorbed two geopolitical shocks in late 1949. As noted previously, the triumph of Mao's forces in China in early October had long been anticipated. Nonetheless, it had a jarring effect on policy makers and the public. Having touted the "communism vs. democracy" line, Truman and Acheson were now hard-pressed to explain why the loss of the world's most populous country was not a disaster. Republicans pounced, with figures like Richard Nixon, Robert Taft, and Joseph McCarthy arguing that communist sympathizers at Foggy Bottom had handed China to Moscow. The attacks were baseless, but they resonated in a highly partisan and ideological climate, and the administration was thrown off-balance. No less problematic, the conclusion of the Sino-Soviet alliance in early 1950 showed the failure of the wedge strategy and led U.S. officials to fear that China might become a launching pad for efforts to destabilize all of East Asia. "From our viewpoint," Acheson noted, "Soviet Union possesses position of domination in China which it is using to threaten Indochina, push in Malaya, stir up trouble in Philippines, and now to start trouble in Indonesia."[86]

Even more unsettling was news of the first Soviet atomic test in August 1949. To a degree that is hard to appreciate now, the Soviet A-bomb fundamentally upset American views of the existing strategic balance. U.S. officials did not think that having the bomb would push Stalin toward general war just yet; a "final showdown" was unlikely, intelligence officials wrote.[87] But this was little cause for comfort. An emboldened Stalin might launch limited probes or proxy wars, or perhaps seek to intimidate Western Europe and Japan into distancing themselves from the United States. "As the Soviet military potential increases relative to that of the United States and its allies," one intelligence estimate predicted, "the USSR will doubtless be willing to take greater risks than before in pursuit of its aims."[88] And once the Soviet nuclear arsenal had matured (presumably sometime around 1954), then there was no guarantee that Stalin would shun the risk of general war in a crisis with the United States.[89]

If such a war did occur, either by accident or by design, then a Soviet nuclear capability could drastically alter the military calculus. After all, the atomic monopoly had been the central pillar upon which U.S. defense policy rested—it had been Washington's only real, if problematic, riposte to massive Soviet conventional superiority in Europe and elsewhere. But with Moscow now having broken the U.S. monopoly, that central pillar had effectively been destroyed. As Marc Trachtenberg has pointed out, it was no longer assured that the United States would win a global war in the end. Rather, Washington would now have to contend with the prospect of Soviet nuclear attacks against American allies and air bases in Europe, and perhaps even against the United States itself. (Soviet long-range bombers could reach the United States on one-way missions.) As George Kennan noted, the prospect of such attacks might even deter the United States from using its own arsenal against the Soviet Union—an outcome that would only magnify effects of American conventional inferiority.[90] In sum, America had lost one of its key strategic advantages vis-à-vis the Soviet Union, and the policy of limited rearmament now looked entirely too risky.

Early 1950 thus saw two momentous developments in U.S. policy. At the end of January, Truman reluctantly approved a program to develop thermonu-clear weapons. The "super" bomb represented a quantum leap in destructive-ness and lethality; scientific advisers condemned it as a "weapon of genocide."[91] Yet given the likelihood that the Soviets would themselves develop the "super," Truman felt that he had no choice but to proceed. "No one wants to use it," he told one aide. "But ... we have got to have it if only for bargaining purposes with the Russians."[92] Having lost the atomic monopoly, Truman would not risk putting the United States on the wrong end of an even more imposing asym-metry. And at the same time that Truman made this decision, he also called for a comprehensive review of U.S. national security policy, the result of which was NSC-68.

Leading historians like John Lewis Gaddis and Melvyn Leffler have long debated whether NSC-68 represented change or continuity in U.S. policy.[93] In reality, the document contained strong elements of both. Paul Nitze, Kennan's successor at the PPS and the primary drafter of NSC-68, reiterated many of the key strategic premises that had heretofore guided Washington. He restated the notion that "Soviet domination of ... Eurasia ... would be strategically and politically unacceptable to the United States." Like his predecessors, he argued that the United States "must lead in building a suc-cessfully functioning political and economic system in the free world." Nitze also reaffirmed an idea that went back to the Long Telegram and the X Article: that the long-range goal of American policy was not simply to contain Moscow, but to increase the strains on the Kremlin, reduce its power, and eventually "foster a fundamental change in the nature of the Soviet sys-tem." And through the entire paper ran the same starkly ideological language that so often characterized U.S. policy during this period. The superpower conflict, Nitze repeatedly wrote, was fundamentally between "the idea of freedom" and the "idea of slavery," between "the most contagious idea in history" and the "perverted faith" of Soviet communism.[94]

Within this general framework of continuity, however, NSC-68 also advocated significant shifts. Whereas the Truman administration had initially been willing to write off peripheral areas like China, Nitze made explicit the idea that had increasingly come to shape U.S. policy in 1949–50: that Washington could not tolerate additional defeats anywhere. Emboldened by the atomic bomb, the Soviets would chip away at the Western world through intimidation, subversion, and proxy wars. If the United States did nothing to contest these advances, Nitze warned, the result would be "gradual withdrawals under pressure until we discover one day that we have sacrificed positions of vital interest." In a bipolar setting, a setback anywhere could have severe consequences everywhere, as frightened allies concluded that they should make their peace with the Kremlin before it was too late. No matter where it was tested, the line therefore had to be held: "The assault on free institutions is world-wide now, and in the context of the present polarization of power a defeat of free institutions anywhere is a defeat everywhere."[95]

Holding that line, in turn, meant accepting the massive military buildup that Truman had so far avoided. "In the face of obviously mounting Soviet military strength ours has declined relatively," Nitze wrote. This ominous trend would certainly tempt the Soviets to behave more aggressively, and within a few years it might even cause Stalin to opt for war. The only acceptable response was "a substantial and rapid building up of strength in the free world" in order to "check and roll back the Kremlin's drive for world domination." If Washington were to make good on its commitments, preserve its global influence, and prevent the geopolitical initiative from passing to Moscow, then it would need outright superiority in both conventional and nuclear arms. "Without superior aggregate military strength, in being and readily mobilizable, a policy of 'containment' ... is no more than a policy of bluff."[96] NSC-68 contained no precise recommendations for military spending, but as Bohlen noted in an analysis of the paper, it "would appear to imply a defense establishment in time of peace which would involve almost full-time war mobilization in the United States and the Atlantic Pact countries."[97]

What NSC-68 represented, then, was an effort to fill the holes that were opening up in the nation's strategic posture as commitments expanded and Soviet military power grew. "What we have had to do," said Acheson, "is to construct a defense with inadequate means, trying to guess where each play would come through the line. The result has been amazingly good, but no team can win a pennant this way."[98] It was essential to restore coherence to policy, by clarifying the ideas on which that policy was based, and by providing the resources that would restore strategic solvency. All vulnerable areas would now have to be protected; a substantial, across-the-board military advantage would be central to the accomplishment of national aims. In these respects, NSC-68 showed just how much U.S. grand strategy had evolved since 1947–48. Whether that document provided a better approach would be tested soon enough.

Timing is everything in politics, and Nitze's timing with NSC-68 was impeccable. Prior to June 1950, Truman had accepted the basic analytical thrust of the paper but had blanched at its budgetary implication—a massive, perhaps threefold increase in defense spending. Then North Korean tanks and infantry streamed south across the thirty-eighth parallel. American officials assumed (correctly) that Stalin must have authorized the attack, and they concluded (also correctly) that the invasion validated some of the key ideas of NSC-68. Stalin certainly did not want to start a global war in June 1950; he approved the invasion only after Acheson's Press Club speech had somewhat misleadingly implied that South Korea was *not* a vital U.S. interest. Yet the Soviet dictator was nonetheless engaging in risky, aggressive behavior; he was supporting proxy wars along the periphery: in short, he was exploiting changing power dynamics much as Nitze had predicted. It was "plain beyond all doubt," Truman declared on June 27, "that communism has passed beyond the use of subversion to conquer independent nations and will now used armed invasion and war." The implication was clear: containment on the cheap would no longer work.[99]

Truman responded to the invasion along two separate tracks. First, he dispatched air, naval, and land forces to defend South Korea, and secured United Nations sanction for the endeavor. The administration had previously avoided any explicit commitment to defend South Korea from military attack, and Pentagon war plans still had the peninsula as a marginal area that would be abandoned in case of global war. Yet given the resources and prestige that Washington had invested in Rhee's regime, the string of setbacks that the United States had absorbed in recent months, and no less the blatant manner in which the attack had occurred, it seemed unthinkable that Truman would allow the country to be overrun. If he did, the president and his advisers almost unanimously agreed, the psychological consequences would be catastrophic. Governments from Paris to Tokyo would question U.S. resolve; allied morale would suffer worldwide. "You may be sure that all Europeans to say nothing of the Asiatics are watching to see what the United States will do," wrote Bohlen. "We must draw the line somewhere," agreed JCS Chairman Omar Bradley.[100]

Yet it was vitally important that the commitment to Korea remain limited, for the second track of U.S. policy consisted of a broader campaign to shore up Western positions around the globe. Once it became clear that the Korean War was not merely prelude to additional Soviet advances elsewhere, officials like Acheson and Nitze came to see the conflict as an opportunity as much as a crisis. The invasion had illustrated, in graphic fashion, the dangers of the current situation and the vulnerabilities of Washington's position. But in doing so, it had also created an opening—at home and abroad—for decisive moves to redress that weakness. The United States must "regain the initiative," concluded a follow-on report to NSC-68. It should "build up the military strength of the free world and step up the implementation of a political, economic, and psychological offensive against the USSR."[101]

The primary thrust of the offensive came in Western Europe, where the priority was to turn NATO into a functioning military alliance capable of actually defending the continent in event of war. This meant creating a unified command structure and appointing an American as supreme commander, both of which initiatives Truman began to pursue in the summer of 1950. More importantly, Truman decided to send at least four additional U.S. divisions, along with accompanying tactical air power, to Europe. These forces, Acheson and Johnson had told the president, must be sent "at the earliest feasible date in order that any doubts of American interest in the defense, rather than the liberation, of Europe will be removed, thus increasing the will of our allies to resist."[102] The administration also made plans to earmark additional aid money to support the buildup of European defense capabilities, and for the first time broached the heretofore taboo subject of West German rearmament. It was obvious that Western Europe could not be defended without German troops; American diplomats now tackled the difficult issue of how to raise those troops without antagonizing Paris and shattering the alliance. "If we wait to solve the details of all these questions it will be too late," warned Acheson.[103]

Western Europe remained the decisive theater, but in the spirit of NSC-68 the administration took immediate action to buttress the U.S. position throughout East Asia as well. Military aid to Indochina increased, and its delivery accelerated, rising from an initial commitment of $10 million in May 1950 to $107 million in August.[104] Truman and Acheson also decided that the United States could no longer tolerate the capture of Taiwan, strategically situated between Japan and Southeast Asia, by Mao's forces. The administration interposed U.S. naval forces between Taiwan and the mainland, "neutralizing" the strait and guaranteeing, for the indefinite future, that Chiang's regime on the island would survive. "Formosa is too dangerous a thing for them to have to play with," said Acheson in late 1950. "We must hold the islands."[105] Finally, and despite Soviet objections, the United States initiated the process of negotiating a peace treaty with Japan so as to end the occupation, firm up that country's relationship with the West, and assure that American forces would have continuing use of Japanese bases. The idea, wrote Assistant Secretary of State Dean Rusk, was to "give the Japanese the feeling of again belonging to the family of nations."[106]

All these initiatives were underpinned by the massive military outlays that NSC-68 had recommended. "For as long as necessary," an NSC report completed in August stated, the United States would need "a level of constant military readiness adequate to support U.S. foreign policy, to deter Soviet aggression, and to form the basis for fighting a global war should war prove unavoidable."[107] His resistance to high defense budgets having finally been broken by the Korean War, Truman now agreed with this analysis. He had initially requested $13.9 billion in defense spending for fiscal year 1951; the final authorization ended up being nearly $43 billion. If the United States were to take the steps necessary to strengthen the noncommunist world, it must have a strong military shield. "The proposed military build-up will not solve our international problems," noted Acheson in October 1950, "but will only give an opportunity to solve them." To be sure, a major U.S. military buildup might alarm the Soviets and heighten Cold War tensions, but given the gaps in the nation's strategic posture, there was no good alternative: "The only thing that was more dangerous than undertaking this program was not undertaking it."[108]

Of course, building what Acheson called "situations of strength" in Europe and Asia required keeping the war in Korea short and contained. For all its symbolic importance, Korea remained materially peripheral to the broader scheme of global power relations. If the fighting there dragged on indefinitely, or if it escalated into a larger war involving Communist China, then American energies and military capabilities would be diverted from more crucial areas like Europe. Worse still, if the Soviet Union entered the fray, the United States might be forced to fight—and perhaps lose—a general war before the buildup associated with NSC-68 had taken full effect. As early as June 1950, Acheson had "pointed to the serious nature of the situation if the difficulties in Korea increased instead of our meeting with quick success."[109] "Elementary prudence," agreed the U.S. ambassador to Moscow, "dictates that we not take on now an obligation, the fulfillment of which may require a U.S. military effort out of proportion to political and strategic importance of Korea."[110]

Yet this, unfortunately, was precisely what happened. After UN forces stabilized the front lines in August 1950, Douglas MacArthur's successful landing at Inchon in September presented the administration with an opportunity to reunify all of Korea under noncommunist rule. Truman and the JCS then allowed MacArthur to race northward toward the Yalu, rather than settling for a return to the status quo ante or the establishment of a more defensible border north of the thirty-eighth parallel but well short of the Chinese and Soviet frontiers. They did so despite warnings from Kennan, Bohlen, and Nitze's PPS (as well as numerous international observers) that this might elicit Soviet or Chinese intervention, and despite reminders from military and civilian officials alike that Korea must be kept "in proper correlation to those other worldwide problems we face."[111] The upshot was a massive Chinese counteroffensive in November 1950 that resulted in one of the worst military defeats in U.S. history, dashed hopes for a quick victory in Korea, and led to fears that nuclear—even global—war might be in the offing. "We are faced with the most terrible situation since Pearl Harbor," Truman said.[112]

Looking back, the failure to settle for a good-enough outcome in Korea was clearly the Truman administration's greatest grand strategic blunder, and one that ultimately incurred a terrible human and financial cost. At the time, however, there were a number of powerful factors pushing the administration along its fateful course. Basic military considerations were certainly among these, for the thirty-eighth parallel was not considered a defensible boundary, and Truman, Marshall (now secretary of defense), and the JCS had little desire to restrict MacArthur's tactical flexibility.[113] Simple emotion was also at work, as the smashing success at Inchon created a surging optimism that made top officials less sensitive to the immense dangers they were courting.[114] And, of course, it should be noted that the administration was acting in an atmosphere of great uncertainty. While Kennan and others warned of disaster if the United States pushed too far north, MacArthur and the CIA offered more sanguine assessments of Chinese and Soviet intentions. Beijing would not come in, the supremely confident general famously assured Truman in October 1950, and if it did, "there would be the greatest slaughter."[115]

Beyond all this, there were two deeper motives behind the administration's policy. The first was a sense that Washington had a momentous geopolitical opportunity before it in Korea. If the United States and its allies triumphed conclusively, State and Defense Department officials predicted, the benefits would be far-reaching. Victory in Korea would teach Stalin a stern lesson, strengthening deterrence and boosting American credibility worldwide. It would show that communism could be rolled back, not just contained. It would cause recriminations within the Soviet bloc and might even set off a reverse domino effect in Asia. All this added up to a tremendously alluring prospect for administration officials, one they did not feel they could squander. At stake, wrote the head of the State Department's Office of Northeast Asian Affairs, was the "courage, intelligence, and morality of the United States.... The issue is clear—we should now decide to stand up to what our

President has called 'raw aggression,' or we should admit that Soviet Communism has won and be prepared to take the consequences."[116] Pushing toward the Yalu could be problematic, Acheson acknowledged in October, but "a greater risk would be incurred by showing hesitation and timidity."[117]

Then there was the political dimension. With McCarthyism in full flower in the fall of 1950 and congressional elections fast approaching, top officials were keenly aware that restraint could prove politically painful. "Public and congressional opinion in the United States might be dissatisfied with any conclusion falling short of ... a 'final' settlement of the problem," one State Department official noted.[118] Acheson may inadvertently have stoked this atmosphere during early 1950, when he made several public addresses on the need for a military buildup. Like NSC-68 itself, these presentations were sharply ideological, designed to rouse the domestic audience to action. "We are children of freedom," he declared at one point. "We cannot be safe except in an environment of freedom. We believe in freedom as fundamentally as we believe in anything in this world.... We believe that all people in the world are entitled to as much freedom ... as we want ourselves."[119] As with the Truman Doctrine, this rhetoric was unlikely to encourage sober thinking about limits and trade-offs. One scholar notes that the secretary "may have helped fuel the flames of McCarthyism."[120] Whatever the case, the administration was operating in a political environment that seemed distinctly hostile to half measures, and the prospects for caution declined accordingly.

The tragedy of U.S. escalation in Korea, writes Acheson's foremost biographer, is that "generally admirable men" were unable to avert disaster because they found themselves "paralyzed ... by the force of cold war passions and hemmed in by circumstances."[121] Truman and his top advisers were a group of highly talented individuals, and they were hardly unaware that rushing toward the Yalu could prove geopolitically counterproductive. Yet amid an overheated domestic climate and an intensifying Cold War, they were nonetheless impelled forward by powerful pressures and beguiling temptations. The administration lost its grand strategic equilibrium at a critical moment, and found itself facing just the wider war it had been so important to avoid.

To its credit, the administration regained its balance in the wake of the Chinese intervention. After much deliberation in late 1950 and early 1951, the president rejected the idea of withdrawing from Korea, as well as MacArthur's insistent calls to expand the war into China. The former option would destroy whatever credibility the United States had accrued by intervening in the first place; the latter, as Bradley memorably put it, would "involve us in the wrong war, at the wrong place, at the wrong time, and with the wrong enemy."[122] Instead, the administration opted to fight a limited war. It would seek to stabilize the front, confine the fighting to Korea, and then negotiate an armistice with the enemy, while simultaneously bolstering key geopolitical positions around the world. "We should not think in terms of Korea alone," Acheson insisted, "but in world-wide terms and what we face around the world, principally in Europe."[123] The global situation was critical, he believed, and the United States could not lose sight of the big picture. Acheson expressed his views forcefully at a high-level meeting in late 1950:

> It would not be too much if we had all the troops that the military want. If we had all of the things that our European allies want it would not be too much. If we had a system for full mobilization it would not be too much. Secretary Acheson said that how we get there he doesn't know, but he feels that the danger couldn't be greater than it is.[124]

Through the end of Truman's presidency, Europe and NATO remained the primary focus of U.S. policy. Washington and its allies could not settle on a formula for German rearmament, which remained elusive until the mid-1950s. But they did decide, in principle, that rearmament would happen at some point, and in the meantime Acheson secured accords that devolved greater authority and sovereignty to the West German government. The administration also took additional steps to strengthen the alliance. Between 1951 and 1953, the United States provided some $20 billion in military assistance to its NATO allies, in effect sponsoring a European buildup to complement the arrival of additional American forces on the continent. By 1952, the alliance boasted fifteen well-equipped divisions, anchored by 180,000 U.S. troops. The southern flank of NATO received attention as well, with the administration extending military aid to Yugoslavia and bringing Turkey and Greece into the alliance in the early 1950s. A "real deterrent to aggression in Western Europe" was taking shape, Dwight Eisenhower (then supreme commander of NATO) believed.[125]

The same sense of urgency and determination characterized U.S. policy in East Asia. Acheson pushed ahead with the negotiation of a peace treaty with Tokyo, along with an accompanying security agreement that brought Japan under the U.S. defense umbrella and guaranteed American forces access to Japanese bases. Japan was "the heart of the whole Far Eastern situation," he explained, and it had to be held "with the West."[126] To assuage the concerns of Japan's former enemies, the United States also concluded security agreements with Australia, New Zealand, and the Philippines. Meanwhile, aid to Indochina continued to rise rapidly. As the Vietminh insurgency intensified, the United States provided tanks, planes, guns, ammunition, and other assets to French forces. "The Military Aid Program to Indochina enjoys the highest priority immediately after the military effort in Korea," noted one State Department official. By late 1952, the United States was paying over one-third of the costs of Paris's war in Indochina, and the proportion soon went up from there.[127]

The United States also began to assume greater responsibilities in the Middle East. The importance of Middle Eastern military bases and oil reserves only loomed larger amid the elevated international tensions caused by the Korean War, while a rising tide of nationalism was destroying London's influence in the region. Worried that British intransigence might channel this nationalism in radical directions, and fearful of potential Soviet moves in the region, U.S. officials considered numerous methods for stabilizing the area. Acheson worked, unsuccessfully, to mediate disputes between London and the governments of Iran and Egypt, while also pushing for significant U.S. aid to win favor with these regimes. State and Defense officials explored a series of regional defense schemes involving Washington, London, and key Middle Eastern countries, while Nitze called for the stationing of U.S. forces in the area. For its part, the CIA developed covert programs to weaken pro-Soviet groups like the Tudeh Party in Iran. Many of these initiatives were stillborn or ineffective during the Truman years, but they presaged growing preoccupation with the region in the period to follow. "The time has come," argued Assistant Secretary of State George McGhee, "for more positive action in the Middle East on our part."[128]

Amid this activity, the American military buildup continued apace. Defense budgets stayed high through the end of Truman's presidency, with the fiscal year 1952 authorization topping out at $56.9 billion, plus another $5 billion for defense-related projects and $6 billion for military assistance. Crucially, the administration devoted the bulk of defense spending to improving general-purpose capabilities rather than to fighting the war in Korea. By the end of that conflict, the Army had grown by nearly one million personnel and ten divisions; the Navy had added some 450 ships and over four hundred thousand sailors; the Air Force roughly doubled in size; and the Marine Corps grew from 74,000 to 246,000 personnel. The U.S. atomic arsenal increased from 299 weapons at the end of 1950 to 841 by 1952, giving Washington a 17-to-1 advantage in nuclear arms, along with dominant margins in strategic and tactical aircraft, naval might, and other power-projection capabilities.[129] "The Soviets respected nothing but force, and would talk and negotiate only in the face of force," Truman commented. "To build such force ... is precisely what we are attempting to do now."[130]

And by the end of Truman's presidency, terrific results had been achieved in several key areas. Western Europe was recovering from its postwar devastation, Germany was gradually being rehabilitated and reintegrated, and U.S. officials were now confident that at least part of the continent could be held in case of war. Soviet and East bloc troops still far outnumbered their Western counterparts, but as Eisenhower noted in 1952, "the tide has begun to flow our way and the situation of the free world is brighter than it was a year ago."[131] In East Asia, the United States was now allied to an independent Japan, whose economy had been kick-started by the reverse-course and by Korean War–generated exports. More generally, American military strength had grown enormously, decreasing—though hardly eliminating—the prospect that the United States and its key allies would be defeated in war or coerced in peace. All told, Truman and his advisers had done much to foster a stable Western community and establish a very strong position against Moscow.

Yet the price of all this was significant, and the administration was still wrestling with the dilemmas of Cold War grand strategy when it left office in early 1953. There was no escape from the Korean War, where the cost of restraint was an expensive and unpopular stalemate that eventually claimed more than thirty-three thousand American lives. Korea was a "great moral question," said Marshall in 1951, but "a very heavy drain on us" as well.[132] The steady accretion of U.S. military power did allow the administration to more aggressively bomb North Korean targets (particularly those close to the Chinese and Soviet borders), but through the end of Truman's presidency, these tactics could not bring the war to a close. As the fighting and peace talks dragged on inconclusively, Truman's military advisers periodically considered escalating the violence in dramatic ways, perhaps by bombing targets in Manchuria or even using nuclear weapons. Truman fantasized about threatening to destroy "every military base in Manchuria" and every major city in China and the Soviet Union if the enemy did not come to terms.[133] The administration prudently declined to implement these ideas, but their mere consideration showed how burdensome fighting a limited war in a peripheral area could be.

The administration's strategy proved problematic in other ways as well. Acheson liked to talk about creating situations of strength, but because U.S. policy emphasized defending virtually every point along the Eurasian perimeter, it inevitably created situations of weakness as well. This was most clearly the case in Indochina, where it was becoming painfully evident that the French could not defeat the Vietminh militarily, and would not devolve power sufficiently to find a political solution to the conflict. Yet because of the area's perceived economic importance, and no less because U.S. planners had come to define their interests so broadly, backing away from Indochina seemed fantastical. During the early 1950s, American officials plunged deeper and deeper into a conflict that they recognized might well be unwinnable. "The French, through their folly ... have left us with the choice of the following two ghastly courses of action," noted one prescient State Department analysis:

1. To wash our hands of the country and allow the Communists to overrun it; or,
2. To continue to pour treasure (and perhaps eventually lives) into a hopeless cause in which the French have already expended about a billion and a half dollars and about fifty thousand lives—and this at a cost of alienating vital segments of Asian public opinion.

In picking the second option, Truman and Acheson firmly established a commitment that would plague U.S. policy for more than two decades to come.[134]

Nor, for that matter, did the continuing military buildup solve the perpetual problem of reconciling means and ends. One of the key implications of NSC-68 had been that Washington needed the conventional capabilities to defeat local, Korea-style attacks along the Eurasian periphery. Yet as long as the administration believed it necessary to respond to these thrusts wherever they might occur, it was hard to see how any amount of military power would ever be sufficient. The United States could conceivably respond to local conflicts by threatening to use its nuclear arsenal against the Soviet Union, but as Kennan had pointed out in 1949, such a strategy would become less attractive as Moscow's own nuclear capabilities matured. In any event, more military power would not necessarily do much to improve the situation in emerging hot spots like Egypt and Iran, where the problem was less one of conventional military aggression than of rising nationalism and political upheaval. (In the Middle East, Acheson once commented, "we had a situation which might have been devised by Karl Marx himself.") For all the progress that had occurred, Nitze lamented in January 1953, the noncommunist world had "not yet achieved adequate security against the several threats posed by the Soviet system."[135]

In certain ways, the quest for military dominance actually proved to be self-defeating. As American officials recognized, many of the initiatives undertaken to strengthen the West during the early 1950s—discussions of German rearmament, the U.S. military buildup, the signing of a peace treaty with Japan—were bound to be threatening to Moscow. If West Germany rearmed under NATO auspices, one intelligence analysis predicted, the Soviet perception would be that "the situation would present a grave threat to the security of the USSR and to the achievement of ultimate Soviet objectives."[136] Not surprisingly, one result of the Western buildup was to spur a corresponding Soviet response. Stalin refrained from precipitating a diplomatic or military crisis over the German issue, likely out of respect for the growth of U.S. and Western military power related to NSC-68.[137] But in January 1951, he announced a five-year plan for greater defense spending, military production—particularly of long-range bombers—and upgrades in East European arsenals. During the mid-1950s, a major nuclear buildup focusing on long-range missiles would follow. Increases in Western military strength led to greater security for Europe and East Asia, but they contributed to a long-running arms race, and thus persistent insecurity, as well.[138]

Even in the short run, the programs associated with NSC-68 were unsustainable. In public, Truman dismissed charges that the military buildup was draining the domestic economy, but in private, the "hard-money man" was not so sure. "Our resources are not inexhaustible," he lamented. "We can't go on like this."[139] Domestic opposition to higher tax rates and growing budget deficits increased as the war went on, while the economic controls imposed in order to fight inflation proved politically unpopular as well. To continue spending at the current levels, the Budget Bureau predicted, "might require a continuation of economic restraints and taxes incompatible with what the public would support over many years in a situation short of all-out war."[140] It was an astute judgment, as Dwight Eisenhower won the presidency in 1952 on a platform pledging to balance the budget. Convinced that excessive defense outlays risked sapping America's underlying economic vitality, he spent much of his time in Washington seeking to bring Pentagon spending down to a more manageable level. Truman, in contrast, left office with some of the lowest approval ratings in modern history, his policies—especially in Korea—receiving criticism on all sides. The "golden age," in other words, did not appear so golden at the time.

So what can all of this tell us about Truman-era grand strategy, and about the broader challenges of grand strategy as an endeavor? First, it is clear that there was real purpose and innovation in U.S. policy during the Truman years. Relatively early on, U.S. officials came to the fundamental grand strategic insights that made up the intellectual core of containment: the realization that there was a middle ground between appeasement and war, and the idea that containing Soviet power meant, first and foremost, securing a favorable geopolitical position in Europe and East Asia. The United States subsequently worked to construct that position through seminal initiatives like the Marshall Plan, NATO, and the rehabilitation of former enemies in West Germany and Japan. It then defended that position through the rearmament program and political-military initiatives undertaken in response to the Korean War and NSC-68. In this sense, the administration's grand strategy did its job: it put American power to essential long-term purposes, and it provided the intellectual rudder that allowed Truman to navigate the dangerous shoals of the early Cold War.

Yet it also bears remembering that Truman-era grand strategy was often a messy affair, and in some ways a deeply problematic one. Just as it is a mistake to argue that there was no overarching grand strategy guiding the administration, it is also an error to downplay the degree of adaptation and improvisation that characterized U.S. policy.[141] American officials had a clear view of geographical priorities and overall strategic goals from 1947–48 onward, but their ideas on how to achieve those goals shifted considerably as time went on. Truman and his advisers did not initially plan on forming a peacetime military alliance with Western Europe; they took this unprecedented step only after realizing that economic assistance would not suffice to stabilize the region. Likewise, the administration did not originally envision undertaking a massive military buildup; it did so only after an accumulation of global responsibilities and the growth of Soviet military power made it seem that the existing approach risked catastrophic failure. Containment, in other words, did not spring forth fully formed from the mind of George Kennan; it was an idea whose practical implications had to be worked out—and reworked out—amid the myriad crises and shocks of the day.

That working-out process, in turn, could be quite troublesome for the Truman administration. The president and his advisers continually struggled to reconcile America's expanding commitments with its finite capabilities, to find that elusive sweet spot in terms of defense spending, and to mobilize support for containment without overheating the political climate at home. They sometimes found it difficult to maintain a sense of proportion in meeting the challenge of the moment—as their shortsighted expansion of the Korean War so dramatically illustrated—and no less to contain the Soviet Union without encouraging a costly arms race or taking on a dead-end colonial conflict in Indochina. The Truman era was a time of grand strategic determination and accomplishment, but it was one of frustration, errors, and trade-offs as well.

This critique must not be taken too far. Mistakes and trade-offs are inevitable in foreign policy, and the administration made great strides toward achieving its overriding geopolitical goals. What all of these issues suggest, rather, is that grand strategy was in Truman's time what it remains today—a disorderly, iterative process that is never easy and demands frequent recalibration if it is to work at all. That process may originate in a flash of geopolitical insight à la Kennan, but those insights must then be translated into action amid the distractions, fears, and crises that perpetually characterize both domestic and foreign affairs. This was something that Mr. X himself understood. "The purposes of foreign policy will always be relative to a moving stream of events," wrote Kennan in 1948. "Thus, any formula for U.S. foreign policy objectives can only be an indication of direction, not of final destination."[142] It was an apt description of Truman-era grand strategy, and of the difficulties of grand strategy writ large.

CHAPTER 2

Travails of the Heroic Statesmen

Grand Strategy in the Nixon-Kissinger Years

If the Truman administration is generally credited with constructing the Cold War order, Richard Nixon and Henry Kissinger had the misfortune of governing as that order was coming undone. Containment was in crisis in the late 1960s. The Vietnam War had exposed the limits of America's power and the depth of its internal divisions, while the international system as a whole was shifting away from the postwar atmosphere of U.S. hegemony. Simply plodding along with inherited orthodoxies was no longer an option; Washington would need truly innovative policies if it were to preserve global stability in an era of relative national decline. "We require a new burst of creativity," wrote Kissinger in 1968.[1]

In many ways, Nixon and Kissinger seemed particularly well suited to this task. Both men brought considerable insight and expertise to the making of foreign policy. Both believed in taking "the long view," in looking beyond the immediate crisis and grappling with the deeper historical forces at play. And, for all their personal differences, both Nixon and Kissinger possessed an abiding faith in the power of inspired statesmanship. Nixon styled himself the practitioner of the "big play," the bold stroke that would cut through the morass of daily policy struggles. For his part, Kissinger believed that great leaders need not simply react to the challenges they confronted, but that they could rise above these trials and impose their own purpose on events. This was the essence of grand strategy—not just matching means to ends, but waging the more profound struggle to "shape the currents of our time in the light of our values."[2]

This was the ethos that Nixon and Kissinger brought to U.S. foreign policy between 1969 and 1977—Nixon as president from 1969 until 1974, Kissinger as an exceptionally influential national security adviser (1969–1975) and secretary of state (1973–1977) in both the Nixon and Ford administrations. During their time in power, the two men pursued a highly ambitious grand strategy, one that was meant to decrease America's burdens and increase its flexibility, while at the same time maintaining global order and keeping radical forces in check. The challenge, Kissinger said, was "to build a new building while tearing down the old beams and not letting the structure collapse."[3] This would be accomplished not by standing athwart historical change, but by deftly exploiting it to create new sources of strength and maneuver. The United States would draw its chief adversaries into a more manageable triangular relationship, shed unsustainable commitments while maintaining credibility, and ultimately position itself as the pivot of a more stable and advantageous global balance. Through dynamic and purposeful statecraft, America would transcend its moment of relative decline.

Doing so, however, would require American leaders to escape the constraints of their own society as well. Nixon and Kissinger doubted that key attributes of the U.S. system—raucous partisan politics, bureaucratic infighting, even traditional concepts of ethics and morality—could be reconciled with the imperatives of creative leadership. Accordingly, they believed that coherent grand strategy required an extraordinary concentration of power. Talented statesmen needed to be given the authority to make bold and controversial decisions; they had to be insulated from disruptions that might sever the link between wisdom and policy. "The statesman is ... like one of the heroes in classical drama," Kissinger wrote. "He must bridge the gap between a people's experience and his vision, between a nation's tradition and its future."[4] Grand strategy, in this view, was a heroic sort of undertaking.

The heroic style had its merits, and during the early 1970s the United States executed a series of moves that bolstered its deteriorating global posture at minimal material cost. On these grounds alone, the Nixon-Kissinger grand strategy must be considered at least a partial success. In the end, though, the performance could not be sustained. Nixon and Kissinger could not ultimately master a difficult global environment, nor could they indefinitely shield the conduct of policy from the people and institutions it was supposed to serve. A "new equilibrium" remained elusive when Kissinger left the State Department in January 1977, and the heroic style had been exposed as deeply problematic in its own right.[5]

Individuals matter in international politics, and during the Nixon-Kissinger era, they mattered more than usual. Nixon and Kissinger dominated American grand strategy during their time in office. From 1969 to 1974, the two men held the reins of authority tightly in their own hands, taking personal control of the conception and implementation of foreign policy. After Nixon's resignation, Kissinger carried on as the preeminent influence in the Ford administration. As a result of all this, the nation's grand strategy showed strong continuity between 1969 and 1977; it was also shaped, in important ways, by the distinctive personalities of its two chief architects.

Both Nixon and Kissinger possessed considerable geopolitical expertise when they arrived in the White House in January 1969. Kissinger, the Harvard academic, had spent nearly two decades thinking about the requirements of a successful foreign policy prior to his appointment as national security adviser. As a graduate student, he had written a dissertation on the forging of a stable international order after the devastation of the Napoleonic wars, a subject with clear parallels to the postwar predicament of the United States. After receiving his doctorate, he went on to grapple with some of the key problems of Cold War statecraft—the uses of nuclear weapons, the relationship between force and diplomacy, the nature of transatlantic relations, and others. These years as an "apprentice statesman" earned Kissinger a reputation as one of the nation's top strategic thinkers; they also allowed him to develop the "intellectual capital" that would drive his decision making once in office.[6]

Nixon, by contrast, was no academic, but he had sharp geopolitical instincts and abundant practical experience. Nixon had served as Dwight Eisenhower's vice president for eight crisis-plagued years in the 1950s, and he had honed his thinking on world affairs by reading, writing, and traveling during his political exile in the 1960s. By the time he returned to power, he had formulated coherent views on policy issues ranging from the Vietnam War to U.S.-China relations. He had also developed a pragmatic streak that belied his reputation as a dogmatic anticommunist. "We live in a new world," he commented in 1967; new approaches would undoubtedly be required.[7]

To be sure, mutual expertise hardly ensured that the Nixon-Kissinger relationship ran smoothly. Kissinger was a Jewish refugee from Hitler's Germany who moved in the august circles of the eastern establishment and had a long-running partnership with Nelson Rockefeller, Nixon's Republican rival. Nixon was a congenital outsider—and casual anti-Semite—who both loathed and envied the eastern elite. Not surprisingly, the dealings between the two men were never comfortable. Kissinger respected Nixon's geopolitical acumen, but considered him to be impetuous and even irratio-nal. Nixon acknowledged Kissinger's talents, but doubted his loyalty and cast aspersions on his Jewish background. As time went on, he also grew increas-ingly envious of the public acclaim that Kissinger received, to the point that he considered firing the national security adviser before the travails of Watergate made it imperative to promote him instead. "I don't trust Henry," Nixon once said, "but I can use him."[8]

As this comment indicates, the Nixon-Kissinger relationship was simulta-neously dysfunctional and symbiotic. Kissinger viewed Nixon as his conduit to power, and he recognized that the president's insecurities could be made to serve his own ambitions. He fulsomely praised Nixon for his boldness and dar-ing, while also shrewdly reinforcing his suspicions of "enemies" like the press and the State Department. Elitist foreign-service officers believed they had "a charter to dominate the conduct of foreign policy," Kissinger wrote to Nixon in 1970; they showed "a general lack of responsiveness ... and a deficiency in personal loyalty to you."[9] Nixon, in turn, planned to direct foreign policy from the White House, and realized that he needed a brilliant mind to shape and coordinate the diverse aspects of American statecraft. This was Kissinger's role in the administration—translating the president's instincts and ideas into workable policies, and weaving these individual policies into a coherent whole. "Above everything else," Nixon wrote of Kissinger, "he is our big gun in the area where we have had our greatest success."[10] Nixon and Kissinger were never personally close, but they depended on each other nonetheless.

This did not mean, however, that there was only mutual exploitation at work in the relationship. For all their personal differences, Nixon and Kis-singer took strikingly similar views of world politics. Both men believed that foreign policy was too important to be left to a self-interested bureaucracy; both were willing to acknowledge the limits of U.S. power. Both men placed a premium on toughness and credibility, even as they agreed that diplomacy and negotiation had been underutilized weapons in America's Cold War arse-nal. Most importantly, both Nixon and Kissinger viewed global affairs as an unforgiving pursuit, a contest in which weakness could be fatal and a stable balance of power was the only guarantee of peace. "Henry and he had an ideological affinity," Kissinger aide Peter Rodman later recalled. "They both looked at the world in the same way."[11]

They also shared a tendency to see foreign policy as a lonely, heroic endeavor. Nixon, writes one scholar, "fancied himself a solitary prophet, tapped for leadership, endowed with uncommon skills to engineer world peace."[12] He believed that the heart of statesmanship was the ability not simply to respond to crises, but to understand—and thereby take hold of—the profound historical trends underlying them. "It is essential to look at the world not just in terms of immediate diplomatic battles and decisions but the great forces that move the world," he told Zhou Enlai in 1972.[13] It was no less essential to possess the fortitude to turn insight into policy. Throughout his career, Nixon liked to see himself as the brave but embattled leader, struggling to move a reluctant nation toward great and necessary ends. For the president, the archetypal role model was Harry Truman. Truman, he wrote to aide H. R. Haldeman in 1970, "will be remembered in history as one of the more successful Presidents, not because of what he did—the Marshall Plan-the Atomic bomb-etc., but because he had 'courage-guts-an outspoken devil-may-care attitude.'"[14]

Kissinger took a remarkably similar—if more intellectual—view of what statesmanship entailed. From the 1950s onward, Kissinger argued that U.S. policy must be guided by a coherent "global strategy." Without such a strategy, policy makers would inevitably become entranced by the immediate at the expense of the enduring, by the trivial to the exclusion of the essential. "The most difficult challenge for a policymaker in foreign affairs is to establish priorities," he wrote after leaving office. "A conceptual framework—which 'links' events—is an essential tool." The statesman was "locked in an endless battle in which the urgent constantly gains on the important"; only through intelligent, purposeful grand strategy was it possible to "rescue an element of choice from the pressure of circumstance."[15]

For Kissinger, however, grand strategy was about more than setting priorities and matching means to ends. It was also about finding the ability to shape events, rather than being shaped by them. "No leader is entitled to resignation," Kissinger wrote. "He owes it to his people to strive, to create, and to resist the decay that besets all human institutions."[16] This was what had distinguished Metternich and Bismarck, the men Kissinger had studied as an academic and upon whom he modeled himself as a statesman, and this theme of salvaging creation from decay was a constant in his writings. "Anyone wishing to affect events must be opportunist to some extent," he observed in 1968. "The real distinction is between those who adapt their purposes to reality and those who seek to mold reality in the light of their purposes."[17]

Needless to say, this was not a task for the mediocre. True statesmen must possess the vision to discern the great historical forces at work and the adroitness to position their nations accordingly. "The successful conduct of foreign policy demands, above all, the intuitive ability to sense the future and thereby to master it," he argued.[18] They must also possess the authority to turn wisdom into action: innovative policy, Kissinger wrote in the 1960s, would be possible "only by essentially arbitrary decisions."[19] In Kissinger's eyes, then, the statesman was a prophetic figure, a lonely visionary with the foresight and courage that his broader community yet lacked. "The ultimate task of a leader is to take his society from where it is to where it has never been," he would write his memoirs. "But this requires a willingness to travel on the difficult road between a nation's experience and its destiny. He is bound to be alone at least part of the way until his society's experience catches up with its possibilities."[20] For Kissinger as for Nixon, grand strategy was about seizing hold of history—and escaping the limitations of one's own society, as well.

The need for inspired statecraft seemed particularly pressing when Nixon and Kissinger assumed office in January 1969. The international environment had evolved considerably since the Truman years, and much to America's disadvantage. The preponderance of nuclear power that Washington had enjoyed during the early Cold War had vanished, as a determined Soviet buildup brought Moscow to the verge of strategic parity. Mao's China had developed nuclear weapons and emerged as a great power in its own right, even as it quarreled openly—and violently—with the Kremlin. U.S.-NATO relations had grown fractious, as France withdrew from the alliance military command and American legislators balked at funding a continued troop presence on the Continent. The Bretton Woods system of international finance was creaking under the weight of its own accumulating imbalances, and throughout the Third World, instability and radical nationalism were on the rise. All around the globe, the United States was confronted with rising threats and challenges that its leaders were hard-pressed to resolve.

Then there was the Vietnam War. During the 1960s, the Johnson administration had deployed some five hundred thousand troops to Southeast Asia to prevent a Communist victory. The upshot was a bloody stalemate that laid bare the limits of U.S. power and shattered the Cold War consensus at home. The war drove LBJ from office, and it combined with racial injustice, poverty, and other festering social issues to provoke riots and demonstrations from Newark to Berkeley. Violence was becoming distressingly normal; there were over six hundred bombings or bombing attempts across the country in 1969, and the number climbed still higher the year after. "This is the way civilizations begin to die," Nixon remarked.[21] Kissinger, too, was deeply troubled, seeing the "inchoate rage of the 1960s" as a telltale sign of national decline. Protest had taken on "a violent and ugly character," he later wrote. "The comity by which a democratic society must live had broken down."[22]

The war had an equally traumatic impact on the American economy. The cost of fighting in Southeast Asia exacerbated the chronic balance of payments problems the United States faced as the anchor of Bretton Woods, and it caused a sharp and sustained increase in inflation at home. Even before LBJ left office, the economic distortions were mounting, and it had become apparent that Washington was in a position of severe overstretch. "Our fiscal situation is abominable," Johnson lamented. If the United States sought to maintain its commitment to Vietnam indefinitely, it would probably wreck the economic power upon which American global influence ultimately rested.[23]

For Nixon and Kissinger, the crises of the 1960s demonstrated two essential truths about U.S. foreign policy. The first was that the global balance of power had shifted fundamentally since the early Cold War. The "problem we face," noted Kissinger in 1969, was "the generally deteriorating strategic position of the United States during the past decade."[24] Moscow was nearing strategic parity, countries like West Germany and Japan were catching up to Washington economically, and new powers like China, Indonesia, and Brazil were gaining diplomatic and political influence. The world was becoming authentically bipolar militarily, and increasingly multipolar in economic and political terms. "We are reaching the end of the post-war era," Kissinger said; an international system shaped by American hegemony was giving way to a more complex and fluid situation.[25] In these circumstances, the United States could no longer bear such preponderant responsibility for world order. As Vietnam had shown, attempting to do so would only lead to exhaustion abroad and chaos at home. "We had to adjust our foreign policy to the new facts of life," Kissinger explained. "It is beyond the physical and psychological capacity of the U.S. to make itself responsible for every part of the world."[26]

The second essential truth was that the United States had so far failed to adapt to this new reality. Rather than revamping American grand strategy in light of a shifting global balance, the Kennedy and Johnson administrations had merely sought to address the symptoms of the underlying problem— and in doing so, they had made the problem all the worse. Committing five hundred thousand troops to Vietnam had honored the central conceit of NSC-68—the idea that America could and should hold an unbroken global perimeter. But it had also robbed the United States of its geopolitical flexibility, exacerbated the effects of relative decline, and presented Moscow with tantalizing opportunities to exploit American overextension. "While the United States is tied down in Viet Nam," Nixon argued, "the Soviets are loose in the World—free to challenge us in the Mediterranean, free to move into the vacuum left by retreating colonial powers in the Middle East and along the vast rimland of the Indian Ocean."[27] No less troubling, the fact that LBJ had repeatedly doubled down in a theater of tertiary importance—"a small peninsula on a major continent," Kissinger termed it—showed that U.S. policy had lost all sense of proportion.[28]

For the new administration, the first task was therefore to restore intellectual coherence, not just to U.S. policy in Vietnam, but to American globalism writ large. It was imperative to "take the long view," Nixon had commented in 1967, to "evaluate the great forces at work in the world and see what America's role should be."[29] "A philosophical deepening" was in order, Kissinger agreed; American leaders needed to peer beyond the daily crises and begin adapting to unmistakable global trends. "We will never be able to contribute to a stable and creative world order unless we first form some conception of it," he wrote in 1968.[30]

The "philosophical deepening" that the administration envisioned contained both conventional and innovative elements. In the former sense, both Nixon and Kissinger saw American power as a force for good in the world. They believed that the United States must remain the most influential actor in the international system, and they recoiled at the prospect of Moscow, Beijing, or other hostile powers being allowed to run wild. "People may want to put their heads in the sand; they may want to clean up the ghettos," said Nixon. "All right, we will get out of the world. Who is left? The two activists, Russia and Communist China."[31] There would thus be no wholesale retreat from containment or from global responsibility more broadly; at a minimum, Washington must remain committed to preserving a stable and congenial international order. "If America were to become a dropout in assuming the responsibility for defending peace and freedom in the world . . . the rest of the world would live in terror," the president warned.[32]

Where Nixon and Kissinger were more creative was in their approach to dealing with the crisis of American power. Even before they arrived in office, both men had conveyed a clear sense that the development of a less U.S.-centric global order need not lead to chaos. If handled properly, it could actually serve as the basis for a new era of stability and even advantage. A more equitable distribution of power, for instance, could facilitate great-power negotiation and lessen the danger of nuclear war. "The years just ahead can bring a breakthrough for peace," said Nixon in 1968; "they must be a time of careful probing, of intensive negotiations, of a determined search for those areas of accommodation between East and West on which a climate of mutual trust can eventually be built."[33] Similarly, the rise of new economic and diplomatic powers would decrease the U.S. share of international influence, but it might also lessen the burdens on American leadership and create space for more flexible statecraft. "A more pluralistic world . . . is profoundly in our long-term interest," Kissinger wrote. "Political multipolarity, while difficult to get used to, is the precondition for a new period of creativity."[34]

   The purpose of American grand strategy, then, should be to work toward a more economical concept of global order, one that could accommodate the shifting geopolitical dynamics while keeping radical forces at bay. "We ... face the problem of helping to build international relations on a basis which may be less unilaterally American," Kissinger argued.[35] The diffusion of power would have to be treated as an opportunity rather than a crisis; U.S. interests and influence would be preserved not by resisting global forces, but by using agile diplomacy to exploit and balance them against one another. "Our deepest challenge," Kissinger had written in 1968, "will be to evoke the creativity of a pluralistic world."[36] In an era of relative national decline, successful grand strategy meant finding the wisdom and dexterity to master historical change.

What this meant in practice took time to fully emerge. Nixon and Kissinger understood that some improvisation was inevitable in foreign policy, that it was futile to seek "a cookbook, a recipe, that can be applied literally to every situation from one day to the next."[37] What they did have, thanks to their years of experience and reflection, was a set of core strategic principles and priorities that structured their dealings with the world. Taken together, these concepts constituted a blend of boldness and restraint. They involved reducing commitments and lessening tensions, but also seizing the initiative through unorthodox and dramatic steps. The basic idea, according to Kissinger, was to enlist creativity in the service of order, to use innovative measures "to clear away the underbush [sic] of the old period ... to construct a new international settlement—which will be more stable, less crisis-conscious, and less dependent on decisions in one capital."[38]
   The cornerstone of this new settlement would be a more sustainable relationship with America's chief rival. Like their Cold War predecessors, Nixon and Kissinger identified the Soviet Union as the most dangerous threat to the United States and its allies. Yet they also thought (as Kissinger put it) that Soviet policy "was being pulled in two directions" during the late 1960s. On the one hand, the attainment of parity and the growth of Soviet power had put Moscow in a position to challenge U.S. interests worldwide. On the other hand, there were several factors arguing for moderation in Soviet policy. An acrimonious dispute with China, upheaval within the Warsaw Pact, the need for foreign trade and technology, and the desire to gain recognition as a superpower with legitimate interests and prerogatives—these trends gave Moscow reason for restraint in its dealings with the West. To the extent that the United States could encourage these latter tendencies and discourage the former, it could hold the line and even place containment on a sounder

footing.[39] The goal, Kissinger noted, should be to lead the Soviet Union "to a realization of the limitations of both its physical strength and of the limits of its ideological fervor"—in other words, to ensure that Moscow's emergence as a true superpower did not destabilize global politics.[40]

Achieving this goal would require the administration to use both positive and negative inducements. Nixon and Kissinger understood that an increasingly powerful Soviet Union was unlikely to act with restraint if its basic security was imperiled or its legitimate demands were ignored. "We must recognize that the Soviet Union has interests," Kissinger wrote in a letter signed by Nixon in February 1969; "in the present circumstances we cannot but take account of them in defining our own."[41] Yet engagement alone would not produce Soviet circumspection, for the Kremlin was equally unlikely to behave it if perceived that there were no sanctions for aggressive behavior. The key, then, was to structure Moscow's incentives so that its leaders would gradually come to appreciate that they had more to gain through moderation than confrontation. "We were determined to resist Soviet adventures," Kissinger later wrote; "at the same time we were prepared to negotiate about a genuine easing of tensions.... We would pursue a carrot-and-stick approach, ready to impose penalties for adventurism, willing to expand relations in the context of responsible behavior."[42]

This was the logic behind the policies collectively known as détente. During Nixon's first term, he and Kissinger pursued several interlocking initiatives meant to satisfy reasonable Soviet interests while also socializing Moscow into a "concept of international order" that the United States could accept.[43] The two countries began negotiations on a series of issues, the most important of which were four-power talks on the still-contested status of Berlin and bilateral discussions on limiting offensive and defensive strategic weapons (the Strategic Arms Limitation Talks, or SALT). The former talks were designed to lessen tensions in a dangerous Cold War hot spot; the latter to legitimize Soviet nuclear parity—a key aspiration of the Brezhnev government—while also imposing bounds on the Kremlin buildup. "We need an agreement," Nixon would tell Brezhnev in 1972, "or we will bankrupt each other in the arms race."[44] In fact, congressional appropriations for a further U.S. buildup were not likely to be forthcoming, so the only way to avoid falling behind was to lock in parity now.

Doing so necessitated a careful balancing act on Nixon's part. The president was painfully aware that the Soviets would have little need to cut a strategic arms deal if they realized that the United States was unwilling to make further improvements to its arsenal in any event. The administration therefore pushed ahead with the deployment of MIRVs (multiple,

independently targeted reentry vehicles) in 1969, while also successfully lob-
bying a reluctant Congress to fund an expanded antiballistic missile (ABM)
system that could then be used as a bargaining chip. At the same time, so as
not to heighten tensions or set off a renewed arms race in which the U.S.
Congress might not be inclined to compete, Nixon signaled that he was not
interested in regaining nuclear superiority over Moscow—"strategic sufficiency" would be enough. "Neither in what we say nor what we do, would
we want to force the pace of armaments," wrote Kissinger.[45]

In hopes of promoting Soviet moderation beyond this single issue, Kissinger devised the concept of linkage, or the idea that SALT and other negotiations must be enmeshed within the broader scheme of bilateral relations.
Progress on arms control and other Kremlin priorities—access to most
favored nation (MFN) status and U.S. trade credits, an East-West conference
that would legitimize the Soviet sphere of influence in Eastern Europe—
would not be determined on the merits of each issue, but would instead be
held hostage to across-the-board Soviet restraint. If Brezhnev wanted SALT,
for instance, he would have to respect American interests in the Third World.
If he pressed for advantage there or elsewhere, he risked provoking a U.S.
reaction and losing all fruits of superpower negotiation. The Soviets "cannot expect to reap the benefits of cooperation in one area while seeking to
take advantage of tension or confrontation elsewhere," Kissinger wrote.[46]
In effect, linkage was a behavior modification policy that was designed to
maximize American leverage. The relative power balance might be shifting,
Kissinger believed, but a subtle, nuanced effort could still allow the United
States to exert great influence over Soviet policy.

In the short term, détente and linkage were meant to provide Moscow
with reasons for adhering to an acceptable code of global conduct. Over the
long term, the "rewards" of détente would reinforce these constraints. As the
Soviets gained access to trade credits and MFN status, they would face greater
risks in antagonizing the United States. The purpose of giving Moscow trade
privileges, Kissinger said, was so that "we can turn it off if their political
behavior becomes threatening."[47] And as the expansion of East-West commerce brought the Soviets deeper into the world economy, the Kremlin would
see still less advantage in challenging the existing order. In theory, the end result
of détente would be a sort of "self-containment," as the Soviets concluded that
a policy of provocation was simply not worth the price. "The structure of
peace," Nixon explained in 1972, "has to be built in such a way that all those
who might be tempted to destroy it will instead have a stake in preserving it."[48]

The counterpart to U.S.-Soviet détente was a parallel opening to China.
Both Kissinger and Nixon had long recognized the impossibility of forging

a stable international order that did not include the world's most populous country. "Taking the long view," wrote Nixon in 1967, "we simply cannot afford to leave China forever outside the family of nations, there to nurture its fantasies, cherish its hates and threaten its neighbors."[49] When Nixon penned these words, Mao's regime was consumed by the radicalism of the Cultural Revolution, and in early 1969 it remained unclear whether there was any real hope for rapprochement. The situation soon changed, however, as the Sino-Soviet split erupted into bloody border clashes and rumors of general war. In August, a Soviet diplomat even asked an American counterpart "what the U.S. would do if the Soviet Union attacked and destroyed China's nuclear installations."[50]

After some initial hesitation, the administration made clear that it would not condone a Soviet war against China. Nixon and Kissinger subsequently began diplomatic overtures to Beijing. They reduced the U.S. military presence in and around Taiwan, revived dormant ambassadorial talks in Warsaw, and sought, through Pakistan and other intermediaries, to move the dialogue to a higher level.[51] The door should be kept open, Kissinger wrote to Nixon, to developments that would "put U.S./Chinese relations on a more rational and less ideological basis than has been true for the past two decades."[52]

These maneuvers were based on a straightforward calculation that it would be disastrous to allow Moscow, the most powerful of America's enemies, to gain an immense geopolitical victory by dominating Beijing. "China's billion people and nuclear potential offer an unpleasant prospect," Nixon had commented in July 1969, "but so does Soviet adventurism in East Asia."[53] "When you have two enemies, we want to tilt towards the weaker, not the strong," he affirmed two years later.[54] The administration's policy also reflected the idea that a better relationship with China would give the United States additional leverage in dealing with a rising Soviet Union. "Right now, we need the Chinese to correct the Russians, and to discipline the Russians," Kissinger noted.[55]

This concept, in turn, was related to the third and most ambitious rationale for the opening to China—the thesis that a triangular great-power relationship would be more stable and beneficial for the United States. If Washington could forge decent bilateral ties with China and Moscow, Nixon and Kissinger believed, it would hold the trump card in dealing with both. Each power would have to contemplate an American partnership with its most dangerous rival; each would therefore need to decrease its radicalism and accommodate itself to a "concept of international order" agreeable to the United States. "In a subtle triangle of relations between Washington, Beijing, and Moscow," Kissinger had written in 1968, "we improve the possibilities of accommodations with each as we increase our options toward both."[56] Nixon agreed: "Best U.S. stance is to play each—not publicly."[57] In an age of limited resources, the United States would shape the global environment via flexible diplomacy rather than raw power. The president put it aptly in his eventual meeting with Zhou Enlai: "The helmsman must ride with the waves or he will be submerged with the tide."[58]

In many ways, then, U.S. policies toward Beijing and Moscow represented two sides of the same coin. In neither case did the administration believe it possible to eliminate bilateral tensions, nor did it mistake the basic nature of its rivals. The Chinese, Kissinger believed, were "tough ideologues who totally disagree with us on where the world is going"; the Soviets were "thuggish bureaucrats," "brutal bastards," and "essentially shits."[59] The purpose of these maneuvers, rather, was simply to temper bilateral competition, harness the more restrained features of Soviet and Chinese policy, and thereby create greater stability at lower cost. "What we are trying to do," Kissinger explained, "is see where there are some specific arrangements that can be made in mutual interest to lessen the tensions and to see whether, in this overall balance that exists, we might not produce a structure that is more stable and less likely to produce war than the preceding one."[60]

Improved great-power relations would presumably help the administration achieve another key goal—getting out of Vietnam. Nixon and Kissinger understood that ending that war was the sine qua non of U.S. grand strategy—it would be vital to restoring the consensus, dexterity, and economy upon which successful statecraft depended. "The war plagues us at home, is costly in our relations with the USSR, and offers all kind of temptations to our politicians," commented Nixon in 1969.[61] Yet simply withdrawing from Southeast Asia was not considered a workable solution, for the massive U.S. investment in Vietnam had made that small, otherwise insignificant country a symbolic proving ground for American power. Were the United States to abandon Saigon, allies might question American resolve, and enemies would surely press for advantage. "In the conduct of long range American policy throughout the world," said Kissinger, "it was important that we not be confounded by a fifth rate agricultural power."[62]

Nixon and Kissinger continually struggled to resolve these conflicting imperatives. In search of a negotiated settlement, they engaged in high-level peace talks with Hanoi. To lower casualties and neutralize antiwar sentiment at home, Nixon also began the process of "Vietnamization"—unilateral troop withdrawals partnered with the rapid training and equipping of South Vietnamese units. By beginning a phased withdrawal, Nixon commented, "maybe we can buy time and perhaps some support."[63]

The obvious problem with these measures was that they would likely weaken South Vietnam and harden Hanoi's desire for complete victory.[64] Kissinger and Nixon thus sought to salvage an acceptable outcome in Southeast Asia by blending great-power diplomacy with dramatic threats and displays of U.S. military power. On the diplomatic front, Kissinger aimed to activate linkage by convincing both Moscow and Beijing that they must push Hanoi toward a settlement or endanger their incipient détentes with the United States. "There would be no special treatment for the Soviet Union until Vietnam was solved," he told Soviet ambassador Anatoly Dobrynin in 1969. While Nixon was sometimes skeptical of this approach, Kissinger held out hope that the fierceness of the Sino-Soviet rivalry would force both powers to accommodate Washington, thereby isolating North Vietnam diplomatically.[65]

The counterpart to this diplomatic activity was the use of sharp, unpredictable military action. Nixon had long espoused a "madman theory" of tactical escalation. "I want the North Vietnamese to believe that I've reached the point where I might do *anything* to stop the war," he commented.[66] Kissinger too saw benefits in threatening that "things may get out of hand." America's rivals must know, he commented in January 1969, "that we are determined to settle this issue one way or the other."[67]

Between 1969 and 1972, this philosophy shaped a series of actions intended to punish the North and signal to Beijing, Moscow, and Hanoi that the war might spin out of control. In late 1969, Kissinger designed a secret nuclear alert meant to convince Soviet intelligence that drastic action was in the offing. The administration also ordered aerial attacks on North Vietnamese positions in Cambodia and Laos, and U.S. planes eventually dropped more ordnance on the former country than Allied forces had used during all of World War II. In 1970–71, U.S. forces conducted or supported ground invasions of the same two countries in an effort to destroy enemy sanctuaries and demonstrate resolve. And when North Vietnamese forces launched a massive conventional assault on the South in early 1972 (the "Easter offensive"), Nixon and Kissinger responded with the sustained bombing of northern cities, including Hanoi, and the mining of Haiphong harbor. "We are not interested in half-measures," wrote Kissinger on the president's behalf; "we want to demonstrate to Hanoi that we really mean business."[68] The United States could find Hanoi's "breaking point," Kissinger believed, but only if it were willing to be brutal.[69]

The effort to achieve "peace with honor" in Vietnam was related to a final strategic challenge confronting the administration—the need to reduce costly commitments without jeopardizing the overall balance of power. By the time Nixon and Kissinger took office, both men were convinced that the United States could not perpetually take the lead in combating instability at every point along the global perimeter. This might have been unavoidable in the 1940s, when America's wealth was unrivaled and its allies were weak, but twenty years later, it was a recipe for disaster. "If we insist on remaining the sole trustee of policy everywhere ... the strain on our resources and ingenuity may well be too great," Kissinger had written in 1965. In these circumstances, Washington should continue to support its friends, but it should also use their growing strength and assertiveness as pillars of a less U.S.-centric global stability. The United States must "contribute to a structure that will foster the initiative of others," Kissinger argued in 1968; "we must seek to encourage and not stifle a sense of local responsibility."[70] Nixon put it more pithily: "We need a new policy to prevent more V. Nams."[71]

This idea was expressed most explicitly in the "Nixon Doctrine." In July 1969, the president ruled out the use of U.S. ground forces in future Vietnam-type wars in Asia, and the administration then revised its overall military doctrine to reflect this change.[72] For both Nixon and Kissinger, however, the basic concept had a broader global significance. In virtually every region of the world, they sought—early on, at least—to make a virtue of necessity by devolving responsibility to friendly governments. In East Asia, Nixon mooted the possibility of Japanese rearmament and called for Tokyo to play a stronger role in global affairs.[73] In Europe, he encouraged Pompidou's France to continue de Gaulle's independent diplomacy. To have "just two superpowers" was "not healthy," Nixon said to Pompidou in 1969. "What we need is a better balance in the West."[74] This same logic even figured, albeit somewhat contradictorily, in the administration's international monetary policy. The decision to abandon the gold standard (and thus Bretton Woods) in 1971 was based on the conviction that the United States had to slough off some of its international economic burdens—and that the Europeans and Japanese were now rich enough to pick them up. "Santa Claus is dead," one U.S. official subsequently commented.[75]

Unfortunately (but unsurprisingly), this particular decision caused real friction with the NATO countries and Japan, and in both cases the administration ultimately settled for just getting by in its relations with major U.S. allies.[76] In consequence, the fullest application of the Nixon Doctrine came in the Third World rather than the First. Here the Nixon and Ford administrations used military sales, economic assistance, and political solidarity to cultivate anticommunist "regional sheriffs" like Brazil, Indonesia, Iran, Israel, and South Africa.[77] None of these regional sheriffs (save Israel) boasted democratic rule, but this did not much trouble Nixon and Kissinger.

On the contrary, they quite preferred dealing with strong, decisive leaders and maintained that abhorrent domestic practices—even torture and political assassination—should not intrude on fruitful partnerships. "Any differences we have are 'in the family,'" Kissinger told Brazilian dictator Emílio Médici. "Our fundamental relationship is of paramount importance."[78] The domestic characteristics of these regimes were unpleasant, but their strong regional leadership could provide stability along the periphery and free Washington for the larger job of managing the global balance. "The United States," Kissinger explained in 1970, "should not be the fireman running from one conflagration to the other, but can address itself to the longer-term problems of a peaceful international structure and leave to local responsibilities the immediate task of construction."[79]

Just how seriously the administration took this imperative of devolving responsibility is evident from its stance on nuclear proliferation. During the 1960s, LBJ had invested significant diplomatic capital in efforts to slow the spread of nuclear weapons, and aides had even considered taking coercive action to rein in the nuclear programs of friends like France as well as rivals like China.[80] Nixon and Kissinger adopted a much different policy. As Francis Gavin notes, they thought it inevitable that vulnerable countries would seek nuclear weapons, and they saw little logic in brawling over the issue just as Washington was encouraging greater self-sufficiency among its clients.[81] (A study prepared by one of Kissinger's top staffers even broached the idea that during a period of selective retrenchment, limited proliferation might be in the U.S. interest.[82]) This general attitude meant that while Nixon did eventually secure ratification of the nuclear Non-Proliferation Treaty (signed under Johnson) in 1970, he made little effort to pressure key allies like Brazil, South Africa, or West Germany to participate in the accord. Moreover, the administration took a tolerant attitude toward Israel's burgeoning nuclear capability, and even provided secret assistance to the French program. "It is too dangerous to have one country as the repository of nuclear weapons," Kissinger told a French diplomat. "We would like France to be a possessor."[83] In effect, Nixon and Kissinger were willing to downplay nonproliferation as the price of stimulating local initiative among friendly powers.

Over the long term, the Nixon Doctrine and its related policies were meant to provide geopolitical order at a decreased price for the United States. In the meantime, however, one could not be so sure. After all, American power and commitments constituted the glue that had held the postwar system together. As the United States rebalanced those commitments and retreated from exposed positions, there was bound to be a period of uncertainty and disorder.

Until the new distribution of responsibility congealed, the United States must therefore demonstrate—to allies and adversaries alike—that it would not allow fluidity to turn to chaos. Washington must move, Kissinger said during one crisis, "to prevent a complete collapse of the world's psychological balance of power."[84] Nixon put the issue even more bluntly in announcing the invasion of Cambodia in 1970: "If, when the chips are down, the world's most powerful nation, the United States of America, acts like a pitiful, helpless giant, the forces of totalitarianism and anarchy will threaten free nations and free institutions throughout the world."[85]

This emphasis on manifesting strength at a time of geopolitical transition fit well with the president's proclivity for tough and unpredictable action, as well as Kissinger's long-standing emphasis on making American power credible.[86] Throughout the Nixon-Kissinger era, this theme underlay a series of strong—even aggressive—policies in the Third World: military strikes on Cambodia following the seizure of the merchant ship *Mayaguez* in 1975; an unsuccessful bid to prevent a Marxist faction, backed by Soviet arms and eventually Cuban troops, from winning a civil war in faraway Angola in 1975–76; even the attempt to overthrow Salvador Allende's socialist (but democratic) government in Chile from 1970 to 1973. "No impression should be permitted in Latin America that they can get away with this, that it's safe to go this way," Nixon declared in the Chilean case. "All over the world it's too much the fashion to kick us around.... There must be times when we should and must react, not because we want to hurt them but to show we can't be kicked around."[87]

The same considerations determined U.S. policy during the South Asian crisis of 1971. The Nixon administration first remained silent as the government of Agha Mohammad Yahya Khan, which was facilitating the U.S. opening to China, brutally murdered hundreds of thousands of its own citizens amid an uprising in East Pakistan. "Here in Dacca we are mute and horrified witnesses to a reign of terror by the Pak military," wrote one U.S. diplomat in disgust.[88] During the war that resulted, Kissinger argued that the administration must prevent India, which was loosely aligned with Moscow, from inflicting a decisive defeat on Pakistan. "I have to tell you honestly I consider this our Rhineland," he said.[89] Even though the administration failed—despite sending a naval task force to the Bay of Bengal, illegally shipping fighter jets to Khan's government, and asking the Chinese to move their troops to the Indian border—to deter India from detaching East Pakistan from West Pakistan, Kissinger nonetheless praised Nixon's handling of the crisis as a "heroic act."[90]

More dramatic still was U.S. policy during the Yom Kippur War. "This is bigger than the Middle East," Nixon commented after Syria and Egypt launched a surprise attack against Israel in October 1973. "We can't allow a Soviet-supported operation to succeed against an American-supported operation. If it does, our credibility everywhere is severely shaken."[91] The U.S. response was striking in its scope and riskiness. After first providing Israel with a massive military resupply, and then encouraging it to press the advantage against battered Arab armies (even to the point of violating a UN-sponsored cease-fire), the administration ordered a strategic nuclear alert to deter Moscow from interceding. Kissinger later outlined the administration's philosophy on handling such crises: "Our general strategy is to make a lot of moves, all at the same time, to give the other side a lot of decisions to make. And then, if we move military forces, to maneuver very danger-ously, so that the other side doesn't think it is riskless to challenge." Or, as he put it on another occasion, "We've got to play it recklessly. That's the safest course."[92] Amid global power shifts and U.S. retrenchment, a daring—even dangerous—approach to crisis management seemed essential.

There was, then, a clearly identifiable grand strategy at work during the Nixon-Kissinger years. From the late 1960s onward, the administration was guided by a set of firmly held, interlocking concepts that gave structure to foreign policy and drove a wide range of U.S. initiatives abroad. And taken collectively, those policies and ideas added up to an ambitious program for ensuring that America could thrive even as its relative power waned. As Nixon and Kissinger saw it, the United States would use bold and innovative actions to reassert control of great-power affairs, end an inherited quagmire in Vietnam, and delegate authority while preserving credibility. It would thereby make itself the pivot of a more manageable global equilibrium, and accommodate profound change in ways that produced stability rather than chaos. In essence, Nixon and Kissinger believed that their country need not fall victim to the forces of historical decline, but that it could summon the virtuosity to transcend them, "to shape events." The United States was no longer simply struggling to keep its head above water, Kissinger wrote in 1972. "We know where we are going. We are moving with history, and moving history ourselves."[93]

The administration's grand strategy also had a crucial domestic compo-nent. There was, of course, the omnipresent issue of Nixon's reelection, something that Kissinger was rarely permitted to ignore. ("Winning an election is terribly important," Nixon helpfully reminded him.[94]) But there was also the larger question of restoring a domestic consensus on foreign policy. By lowering international tensions and reducing the burdens of glo-balism, Nixon and Kissinger hoped to defuse radical criticism and deflect pressures for dramatic retrenchment. The goal, said Nixon, was to "stay in the world, not ... get out of the world."[95] More positively, Kissinger expected that constructive diplomacy would help restore the national self-confidence and cohesion that had been so corroded by Vietnam, decreasing internal tensions and making possible a more assertive global posture over the long run. His purpose, he commented in 1971, was to promote the "reintegration of American society," to provide "a feeling ... that the nation is a unified and functioning entity."[96]

Yet here the administration's optimism ended. Kissinger and Nixon hoped that creative diplomacy could have a restorative effect at home, but they also worried that the nation might be so traumatized by Vietnam that it would fail to back an activist policy of any sort. The issue, Nixon had said in 1967, was "whether America has the national character and moral stamina to see us through this long and difficult struggle." More profoundly still, both men saw some of the most prominent features of U.S. politics—the bureaucratized nature of the government, the furies of partisan politics, the tendency toward highly moralistic definitions of national purpose—as threats to the coherence of policy. "A philosophical deepening will not come easily to those brought up in the American tradition of foreign policy," Kissinger predicted.[97]

Congress and the bureaucracy were targets of particular suspicion within the administration. For Kissinger, the requirements of successful statecraft—speed, secrecy, unity of purpose, the ability to act unpredictably when necessary—were incompatible with laborious bureaucratic procedures and timely democratic oversight. "One cannot put a negotiation before forty-five members of the House Foreign Affairs Committee," he told a group of congressmen.[98] Nor would purposeful statecraft be possible if every initiative had to be vetted by a cumbersome interagency process in which each player had its own institutional prerogatives and interests: "The bureaucracy is the curse of the modern state," he said in 1970.[99] As usual, Nixon was even more vehement on these counts. Congress was "cumbersome, undisciplined, isolationist, fiscally irresponsible, overly vulnerable to pressures from organized minorities, and too dominated by the media"; the State Department was full of "impossible fags" who were determined to obstruct his policies.[100]

Then there was the issue of morality. Kissinger and Nixon never doubted that the United States had the better of the moral argument with its enemies, and they believed that seeking peace and stability was itself a moral good. This was America's "summons to greatness," the president declared.[101] Both he and Kissinger were deeply skeptical, however, that morality could be directly translated into day-to-day policies. After all, navigating global politics would often require an amoral ethos—accepting the legitimacy of repressive governments in Beijing and Moscow, cooperating with murderous autocrats, subverting democratic governments, and so on. The United States had to "find ways of living in the real world," Nixon told NATO leaders in 1969.[102] "Totally ruthless people are successful," Kissinger later agreed.[103]

As a result of these concerns, Nixon and Kissinger took extraordinary steps to shield their foreign policy from the allegedly pernicious aspects of the American system. They attempted to keep many of their most significant moves—the opening to China, the "tilt" toward Pakistan, the high-level negotiations to end the Vietnam War, the bombing of Laos and Cambodia, the 1969 and 1973 nuclear alerts, the destabilization of a democratic government in Chile—hidden from public view, often to the point of simply lying about their intentions and actions. The administration also made deliberate efforts to obstruct meaningful congressional oversight. "Henry has made a commitment to Congressman MacGregor of Minnesota to provide him with some position papers," Kissinger aide Alexander Haig wrote to another staffer in 1970. "Would you please work with the various substantive offices involved and prepare a series of papers. We just have to provide some unsubstantive pap."[104] According to one historian, Kissinger even instructed subordinates to stonewall Congress on the human rights abuses of U.S. allies during the mid-1970s.[105]

The same conspiratorial ethos prevailed within the administration. Prior to the inauguration, Nixon and Kissinger had skillfully staged a "palace coup" that gave the NSC—and thus the White House—control over all of the crucial interdepartmental coordinating bodies. They subsequently delighted in marginalizing, confusing, or simply ignoring the bureaucracy, busying subordinate agencies with requests for lengthy staff studies while making virtually all the important decisions themselves. Even senior officials—Secretary of Defense Melvin Laird, Secretary of State William Rogers, CIA Director Richard Helms, the JCS—often found themselves excluded from the policy process. "Dr. Kissinger alone enjoys both the intimate day-to-day contact and confidence of the President," one JCS staffer commented.[106] Kissinger personally conducted negotiations with the Soviets, Chinese, North Vietnamese, and other countries through back channels that were kept secret even from Rogers and the diplomats who were nominally charged with pursuing these talks. The State Department, complained one official, was simply "left in the dark."[107]

Personality quirks and self-interest certainly played a role in this modus operandi. Nixon's well-documented paranoia, his fear of direct confrontations with subordinates, and his penchant for self-isolation all inclined him to prefer a centralized system where nearly all important issues ran through a single aide. Kissinger, in turn, used these arrangements to concentrate unparalleled power among presidential advisers, build his own public image, and humiliate rivals like the much-abused Rogers. (Kissinger, Nixon remarked, was "psychopathic about trying to screw Rogers."[108]) And, of course, this system reflected the great confidence that Nixon and Kissinger had in their own abilities, and no less the heroic notion of statesmanship that both men possessed.

"As in all tragedies," Kissinger had written in the 1950s, "many of our problems have been produced in spite of our good intentions and have been caused, not by our worst qualities, but by our best."[109] This was the central dilemma of the administration's grand strategy. Nixon and Kissinger believed that the United States could accomplish great things and restore its sense of national purpose. Yet they also believed that this would be possible only if American leaders could operate outside the constraints of their own polity and society. Grand strategy was about moving a nation, but in the Nixon administration, it remained a lonely pursuit.

For a time, this style worked remarkably well, especially when it came to great-power relations. By mid-1972, Nixon and Kissinger had successfully made the opening to China. They had also finalized SALT and the ABM Treaty with Moscow, concluded an accord that removed Berlin as a super-power flashpoint, and inked another that laid the basis for expanded East-West commerce. These concurrent détentes culminated with a flourish, as Nixon and Kissinger traveled to Beijing for a successful summit in February 1972, then repeated the performance in Moscow three months later. The novelty of the entire spectacle was considerable. The president who termed himself "the original anti-Communist" was now toasting Mao and Brezhnev and hailing the advent of a "generation of peace."[110]

As these impressive results demonstrated, triangular diplomacy was well suited to the climate of East-West relations in the early 1970s. The war scare of 1969 had accentuated Chinese vulnerability, and a worried Mao was quick to pick up on U.S. overtures. "Isn't it true that the American global strategy has been sending out signals?" he asked.[111] Chinese officials reciprocated American feelers during 1969–70, leading to Kissinger's secret visit to Beijing in July 1971 and the Nixon-Mao summit the following February.

For Kissinger and Nixon, these encounters represented the essence of heroic diplomacy. As Kissinger explained to Zhou in July 1971, it was imperative that world leaders be able to converse "unencumbered by bureaucracy, free of the past, and with the greatest possible latitude." Freed from these constraints, realistic statesmen could retreat from outdated positions—Kissinger by promising that the United States would distance itself from Taiwan; Zhou and Mao by conceding that American power was a stabilizing factor in the western Pacific. They could also dispense with the ideological vitriol that obscured a common interest in containing Moscow, a fact that Nixon emphasized during the Beijing summit in 1972. "We have broken out of the old pattern," he said. "We look at each country in terms of its own conduct rather than lumping them all together, and saying because they have this kind of philosophy they are all in utter darkness."[112]

The merits of this approach were difficult to deny. The opening to China made Kissinger a global celebrity, and established Nixon's reputation as a peacemaker in the run-up to the 1972 election. More substantively, Sino-American rapprochement was a grand strategic coup of the first order. In the 1960s, U.S. policy had been groaning under the weight of containing two powerful rivals; now it was the Kremlin that had to bear this cross. "We can work together to commonly deal with a bastard," Mao told Kissinger.[113] Although full normalization of relations would be delayed until after Ford and Kissinger left office, this anti-Soviet alignment would endure and expand under their successors. The basic line-up of the Cold War had shifted fundamentally.

The opening to China also made Moscow somewhat more tractable. Kissinger later exaggerated the degree to which the "China card" influenced U.S.-Soviet relations, for the arms control and Berlin talks had already begun to show significant progress before July 1971. Once news of Nixon's China gambit broke, however, Moscow did hasten to achieve its own détente with the United States. Upon learning of Kissinger's initial trip to Beijing, Dobrynin wrote that Sino-American rapprochement was "unquestionably of major international significance" and urged that Moscow endeavor "to check possible sliding into anti-Sovietism by the U.S."[114] The Berlin, SALT, and ABM agreements were soon concluded, and when Nixon responded to the Easter offensive by ordering massive aerial attacks on North Vietnam, the Soviets surprised even Kissinger by deciding not to cancel the upcoming summit. The United States was "building a new strategic alignment of forces in international politics in Asia and in the world as a whole," Dobrynin had noted just weeks before this episode, and Moscow needed to keep pace.[115]

When Brezhnev and Nixon met shortly thereafter, they signed a document titled "Basic Principles of Relations between the United States of America and the Union of Soviet Socialist Republics." The charter, formulated by Kissinger and Soviet foreign minister Andrei Gromyko, had a strikingly cooperative tone that contrasted sharply with the crises and rhetoric of earlier years. It pledged the two sides to "peaceful coexistence" and "normal relations." In the nuclear age, Washington and Moscow must avoid "situations capable of causing a dangerous exacerbation of their relations" and forswear "efforts to obtain unilateral advantage at the expense of the other."[116] Just as Kissinger had emphasized the need for an agreed "concept of international order" in U.S.-Soviet affairs, the basic principles called for restraint and mutual accommodation—a superpower concert of sorts—in the service of global stability. The principles, he wrote in 1973, constituted a "code of conduct" for U.S.-Soviet affairs.[117]

What was remarkable about détente, though, was how quickly this "code of conduct" broke down. Even before the 1972 summit, the Brezhnev Kremlin had done several things—supporting India in its 1971 war against Pakistan, providing the equipment necessary for Hanoi's 1972 offensive—that cast doubt on the extent of Soviet restraint. The doubts only worsened from there. Moscow backed the Arabs (albeit without great enthusiasm) in the Yom Kippur War, tacitly abetted Hanoi's eventual takeover of South Vietnam in 1975, and airlifted arms—along with thousands of Cuban troops—to intervene decisively in the Angolan civil war. Clearly, détente had not translated into greater stability in the Third World. Nor did it provide a solid basis for U.S.-Soviet bilateral ties. The Kremlin aggressively MIRVed and modernized its strategic forces during the mid-1970s (such qualitative improvements were permitted under SALT), gaining what many considered to be a significant edge in the arms race. Intensive negotiations failed to produce a second arms deal to replace SALT (set to expire in 1977) before Ford left office, and détente became the subject of widespread political opprobrium, particularly on the right, in the United States.[118] And as U.S.-Soviet relations worsened in the mid- and late 1970s, triangular diplomacy gradually came undone, with Kissinger and then his successors increasingly seeking to align with China against a troublesome Moscow rather than flexibly playing the two rivals off one another.

Why did U.S.-Soviet détente, a policy that had seemed so successful, end up unraveling so quickly? American opportunism was partially to blame. Nixon and Kissinger undermined their own "code of conduct" during and after the Yom Kippur War, when they first threatened Moscow with a strategic nuclear alert and then maneuvered diplomatically to evict the Soviets from the region. "The situation in this area is poisoning the general atmosphere of détente," Brezhnev complained.[119] The China card also lost some of its effectiveness as the initial shock wore off and political issues— particularly lingering GOP support for Taiwan—slowed the pace toward full normalization. Fundamentally, though, détente foundered because a messy and dynamic world simply could not be manipulated to the extent that Nixon and Kissinger presumed.

This problem was apparent in many of the Third World crises that tested détente during the 1970s. As Kissinger envisioned it, détente was supposed to give the Kremlin an incentive to avoid military or diplomatic adventures abroad. The liability of this approach was that Moscow could not necessarily control its allies, who often launched these crises, any better than Washington could. The Soviets did not instigate the Yom Kippur War in 1973; they were thrust into the crisis by a determined Anwar Sadat, whose drastic action confronted Brezhnev with a choice between backing a troublesome client and seeing that client defeated—perhaps destroyed—by a U.S. ally. Likewise, historians still debate the genesis of East-bloc intervention in Angola, but it is worth recalling that the primary contribution came from Fidel Castro, a perennially independent-minded leader who cared less about détente than about pushing his own revolutionary agenda. The type of stability that Kissinger desired, in other words, was vulnerable to precisely the sort of local initiative that he and Nixon sought to encourage.[120]

Nixon and Kissinger—especially the latter—also expected too much in terms of their ability to influence the Soviets themselves. Kissinger understood that détente and harmony were not synonymous, but he still believed that Moscow could be brought into a concept of order devised largely by the United States. The hitch was that Soviet officials, perceiving their country's influence to be on the rise, never fully accepted this logic. They rejected the idea that détente represented a guarantee of the global status quo, instead seeing it as a way of achieving international legitimacy, limiting the dangers of war, and paving the way for advances in other areas—particularly the Third World. As Brezhnev put it, "We make no secret of the fact that we see détente as the way to create more favorable conditions for peaceful socialist and communist construction."[121] And with the United States being defeated in Vietnam and the Portuguese empire in Africa collapsing, the mid-1970s seemed an auspicious time for such construction. The sense in the Kremlin, one official later recalled, was that "the world was turning in our direction."[122] At a time when the global balance was shifting and Soviet influence seemed to be waxing, it was beyond American power to set the terms of world order.

In theory, linkage offered a mechanism for dealing with this problem. If the Soviets wanted any part of détente—and they did—they would have to accept all of it. Yet linkage, like so much of the Nixon-Kissinger grand strategy, demanded a massive concentration of executive power. If linkage were to be implemented successfully, U.S. officials had to have the authority to bestow the requisite rewards and punishments. For the concept to be credible, they even needed to be able to bring détente to a halt if Soviet behavior warranted.

Herein lay the trouble. Even before the 1972 Moscow summit, it was simply wishful thinking to assume that the United States could really derail détente if Moscow misbehaved. The United States needed SALT to avoid falling behind in the arms race; Nixon needed foreign policy successes to win reelection. Accordingly, linkage worked both ways: it provided the United States with leverage on Moscow, but the reverse was also true. The Kremlin could thus brush aside American objections to Indian conduct in late 1971, noting, as one Foreign Ministry official did, that "the Soviet Union, not the United States, will gain all the political benefits" from Pakistan's humiliation.[123] Similarly, the Soviets felt little pressure to rein in North Vietnam during the Easter offensive in 1972, secure in the knowledge that, as Dobrynin put it, the upcoming summit was "becoming increasingly valuable to Nixon."[124] The way that politics could intrude on grand strategy was equally apparent after the summit, when Nixon's Department of Agriculture—with an eye to gaining farmers' support for the president in November—sold massive quantities of grain to Soviet customers before Kissinger could extract a bilateral quid pro quo from the Kremlin. In these conditions, the precision diplomacy that linkage presupposed proved elusive.

Nor was the presumption of executive dominance realistic. Détente played well politically at first, helping Nixon win reelection in 1972. Yet once the initial aura wore off, détente proved poorly suited to U.S. politics. By combining containment with negotiations, détente moved foreign policy to the political center, but it did so at a time when the center was becoming a lonely place. Many liberals turned more dovish amid the anguish of Vietnam, and so they supported great-power negotiations but called for greater military and diplomatic retrenchment. Many conservatives and neoconservatives took the opposite lesson from the war and became more hawkish. Led by Senator Henry Jackson, they contended that détente was immoral, because it downplayed Moscow's repressive practices at home, and imprudent, because it emphasized arms control over U.S. military superiority. As the 1970s went on, Kissinger—now effectively running foreign policy in the Ford administration—found himself trapped in the middle.[125]

He also found himself caught in a backlash against presidential supremacy. Some such backlash was inevitable as a response to LBJ's deception regarding Vietnam, but this reaction intensified immensely as a result of Watergate. The train of events leading to that scandal had started with Nixon's attempt (encouraged by Kissinger) to preserve White House power by finding and punishing those responsible for leaking information on the secret U.S. war in Cambodia. When the extent of the crimes that eventually resulted became clear during 1973–74, the result was to tar executive authority writ large. It was a classic self-inflicted wound. At precisely the time that Nixon and Kissinger had hoped to centralize power in the White House, Congress was reasserting its own prerogatives through the War Powers Act, the Pike and Church committee investigations into CIA covert action, and other such devices. "Our policy has been whenever Russia puts a toe across the line, we cut it off," said Kissinger in October 1974. Yet cutting off Soviet toes required decisive executive authority, and by the mid-1970s that authority was unmistakably in eclipse.[126]

This combination of headwinds and crosscurrents left Kissinger struggling to hold a steady course. Congress steadily whittled away at military expenditures during the early and mid-1970s, just as Moscow was pushing ahead with major conventional upgrades and qualitative improvements to its nuclear forces. The Soviets were building an increasingly global naval presence and an authentic power projection capability, while also carrying out a determined MIRV program and making dramatic advances in the accuracy and lethality of their strategic arsenal. "The current Soviet programs for development of intercontinental attack weapons are unprecedented in scope," CIA Director William Colby reported. Meanwhile, the American nuclear arsenal failed to keep pace, and U.S. conventional capabilities were in decline. The number of individuals in the U.S. armed forces fell from 3.4 million to 2.1 million between 1968 and 1975, and levels of ships, planes, and divisions declined commensurately.[127] In 1971, Nixon had commented that "the main purpose of our forces is diplomatic wallop." By the time he resigned three years later, the United States had less diplomatic wallop relative to the Kremlin than at any previous time in the Cold War.[128]

Worse was still to come. Nixon and Kissinger had always expected that the promise of permanent MFN status and trade credits would allow the United States to exert a powerful moderating force on Soviet behavior. This package, however, required congressional approval, and Jackson seized the opportunity to undermine détente and embarrass the White House at a single stroke. In 1974–75, he torpedoed this central economic component of linkage by attaching harsh conditions on Soviet Jewish emigration to the bilateral trade agreement signed in 1972. The Soviets, incensed, rejected the entire deal, depriving Kissinger of a key point of potential diplomatic influence. "We have now lost the leverage," he acknowledged.[129]

The constraints on executive action became even more painfully clear amid a series of Third World crises in 1975. Early that year, Congress prevented

Ford from obtaining a massive infusion of aid for a teetering South Vietnam or taking other steps to prevent the country's collapse. In December, a bipartisan majority terminated U.S. covert involvement in the Angolan civil war, contributing to the victory of Soviet- and Cuban-backed fighters the following year. "We are living in a nihilistic nightmare," Kissinger lamented. "We are being deprived of both the carrot and the stick."[130] Détente was supposed to rest on the ability to wield both positive and negative incentives, but amid the general reassertion of congressional power, Kissinger and Ford were hard-pressed to avail themselves of either.

The political frailty of détente was amply confirmed by the domestic reaction to the signing of the Helsinki Final Act in mid-1975. The Helsinki accords were a collection of East-West agreements on trade, security, and political issues, hammered out in arduous negotiations between Washington, Moscow, and their respective European allies. The agreements contained provisions for protecting human rights and political freedoms in the Soviet bloc, and they eventually created space for the dissident movements that would help destroy the empire from within during the 1980s. Unfortunately for Ford and Kissinger, the accords also conferred U.S. recognition of the Cold War borders of Europe. Right-wing critics pounced, charging, in the words of former California governor and GOP presidential candidate Ronald Reagan, that Ford had "put the American seal of approval on the Red Army's Second World War conquests."[131]

The whole episode was genuinely perplexing to Kissinger, who had seen Helsinki largely as a bargaining chip for Soviet concessions on arms control or other issues. "Who does not recognize those frontiers?" he complained. "Is the U.S. going back to the Dulles era?"[132] Nonetheless, the fallout from Helsinki energized moral critiques of U.S. policy, particularly on the right, and forced Ford to distance himself from détente. The president stripped Kissinger of his duties as national security adviser (but not secretary of state) in late 1975.[133] Faced with a strong challenge from Reagan in the GOP primaries, as well as mounting opposition from the JCS and the Pentagon, he also gave up on concluding SALT II before the 1976 elections. The now-tarnished word "détente" was even dropped from the administration's vocabulary.[134]

At the time, Kissinger blamed the travails of détente on the political opportunism of Jackson and other domestic opponents. "I sometimes despair . . . whether it is possible in a democracy any more to conduct a thoughtful foreign policy," he said.[135] Political ambition certainly played a role in many critiques of détente; on this point, Kissinger was right. The fact was, though, that the Nixon-Kissinger grand strategy was politically unrealistic.

It demanded discipline and acquiescence from a system premised on divided power and noisy electoral competition, all at a time when the key tenet of administration statecraft—that wise elites knew best—seemed downright preposterous to many citizens. In this context, Nixon and Kissinger were bound to encounter severe difficulties in implementing their grand strategy. Frustration was virtually guaranteed.[136]

None of this should detract from American accomplishments in great-power relations during the Nixon-Kissinger years. The opening to China would redound to America's benefit through the end of the Cold War and beyond. And for all its failings, détente reduced superpower tensions and provided a much-needed breather for a country suffering from strategic exhaustion. The fact that Nixon and Kissinger achieved all this without any major expenditure of resources, and at a time when American power was generally thought to be on the wane, made their performance all the more impressive. Ultimately, though, the key goal of détente—obtaining Soviet restraint and a time of growing Soviet influence—proved elusive. American policy fell victim to its own conceptual shortcomings, the tyranny of shifting global power dynamics, and the frictions of democratic politics. Heroic statecraft was impossible to sustain.

The frustrations of the administration's grand strategy were even more pronounced in Vietnam. The administration did achieve a negotiated settlement in early 1973, one that left a noncommunist government in power in the South, brought home American POWs, and allowed Nixon to claim that he had delivered peace with honor. The triumph was illusory, though, because the agreement was so flawed that it presaged the fall of Saigon just two years later. In Vietnam, Nixon and Kissinger ended up with the worst of both worlds—four more years of fighting at a cost of over twenty thousand American deaths and immense political divisiveness at home, followed by just the outcome they had hoped to avert.

In fairness, the root of the U.S. failure in Vietnam was a factor beyond the administration's control: the fact that despite massive outlays of American aid, the Saigon regime remained too weak to stand on its own. In consequence, the administration's approach to the war always rested on a glaring contradiction. A steady military drawdown was vital to decreasing casualties and ensuring that domestic support for the war did not collapse altogether, yet that same process weakened Saigon and guaranteed that Hanoi would gain much of what it wanted—a unilateral American withdrawal—without making concessions of its own. "To be in a hurry when your opponent is not puts one in a very weak negotiating position," commented one U.S.

official.[137] In effect, the administration was confronted with a classic time horizon problem in Vietnam: the domestic will to fight the war was ebbing faster than the enemy's capacity to wage it.

Kissinger and Nixon had hoped that bold, sometimes brutal statecraft could permit the United States to wriggle out of this dilemma, and these tactics were largely responsible for what progress occurred between 1969 and early 1973. While several U.S. escalations fell flat—notably the 1969 nuclear alert and the attacks into Laos and Cambodia—others were more productive. The 1972 bombing of North Vietnam "completely obliterated our economic foundation," said one Hanoi official, forcing the regime to take the peace talks seriously.[138] As triangular diplomacy matured, moreover, both Beijing and Moscow came to view the war as an obstacle to better relations with Washington. They advised North Vietnam that military victory was unattainable with U.S. troops in the South, and that Hanoi should drop its demand that President Nguyen Van Thieu be deposed as the price of peace.[139]

Yet there remained two fundamental liabilities of U.S. strategy. The first was that the logic of triangular diplomacy proved more complex than Kissinger had expected. In a conversation with the national security adviser in 1969, Dobrynin had bluntly explained the problem. "While the Soviet Union might recommend certain steps," he said, "it would never threaten to cut off supplies.... Communist China was constantly accusing the Soviet Union of betraying Hanoi. The Soviet Union could not afford to appear at a Communist meeting and find itself accused of having undermined a fellow Socialist country."[140]

And so it went. Chinese and Soviet officials urged Hanoi to negotiate, but they did so on the rationale that it would be easier (and less damaging to détente) to unify the country once U.S. troops had gone home. "The most important [thing] is to let the Americans leave," Zhou told North Vietnamese officials in January 1973. "The situation will change in six months or one year."[141] And insofar as triangular diplomacy had the effect of encouraging competition between Moscow and Beijing, it quite logically fueled their rivalry over Communist allies like Hanoi. Material support to North Vietnam thus *increased* in the early 1970s. In 1971, Chinese weapons shipments to Hanoi rose dramatically: "Shipments of artillery pieces rose by 257 percent, rifles by 41 percent, tanks from zero to 80 units, and vehicles from zero to 4,011."[142] The Kremlin kept pace; its infusions of matériel made possible the Easter offensive of 1972. The Chinese again increased their aid as that offensive unfolded, and dispatched minesweepers to reopen ports that were closed by U.S. attacks.[143] When it came to ending the Vietnam War, the effects of triangular diplomacy were as perverse as they were productive.

The second liability was that the administration's tactics quickly came to subvert its broader ends. Sharp military action did punish the enemy, but it also compounded the crisis of American foreign policy at home. Each of the major escalations undertaken between 1969 and 1971 produced a severe domestic backlash that polarized the country, increased the political pressure on Nixon, and undercut prospects for renewed consensus on U.S. diplomacy writ large. The invasion of Cambodia in 1970 was particularly incendiary. It kick-started serious congressional activism to end the war and led to demonstrations and riots nationwide, culminating in the tragic shooting of students at Kent State University. As Nixon later recalled, "The daily news reports conveyed a sense of turmoil bordering on insurrection."[144] By 1971–72, Nixon was therefore desperate to end the war by any means available. "We've got to get the war the hell off our backs in this country," he told Kissinger and Haig. "That's all there is to it."[145] Determined grand strategy did not rescue the United States from the contradictions of Vietnam; it only exacerbated them.

This was also true of the war's effect on Southeast Asia as a whole. A key U.S. rationale for fighting in Vietnam had always been that the failure to do so would set the dominoes to falling throughout the area. Kissinger and Nixon accepted this thesis, and both claimed—with some plausibility—that the U.S. intervention in 1965 had bought time for countries like Thailand and Indonesia to set their affairs in order.[146] What they failed to acknowledge was that U.S. actions did much to *destabilize* other countries in the region. The military operations that Kissinger and Nixon ordered did not start the civil wars in Laos and Cambodia, nor did they fully determine the outcomes. But the devastating attacks unleashed on these countries, particularly Cambodia, did rend the political fabric, fuel polarization, and thereby facilitate—however unintentionally—the bloody leftist takeovers that eventually occurred. As Yale historian Ben Kiernan concludes, U.S. intervention in Cambodia was "probably the most important single factor in Pol Pot's rise."[147] In two senses, tactical escalation proved strategically counterproductive.

By 1971–72, these frustrations and failures had produced a significant shift in policy. Nixon and Kissinger accepted that the long-term survival of South Vietnam was unlikely, and resigned themselves to seeking a "decent interval" between a peace agreement and a potential collapse. "If a year or two years from now North Vietnam gobbles up South Vietnam, we can have a viable foreign policy if it looks as if it's the result of South Vietnamese incompetence," Kissinger told Nixon in 1972. "So we've got to find some formula that holds the thing together a year or two, after which ... Vietnam will be a backwater. If we settle it, say, this October, by January '74 no one will give a damn."[148] Kissinger even conveyed this message to the Soviets and the Chinese. "We want a decent interval," he wrote on a briefing book for the 1971 trip to China. "You have our assurance."[149] Along these lines, the administration abandoned its insistence on a mutual withdrawal of foreign forces from South Vietnam—the Americans had been the only ones withdrawing, anyway—instead accepting the principle of a unilateral U.S. pullout.

This shift, combined with the effects of U.S. bombing in 1972–73, did eventually bring about the peace agreement. Yet the accord was fatally flawed. Among other things, it allowed North Vietnamese and Vietcong troops to remain in place in the South, and it included a promise of economic assistance for Hanoi that the U.S. Congress ultimately declined to approve. Thieu realized that the deal was unlikely to hold—he had to be cajoled and practically coerced into signing off on the accord—and, later denials notwithstanding, so did Kissinger. "This thing is almost certain to blow up sooner or later," he predicted.[150] Quite right; the accord, promptly violated by both sides, had largely broken down by late 1973. Kissinger held out some hope that extensive aid to South Vietnam, perhaps accompanied by U.S. air support, might stave off a collapse, but the political climate created by Watergate and general domestic disillusion with the war made both of these measures impossible. In early 1975, a massive North Vietnamese offensive overran what remained of South Vietnam. Whatever credibility Washington had won by fighting for four more years presumably evaporated amid the desperation evacuation from Saigon.[151]

Kissinger and Nixon came into office convinced that the Vietnam War needed to be reduced to its proper significance, that a "shit-ass little country" (in Nixon's phrasing) could no longer be permitted to dominate the nation's foreign policy.[152] Yet their management of the war demonstrated the limits, not the promise, of their grand strategy. In the end, ruthless military action and creative triangular diplomacy could not rescue the United States from its predicament in Vietnam. The administration did extricate the United States from the war, but only in a way that prejudiced South Vietnam's survival, destabilized Laos and Cambodia, and exacerbated the turmoil at work in the United States. When Kissinger spoke of imposing purpose on events, this was not, presumably, what he had in mind.[153]

As events in Vietnam demonstrated, the Third World was often resistant to the logic of the Nixon-Kissinger grand strategy. Intellectually, Nixon and Kissinger seemed well aware that any single design was probably inadequate for dealing with "an increasingly complex and pluralistic international environment" in which countries from Peru to Pakistan were playing a larger part.[154] In practice, however, their emphasis on credibility and "the psychological balance of power" permitted little sensitivity to the nuance of a messy world. This effect was particularly apparent during the South Asian crisis of 1971, when Nixon and Kissinger determined that maintaining America's reputation required tilting toward a Pakistani regime that had massacred its own citizens and started a war against India that it had little chance of winning. (Nixon's strong diplomatic support for Khan may actually have helped persuade the Pakistani leader to launch that war in the first place.) The results were ugly—the United States associated itself with a losing cause, while also substantially isolating itself from global opinion. Backing Pakistan entailed a "high possibility" of "disaster," Kissinger admitted, "but at least we're coming off like men."[155] Grand strategy, in this context, was more of a hindrance than an aid to policy.

The South Asian affair also showed that the Nixon-Kissinger grand strategy could even bring an element of absurdity into American statecraft. In reality, the potential geopolitical consequences of a Pakistani defeat were never as grave as the administration feared.[156] But because Nixon and Kissinger were so fixated on maintaining American credibility, they countenanced a series of actions—most notably encouraging Beijing to move its troops toward the Indian border—that threatened to turn a local crisis into a global one. Nixon recognized as much at one point, noting that if the Chinese did what Kissinger was asking them to do, then the Soviets might feel forced to respond. "So what do we do if the Soviets move against them?" he asked Kissinger. "Start lobbing nuclear weapons in, is that what you mean?" This sobering prospect momentarily caused Kissinger to consider de-escalating the crisis, but the dictates of the "psychological balance" permitted no such flexibility. If Pakistan and China were humbled, Kissinger concluded, the result would be "a change in the world balance of power of such magnitude that the security of the United States" would be undermined "maybe forever, certainly for decades." Luckily, the Chinese stayed put and the crisis soon passed, but the incident nonetheless illustrated just how constricting and even dangerous this aspect of the administration's grand strategy could be.[157]

Similar problems were at work four years later, during the Angolan civil war. Even before Congress terminated U.S. involvement in that conflict, Kissinger had made a series of questionable judgments that flowed naturally from his approach to global affairs. Convinced that the United States needed to make a stand *somewhere* following the collapse of South Vietnam in April 1975, he laid aside the advice of numerous area experts in the State Department and persuaded Ford to make Angola a test of American credibility. The

CIA (which was already playing a minor role in the conflict) subsequently began a larger-scale covert initiative meant to aid two unsavory Angolan factions in hopes of defeating a third group with ties to Havana and Moscow. It was not a winning policy, because it was unlikely that Congress would support the intervention if word of the covert undertaking leaked (as it did), and perhaps even less likely that U.S. assistance would be enough to secure victory in any event. The result, as in the subcontinent, was to embroil the United States in a conflict from which there was little to gain and much to lose. Indeed, American meddling may actually have provoked greater Soviet and Cuban intervention in Angola. Whatever the case, Congress ended U.S. covert aid in late 1975, and the Soviet- and Cuban-backed forces won the civil war soon thereafter. Kissinger considered the episode a humiliation for the United States, but it was a humiliation that he had done much to cause.[158]

In other parts of the Third World, American policies were initially more successful. The regional sheriff strategy paid dividends in the Persian Gulf, as the Shah's Iran used its own military capabilities (including U.S.-supplied helicopters) to help stifle a leftist revolt in Oman. "The Shah is a tough, mean guy," Kissinger told Ford in 1974. "But he is our real friend."[159] Another such friend, Indonesia's Suharto, was equally helpful. With encouragement from Kissinger and Ford, Indonesia invaded East Timor in 1975, snuffing out—at the eventual cost of perhaps two hundred thousand lives—an independence movement with suspected communist leanings. "We understand the problem you have and the intentions you have," Ford told Suharto just before the invasion.[160] As Nixon and Kissinger had hoped, friendly dictators put out fires and relieved the strain on American resources.

The promise and perils of this approach were most pronounced in Latin America. During the early 1970s, the partnership with the Brazilian dictatorship was a fruitful one. Brazil's anticommunist generals energetically targeted leftist movements at home and in neighboring countries, and they viewed Washington as a natural partner in the endeavor. "Any disagreement between the U.S. and Brazil should be considered a 'lovers' quarrel,'" Médici told Nixon and Kissinger.[161] In 1971, the Brazilian military conspired with Bolivian conservatives to overthrow the left-leaning government in La Paz, and stationed thousands of troops on the Uruguayan border in case a popular front organization took power via elections in that country. "I wish he were running the whole continent," Nixon said of Médici.[162]

U.S.-Brazil cooperation notched another victory in September 1973, with the overthrow of Chile's Allende. The U.S. campaign to unseat Allende, while technically covert, had always been closely linked to the administration's stress on manifesting strength and vitality. "Our failure to react to this situation," Kissinger told Nixon in 1970, would be seen "as indifference or impotence in the face of clearly adverse developments in a region long considered our sphere of influence." Nixon concurred, and over the next three years, the United States employed economic pressures, CIA subsidies, and other skullduggeries to encourage the overthrow of a flawed but democratically elected government.[163] Médici, for his part, agreed that "something should probably be done ... very discreetly and very carefully," and Brazil provided support to right-wing groups opposing Allende. While neither Washington nor Brasília directly instigated the coup that eventually toppled Allende, their destabilization tactics helped foster the atmosphere of chaos that preceded it.[164]

Kissinger subsequently established warm relations with Chilean dictator Augusto Pinochet, praising him for his "great service to the West" in toppling Allende and encouraging his vicious campaign of repression against the political Left. "We are sympathetic with what you are trying to do here," he said. "We are behind you," Pinochet assured Kissinger in response. "You are the leader."[165] In late 1975, Pinochet's intelligence services joined with several other South American militaries to launch Operation Condor, a transnational alliance dedicated to tracking, jailing, and killing Marxist guerrillas and other political opponents. Kissinger probably played no direct role in formulating Condor, but it was precisely the sort of "local initiative" he and Nixon had long encouraged. The CIA apparently provided modest technical assistance for the endeavor, and Kissinger blocked State Department efforts to criticize Chile or its allies for their abhorrent human rights practices. "I have an old-fashioned view that friends ought to be supported," he told the Argentine foreign minister in 1976, just as that junta was waging its own "dirty war" that would ultimately claim nearly thirty thousand lives.[166] Repression was unpleasant, Kissinger believed, but instability would be worse.

Yet this policy was itself unstable, because it ran head-on into the rise of a powerful global human rights movement. In the United States, this movement was catalyzed by the moral anguish provoked by Vietnam, and it was sustained by an infrastructure of activists, nongovernmental organizations, and rights-minded politicians. By the mid-1970s, as neoconservatives like Jackson were using human rights issues like Jewish emigration to wage Cold War against the Soviets, liberals like Tom Harkin, Donald Fraser, and Edward Kennedy were mobilizing against the practices of allies like Médici and Pinochet. "Basically we feel it's very difficult to continue to support foreign assistance programs to governments which oppress their own people," Fraser told Kissinger.[167] AFL-CIO president George Meany decried

Chile's "savage repression of its own people," declaring that these citizens had become "one of the globe's endangered species." During the 1976 presidential campaign, Jimmy Carter singled out U.S. ties to Brazil as "a good example of our present policy at its worst."[168]

Kissinger, now secretary of state under Ford, struggled to understand these criticisms or react effectively to them. In his mind, human rights represented a secondary or even tertiary interest—a laudable objective, but something that should only be pursued once first-tier interests like order and security had been achieved. Like Nixon, then, he believed that human rights advocacy was "sentimental nonsense" at a time when the global balance seemed to be shifting in Moscow's favor, and he argued that U.S. officials who prioritized the issue were dangerously naïve and moralistic.[169] "The State Department is made up of people who have a vocation for the ministry," he told the Chilean foreign minister. "Because there were not enough churches for them, they went into the Department of State."[170] Nor did Kissinger think it proper for the legislative branch to interfere with productive diplomatic alliances forged by the executive: "I don't yield to Congress on matters of principle."[171]

Kissinger thus responded to the human rights issue in obstinate and self-defeating ways. Refusing to listen to aides who advocated compromise with Kennedy and Fraser, Kissinger tried to ignore the problem. According to the historian Barbara Keys, he deliberately sought to withhold information on allies' human rights abuses from Congress, and he ensured that the State Department office for human rights was underfunded and understaffed. At a time of growing congressional assertiveness, however, this stance was counterproductive. Fraser and his allies responded by passing legislation that linked foreign aid allotments to human rights performance, compelled the State Department to issue reports on rights abuses in countries that received American assistance, and restricted, reduced, or terminated U.S. aid to Santiago, Buenos Aires, and other capitals.[172] The statesman who prided himself on vision did not understand that he was living amid a human rights revolution, and his policies proved politically untenable as a result.

The problem of assimilating revolutionary change was also at the core of U.S. dealings with the Middle East. Here Kissinger, effectively running foreign policy as Nixon grew consumed by Watergate in 1973, had scored a major triumph during and after the Yom Kippur War. He did not do so by confronting Moscow with a strategic nuclear alert, for Brezhnev had never really planned to intercede militarily, but by intuiting that the shock of the Arab attack had opened the door to a postwar diplomatic process.[173] Kissinger's wartime actions were therefore designed to give the United States maximum leverage over both Arabs and Israelis. To Egypt and Syria, the

American airlift to Israel demonstrated that the United States would not permit its ally to be defeated militarily, that Soviet arms would not enable them to regain their lost lands, and that the road to Israeli concessions ran through Washington rather than Moscow. To the Israelis, the course of the fighting showed that their country could not defend itself without American backing. "We had two objectives in the war," Kissinger explained; "to maintain contact with both sides."

> For this the best outcome would be an Israeli victory but it would come at a high price, so we could insist that they ensure their security through negotiations, not through military power. Second, we attempted to produce a situation where the Arabs would conclude the only way to peace was through us. But during the war we had to show the Israelis they had to depend on us to win and couldn't win if we were too recalcitrant.[174]

The war thus led to a painstaking process of personal diplomacy, with Kissinger spearheading separate negotiations between Israel and its two Arab antagonists. The purpose of the talks was to produce a deliberate, step-by-step disengagement process that would divide the Arabs and divert pressure for an overarching settlement, while still giving them enough tangible gains to ensure that Damascus and Cairo (particularly the latter) came to view the United States, rather than the Soviet Union, as their principal interlocutor.[175] The discussions were tortuous, but by 1975 Kissinger had used American leverage, along with the combination of charm, obsequiousness, and blunt talk that made up his negotiating style, to make substantial headway. His diplomacy achieved the disengagement of Israeli and Arab forces, initiated the process by which Egypt and Israel would eventually make peace, and rendered Moscow largely irrelevant to regional negotiations.[176]

The disengagement accords cemented Kissinger's reputation for diplomatic brilliance—"Super K," as *Newsweek* famously called him. Kissinger himself interpreted the episode as confirmation that the sharp-eyed statesman could look beyond the curve of events and thereby imprint his own stamp upon them. "If one studies our tactics carefully and thoughtfully," he told Israel's Golda Meir, "one must come to the conclusion that our way of dealing with a crisis is to try to judge the crest of the crisis and try to anticipate the events that are happening and thereby dominate them."[177] Heroic diplomacy, Kissinger believed, had allowed Washington to transform the Middle East.

Yet the 1973 war and its aftermath also transformed the region—and the larger global system—in ways that American officials had not expected.

The Yom Kippur War and U.S. support for Israel precipitated an Arab oil embargo. Combined with a major price hike engineered by the Shah of Iran, the result was a quadrupling of world oil prices and severe economic distress in the West. While petro-states like Venezuela, Saudi Arabia, and Iran enjoyed unprecedented profits and a new sense of global influence, the United States and its Western allies experienced high inflation and depressed growth. By the mid-1970s, world lending capacity was stretched thin as petroleum consumers scrambled to cover rising import bills, and U.S. officials feared that several NATO allies were on the verge of financial disaster. "I'm convinced that the biggest problem we face now is possible economic collapse," Kissinger said: "fall of the western world."[178]

The oil shock was not the type of crisis that Kissinger had expected to face (economic issues were not his strong suit), and this episode tested some of the core tenets of his worldview. For one thing, it upended his beliefs about Cold War loyalties in the region, as both Iran and Saudi Arabia—Washington's "twin pillars" of Gulf stability—exploited the economic vulnerability of the West. More profoundly, it inverted Kissinger's assumptions about the nature of power in the international system. Small, underdeveloped countries exercised unprecedented influence over world affairs, while the major industrial democracies found themselves impotent. "It is intolerable that countries of 40 million can blackmail 800 million people in the industrial world," he fumed. As Western economic distress increased, Kissinger even considered coercive action to seize the Saudi oil fields.[179]

Kissinger and Ford never adequately solved the problems of the global oil crisis. The secretary of state did manage to foster some cooperation among the major petroleum consumers, thereby averting complete chaos in the oil markets, but the United States still struggled to make its leverage effective. The Shah, America's "real friend," refused U.S. entreaties to hold off on further price hikes. "He was *our* baby, but now he has grown up," one U.S. intelligence official remarked. Desperate, Kissinger and Ford turned to Saudi Arabia, prevailing on the kingdom to keep oil prices steady, and sweetening the plea with the sale of advanced weapons. The gambit eventually worked, but in doing so it blew a hole in the Iranian national budget, leading to rising unemployment and unleashing the discontent that would soon sweep the monarchy from power. In their efforts to grapple with one revolution, Ford and Kissinger inadvertently encouraged another.[180]

Kissinger's approach to grand strategy was premised on the idea that gifted statesmen could peer through the haze of crisis and impose their own meaning on history. Events in the Third World put this conceit to the test. Kissinger skillfully seized the opportunities presented by the Yom Kippur War, and the friendly-dictators policy was a cost-effective approach to maintaining stability in Latin America and other regions. In the end, though, he struggled to deal with the new and unfamiliar challenges posed by issues like human rights and petro-politics. Kissinger emphasized heroic diplomacy, but he ultimately found himself buffeted by forces that he could not control.

As all of this indicated, the heroic style ended up being a mixed blessing for the conduct of grand strategy. To be sure, Nixon and Kissinger reaped enough success to show that their methods had real utility. The U.S.-Soviet back channel, for instance, was essential in developing détente and bringing SALT to a conclusion. It allowed for rapid communication, the ability to elevate negotiations to a higher level of authority, and the emergence of rapport between Dobrynin and Kissinger. "Without that channel," Dobrynin later wrote, "it would hardly have been possible to reach many key agreements in a timely manner or to eliminate dangerous tensions that arose periodically."[181] Similarly, even administration critics have since allowed that secrecy and personal diplomacy were crucial to moving toward accommodation with Beijing without exposing the process to interference by actors—the Taiwan lobby, U.S. allies in Asia, Soviet experts in the State Department—with an interest in disrupting it.[182] Finally, there is little doubt that Kissinger's ability to act with "quasi-presidential" authority in 1973–74 allowed him to tie together the various implements of American power in managing the Yom Kippur War and choreographing the delicate disengagement talks that followed.[183]

Yet the heroic model also caused as many problems as it solved. It fostered a thoroughly dysfunctional climate within government, as the White House waged what amounted to a permanent war against the agencies that were meant to serve the president. In 1972, Nixon promised that his "one legacy is to ruin the foreign service. I mean ruin it—the old foreign service—and to build a new one."[184] The consequences of this attitude were predictable. The undisguised disdain that Nixon and Kissinger showed for the bureaucracy—and no less their tendency to transfer or otherwise sanction employees who questioned their decisions—were lethal to morale, particularly in the State Department. "The Foreign Service is in an advanced state of depression," Kissinger quipped after moving over to Foggy Bottom, "because they have a Secretary who takes an interest in the conduct of foreign policy."[185]

Kissinger joked, but the ramifications were serious. Once he and Nixon made clear that they would ignore or punish dissenters, a sort of self-censorship took effect, as State Department and CIA officials—including CIA Director Richard Helms—became understandably reluctant to hazard contrary opinions. Those who decided to fight back, conversely, adopted their own methods of intra-governmental warfare. Laird, no less of a bureaucratic brawler than Kissinger, used electronic intercepts from the National Security Agency to stay abreast of administration policy. JCS staffers resorted to more old-fashioned methods, stealing documents from the NSC. Frustrated by the White House tendency to run roughshod over Pentagon concerns about arms control, Laird's successors—James Schlesinger and then Donald Rumsfeld—turned the tables on Kissinger by using leaks, intentional delays, and other methods of obstructing the decision-making process. As Chief of Naval Operations Elmo Zumwalt noted, administration politics had devolved into low-intensity warfare. "What I find hard to believe," he wrote, "is that rational men could think that running things like that could have any other result than 'leaks' and 'spying' and all-around paranoia. Indeed they had created a system in which 'leaks' and 'spying' were everyday and essential elements."[186]

This atmosphere might have been an acceptable cost of doing business had it not detracted from the overall quality of policy. Inevitably, however, it did. Centralizing the decision-making process allowed greater flexibility, but it also deprived top officials of expertise and information from the bureaucracy. This liability marred American dealings with Southeast Asia between 1969 and 1971, when Nixon and Kissinger repeatedly shut out State Department and intelligence officials who might have warned that attacking Laos and Cambodia would do little to improve the military situation but much to destabilize these countries. "State is to be notified only after the point of no return," Nixon declared during the run-up to the bombing of Cambodia in 1969.[187] The problem recurred during the South Asian crisis in 1971, when Kissinger blithely ignored regional experts who warned that the administration's policies would lead to grief.[188] In numerous other episodes, the story was similar.

The same issue even intruded on the management of great-power relations, which Nixon and Kissinger considered their area of particular expertise. During the SALT negotiations, Kissinger's insistence on operating behind the backs of his own experts led him to make a major substantive error that allowed the Soviets to obtain a very generous ceiling on the number of submarine-launched ballistic missiles (SLBMs) they were permitted.[189] (That error, in turn, would be ruthlessly exploited by hawks who opposed détente.) And during the SALT II process in the Ford years, the combination of leaking, bureaucratic intrigues, and the accumulated resentment of Pentagon officials played havoc with Kissinger's efforts to formulate a workable negotiating posture. "The SALT debate is unbelievable," he told Ford in early 1976. "How can we negotiate when every position is in the press?"[190] As Kissinger eventually discovered, it was difficult to make policy in a den of conspirators.

As these and other incidents showed, a key liability of a centralized decision-making process is that the weaknesses of the person or people at the center become the weaknesses of the system as a whole. Nixon and Kissinger were undoubtedly gifted strategic thinkers, and they made the conspiratorial model work quite well in a number of areas. Yet like all policy makers, Nixon and Kissinger also had their blind spots—human rights, economics, the intricacies of regional affairs in the Third World, the technical details of arms control. And like everyone else, they could be rash and impulsive rather than cool and deliberate. "Henry is very excitable, very emotional almost," noted U.S. ambassador to the United Nations George H. W. Bush in 1971. "He has a great sense of humor and is tremendously relaxed and buoyant. Often, however, he hits the ceiling and raises hell.... He is paranoid about the Department."[191] Kissinger, like Nixon, was a man of great talents and serious flaws. Centralizing policy ensured that both sets of characteristics worked their influence on American grand strategy.

What was ultimately the biggest flaw of the heroic model was its central premise—that successful grand strategy was something that had to be executed independently of, and even in opposition to, the institutions and traditions of the society it was meant to serve. Nixon and Kissinger were undoubtedly right in thinking that the United States needed creative leadership during a traumatic time. They were also correct in identifying some of the potentially pernicious qualities of the American system. Where they went wrong was in thinking that a model of statecraft that flouted that system could itself be long maintained.

Take, for instance, the issue of morality. One can debate whether the more controversial policies pursued during this period—the air attacks on North Vietnam, the bombing and invasion of neutral countries, the support for brutal governments in Pakistan and Argentina, the determined efforts to overthrow Allende—were really as immoral as the critics charged. What can be said with certainty is that these policies were self-defeating politically, because they put the Nixon and Ford administrations seriously at odds with the post-Vietnam mood in the United States. At a time when a nation scarred by division and defeat craved moral reassurance, these administrations' policies on human rights, covert intervention, and other subjects exemplified the same end-justifies-the-means calculus that seemed so terribly discredited by recent events. As a result, the cumulative impact of these initiatives was to produce in many observers a sense that U.S. foreign policy had become morally bankrupt. When State Department officials took soundings of public opinion in 1976, they discovered a "deep-seated yearning that the moral aspect of foreign policy issues should be a significant factor in policy decisions," the clear implication being that recent diplomacy had not satisfied this concern.[192]

The same point could be made about official secrecy and the centralization of power. The fact that these methods could boomerang was most painfully demonstrated by Watergate, which shattered the very executive authority that Nixon and Kissinger had so jealously sought to defend. More broadly, the antidemocratic tendencies of the Nixon-Kissinger grand strategy occasioned growing resistance as this period went on. Media reports and congressional inquiries eventually unveiled most of the administration's covert pursuits—the bombing of Cambodia, the tilt toward Pakistan, the destabilization of Chile, and others. These exposés revealed that the administration had often been deceptive if not downright dishonest with the American people, and they fed a sense that the nation's foreign policy had lost its democratic moorings. As Jimmy Carter charged during the 1976 campaign, Kissinger was pursuing "a kind of secretive, 'Lone Ranger' foreign policy, a one man policy of international adventure."[193] Similarly, it may or may not have been wise for Fraser and his allies to inject human rights concerns into American diplomacy in the mid-1970s, but when Kissinger refused to take the issue seriously, he simply confirmed for his critics that executive power had to be checked.

The ironic result of all this was to undermine the realpolitik that Nixon and Kissinger had sought to practice and the heroic model they sought to utilize. The War Powers Act, which curbed the executive's authority to use military force; the Pike and Church committee investigations, which imposed new constraints on CIA covert action; the human rights legislation that restricted aid to dictatorial governments: all of these course corrections flowed, not wholly but partially, from disillusion with the methods of American grand strategy during the Nixon-Kissinger years. And it was just this discontent that Carter tapped into in 1976 when he lambasted the secrecy and amorality of his predecessors' diplomacy and promised the American people a more transparent and ethical foreign policy. Nixon and Kissinger had hoped to forge a new consensus on American grand strategy, but their operating style helped ensure that this ambition went wanting.[194]

"We are the ones who have been operating against our public opinion, against our bureaucracy, at the very edge of legality," Kissinger exclaimed during one crisis in 1971.[195] This heroic ethos proved its merit in facilitating the triumphs of the period, but in the end, it also played a key role in making the Nixon-Kissinger grand strategy unsustainable.

Richard Nixon and Henry Kissinger believed that inspired grand strategy could allow the United States to rise above its crisis of relative decline and shape the contours of a more stable global order. Theirs was an ambitious design, and one that delivered significant results. The opening to China, the conclusion of SALT and other negotiations with Moscow, the handling of the Yom Kippur War and its aftermath, even the devolution of responsibility to local allies in the Third World: all of these initiatives benefited a superpower in distress, all came at a relatively low material cost, and all of them flowed from the ideas and methods that Nixon and Kissinger advocated. Legacies have been forged from far less. To appreciate the merits of their grand strategy, one has only to consider how much America's international position would have deteriorated without these advances.[196]

In the end, however, the geopolitical virtuosity that the administration aspired to remained beyond reach. Nixon and Kissinger could not translate the early triumphs of détente and triangular diplomacy into a lasting structure of Cold War stability. Nor could they liberate America from the Vietnam War in a way compatible with the country's broader needs. Nor, for that matter, was their statecraft well suited to various Third World crises or emerging issues like human rights and the oil shocks. By the mid-1970s, the Nixon-Kissinger strategy was running out of gas. The United States had not transcended its traumas and mastered the shifting geopolitical currents; it was struggling just to deal with the crises and divisions of the day.

The frustrations that Nixon and Kissinger encountered were not solely their fault, but they nonetheless revealed two basic problems with their approach to grand strategy. The first was that there was simply a limit to what even bold, purposeful statecraft could accomplish in a complex—and often difficult—operating environment. Nixon and Kissinger had hoped that imaginative leadership could allow the United States to surmount the challenges of U.S.-Soviet relations, the Vietnam War, and other difficult issues. In the event, however, their efforts repeatedly ran afoul of domestic political constraints, the actions of opponents and rivals, and the general stubbornness and unpredictability of a world in which American power was no longer so great. "The gods are offended by hubris," Kissinger would later write. "They resent the presumption that events can be totally predicted and managed." It was presumably an insight born of experience, for the Nixon-Kissinger years offered abundant proof of the tension between grand designs and hard reality.[197]

The second and related problem was that shielding grand strategy from the very government and society it was meant to benefit was an inherently fraught proposition. Concentrating power permitted boldness and dexterity, but it also created a poisonous mood within government and limited the collective wisdom that could be brought to bear on difficult problems. In any event, it ultimately proved impossible to maintain the degree of secrecy, centralization, and tactical ruthlessness that Nixon and Kissinger thought necessary, and the effort to do so was politically self-defeating in the end. When it comes to grand strategy, working within the strictures of the American system is difficult enough. As the experience of Nixon and Kissinger showed, seeking to circumvent those strictures can be just as dangerous.

CHAPTER 3

Was There a Reagan Grand Strategy?

American Statecraft in the Late Cold War

Few of Kissinger's critics were more outspoken than Ronald Reagan, the former California governor who emerged as a leading GOP figure following Nixon's resignation in 1974. During the 1976 Republican primaries, Reagan had attacked détente as an abdication of America's moral heritage and a dangerously naïve approach to the Cold War. He maintained this position after Jimmy Carter took office in 1977. In radio addresses and other public commentaries, Reagan warned that the United States was falling perilously behind in the strategic arms race, and that the Soviets were exploiting détente to gain advantage in the Third World. He argued that the United States could reverse these trends and retake the geopolitical advantage over Moscow, but only if it developed a "long-range diplomatic strategy" for contesting the Cold War. The recent record of U.S. diplomacy had been one of "vacillation, appeasement, and aimlessness," he declared; America would need a more purposeful and coherent design in the years to come.[1]

Whether President Reagan actually brought these qualities to U.S. policy remains a subject of intense dispute. Historical assessments of Reagan vary widely, ranging from glowing portrayals of a visionary statesman to biting depictions of an ideologue who was more fortunate in his timing than skillful in his statecraft. Observers disagree on whether it was the president or his advisers that drove American diplomacy, whether there was ever something coherent enough to be called a Reagan grand strategy, the extent to which the administration shifted its approach to Moscow in the mid-1980s, and the contribution that Reagan and his policies made to ending the Cold War.[2] These debates have sometimes grown quite heated: in one recent book, a prominent diplomatic historian asserts that pro-Reagan accounts suffer from a lack of scholarly objectivity.[3] A quarter century after he left office, Reagan is still a polarizing figure.

This much is clear: Reagan presided over a truly astounding improvement in America's geopolitical fortunes, a turnabout that most observers would have thought highly unlikely when he took office in 1981. At the outset of Reagan's presidency, the Cold War appeared very clearly to be going Moscow's way, and America and its allies were stuck on the defensive. Just eight years later, it was the Soviets who were retreating on virtually all fronts, and bilateral tensions had eased so much that both Reagan and Mikhail Gorbachev were proclaiming the Cold War's end. The purpose of this chapter, then, is to use a range of historical sources—recently declassified documents, Reagan's pre-presidential writings, the relevant memoir and secondary literature—to assess whether there was in fact a Reagan grand strategy, and if so, how it influenced the trajectory of superpower affairs during the 1980s.

These sources illustrate that there was a Reagan grand strategy—a comprehensive, long-term vision for U.S. policy toward Moscow. This strategy drew heavily on Reagan's own ideas and involvement, and it utilized all elements of national power. It was premised on the idea that the Soviet Union was far weaker than it had looked in the late 1970s, and that the United States could take advantage of that weakness by exerting pressure in the military, economic, political, and ideological realms. This was the unifying rationale behind the major elements of Reagan's statecraft, from his enormous military buildup, to his eponymous doctrine of supporting anti-Soviet insurgents in the Third World, to his strident rhetorical condemnations of Moscow and other measures. The primary goal of these initiatives was not to force the collapse of the Soviet Union (as some hard-liners advocated), but to provide diplomatic leverage that could be used to moderate Soviet behavior and reduce Cold War tensions on terms favorable to the United States. In essence, Reagan's grand strategy—spelled out in presidential decision directives issued in 1982 and 1983—was meant to capitalize on America's competitive advantages vis-à-vis Moscow, to reverse the tide of the Cold War, and then to begin the process of forging a more stable superpower relationship.

When Reagan left office, this vision had largely been realized. This did not mean, however, that events followed a straight line from the formulation of his grand strategy to the end of the Cold War, for the history of the period was more complex than that. During the early 1980s, the administration was quite effective in reasserting U.S. strength, exploiting emerging Soviet vulnerabilities, and seizing a position of geopolitical advantage. In this sense, Reagan's statecraft served as an excellent example of what the focused, multidimensional application of power could accomplish. Unfortunately, the president could not initially translate these gains into productive diplomacy with Moscow. Quite the opposite, in fact: the very aggressiveness of his policies frightened the Soviet leadership and thereby *reduced* the near-term prospects for improved superpower relations. The result was a dangerous escalation of Cold War tensions, culminating in the Able Archer crisis of late 1983.

What ultimately allowed Reagan's grand strategy to succeed was his ability to learn from these early experiences and recalibrate accordingly. This constituted less of a "reversal" than sometimes claimed, for Reagan persisted in many of his basic policies, and he had always planned to negotiate with Moscow eventually.[4] But beginning in late 1983 and early 1984, the president did execute a key tactical shift by toning down his incendiary rhetoric, calling for an expanded bilateral dialogue, and seeking to build trust with the same Kremlin leadership he had so vociferously condemned. From this point onward, his statecraft was characterized by efforts not simply to preserve American strength and leverage, but to reassure and conciliate his Soviet counterparts as well.

This revised approach left the administration well-placed to respond when Gorbachev became general secretary in 1985. In retrospect, the subsequent improvement of superpower relations had much to do with Gorbachev's personality, his intellectual makeup, and his determination to achieve a "breathing space" that would allow him to address the advancing crisis of the Soviet system. Yet Reagan's policies also played a key role. From 1985 onward, the administration—led by Reagan and Secretary of State George Shultz—maintained a hard enough line to ensure that Gorbachev could get the détente he wanted only by making significant changes to Soviet policy, both at home and abroad. But no less crucially, they also worked to construct a climate of respect and even trust with Gorbachev, and to convince him that constructive actions would bring about a more beneficial relationship with the West. In effect, the administration underscored Gorbachev's incentives— both positive and negative—for moderation and reform, and thereby promoted the transformation of U.S.-Soviet affairs.

In the end, Reagan thus succeeded in combining vision with flexibility, strength with diplomacy, and in bringing his grand strategic agenda to fruition. It was hardly a flawless performance, though, because in doing so the president incurred significant costs: military expenditures that led to a record-breaking accumulation of national debt, partnerships with morally questionable allies in the Third World, and inattention to—even encouragement of—rising threats like nuclear proliferation and Islamic extremism. These pernicious legacies did not invalidate the administration's very real achievements in U.S.-Soviet relations. They did indicate, however, that Reagan's grand strategy had its price.[5]

The Reagan administration came to power at a low point in America's Cold War fortunes. Détente had collapsed during the late 1970s, and Soviet power seemed very much on the ascent. Moscow was enjoying a run of successes in the Third World, as Marxist movements seized power in locales from Nicaragua to Angola to South Yemen. Soviet military might was also on the upswing. Having already attained strategic parity, the Kremlin continued to push forward by deploying heavier, more accurate ICBMs, fielding SS-20 intermediate-range missiles (IRBMs) that menaced all of the NATO countries, and improving its naval and air forces. In the West, these developments created fears that the strategic balance was tipping toward Moscow, a concern that was magnified when Soviet troops invaded Afghanistan in 1979. The invasion raised the specter of a Kremlin thrust toward the Persian Gulf, and it punctuated what seemed to be a growing Soviet militancy. "This more assertive Soviet international behavior is likely to persist as long as the USSR perceives that Western strength is declining and as it further explores the utility of its increased military power as a means of realizing its global ambitions," U.S. intelligence analysts wrote in 1981.[6]

It later turned out that Moscow's invasion of Afghanistan was not part of an aggressive bid to dominate the Gulf, but a desperate maneuver to preserve the crumbling Communist regime in Kabul. On the whole, though, Soviet officials did believe that the strategic momentum was on their side in the late 1970s. Moscow appeared to be making gains both militarily and diplomatically, while the United States was struggling with "stagflation" and post-Vietnam malaise. The Politburo, Dobrynin later recalled, "lived in the certainty that a historical process was under way: the collapse of the old colonial empires and general weakening of the capitalist system."[7] Brezhnev and his colleagues expected that growing Soviet power would enable still greater advances in the Third World, and they even hoped that the SS-20s might intimidate Western Europe and undermine NATO cohesion. Yuri Andropov (Brezhnev's successor) later looked back on the 1970s as "a time of further growth in the power and influence of the socialist commonwealth," years of "major positive developments in international relations."[8]

As superpower relations deteriorated, the Carter administration struggled to respond. The problem was not any reticence to take strong steps. Carter imposed a raft of sanctions on Moscow following the invasion of Afghanistan, and as détente unraveled he initiated a number of the countermeasures—from increased military spending to support for the anti-Soviet mujahideen in Afghanistan—that would later loom large in Reagan's policy. The trouble, however, was that because Carter had previously argued that the United States should move *away* from containment, these maneuvers looked like knee-jerk reactions to unexpected events rather than parts of an integrated strategic program. As Raymond Garthoff has written, Carter's post-Afghanistan policy was "thrown together hastily . . . without much thought of the implications and consequences."[9] Détente was dead when Carter left office, but the United States lacked a coherent grand strategy for managing the renewed Cold War that followed.

In many ways, Reagan seemed uniquely unqualified to provide this strategy. The septuagenarian president was no one's idea of a geopolitical mastermind when he took office. As one biographer notes, Reagan often displayed an "encyclopedic ignorance" of policy specifics, and he had a number of personal characteristics—his age, his background in television and movies, his penchant for expressing complex ideas in moralistic and highly ideological terms—that caused critics to consider him an intellectual impotent. Even advisers sometimes doubted his competence. Paul Nitze, one of Reagan's lead arms control officials, put it bluntly. "When I first met Reagan," he said, "I thought he was just a born loser."[10]

As Nitze later conceded, however, this impression of superficiality was itself superficial. Reagan had no knack for the finer points of policy, but he possessed sharp geopolitical instincts and an ability to grasp the essence of difficult issues. The president had "an amazingly intuitive mind," chief science adviser George Keyworth later said. "He can sift out what matters from ten thousand bureaucratic details in a remarkable manner."[11] Another contemporary put it in almost identical terms: "Reagan is extremely intelligent. He is quick, and not easily sidetracked, able to get to the center of a complicated problem almost abruptly."[12] And while Reagan was no policy wonk, he had spent a great deal of time in the 1960s and 1970s—first as a General Electric spokesman, then as a presidential candidate and GOP leader—refining his core beliefs on America's role in the world. To an extent that not even his closest aides then appreciated, Reagan had actually developed the key intellectual precepts of his foreign policy before he ever arrived in Washington. "If you look at [his pre-presidential writings and speeches]," Shultz later noted, "you can see the whole kind of conceptual understructure of the Reagan administration right there."[13]

At the core of this "conceptual understructure" was an appreciation of the need for an integrated, coherent grand strategy for waging Cold War. Reagan saw the superpower rivalry as a defining global struggle—a Manichean clash between the forces of freedom and those of totalitarian evil.[14] If the United States was to prevail, it would need a "long-range diplomatic strategy" that would allow it to regain the global initiative and restore a favorable balance of power. "We must above all have a grand strategy," he declared in 1980: "a plan for the dangerous decade ahead."[15] The United States must connect its short-term policies to a longer-term vision for reducing the Soviet threat; it must also synergize its various initiatives so as to maximize the impact of American power. "The essential ingredients of any successful strategy," Reagan commented, "include political, economic, military and psychological measures."[16]

From the 1970s onward, Reagan's approach to grand strategy rested on a seemingly paradoxical idea—that the Soviet Union was simultaneously strong and weak. Like many conservative commentators, Reagan was deeply worried by the growth of Soviet military power and its potential geopolitical consequences. He believed that the loss of strategic superiority had deprived the United States of essential diplomatic leverage, and he feared that the Soviets were becoming strong enough to intimidate and divide the noncommunist world. He saw recent Soviet gains in the Third World as proof of a deteriorating global balance, and in radio commentaries and other public addresses he cited long lists of statistics meant to demonstrate creeping U.S. military weakness. "The evidence mounts," he said in 1976, "that we are Number Two in a world where it is dangerous, if not fatal, to be second best."[17]

The shifting nuclear balance was a subject of particular concern for Reagan. Whereas some contemporary observers contended that nuclear superiority was essentially irrelevant to geopolitical outcomes, Reagan took a much different view. He believed that the ability to dominate the escalatory process conferred real coercive leverage, and he cited the U.S. experience in Berlin, Korea, and the Cuban missile crisis as support for this argument. "The nuclear weapon," he said in one radio broadcast, "was always a decisive factor in the background." Unfortunately, it followed that the growth of Soviet strategic capabilities posed enormous problems for the United States. Moscow would be emboldened to take greater risks, and American allies would question the credibility of Washington's nuclear guarantees. The potential consequences were frightening to contemplate. "The Russians are pursuing a program to achieve clear-cut military superiority over the West," Reagan warned in 1979. "Once this is accomplished they will intimidate, 'Finlandize,' and ultimately neutralize Western Europe."[18]

From a military perspective, then, the United States was fast approaching a dangerous window of vulnerability vis-à-vis Moscow. From a longer-range and more holistic perspective, however, Reagan remained far more sanguine about America's Cold War prospects. Better than many contemporaries, he intuitively understood that Moscow's growing military capabilities rested atop a rotting political-economic foundation. Throughout the 1970s, he argued that Moscow's "incompetent and ridiculous" system was growing increasingly sclerotic, and that the Soviet economy could never compete with the West over the long run. "Nothing proves the *failure of Marxism more than the Soviet Unions* [sic] inability to produce weapons *for its mil. ambitions and at the same time provide* for their peoples [sic] everyday needs," he wrote.[19] Similarly, Reagan adduced the vitality of the Soviet dissident movement as evidence that the political system was also vulnerable. Together, these ideas led him conclude that Soviet communism would not be a permanent fixture of the international scene. "Communism is neither an economic nor political system—it is a form of insanity—a temporary aberration which will one day disappear from the earth because it is contrary to human nature," he told a radio audience in 1975.[20] The near-term threat was undoubtedly severe, but if the United States kept its guard up and its powder dry, then the forces of history would ultimately be on its side.

It was precisely for these reasons that Reagan so vehemently criticized détente during the 1970s. Reagan did not oppose a decrease in global tensions per se, but he felt that détente had allowed the Soviets to increase their military strengths while masking their underlying weaknesses. In his view, arms control agreements had not prevented Moscow from MIRVing its missiles, but they had given Americans a false sense of comfort that discouraged "appropriate responses to defend our security interests."[21] Meanwhile, the Soviet bloc had gained greater access to Western loans and technology, while largely escaping—under Kissinger, at least—moral condemnation of its abhorrent internal practices. "Are we not helping a Godless tyranny maintain its hold on millions of helpless people?" he asked. "Wouldn't those helpless victims have a better chance of becoming free if their slave masters [sic] regime collapsed economically?"[22]

For Reagan, the key to a successful grand strategy thus lay in redressing America's temporary weaknesses while also exploiting the more profound debilities of the Soviet Union. By the time he was elected president, Reagan had already begun to outline the measures he deemed necessary to accomplish these goals. He consistently argued that the United States would have to rebuild its military power and regain strategic superiority over Moscow, while also restoring the national self-confidence that had been sapped by Vietnam. "Only by mustering a superiority, beginning with a superiority of the spirit, can we stop the thunder of hobnailed boots on their march to world empire," he said in 1977.[23] With respect to the Third World, he called for unstinting support to anticommunist allies that were menaced by Marxist insurgents, as well as aid to those who were rebelling against pro-Soviet governments in Afghanistan, Nicaragua, and elsewhere.[24]

Most notably, Reagan advocated steps to pressure the Soviet system itself. During his pre-presidential years, he called for tighter controls on East-West commerce to deny the Soviet bloc badly needed capital and technology. Similarly, he argued that Washington should wage political warfare by encouraging Soviet dissenters—this "might be worth a lot of armored divisions"—and by conducting a vigorous public diplomacy that would paint the Kremlin dictatorship in its most unflattering hues: "It's time to remind *ourselves & others* of the difference in culture, in morals and in the levels of civilization between the free world and the communist ant heap."[25] Reagan understood that these measures would not cause immediate upheaval in Moscow, but he believed that they would drive home the failures of communism, strengthen liberalizing tendencies within the Soviet system, and eventually make the Kremlin a more manageable and predictable opponent. "We could have an unexpected ally," he predicted, "if citizen Ivan is becoming discontented enough to start talking back."[26]

Needless to say, these proposals implied a significant escalation of superpower tensions, at least in the near term. As Paul Lettow has noted, however, Reagan did not believe that an indefinite Cold War was either desirable or inevitable. More so than many contemporaries realized, Reagan was genuinely horrified by the prospect of nuclear war, and he regarded mutual assured destruction (MAD) as strategic lunacy. MAD, he said, was like "two westerners standing in a saloon aiming their guns at each other's head—permanently."[27] Reagan had voiced a desire to abolish nuclear weapons during the 1960s and 1970s, and even as he called for a military buildup he expressed hope that nuclear arsenals could eventually be lowered dramatically. "Currently the only way to deter nuclear war was to arm as strongly as the potential opponent," he said privately in 1981. "However, this was not good enough. There could be miscalculations and accidents. It was necessary to reduce the number of forces on both sides."[28]

For Reagan, then, reversing the momentum of the Cold War was not an end in itself. It was a means to the longer-term goal of *reducing* superpower

tensions on American terms. If the United States reestablished its strength
and increased the strains on the Soviet system—in short, if it showed that
Moscow could not win the Cold War—then the Kremlin would eventually
have to moderate its conduct and accept a modus vivendi. As Reagan had
written in the 1960s, his policy rested "on the belief . . . that in an all out
race our system is stronger, and eventually the enemy gives up the race as a
hopeless cause. Then a noble nation believing in peace extends the hand of
friendship and says there is room in the world for both of us."[29] This theme
was one to which he returned repeatedly. "There was no miracle weapon
available with which to deal with the Soviets," he said in 1981, but "we
could threaten the Soviets with our ability to outbuild them . . . Once we had
established this, we could invite the Soviets to join us in lowering the level
of weapons on both sides."[30] In Reagan's mind, a determined geopolitical
offensive could set the stage for a more durable international peace.

Translating ideas into policy is rarely an easy process, and the early experience
of the Reagan administration was no exception. To all outward appearances,
there was no grand strategy during the opening innings of Reagan's presidency. "Hard-liners" battled with "moderates" over the direction of U.S.
policy toward Moscow, and the president, who disliked confrontations with
his advisers, proved reluctant to halt the bickering. The result was nonstop
leaking and infighting, and a widespread sense that U.S. diplomacy lacked
any compass at all. "The entire first year and a half of the administration
passed in an atmosphere of unremitting tension," NSC staffer Richard Pipes
recalled. When Secretary of State Alexander Haig resigned after just over a
year in office, it seemed obvious that Reagan's policy was off to an inchoate
and inauspicious start.[31]

The bureaucratic warfare and disorganization were no illusion, and these
tendencies would remain a problem for the administration. Yet there was a
certain method to the madness. Reagan may not have dominated the bureaucratic process, but as key NSC adviser Jack Matlock later observed, he "knew
very well what he was doing, and why."[32] "I have a foreign policy," Reagan
wrote in 1981. "I just don't happen to think that it's wise to always stand up
and put in quotation marks in front of the world what your foreign policy
is."[33] Indeed, it now seems that Reagan's refusal to side definitively with any
one group of advisers was not a product of indecisiveness, but rather an effort
to avoid becoming the captive of any single faction.[34] For even as conflict
swirled around him, Reagan was working with a diverse set of hard-liners
and moderates alike—William Casey at the CIA; Shultz at State; Pipes,
Robert McFarlane, and later Matlock at the NSC; Caspar Weinberger and

others at the Pentagon—to enact the components of a grand strategy meant to reassert American power, pressure the Soviet Union, and fundamentally alter the course of the Cold War.

The first element of this grand strategy was the major military buildup that Reagan had long been advocating. The U.S. defense budget increased from $155.2 billion in 1980 to $319.8 billion in 1988—in constant dollars, a rise of more than 50 percent. Weinberger's Pentagon used this money to procure an array of advanced weapons and platforms, including Trident nuclear submarines, Trident II SLBMs, MX intercontinental missiles, and B-1 and B-2 bombers.[35] In addition, Reagan adopted a Carter-era plan to deploy Tomahawk cruise missiles and Pershing II IRBMs (which could strike targets deep inside the Soviet bloc in a matter of seven or eight minutes) to Western Europe to offset the shadow cast by the SS-20s.[36] Reagan was prepared to enter into arms-control negotiations on these and other weapons, but in the meantime he deemed it imperative to restore the leverage that came with military power. "A sound East-West military balance is absolutely essential," he stated; strength was the indispensable precondition to everything Reagan hoped to do.[37]

As the Reagan administration pursued an improved military balance, the armed services embraced new doctrinal concepts meant to maximize U.S. advantages and minimize long-standing weaknesses. Building on ideas and technologies developed during the 1970s, the Army promoted "Air-Land Battle," an approach premised on utilizing U.S. strengths in precision-guided munitions and deep strike capabilities to blunt a prospective Soviet thrust into Western Europe without having to resort to nuclear escalation.[38] For its part, the Navy advanced an aggressive "Maritime Strategy" that threatened Moscow with rapid geographical expansion of any conflict that began in the European theater. If the Kremlin struck in Europe, American naval forces would not simply assist in the NATO response; they would also conduct offensive operations against vulnerable targets in the Soviet Far East and potentially elsewhere. "To deter is to threaten," Navy officials explained in a 1982 presentation; the Maritime Strategy was one of "full forward pressure."[39] Reagan fully approved of the underlying theme. "If they know that we might respond to them by hitting them anywhere in the world, that's a strong deterrent," he remarked at an NSC meeting in April 1982.[40]

Beyond strengthening deterrence and improving American leverage, the military buildup also had an important secondary objective: to increase the strains on a deteriorating Soviet economy. By 1981–82, intelligence was piling up that the Soviet economy was (in Reagan's words) "approaching the brink of collapse," in part because of military expenditures upward of 20 percent of GNP.[41] In concert with officials like Henry Rowen at the CIA and Weinberger and Andrew Marshall at the Pentagon, Reagan believed that the U.S. buildup could be used to widen "these cracks in the Soviet system" by forcing the Kremlin to invest in new weapons programs it could not afford. This "cost-imposing strategy," as Marshall called it, was enshrined in an early Pentagon planning document that advocated the development of systems that would be "difficult for the Soviets to counter, impose disproportionate costs, open up new areas of major military competition and obsolesce previous Soviet investment." Or as Weinberger noted in a memo written in late 1982, the United States should pursue strategic modernization "in such a way that will force the Soviets into an expensive program of research, development and deployment to overcome it." If carried through, this approach would confront Soviet officials with a painful dilemma—they would either have to concede defeat in the arms race, or overstress their economy in an effort to keep pace.[42]

This logic also figured in the signature military initiative of Reagan's presidency—his announcement of plans to develop an antimissile shield that would render nuclear weapons "impotent and obsolete."[43] As was often the case with Reagan, the proposal for a Strategic Defense Initiative (SDI) drew on numerous motives. The idea certainly reflected his long-standing antinuclearism, and his desire to move toward something better than the grim reassurance of MAD. There was a "moral context" to missile defense, Reagan told British prime minister Margaret Thatcher in 1984. "We cannot and should not . . . have to go on living under the threat of nuclear destruction."[44] A missile shield could allow the United States to defend itself should war occur, while also dramatically reducing the utility of the most dangerous and destabilizing weapons—ICBMs. Eventually, SDI might thereby lead to the reduction—even elimination—of nuclear arsenals. The idea, Reagan would tell Gorbachev in 1986, was to "give the world a means of protection that would put the nuclear genie back in his bottle."[45]

Yet SDI was also conceived with malice aforethought. As officials like McFarlane pointed out, a substantial U.S. investment in missile defense would present the Soviets with only unattractive options. They could develop their own shield, but this would be a technology- and innovation-intensive endeavor for which a creaking command economy was poorly suited. Or they could engage in an ICBM buildup to overwhelm SDI, but this too would strain Kremlin finances. In sum, SDI was precisely the sort of program that would escalate strategic competition in ways that Moscow could not readily match. The Soviets "must be concerned about our economic strength," Reagan told Thatcher during their discussion of SDI. "It will be especially difficult for them to keep spending such vast sums on defense."[46]

If intensified military competition represented the first prong of Reagan's strategy, intensified competition in the Third World constituted the second. The president and advisers like Casey believed that recent Soviet advances had made the Third World a crucial battleground, and they worried that issues like human rights had placed Washington at a disadvantage in waging this struggle. From the outset, Reagan resolved that he would henceforth be holding the line in places like Latin America, even if it meant partnering with otherwise abhorrent regimes. "We don't throw out our friends just because they can't pass the 'saliva test' on human rights," he told the NSC in 1981.[47] The administration initially sought to repair relations with pariah states like Argentina and Chile, and it poured billions of dollars in economic and military aid into El Salvador, where a murderously repressive army was fighting a powerful Marxist insurgency. For Reagan, this conflict was a crucial test of America's ability to blunt Soviet geopolitical momentum. "El Salvador is a good starting point," he said. "A victory there could set an example."[48]

As this comment indicated, there was also an offensive component to U.S. policy. Reagan had long been taken with the idea that Washington could seize the initiative in the Third World by turning Moscow's own tactics against it.[49] With his encouragement, Casey and like-minded officials fashioned this idea into a wide-ranging policy of destabilization. In Afghanistan, Nicaragua, and elsewhere, the CIA provided money, weapons, and training to anticommunist insurgents struggling against vulnerable pro-Soviet regimes. In the Nicaraguan case, administration officials clearly hoped to overthrow the Sandinista government; in Afghanistan, the initial goal was simply to "bleed" Moscow and increase the burdens of empire. "At a very low cost, without a big investment on our part, we can make it very hard for them in these places," explained Pipes in 1981.[50] This concept was subsequently integrated into a major NSC study. "The U.S. should not accept the notion that, once a Communist or pro-Soviet regime has come to power in a state, this situation is irreversible," the document asserted.[51]

For the most part, Reagan shied away from using U.S. troops to accomplish this aim. The president understood that he had come to power at a politically propitious time, in that Soviet advances had re-created something of a Cold War consensus at home. Yet he also knew that costly military misadventures could easily rupture that consensus. In consequence, he tried to keep U.S. military operations short and contained, and only once—in Grenada in October 1983—did he use American forces to overthrow a pro-Soviet government. This particular intervention had less to do with rollback than with ensuring the safety of U.S. citizens on the island, and it was such a colossal mismatch that the outcome was never in doubt. Even so, the operation punctuated Reagan's more aggressive posture, and it gave him a military triumph he could use to bolster American self-confidence after Vietnam and another disastrous intervention in Lebanon during his first term. "Our days of weakness are over," he proclaimed.[52]

Meanwhile, the administration was also pursuing a third aspect of Reagan's grand strategy: efforts to undermine Kremlin authority at home and in Eastern Europe. By mid-1981, Reagan's conviction that communist systems were inherently vulnerable was being reinforced by growing popular unrest in Eastern Europe and a flood of intelligence reports on social and economic problems in the Soviet Union. "We are seeing the first, beginning cracks," he said in July, "the beginning of the end." A high-level study the next year concluded that "the ideological underpinnings of the system have clearly been eroding" and argued that the United States should compound these problems and promote liberalizing trends within the Soviet bloc.[53]

The first opportunity to do so came in Poland in 1981–82. The rise of the independent trade union Solidarity, with its political activism and demands for reform, presented Moscow with a grave challenge. "Here is the 1st major break in the Red dike," Reagan wrote in his diary.[54] During 1981, the administration sought to encourage liberalization in Eastern Europe by lending quiet moral support to Solidarity, while also warning Brezhnev that there would be severe diplomatic consequences if Soviet forces intervened. When the Politburo circumvented this issue by inducing the Polish government to declare martial law, Reagan was nonetheless determined to respond. "This is the first time in 60 years that we have had this kind of opportunity," Reagan told the NSC. "There may not be another in our lifetime." U.S. officials provided covert assistance to Solidarity (now forced to operate underground), stepped up Voice of America broadcasting, and slapped economic sanctions on the Polish and Soviet governments. An NSC directive completed in 1982 affirmed that the U.S. goal in Eastern Europe was to "loosen the Soviet hold on the region and thereby facilitate its eventual reintegration into the European community of nations."[55]

The successful crackdown in Poland ensured that this remained a long-term aspiration, but it also provided Reagan with an opportunity to exacerbate Moscow's economic problems. "The Soviet Union is economically on the ropes—they are selling rat meat on the market," he told advisers. "This is the time to punish them."[56] In addition to imposing sanctions, the administration discouraged international lending to Poland in the wake of the crackdown, so as to force the Soviets to pay the cost of stabilizing the country. While rejecting the extreme option of declaring Poland to be in default on its debts (a move that might have destabilized the international financial system), the Reagan team did prevent Poland from becoming a member of the IMF, and it suspended upcoming negotiations to reschedule the government's debt. As Kenneth Rodman writes, "Each of these measures closed avenues that would have alleviated Poland's debt problem, and their removal was linked to the end of martial law." The administration simultaneously urged commercial banks to impose more stringent controls on lending to Poland, while issuing public warnings that the Soviet bloc was a bad credit risk.[57]

There were initially desires to go even further, to cripple Soviet hard currency earnings by persuading—or simply pressuring—key NATO allies to back out of an agreement to help Moscow construct a natural gas pipeline connecting Siberia and Western Europe.[58] Unfortunately, this initiative soon foundered amid angry protests from governments that were not eager to hurt their own economies by curtailing trade with Moscow, and the entire incident demonstrated how alliance politics could impose constraints on U.S. policy. There were, the National Intelligence Council acknowledged, substantial "differences between the United States and our West European allies." But to his credit, Shultz did eventually secure an agreement to limit the provision of credits and certain strategic goods to the Soviets, and in 1984–85 the alliance mounted a successful counterespionage program to arrest illicit KGB acquisitions of sensitive technology abroad.[59] Meanwhile, U.S. officials were undertaking more unilateral—and less publicized—measures against the Soviet economy. The CIA used specially designed computer software to sabotage a branch of the Siberian pipeline, resulting in "the most monumental nonnuclear explosion and fire ever seen from space." Additionally, the administration apparently lobbied Saudi Arabia to increase its oil production and thereby drive down the energy-related export earnings that were so critical to the Soviet economy.[60] All told, this campaign of economic warfare was less thoroughgoing than Reagan and some of his hard-liners might have liked, but it still represented the most determined U.S. effort since the early Cold War.

Throughout the 1980s, Reagan used human rights as another coercive tool. While the administration was initially dismissive of human rights concerns in the Third World, top officials saw the issue as a point of leverage in dealing with Moscow. The idea of human rights "conveys what is ultimately at issue in our contest with the Soviet bloc," one State Department memo explained, and must "be central to our assault on them." American diplomats used the Conference on Security and Cooperation in Europe (CSCE) as a forum for publicizing rights violations behind the Iron Curtain, and they worked with the NATO allies to link the expansion of East–West commerce—something Moscow greatly desired—to the easing of political controls in the Warsaw Pact countries. There were few expectations that these tactics would produce immediate results, but U.S. officials nonetheless hoped that Western advocacy would energize dissidents and make repression more diplomatically and economically costly for the Soviet bloc.[61]

This diplomatic campaign was complemented by a high-volume rhetorical assault by the president himself. Between 1981 and 1983, Reagan publicly condemned the Soviet Union in stark and unapologetic terms. There was no moral equivalency between the superpowers, he asserted in 1983; the Soviets were "the focus of evil in the modern world." Moscow would not thrive in coming years; its system would wither as its failures became impossible to conceal. "The West won't contain communism," he declared in 1981, "it will transcend communism. It won't bother to . . . denounce it, it will dismiss it as some bizarre chapter in human history whose last pages are even now being written." Reagan was loudly telling the world that the Soviet Union was a fundamentally malign force—and a fundamentally spent force, too.[62]

He was doing so for multiple reasons: to restore Americans' sense of confidence and mission after the travails of Vietnam, to deny Soviet leaders the international legitimacy they craved, to invigorate dissidents within the Soviet bloc, and above all, to remind observers on all sides of the Cold War that communism was not the wave of the future but something that would be left, as Reagan memorably put it, "on the ashheap of history." An NSC report on U.S.-Soviet relations stated the basic goal: "The U.S. should stress that, 65 years after the October Revolution, the Soviet regime continues to deny its people fundamental human rights and to pour enormous economic resources into the military sector at the cost of continuing to fall behind. . . . The U.S. must make clear to the world that democracy, not Communism, is mankind's future." For Reagan, words were a low-cost way of waging ideological combat and driving home the failures of the Soviet regime.[63]

All of these policies were meant, as National Security Adviser William Clark put it in January 1983, to "re-establish American ascendancy" and turn the tide of the Cold War.[64] That position of power would then be leveraged to accomplish a fourth and final aspect of Reagan's grand strategy—persuading Moscow to moderate its conduct and accept a less confrontational relationship with the West. Unlike hard-liners Casey and Pipes, who believed that the goal of U.S. policy should be to seek the collapse of the Soviet empire, Reagan saw strength as a prerequisite to—not a substitute for—successful diplomacy. "The West has a historic opportunity, using a carrot and stick approach, to create a more stable relationship with the USSR," he told West

German officials in 1982. In a subsequent diary entry, Reagan criticized those who "don't think any approach should be made to the Soviets. I think I'm hard-line & will never appease but I do want to try & let them see there is a better world if they'll show *by deed* they want to get along with the free world."[65] Shultz, a strong proponent of eventual negotiations, stressed the same theme. "Strength and realism can deter war," he argued, "but only direct dialogue and negotiation can open the path toward lasting peace."[66]

The idea of using a confrontational policy now to enable a relaxation of tensions later was most evident in Reagan's approach to the arms race. From the start, he believed that a determined buildup would force the Soviets to embrace an economically disastrous competition or else accept deep cuts in existing arsenals. "The message to the Soviets is that if they want an arms race, the U.S. will not let them get ahead," he told the NSC. "Their choice is to break their backs to keep up, or to agree to reductions."[67] From 1981 onward, Reagan thus paired increased defense spending with calls for negotiation. The administration proposed Strategic Arms Reduction Talks (START) focused on the idea of a 50 percent cut in strategic ballistic missiles, and pushed an Intermediate-Range Nuclear Forces (INF) pact that would eliminate theater nuclear forces in Europe. "Let us see how far we can go in achieving truly substantial reductions in our strategic arsenals," Reagan announced in late 1981.[68]

To be sure, there were limits to the administration's willingness to negotiate. Reagan wanted any agreement to favor U.S. interests, and he did not believe that this would be possible until Washington had restored an advantageous strategic balance. Accordingly, U.S. negotiators staked out maximalist positions in both START and the INF talks—indeed, hard-liners like Weinberger and Richard Perle seem to have supported these positions precisely because they believed them to be unacceptable to Moscow—and the administration rejected potential compromises during the early 1980s.[69] Reagan also lobbied strenuously against the "nuclear freeze" movement, because it would free Moscow from the threat of a continuing arms race. "How can we expect to make further progress towards arms reductions if the [Soviets have] no incentive to reduce?" he asked congressional leaders.[70]

At the same time, however, Reagan sent signals that he was interested in something more promising than an unending Cold War. In April 1981, he lifted the grain embargo put in place after the invasion of Afghanistan, even though this decision cut across his policy of economic pressure. The same month, he wrote a letter to Brezhnev calling for "meaningful and constructive dialogue which will assist us in fulfilling our joint obligation to find lasting peace."[71] Reagan subsequently sought a summit meeting with Brezhnev's successors, and in early 1983, he approved an NSC directive stating that U.S. power had to be related to a longer-term program for easing Cold War hostilities. "The U.S. must convey clearly to Moscow that unacceptable behavior will incur costs that would outweigh any gains," the directive stated. "At the same time, the U.S. must make clear to the Soviets that genuine restraint in their behavior would create the possibility of an East-West relationship that might bring important benefits for the Soviet Union." If the Soviets acted "in a responsible fashion," Reagan affirmed, "they will meet a ready and positive response in the West."[72]

It is clear, then, that Reagan did have a grand strategy, one that utilized all elements of national power, related short- and medium-term policies to long-range goals, and drew deeply on the president's own thoughts and influence. The key elements of this strategy were drawn together in two major decision directives issued in 1982–83. The first, NSDD-32, outlined the "development and integration of a set of strategies, including diplomatic, informational, economic/political, and military components." It argued that American objectives must be to "strengthen the influence of the U.S. throughout the world," "to contain and reverse the expansion of Soviet control and military presence throughout the world," to "discourage Soviet adventurism, and weaken the Soviet alliance system by forcing the USSR to bear the brunt of its economic shortcomings, and to encourage long-term liberalizing and nationalist tendencies within the Soviet Union and allied countries." These efforts would take time, but the eventual payoff might be substantial: "The decade of the eighties will likely pose the greatest challenge to our survival and well-being since World War II and our response could result in a fundamentally different East-West relationship by the end of this decade."[73]

The same ideas were refined and reaffirmed by NSDD-75, drafted largely by Pipes and the NSC staff and signed by Reagan in January 1983. Better than any other document, NSDD-75 explicitly laid out the essential goals and stages of Reagan's policy:

1. To contain and over time reverse Soviet expansion by competing effectively on a sustained basis with the Soviet Union in all international arenas—particularly in the overall military balance and in geographical regions of priority concern to the United States . . .

2. To promote within the narrow limits available to us, the process of change in the Soviet Union toward a more pluralistic political and economic system in which the power of the privileged ruling elite is gradually reduced . . .

3. To engage the Soviet Union in negotiations to attempt to reach agreements which protect and enhance U.S. interests and which are consistent with the principle of strict reciprocity and mutual interest.

This policy was "one for the long-haul"; it would require persistent efforts in the military, economic, political, diplomatic, covert, and ideological realms. The desired result was not an "open-ended, sterile confrontation with Moscow," but rather to find a more "stable and constructive long-term basis for U.S.-Soviet relations." This was Reagan's vision for U.S. policy; whether he could bring it off in practice remained to be seen.[74]

The administration was quite successful in achieving the first major goal of its grand strategy, which was to reassert American strength and reverse the momentum of the Cold War. In 1980, there had been a widespread sense that the United States was in retreat and the Soviet Union was on the march; by 1983–84, that perception had been largely inverted. Soviet officials no longer evinced confidence that the "correlation of forces" was in their favor, and American policy now boasted a spirit of power and confidence. The United States, Reagan declared in January 1984, was "in its strongest position in years."[75]

In many ways, this turnaround validated both the intellectual premises and the specific policies of Reagan's grand strategy. The president had long argued that Moscow was far weaker than it looked, and during the early 1980s events began to make him look like a prophet. The Soviet economy was gradually but unmistakably slipping into stagnation and obsolescence, while Soviet society was wracked with ills ranging from rampant alcoholism to signs of incipient civil unrest. These problems were compounded by a bloated military budget that soaked up badly needed resources, and by the dismal leadership of a feeble and rigid gerontocracy. The geopolitical significance of all this was profound: a regime that had so recently touted the irreversible ascent of socialism was now trapped in a systemic crisis that it appeared powerless to escape. "Soviet leaders are starting to recognize that something has gone hideously wrong," one top U.S intelligence official wrote in 1984. "History is no longer on Moscow's side—if ever it was—and Soviet leaders sense they lack the wit, the energy, the resources, and above all the time, to win it back ... The Soviet Union is the world's last empire, and after 67 years of communism it has entered its terminal phase."[76]

Reagan's grand strategy did not cause this crisis of Soviet power, but it did allow the United States to exploit its geopolitical effects. This was certainly true in the Third World, where U.S. policies significantly worsened the problems confronting Moscow and its allies. To be clear, the Reagan Doctrine was never the silver bullet it was sometimes made out to be, and American-backed "freedom fighters" were sometimes just thugs of an anti-communist variety.[77] Nevertheless, U.S. intervention did serve strategic purposes. If nothing else, U.S. policy in Central America helped break the perception of Soviet momentum in the Western Hemisphere by preventing the collapse of the Salvadoran government and keeping the Kremlin-supported regime in Nicaragua under constant duress.[78] More important, the Reagan Doctrine significantly strengthened the Afghan mujahideen and helped ensure that this particular conflict became a bloody, expensive, and thoroughly demoralizing quagmire for the Soviet Union.[79] Indeed, the costs that U.S. policies imposed on Moscow were ideological as well as material. As the attractiveness of the Soviet economic model faded and U.S. pressure on Kremlin clients from Kabul to Managua increased, Moscow's view of the Third World dimmed considerably. In the late 1970s, Soviet officials had looked forward to further socialist gains; by 1983–84, their assessments had grown pessimistic. "It is one thing to proclaim socialism as one's goal," Andropov acknowledged, "and it is quite another to build it." A leading Soviet specialist on the Third World put it more explicitly, citing Reagan's "universal anti-Soviet strategy" as a reason why "there is no guaranteed 'automatic' revolutionary potential there."[80]

U.S. policies increased the strain on Moscow in other ways as well. In Eastern Europe, covert support for Solidarity helped keep that organization alive after the Polish crackdown, much to the discomfiture of bloc officials. Reagan's economic warfare policies had a similar effect. While there is much debate about whether U.S.-Saudi collusion was responsible for the drop-off in world oil prices from mid-decade onward, there is no arguing that this decrease greatly intensified the pressure on Soviet export earnings at a time when the economy was already vulnerable.[81] Even before that, sabotage of the Siberian pipeline and other industrial facilities had added to Moscow's economic problems, while restrictions on loans to Eastern Europe forced the Kremlin to assume the rising costs of stabilization in that region.[82] By the mid-1980s, notes one scholar, "Soviet subsidies to the region were becoming an intolerable burden."[83] And although the president's rhetorical offensive had little material impact, it did serve as a constant reminder—to Moscow, to the West, to dissidents within the bloc—of just how morally and economically bankrupt the Soviet system had become. Soviet leaders were "extremely thin-skinned" on this score, Dobrynin later acknowledged.

Reagan was "giving them a dose of their own medicine," and they found it hard to stomach.[84]

Then there was the effect of the U.S. military buildup. Although Soviet officials were loath to admit it publicly, ramped-up U.S. defense programs posed real strategic dilemmas for the Kremlin. During the 1970s, Soviet force planners had operated on the assumption that their ongoing buildup would provide Moscow with a measure of strategic superiority over Washington, with increased coercive leverage to match.[85] But as the United States began to sprint forward with new capabilities under Carter and then more significantly under Reagan, it was the Kremlin that had to reckon with an approaching window of insecurity. In the European theater, for instance, the Pershing IIs were faster and more accurate than the SS-20s they were meant to offset; the Soviets were thus coming out of the "Euromissile" episode *more* vulnerable than before. The Pershing deployment, Gorbachev later wrote, was "a pistol held to our head."[86]

SDI appeared even more threatening. If Washington could develop the system—and Soviet officials feared that this might be possible—it would render Moscow's ICBM force irrelevant and potentially expose the Soviet Union to a debilitating first strike. Nor was there much chance that the struggling Soviet economy could compete with the United States in such a high-technology arena. SDI "played a powerful psychological role," one KGB general recalled. "It underlined still more our technological backwardness." Soviet officials evinced confidence that they could counter SDI with an offensive buildup, but even this would imply significant new expenditures at a time when resources were growing scarce.[87] Moscow had spent decades seeking equality and then advantage in the arms race, only to find the strategic balance once again tilting toward Washington. William Odom, the U.S. Army's assistant chief of staff for intelligence, captured the Soviet predicament aptly:

> Like Sisyphus, who was condemned in Hades to push a rock up a hill only to see it roll back down, causing him to repeat the task, the Soviet General Staff seems to see the rock of its military labor rolling back to the bottom of the hill, presenting the Soviet military with a repetition of the same task: a long-term new force building task.[88]

During the early 1980s, all of these issues were just beginning to affect the material balance of power. Yet they were already exerting a profound influence on *perceptions* of relative strength. "We are facing one of imperialism's most massive attempts to slow down the process of social change in the world, to stop the advance of socialism or even to push it back in some places,"

Andropov told Warsaw Pact leaders in 1983. He acknowledged that Moscow was feeling "the increased activity of the ideological centers of imperialism," and conceded that the West was exploiting "the growth of foreign debts, the food situation, our technological lag in certain areas and a series of other bottlenecks" in the Soviet economy. He even hinted that Moscow could not long sustain the superpower strategic competition. "More than others, the Soviet Union probably feels the burden of the arms race ... For Reagan it is not a problem to take tens of billions of appropriations for social needs and pass them on to the military-industrial complex. But we cannot help but think about the well-being of workers." As Andropov recognized, the geopolitical initiative had shifted, and Moscow now found itself on the defensive.[89]

Reagan's grand strategy thus showed how the coordinated application of U.S. power, in the right places and at the right time, could capitalize upon Soviet frailties and produce a rapid shift in the trajectory of the Cold War. Through the early 1980s, however, there were few signs that these changing power dynamics were facilitating the administration's second goal—moderating Soviet behavior and easing superpower tensions. In fact, just the opposite was happening. The Kremlin showed no outward inclination to withdraw from Afghanistan, or to decrease support to its Third World allies. Moscow brushed aside U.S. concerns about human rights— "We have no intention of discussing our internal affairs with anyone," Gromyko remarked—and political repression intensified.[90] Nor was there progress toward arms control. Moscow effectively suspended the START and INF talks once the deployment of the Pershings began in late 1983, and announced plans for increased military spending and its own "counter-deployment" of additional IRBMs. "The prospects for an improvement in U.S.-Soviet relations are dismal over the next 12 months," said CIA deputy director for intelligence Robert Gates in November. Matlock later recalled that "relations with the Soviet Union seemed about as tense as they could be short of actual conflict."[91]

These frictions were not altogether unexpected in Washington; Reagan had understood that a confrontational policy might initially elicit an intransigent response. What the president had not realized, however, was precisely how menacing his geopolitical offensive looked in Moscow. Reagan certainly believed that his own intentions were purely peaceful, and he had no patience for the suggestion that Soviet leaders might think otherwise. There was not "any truth to the belief ... that the Soviet Union is motivated by fear of the West," he commented in 1982.[92] Unfortunately, Kremlin officials begged to differ. Brezhnev's generation had come of age during the horrors of World War II and had resolved never again to permit their country to be weak and vulnerable. From their perspective, U.S. policies represented an effort to overturn the balance of power, drastically weaken if not liquidate the socialist system, and perhaps set the stage for a surprise military attack. "They are trying to destroy us," Gromyko said, "and we really have to do something about it." In this atmosphere, the dominant sentiment in Moscow was that accommodation would only lead to disaster. "If we begin to make concessions," Andropov remarked in 1983, "defeat would be inevitable."[93]

This dynamic pointed to a key contradiction in Reagan's grand strategy. The president's approach was basically one of coercive diplomacy. He aimed to achieve negotiation by way of confrontation, to use American power to convince the Soviets that it was in their best interest to behave with restraint. The problem, however, was that the first part of the strategy obscured the second: because Reagan pursued the coercive aspects of his policy so zealously, Soviet leaders doubted that he would *ever* seriously negotiate. During the early 1980s, they dismissed his occasional overtures for precisely this reason. There was a "contradiction between words and deeds that greatly angered Moscow," Dobrynin later wrote, "the more so because Reagan himself never seemed to see it."[94] Reagan's "sticks" were credible, but his "carrots" were not.

The disorder within the administration only made matters worse. The great advantage of Reagan's management style was that it allowed him to float above internecine disputes and engage with various factions as he saw fit. The disadvantage was that this approach did nothing to resolve the underlying struggles—it encouraged them by ensuring a continuing competition for Reagan's ear. Internal warfare thus raged throughout the early 1980s. Hard-liners like Weinberger feuded with Shultz and his allies, and they made plain their displeasure with the idea of meaningful negotiations. The former group "did everything they could do to prevent or to stop or to turn back any attempt to even talk, even meet, even be in the same city with the enemy," one Shultz loyalist recalled.[95]

As a result, U.S. policy was continually plagued by mixed messages and inflammatory statements. Pipes at one point implied that conflict was inevitable unless the Soviets changed their sociopolitical system, while Weinberger and others talked casually of "winning" a nuclear war. All Americans needed to do to survive such a war, one official helpfully suggested, was to build backyard bomb shelters: "If there are enough shovels to go around, everybody's going to make it."[96] It was a foolish statement, but no more so than Reagan's own quip—captured on a live microphone—that he had "signed legislation that will outlaw Russia forever. We begin bombing in five minutes."[97] No wonder the Soviets doubted Reagan's good intentions.

The potential liabilities of Reagan's grand strategy became frighteningly clear in 1983. Throughout that year, U.S.-Soviet relations worsened steadily. Reagan delivered his "evil empire" speech in March, followed by the announcement of SDI two weeks later. Amid heightened tensions, Soviet fighter jets then shot down a South Korean airliner that had strayed off course in September. Reagan called it an "act of barbarism" and a deliberate "crime against humanity"; Andropov countered by alleging that the incident was a "sophisticated provocation" by U.S. intelligence.[98] A month later, the United States invaded Grenada, and in November, the first shipments of Pershing IIs reached West Germany. As if this were not enough, Soviet warning systems malfunctioned during the fall of 1983, several times showing that U.S. missiles were incoming. The international climate had become "white hot, thoroughly white hot," one Politburo member declared. "Many in the Soviet public are asking if war is imminent," another observer reported.[99]

It was in these conditions that NATO conducted Able Archer 83. The exercise was designed to simulate a general East-West conflict, and it featured a command-post scenario in which Reagan and other top officials would rehearse the steps needed to initiate nuclear war. For a frightened Soviet leadership, the preparations for Able Archer looked extremely ominous, and high-ranking military officials feared that the exercise might be a cover for a surprise first strike. Soviet forces—including nuclear forces—went on heightened alert, and the crisis passed only when Western officials belatedly became aware of the danger and scaled back Able Archer.[100] Nonetheless, the episode stood as a terrifying example of how badly superpower relations had deteriorated, and how much Reagan's policies had contributed to this situation.

The Able Archer crisis was a searing experience for Reagan, and an enlightening one as well. He realized that while a confrontational policy might be a prerequisite to negotiations, it could also lead to catastrophic miscalculations that might prevent those negotiations from ever occurring. He now understood, as he later wrote, that "many Soviet officials feared us not only as adversaries but as potential aggressors who might hurl nuclear weapons at them in a first strike." The implications were appalling: a Pentagon briefing Reagan received at roughly the same time revealed that even a "successful" nuclear war would cause horrendous American casualties.[101]

Accordingly, the period following Able Archer saw a crucial recalibration of U.S. policy. This did not mean that it was only in late 1983 that Reagan saw the value of negotiation, or that this period saw a dramatic "reversal" of his strategy. What happened, rather, was that Reagan grasped that successful negotiations would only be possible if he toned down his rhetoric and reduced the tensions that his own policies had helped foster. "I feel the Soviets are so defense minded, so paranoid about being attacked that without being in any way soft on them we ought to tell them no one here has any intention of doing anything like that," he wrote in his diary. ("What the h—l have they got that anyone would want," he added.) If meaningful negotiations were to be possible, Matlock wrote in an influential memorandum during this same period, the United States would need to "establish minimal level of trust" with Moscow. Reagan should maintain his firm policies, but he should also marry strength with reassurance by showing that he did not intend war or "forcing collapse of the Soviet system."[102] The idea was not to junk the overall grand strategic framework that Reagan had developed, but to modify the degree of emphasis placed on the various elements of that framework.

Other factors were simultaneously pushing the president in the same direction. Reagan was facing what initially looked to be a difficult reelection campaign, and he was sensitive to the prospect that unrestrained Cold War tensions might make him vulnerable politically. "The Public is increasingly concerned that the President does not genuinely desire to negotiate with the Soviet Union on nuclear arms," one official had earlier reported. Likewise, NATO allies like West Germany and the Netherlands had faced vocal domestic opposition to the Tomahawk and Pershing II deployments, and they too desired reassurance that Reagan envisioned something other than an indefinite nuclear standoff.[103]

The result of all this was a series of initiatives meant to lower the temperature of superpower relations and open the door to diplomacy. In December 1983, Reagan acknowledged that his "evil empire" speech had been too provocative. In January 1984, he gave a remarkably conciliatory speech in which he stressed the dangers of nuclear war, called for renewed arms control talks, and emphasized that "dialogue" must go hand in hand with "realism" and "strength." "The fact that neither of us likes the other system is no reason to refuse to talk," he said. "Living in this nuclear age makes it imperative that we do talk."[104] After an obviously ailing Andropov died in February, Reagan struck up a correspondence with his successor, Konstantin Chernenko. He reassured the Soviet premier that "neither I nor the American people hold any offensive intensions toward you or the Soviet people" and pledged his "profound commitment" to improving relations. Efforts to arrange a summit with Chernenko went nowhere, but in September the president met with Gromyko for several hours. "We have no aggressive intent toward anyone," he told the Soviet foreign minister. "The time has come to clear the air, reduce suspicions, and reduce nuclear arms."[105]

Reagan also belatedly moved to impose discipline on the bureaucracy. The president was never ruthless enough to stamp out the internal conflicts between his advisers, but he did make sure that key hard-liners like Weinberger and Casey understood that negotiations were integral to his grand strategy. In consequence, Shultz gradually began to emerge as Reagan's single most important adviser. From late 1983 onward, one rival later noted, the secretary's influence "grew steadily with the President, to the point where he lost virtually no important strategic battle he carried to the Oval Office."[106]

The immediate results of this shift were not overwhelming, for Chernenko, like Andropov and Brezhnev, was far too decrepit to undertake any major departures. Yet there were promising signs. Washington and Moscow upgraded the bilateral "hotline" in July 1984 and signed several small, confidence-building measures. In the fall, Gromyko agreed to revive the START and INF negotiations.[107] And while Chernenko's all-too-apparent debility was an obstacle to improved relations in the short term, it did raise hopes that a long-awaited generational shift in Moscow was about to occur. Since 1982–83, U.S. officials had predicted that the most opportune time to talk would be after Brezhnev and his successors gave way to a less sclerotic cohort. As Chernenko mumbled and stumbled his way through his reign, this transition began to look more and more likely. It was possible that the United States would soon find itself dealing with "younger men who might have a significantly different outlook," Shultz informed Reagan in mid-1984. They would be "post–World War II people," more flexible than their predecessors. "It will pay dividends to treat them with civility."[108] Within months, Chernenko had died, and Mikhail Gorbachev had taken his place.

Gorbachev's accession initiated a new era in U.S.-Soviet affairs. Prior to March 1985, Reagan had seized the geopolitical high ground but not achieved any meaningful reduction of tensions. After March 1985, superpower rapprochement came with surprising speed and thoroughness. Reagan and Gorbachev held five summits between 1985 and 1988, with their vigorous presidential diplomacy matched at the lower levels of government. The results were amazing. By the time Reagan left office, Gorbachev had agreed to eliminate all intermediate-range nuclear forces and accepted the principle of deep cuts in broader strategic arsenals. Moscow was also withdrawing from Afghanistan and other Third World conflicts, unilaterally reducing its conventional forces, signaling its commitment to self-determination in Eastern Europe, and permitting unprecedented liberalization at home. Through all this, the tone of the relationship changed dramatically. The two countries were "'doomed' to cooperate," Gorbachev remarked in 1988. Reagan was more explicit still: "The Cold War is over."[109] Reagan's goal had been to lower tensions on American terms; by the close of his presidency, this was exactly what had happened.

The reasons *why* it happened are still difficult to disentangle. In retrospect, Gorbachev deserves enormous credit. If Reagan's goal was to find an interlocutor in the Kremlin, he could hardly have asked for anyone better than Gorbachev. The new general secretary was energetic, good-humored, and flexible—everything his predecessors were not. Unlike Brezhnev and Andropov, he was willing to question old verities, abandon untenable positions, and rethink ideological precepts. "Now we have a real find of a leader," wrote Anatoly Chernyaev, one of Gorbachev's closest aides, in 1986. "Myths and taboos ... are nothing for him. He could flatten any of them."[110]

Most important of all, Gorbachev saw that the Cold War had become unsustainable for Moscow. He understood that the Afghan war was a "bleeding wound" for an already hobbled superpower, that the nuclear arms race was an increasingly dangerous competition that the Kremlin could no longer afford, and that the costs of dominating Eastern Europe increasingly outweighed the benefits.[111] Above all, he believed that the Soviet Union could remain a superpower only if it revitalized its economy, and that the resources and breathing space necessary to do so could only be obtained by reducing tensions with Washington. The prerequisite for *perestroika,* Gorbachev later wrote, was to "clear up the 'snow-drifts' left over from Cold War times and to alleviate the pressure that had borne down on us due to our involvement in conflicts all over the world and in the debilitating arms race."[112]

It seems that Reagan's first-term policies helped Gorbachev reach this conclusion. There is no question that the general secretary was primarily motivated by a desire to deal with the creeping enervation of the Soviet system, a challenge he would have faced regardless of what Reagan did. Yet Gorbachev was also quite preoccupied with easing the pressure that U.S. grand strategy had exerted. Political scientist Archie Brown has noted that one reason Gorbachev was determined to relax tensions was his fear that the United States was on the verge of SDI-related technological breakthroughs that would leave the Soviets at a permanent strategic disadvantage.[113] If Moscow did not compromise, Gorbachev said in 1986, "we will be drawn into an arms race that we cannot manage. We will lose, because right now we are already at the end of our tether."[114] More broadly, leading Soviet journals acknowledged that the country had suffered "enormous losses" as a result of the Western reaction to Brezhnev-era policies, and that it was now facing "unprecedented new pressure from imperialism." Plodding along was no longer an option, Gorbachev said in late 1985; Moscow must "take into account the changing situation ... face the reality without any bias, objectively appraise current events, and flexibly react to the demands of the moment."[115]

What is often forgotten about the 1985–86 period, however, is that this desire for détente did not translate into any immediate accommodation with the United States. To be sure, Gorbachev wanted room to breathe. But he was wary of Soviet hard-liners, he worried that Reagan was an unreformed militarist who would ruthlessly exploit signs of weakness, and he hoped that creative diplomacy might allow him to get his breathing space, as CIA analysts assessed, "on the cheap."[116] Consequently, Gorbachev's early peace proposals—such as the idea for an IRBM "freeze" or a mutual troop withdrawal from Europe—were meant to benefit Moscow disproportionately if accepted, and to expose Reagan as a dangerous ideologue if not.[117] Similarly, while Gorbachev called for superpower cooperation, he simultaneously staked out a hard line on key policy questions. He initially refused to negotiate on human rights issues, and declared that any arms control deal would have to preclude missile defense. "The USSR cannot simply reduce and will not reduce nuclear weapons to the detriment of its security, when the SDI program is being implemented in the U.S.," he wrote in late 1985. Gorbachev also allowed the military to escalate the war in Afghanistan in 1985–86, and he increased Soviet assistance to Nicaragua and the Salvadoran rebels. "We cannot afford to lose," he explained. "Even if we cannot move decisively ahead, we still can and should keep what we already have." Gorbachev wanted a calmer international climate, but he did not want to give up much to get it.[118]

There were three main reasons why Gorbachev became steadily more accommodating as the late 1980s progressed. The first—and most important—was the worsening crisis at home. Gorbachev had understood that the Soviet Union was in trouble when he took office, but his remedies almost invariably made things worse. His initial economic reforms did not fix the underlying structural problems, but they did help to turn Moscow's fiscal problems into an exploding fiscal calamity. Similarly, political liberalization was meant to revitalize Soviet communism and provide space for economic perestroika, but it progressively eroded the stability of the system instead. These processes would eventually destroy the Soviet Union altogether. In the short term, they powerfully underscored the rationale for détente with the West—to free up resources, expand access to foreign trade and technology, shore up the diplomatic scene while focusing on the domestic, and achieve successes that would insulate Gorbachev from growing criticism by hard-liners and liberals alike. As time went on, Gorbachev thus became desperate for good relations with Washington, even if it meant sacrificing long-held positions. "As difficult as it is to conduct business with the United States, we are doomed to it," he acknowledged in early 1987. "We have no choice."[119]

Second, Gorbachev became more radical intellectually as time went on. The general secretary had long exhibited a humanistic streak, a receptivity to Western ideas, and an abhorrence of the nuclear arms race. As he consolidated power and interacted with kindred spirits like Chernyaev and Foreign Minister Eduard Shevardnadze, he gradually fashioned these and other concepts into his "new political thinking." Among other things, the new thinking emphasized the indivisibility of global security, the importance of lowering tensions and reducing the risk of war, the imperative of opening the Soviet Union to outside influences, and the need to take legitimate U.S. and Western concerns into account in pursuing Moscow's own security interests. It is still difficult to tell how much of the new thinking was genuine and how much was a rationalization for steps that were taken of necessity.[120] Whatever the case, these concepts helped ease the zero-sum, Cold War mentality in Moscow, they lent ideological sanction to Gorbachev's dramatic departures at home and abroad, and they therefore played an important role in facilitating the transformations of the late 1980s and after.

These internal and intellectual influences interacted with a third key factor—U.S. policy. From the outset, Reagan had seen Gorbachev's ascension as a possible turning point in the Cold War. The president did not yet trust Gorbachev—the general secretary was "totally dedicated to traditional Soviet goals," he believed—and he did not foresee the full extent of the changes that would soon occur. Yet the fact that someone so vibrant and unconventional had risen atop the Kremlin hierarchy gave Reagan hope that the time for dialogue had arrived. He proposed a summit immediately after Gorbachev took power, and the two leaders eventually met in Geneva in November. For Reagan, this meeting was not meant to be "a watershed event in and of itself," but simply "an important part of a vital long-term process" of negotiation.[121]

Reagan's goal in these talks was to translate the position of strength that the administration had built during the first term into a broad-based moderation of Soviet conduct. As early as 1981, he had told Thatcher that any summit could not "be confined to arms control matters: rather it would also have to cover issues such as Afghanistan and Soviet backing for Cuba's effort to export revolution."[122] In 1983–84, Shultz and Matlock had turned this guideline into a four-part agenda for negotiations. The idea was that the administration should force Moscow to address a wide range of external and internal questions—arms control, Third World conflicts, human rights and political liberties within the Soviet Union, and bilateral economic and cultural ties—rather than allowing the Kremlin to discuss only its preferred subjects (arms control and trade). This did not mean that Reagan was reviving the explicit "linkage" used during the Kissinger years, Shultz stressed in a major speech in late 1984, but simply that Washington would not let any one part of the agenda progress too far ahead of the others.[123]

The methods that Reagan used in the negotiations reflected the continuing evolution of his grand strategy. On the one hand, he and Shultz believed that power and pressure remained fundamental to successful diplomacy. "The strategic reality of leverage," Shultz explained, "comes from creating facts in support of our overall design."[124] During the second term, the administration labored to preserve and even increase its leverage on Moscow. It maintained—and sometimes expanded—its support to anticommunist guerrillas, continued to emphasize military preparedness and SDI, and resolved to delay significant progress on East-West trade until the Soviets were more forthcoming on the rest of the superpower agenda. The right approach, Reagan wrote in 1985, was one of "just hanging back until we get some of the things we want."[125] The administration also set a high standard for what would constitute progress on key issues ranging from human rights to arms control to Afghanistan. The focus, Shultz believed, should not be on accords that would paper over fundamental disagreements or allow the Soviets to escape their current predicament, but on steps that "could bring about real change in Moscow's approach to the world and its own citizens." If Gorbachev wanted a reduction in tensions, he would have to pay for it.[126]

Reagan also realized, however, that pressure alone would not make Gorbachev cooperate. The takeaway lesson of the first term had been that Soviet leaders would not negotiate if they felt that Reagan aimed to coerce, intimidate, or perhaps even destroy their regime. It was imperative, the president had told Thatcher in late 1984, "to convince the Soviets that we mean them no harm."[127] American officials must avoid issuing public ultimatums, they must show that they were serious about reducing superpower tensions, and they must demonstrate that constructive Soviet behavior would bring about rewards in the form of a more beneficial relationship with the West. In essence, Reagan would have to convince Gorbachev that it was both necessary *and* desirable to reach an accommodation. The president later laid out his philosophy on negotiations: "You shouldn't back your adversary into a corner, embarrass him, or humiliate him; and sometimes the easiest way to get some things done is for the top people to do them alone and in private."[128]

Along these lines, much of Reagan's second-term diplomacy can be seen as an effort to establish trust and rapport with Gorbachev. Reagan refused to abandon SDI, for instance, but he continually stressed its defensive character and offered to share the technology if the two sides could eliminate their disagreements. He pushed Gorbachev to respect human rights, but he generally did so in private, and he pledged not to trumpet any Soviet concessions for propaganda purposes. The United States must not "force Gorbachev to eat crow and embarrass him publicly," Reagan wrote. "We must always remember our main goal and his need to show his strength to the Soviet gang back in the Kremlin."[129] Above all, the president sought to forge a personal bond with Gorbachev during their numerous private meetings, and he repeatedly assured the general secretary that he wanted something better than a continuing Cold War. "We harbored no hostile intentions toward the Soviets," he said in 1986. "We recognized the differences in our two systems. But the President felt that we could live as friendly competitors."[130] And as U.S.-Soviet relations gradually began to warm, these conciliatory aspects of Reagan's diplomacy would become more pronounced.

As in the first term, implementation of this strategy was not always smooth. Bureaucratic gamesmanship remained a problem until Weinberger resigned in 1987, and Shultz was close to quitting at times. Politics also intruded on policy: the need to retain right-wing support for negotiations occasionally caused Reagan to take a more strident public tone toward Moscow.[131] On the whole, though, the president and Shultz managed to hit the right balance of strength and reassurance in dealing with Gorbachev. By doing so, they were able to exploit the growing weakness of the Soviet system, underscore both the positive and negative inducements for Gorbachev to modify policy, and facilitate the emergence of a profoundly different superpower relationship.

This approach first began to pay dividends at Geneva. The summit did not produce any major agreements on arms control, human rights, or Third World conflicts, and the discussions of these issues often grew quite heated.[132] Yet the meeting nonetheless served an important purpose. It allowed Reagan to conclude that Gorbachev was really a "different breed" of Soviet leader, one who was less rigid than his predecessors and might "make some practical agreements."[133] Gorbachev remained more suspicious of Reagan, but their conversations did convince him that the president was at least willing to engage in respectful dialogue. Reagan was "a man who was not as hopeless as some believed," the general secretary concluded. The meeting resulted in a joint communiqué that promised subsequent summits and affirmed that "a nuclear war cannot be won and must never be fought." Geneva, Gorbachev commented, "introduced a certain stabilizing element to the relations between the USSR and USA and the world situation in general."[134]

This gradual thaw continued the next year at Reykjavík. By 1986, the Soviet leader was desperate to reduce defense expenditures via arms control.

"If we don't back down on some specific, maybe even important issues … we will lose in the end," he told his Kremlin colleagues. Gorbachev was also driven to negotiate by the reactor explosion at Chernobyl in April, a disaster that showed, in his words, "what nuclear war can be."[135] Having previously proposed the complete elimination of nuclear weapons by the year 2000, Gorbachev arrived in Iceland with another bold idea: the two sides should eliminate intermediate-range nuclear forces in Europe, and make 50 percent cuts in *all* strategic weapons. His own antinuclearism aroused, Reagan countered by suggesting the elimination of all offensive ballistic missiles over the next decade.[136] Gorbachev then offered to do away with all strategic weapons, after which the two leaders briefly agreed to eliminate nuclear weapons altogether. It was an astounding moment, but one that did not last because Gorbachev insisted that his entire offer was contingent on restricting SDI. Reagan was unwilling to do so—he was as attached to SDI as Gorbachev was threatened by it—and the meeting ended in acrimony.[137]

It seemed like a major setback for superpower relations, and an enormous lost opportunity for disarmament. In reality, though, any agreement to ban nuclear weapons probably would have proved militarily and diplomatically unworkable in practice.[138] And as Reagan and Gorbachev both quickly realized, the real significance of the meeting lay not in their failure to reach an accord, but in the fact that they had come so close. If the two leaders could seriously discuss eliminating their countries' ultimate weapons, then the antipathy and mistrust between them must surely be easing. "The progress that we made would've been inconceivable just a few months ago," Reagan commented.[139] Gorbachev likewise interpreted the proceedings as evidence that Reagan was not a right-wing lunatic who might attack the Soviet Union, but a visionary leader who shared his revulsion at the arms race. "After Reykjavík," he told the Politburo, "we have reached a new level of understanding." It was at this point, Dobrynin wrote, Gorbachev "decided that he could and would work with Reagan."[140]

Reykjavík laid the groundwork for progress in more ways than one. The administration's negotiating posture was premised on the idea that the United States was ascendant, and that Gorbachev's bargaining position would only deteriorate as the Soviet economy faltered. "We have the advantage everywhere," Shultz had commented in early 1986.[141] Reykjavík showed that this assessment was correct, for in attempting to break the impasse on arms control and SDI, Gorbachev had made several key concessions. He had accepted the "zero option" for INF in Europe, something Soviet diplomats had earlier called "a formula for unilateral disarmament by our side and, frankly, an insult to our intelligence."[142] (Gorbachev had himself written that "the lop-sidedness" of the proposal "is obvious to everybody."[143]) He also indicated that he would be willing to cut Soviet IRBM forces in Asia as part of a broader INF deal, and moved closer to the U.S. position on START. "We may have made some truly historic breakthroughs on a number of key issues," wrote National Security Adviser John Poindexter.[144] SDI remained the crucial stumbling block, but the meeting nonetheless showed that all the momentum was on Washington's side.

In fact, Gorbachev soon concluded that further delay in arms control would prove far more injurious to his interests than to Reagan's. "Our main problem is to remove the confrontation," he told the Politburo in February 1987. "This is the central issue of our entire foreign policy." Gorbachev made one last effort to derail missile defense, but he relented after Shultz warned him "to weigh carefully the advisability of tying the entire relationship with the United States to SDI."[145] With this issue set aside, the two sides soon agreed to eliminate all of their intermediate-range nuclear forces globally, a pact that required Moscow to destroy roughly four times as many warheads as Washington and vindicated the position Reagan had first proposed in 1981. Gorbachev also dropped a previous Soviet demand by excluding British and French nuclear forces from the deal, and he shocked his own military advisers by agreeing to destroy the shorter-range SS–23 missiles as well. "U.S. policy is one of extorting more and more concessions," he complained at one point. "I'm weeping for you," Shultz replied.[146]

This hard-nosed negotiating style rankled Gorbachev, but the general secretary nonetheless profited from the INF Treaty. The accord removed the threat posed by the Pershings, and it allowed him to begin cutting defense costs as part of a pathbreaking international agreement. Reagan was also careful to ensure that the treaty was portrayed as a victory for both countries. "Let there be no talk of winners and losers," he had warned in 1985. "Even if we think we won, to say so would set us back."[147] In a politically significant gesture, Reagan personally intervened to persuade the West German government to destroy several dozen aging missile launchers that Gorbachev had wanted included in the deal. And when Gorbachev arrived in Washington to sign the accords in December 1987, he was feted with all the trappings of a state visit, including a twenty-one-gun salute, meetings with congressional leaders, and the sight of Soviet and U.S. flags flying side by side. These were atmospherics with a purpose—they showed the Soviet leadership that cooperation would bring respect and prestige, and they gave Gorbachev a symbol of his ability to do business with the West as he began to face rising dissent at home. It all left a lasting impression on the general secretary. The INF Treaty was "the first harbinger of the new times," he later wrote; its signing marked "a new level of trust in our relations with the United States."[148]

By the time of the Washington summit, Soviet policy toward the Third World was also beginning to change. Gorbachev had long understood the liabilities of Soviet involvement in Afghanistan and other regional conflicts, but he had initially resisted a dramatic retrenchment. Both Washington and Moscow had Third World allies, he wrote to Reagan in December 1985. "Why apply a double standard and assert that Soviet assistance is a source of tension and U.S. assistance is beneficial?"[149] This attitude showed up particularly in Soviet policy toward Afghanistan. The general secretary was determined to extricate Moscow from the war, but he was equally determined not to leave in defeat. Aside from increasing the intensity of Soviet military operations in 1985–86, Gorbachev repeatedly insisted that Soviet troops would not depart without a U.S.–Pakistani pledge to cease supplying the guerrillas and destabilizing the Kabul regime. "Soviet withdrawal was definitely linked to an American obligation to cut off support for opposition forces on the date Soviet troop withdrawal started," he told Reagan in December 1987. "They should find a balance of concessions."[150]

Even as Gorbachev made this demand, however, his negotiating position was becoming untenable. The unavoidable fact was that prolonging the agony in Afghanistan would only mean weakening the Soviet Union and further tarnishing its image abroad, neither of which outcomes the general secretary could afford. U.S. policies reinforced this reality. The provision of increased assistance—including Stinger missiles—to the Afghan resistance was not as decisive as some Reagan acolytes later claimed, but it did impose additional costs on Moscow and help ensure that the Soviets could not escalate their way out of the conflict.[151] Meanwhile, Reagan and Shultz played a carrot-and-stick diplomatic game meant to emphasize Moscow's incentives for withdrawal. They hammered home the point that continued Soviet involvement in Afghanistan and other conflicts would hamper the overall improvement of relations, but that greater restraint could ease lingering Western mistrust. The U.S. position, one presidential directive stated, was that "the absence of any progress on regional issues is a fundamental impediment to a general improvement of our relations."[152] "At every U.S.-Soviet summit," Gorbachev aide Andrei Grachev later confirmed, "the American administration raised the issue of 'regional conflicts' with almost the same regularity as the subject of human rights violations within the Soviet Union." Coming at a time when the Soviet Union badly needed a relaxation of Western trade controls and a more stable superpower relationship, this tactic made the overall case for retrenchment seem all the more persuasive.[153]

By the end of 1987, Gorbachev was seeking to eliminate Third World issues as a drain on Soviet strength and a source of East-West tensions. His representatives asked for U.S. help in settling conflicts in Namibia and Angola, and Gorbachev told the Nicaraguan leadership that it should not expect additional Soviet aid. "We have much internationalism, but not enough means," he said; it was necessary to show the world that Nicaragua was not "a Soviet base." And in May 1988, Soviet troops began the withdrawal from Afghanistan, an initiative that Gorbachev had come to see as imperative to reforming his country's image and developing the relationship with the West. "It is difficult to overestimate the political significance of solving the Afghanistan problem," he told the Politburo. "In this way, we deprive our enemies and opponents of their most powerful argument."[154] To Gorbachev's chagrin, the Reagan administration refused to renounce U.S. support for the mujahideen, but it did ease the sting by sponsoring face-saving international accords that allowed Shevardnadze to portray the pullout as part of a diplomatic settlement and a vindication of the "new thinking." "No agreement would be able to put an end to this 'aid,'" Chernyaev conceded privately, but the Soviet withdrawal would still "be easier and more graceful to do ... within the framework of an agreement."[155]

The shifting dynamics of U.S.-Soviet relations were perhaps most evident when it came to the contentious subjects of human rights and political reform. Reagan had consistently argued that internal liberalization would have a moderating effect on Soviet foreign policy, and throughout the late 1980s, he and Shultz kept the issue at the center of the bilateral agenda. Reagan never let a summit pass without raising human rights; Gorbachev was soon complaining that Americans had "an almost missionary passion for preaching" on that subject.[156] The administration pressed Moscow to take a variety of specific steps: to rescind anti-dissident laws and release political prisoners, to shut down psychiatric institutions used to hold critics of the regime, to permit greater freedom of worship, and to allow increased emigration by Soviet Jews and other groups.[157] To encourage a forthcoming response, Reagan and Shultz explained that "lack of progress will only hold us back," and they reinforced this message by taking a very gradual approach to the relaxation of controls on U.S.-Soviet trade. The key was to "create political pressure for the Soviets to take positive steps," one presidential directive stated.[158]

Yet Reagan also appreciated that this "political pressure" had to be generated in a subtle and nonconfrontational manner, for the Kremlin surely would not liberalize if it felt that it was under siege. "Front page stories that we are banging away at them on their human rights abuses will get us some cheers from the bleachers," he wrote in 1985, "but it won't help those who are being abused."[159] Reagan and Shultz were thus unfailingly polite in discussing this issue with Gorbachev. They kept the human rights dialogue largely confined to private channels, and the president assured Gorbachev that "he had no intention of saying publicly that he had demanded anything" from Moscow.[160] In the same fashion, the president preferred to discuss the human rights issue not in terms of requirements that Gorbachev had to meet, but as steps that he, as a strong and independent leader, could take to improve his country's international position. If Gorbachev could guarantee religious freedom, Reagan told the general secretary at one point, "much of the feeling against his country would disappear like water in hot sun."[161] Shultz took this tactic a step further, holding a series of "seminars" in the Kremlin in which he contended that human rights improvements were in Moscow's interest because a freer society would be better able to compete in the information age.[162]

None of this was necessary to convince Gorbachev that some sort of political liberalization was imperative. The general secretary had hinted at this point since 1984, and by 1986–87 he was acutely aware that his economic reform program would fail without it.[163] As scholars and former Soviet officials have attested, though, U.S. policy did play an important role in strengthening and broadening the impetus toward liberalization. In one sense, the informal linkage between human rights, trade, and arms control underscored the costs of Soviet intransigence on specific issues like Jewish emigration and repression of dissent, and thereby helped turn the internal balance of power on these issues in favor of reformers like Shevardnadze. By 1987, even KGB hard-liners accepted that foreign policy concerns necessitated progress on human rights; by 1988, Shevardnadze and his subordinates were encouraging the State Department to make *more* requests that could then be used as a lever in Kremlin debates. "Can the Department provide me a list of prisoners that I could pass on to Kashlev?" one U.S. diplomat asked after meeting with Soviet negotiators. "I take it that he would like to use it to put some additional pressure on Moscow."[164] Similarly, by continually emphasizing the need for greater political freedoms, the administration subtly pushed Gorbachev to live up to the rhetoric of glasnost and perestroika by taking concrete steps to ease internal repression. Years later, Chernyaev underlined the importance of U.S. diplomacy in advancing the cause of Soviet reform:

> Our policy did not change until Gorbachev understood that there would be no improvement and no serious arms control until we admitted and accepted human rights, free emigration, until glasnost became freedom of speech, until our society and the process of perestroika changed deeply.[165]

By 1987, Gorbachev was moving to defuse the human rights issue, telling Shultz that "the Soviet side is prepared to consider any proposal that emerges in the humanitarian area." Over the next two years the Soviets would free hundreds of political prisoners—many of whose release had been specifically requested by the United States—and the number of exit visas increased from around one thousand in 1986 to eighty thousand in 1988. The CIA, normally skeptical of Gorbachev's intentions, admitted that progress on human rights had been "remarkable."[166]

Of course, it is doubtful that any of this could have occurred without the emergence of at least minimal trust between Reagan and Gorbachev, and had the Soviet leader not perceived that these changes would bring some payoff in the larger relationship. And in fact, as it became clear that Gorbachev was quite serious about political reform, the administration's position gradually shifted from one of quiet pressure to one of public support and encouragement. By late 1987 and early 1988, Gorbachev was announcing his intention to go far beyond scattered improvements in human rights practices and make fundamental changes in the nature of the Soviet political system—permitting democratic elections, strengthening individual protections and liberties, and other measures. As these reforms caused growing polarization at home, the Soviet leadership looked to bolster its position by receiving a sign of approval from abroad. In early 1988, Dobrynin passed a message to Washington asking whether Reagan might signal that he no longer thought of "the USSR as an evil empire whose social and political positions have placed it on the 'ash heap of history.'" The Soviet government was willing to take "concrete steps . . . over the next few months to prompt such a statement."[167]

At the Moscow summit in May 1988, Reagan used the leverage this request gave him to continue pushing for the expansion of individual liberties in the Soviet Union. Yet because the president (along with officials like Shultz and Matlock) now grasped that Gorbachev was trying to change that country in ways that might be impossible to reverse, he made sure to provide the Soviet leader with precisely the vote of confidence he had been seeking.[168] The "evil empire" speech, Reagan told reporters in Moscow, was a remnant of "another time and another era." At a subsequent press conference, he affirmed that there had been "profound change" in the Soviet Union, credited Gorbachev for the improvement, and averred that superpower tensions "continue to recede." These words had their desired effect—they strengthened Gorbachev before an upcoming party congress, gave him political capital that could be used to push ahead with reform, and provided him with proof that his more accommodating policies were strengthening Soviet relations with the West.[169] "Ronald Reagan's acknowledgement," Gorbachev wrote, "was one of the genuine achievements of his Moscow visit."[170] The symbolism was certainly remarkable—Reagan and Gorbachev had become partners in promoting the reform of the Soviet system.[171]

The extent to which the U.S.-Soviet relationship had improved became clear with Gorbachev's landmark address to the United Nations in December 1988. Prior to this speech, the Soviet government had already begun to scale back its military posture, adopting a policy of "reasonable sufficiency" and announcing that the Warsaw Pact would henceforth adhere to a solely defensive doctrine.[172] In his UN address, Gorbachev went further still. He renounced class struggle as a driver of Soviet foreign policy, and pledged his support for "freedom of choice" for all peoples. Most tangibly, he announced that Moscow was reducing its conventional forces by five hundred thousand troops, including several divisions in Eastern Europe. The Soviet Union, he explained, was moving "from the economy of armaments to an economy of disarmament."[173] This shift reflected growing financial stringencies as well as Gorbachev's determined effort to improve Moscow's international image. It also owed, however, to the atmosphere of respect and even trust that he and Reagan had built. "Parity is parity, and we must preserve it," Gorbachev had told his advisers earlier that year. "But we also need to disarm. And now that is possible. Because politically we have entered a new situation in our relations with the United States." This process had "all begun at Geneva," he told Reagan at their last meeting in December 1988.[174]

In an article on personality and the end of the Cold War, George W. Breslauer and Richard Ned Lebow appropriately highlight Gorbachev's indispensability to the relaxation of superpower tensions in the late 1980s. They also note, however, that "it is worth considering the proposition that it was Reagan's maximalism and resolve, coupled with his willingness to strike deals and abandon hostile rhetoric when his maximalist demands were met, and the personal rapport and vision he shared with Gorbachev, that ended the Cold War when and how it did."[175]

Leaving aside the question of who contributed *more* to the end of the Cold War, this stands as a good summary of Reagan's role in the process. The president first used numerous tools of statecraft to exploit the emerging crisis of Soviet power and put the United States in a strong negotiating position. During the mid- and late 1980s, he then employed a mixture of pressure, hard bargaining, conciliation, and reassurance to encourage Soviet moderation and help shape a superpower rapprochement on highly favorable terms. Even if we account for the obvious truths that Reagan was very fortunate to have Gorbachev as a negotiating partner, and that his statecraft was only one of several factors that contributed to the easing of U.S.-Soviet tensions, it was nonetheless an impressive performance.

With respect to grand strategy, Reagan's performance also showed that flexibility could be no less important than perseverance. Reagan's long-term vision and his consistent emphasis on strength were central to his ultimate success in dealing with the Soviet Union. So too, however, was his willingness to learn from his early experiences and shift to a less aggressive-looking posture from late 1983 onward. Without this recalibration, even Gorbachev's emergence might not have allowed Reagan to escape the mire of superpower confrontation. Strategic purpose and tactical adaptation had both been imperative as the Truman administration negotiated the difficulties of the early Cold War; this combination was no less essential as Reagan sought to bring that conflict to a close.

This is not to say, however, that Reagan was fully the grand strategic virtuoso that some writers have recently described. The president ultimately achieved real success in the area of greatest geopolitical importance to his country—in this sense, his grand strategy was surely an effective one. Yet throughout the 1980s, the policies that Reagan employed to deal with Moscow often entailed distinct second-order liabilities as well. In some cases, these liabilities were evident at the time; in others, the full price would be known only years after the fact.

The cost of Reagan's grand strategy was most immediately (and literally) apparent when it came to the perpetual dilemma of reconciling strategic and fiscal priorities. From the outset, the president understood that his proposed defense buildup would be expensive. He "was afflicted with two allergies: the allergy of wanting to control government spending and the allergy of wanting to increase our national security posture," Reagan told advisers in 1981.[176]

The president made good on the latter goal, but only by sacrificing the former. Big-ticket items like the B-2 bomber, the MX missile, SDI, and the building of a "600-ship Navy" were designed to provide strategic advantage and strain the Soviet economy. But when combined with Reagan's tax cuts, they exerted great pressure on *American* finances as well. By 1985, the country was running an annual budget deficit of around $250 billion, or five times what Reagan's team had originally forecast.[177] In response, Congress began to enforce modest reductions in defense spending during the late 1980s, and funding for SDI tapered off after the arms control negotiations began to bear fruit. Even so, by one accounting Reagan incurred twice as much debt as all his predecessors combined. When he left office, the United States was a debtor nation for the first time since World War I, and Reagan himself said that "his biggest concern was the budget deficit."[178]

In other areas, the price of Reagan's policies was more moral and human than financial. In monetary terms, the Reagan Doctrine was a cost-effective way of making life difficult for Moscow and its allies, and of reversing the perception that the Soviets were ascendant in the Third World. Yet despite Reagan's defense of anti-Soviet guerrillas as "the moral equal of our Founding Fathers," the fact was that the administration aligned itself with some truly awful characters.[179] The Salvadoran army was notorious for its brutality; that institution, along with right-wing death squads, killed—often in cold blood—the vast majority of the more than seventy thousand citizens who died during the civil war. "Summary execution of prisoners is a standard practice," noted one CIA assessment. "Widespread, and often random, violence by private rightwing groups is viewed as part of government repression because there is no official move to curb it." In Nicaragua, the contras raped and killed government literacy volunteers during the early 1980s, and they continued to practice summary execution, sabotage, and other such techniques thereafter. It is still debatable whether the contras were "better" or "worse" than the Sandinista government, but it is beyond question that by supporting these insurgents Reagan fueled the hellish devastation that wracked Nicaragua throughout the decade. As one historian has noted, the contra war claimed some thirty thousand Nicaraguan lives—in proportional terms, more than the United States lost in the Civil War, the world wars, and the Korean and Vietnam wars *combined*.[180]

The contra war also took a toll—albeit a less ghastly one—on the United States itself. Congressional Democrats were never enthused with this application of the Reagan Doctrine, and the administration had to become ever more creative in securing funding as time went on. The eventual outcome of this process was the Iran-contra episode, in which Reagan's aides illegally diverted the proceeds from covert arms sales to Iran (itself a dubious enterprise) to sustain the war in Nicaragua. When the scheme was exposed in 1986–87, it caused the worst constitutional crisis since Watergate.

Reagan himself ended up avoiding censure or even impeachment over Iran-contra, because there was no proof that he had known of the illegal diversion.[181] Still, his fervent anticommunism and devotion to the contra cause fostered the anything-goes Cold War mentality that informed the initiative. "We must obtain the funds to help these freedom fighters," he had told aides in 1984.[182] Moreover, the entire episode demonstrated the downside of Reagan's lax management style, as the absence of proper bureaucratic oversight made it all too easy for officials like Oliver North to engage in activities that were illegal and full of risk for the administration.[183] The resulting scandal may have prevented Reagan from pushing ahead with broader strategic arms reductions (which had to wait until the Bush years) after Reykjavík, and the president was extremely fortunate that Iran-contra did not wreck his overall diplomatic agenda.[184] As it was, the episode stood as an example of how Reagan's determined anti-Soviet offensive brought with it the potential for serious blowback.

Blowback also resulted from the initiative that was rightly considered one of the signal triumphs of the Reagan years—the semi-covert war against the Soviets in Afghanistan. U.S. support for the mujahideen was the crown jewel of the Reagan Doctrine, and probably ranks as one of the most effective uses of American power during the entire Cold War. Over the longer term, however, this policy had profoundly perverse side-effects. Because the administration relied on Pakistan as an intermediary between the United States and the guerrillas, it could only look the other way as the Islamabad government of General Muhammad Zia-ul-Haq raced forward in its pursuit of a nuclear arsenal. "We must remember that without Zia's support, the Afghan resistance, key to making the Soviets pay a heavy price for their Afghan adventure, is effectively dead," Shultz wrote to Reagan in November 1982. "We must also recognize that how we handle the nuclear issue can have a profound effect on our ability to continue to cooperate with Pakistan in supporting the Afghan freedom fighters." As one scholar aptly puts it, the president's "willingness, in the name of *realpolitik,* to court Pakistan's support for an insurgency had the practical consequences of allowing the further spread of nuclear weapons to one of the most volatile areas on the planet."[185]

Supporting the Afghan resistance also meant strengthening religious fundamentalists who were deeply hostile not just to Soviet communism, but to the United States as well. Some of America's putative Afghan allies, one top intelligence official acknowledged, were determined to "get the Russians out of their country," but even at the time it was apparent that they were "borderline crazies" who were no friends of the United States or Western modernity. By providing Stinger missiles, explosives, and other assistance to these groups, the Reagan team was combating one threat by helping to create another. More broadly, the Afghan war catalyzed development of a transnational network of Arab jihadists, many of whom would go on to fight on other battlefields during the 1990s, and some of whom would eventually turn their sights on America. "Our operations," Gates later acknowledged, "had lingering and dangerous aftereffects."[186]

The administration might have mitigated these effects in the late 1980s, had it heeded Gorbachev's pleas to create a coalition Afghan government (which would have included some Communist elements) that could survive a Soviet withdrawal. "Both the Soviets and the United States have said Islamic fundamentalism is a dangerous phenomenon," the general secretary reminded Shultz in 1988. But because Reagan and Shultz were understandably desirous of scoring a decisive victory in Afghanistan, and because they were under right-wing pressure not to make any concessions to a weakened Gorbachev, they focused their attention on compelling an essentially unilateral Soviet withdrawal and overthrowing the regime in Kabul rather than addressing the instability that was bound to follow. As Shultz put it at the time, "Our top priority must be to get the Soviets out of Afghanistan as soon as possible."[187] The result was to miss whatever opportunity there was for a post-withdrawal settlement, and to encourage the rampant internal strife that would ultimately bring the Taliban to power.

Reagan cannot be blamed fully for the eventual outcome in Afghanistan, for that conflict had its own internal dynamics, and his successors also missed opportunities to follow a more constructive course. Rather, what all these examples indicate is that Reagan's grand strategy had both positive and negative effects on American statecraft. On the one hand, the president's intense Cold War mind-set and his determination to exert pressure on Moscow provided the conceptual focus that allowed him to bring a wide array of policies into concert. On the other hand, this very single-mindedness also encouraged a number of more problematic tendencies: budget-busting defense spending, partnerships with dubious Third World allies, the illegal and counterproductive Iran-contra affair, and an inability or unwillingness to tackle emerging threats in Pakistan and Afghanistan. These drawbacks did not necessarily invalidate the benefits of Reagan's statecraft, for his achievements in superpower relations contributed to a dramatic reduction in the top-level threat to American security.[188] But they did show that his grand strategy—and the fervency with which he pursued it—could be a double-edged sword.

Ronald Reagan was hardly the prototypical strategic savant. He led on the basis of instinct and intuition rather than expert knowledge or careful analysis, and he occasionally stunned his own advisers with his ignorance of technical matters. Yet for all his foibles and idiosyncrasies, Reagan possessed a combination of shrewd geopolitical insights. He understood that the Soviet Union was militarily strong but economically, politically, and ideologically weak; that reversing the trajectory of the superpower struggle required bringing all elements of national power to bear on that competition; and that an initial move toward confrontation could foster a longer-term transition to negotiation and a more stable peace. During the early 1980s, Reagan explicitly and deliberately transformed these insights into policies that reasserted American ascendancy; in the years that followed, he blended strength with conciliation and worked toward a dramatic reduction of Cold War tensions.

If grand strategy involves making power serve essential long-term ends, then Reagan's grand strategy was immensely productive.

Qualifications, however, are necessary. It is profoundly misleading to see this story as one of Reagan formulating a seamless long-range plan and then moving confidently from success to success. As noted above, the history of the period was far more tortuous. The president continually struggled with bureaucratic conflict during the 1980s; one might well say that he succeeded despite as much as because of his management style. Partly because of this problem, Reagan's grand strategy initially led to a more volatile and danger-ous Cold War, and it took time—and no little good fortune—for him to find the right mix of policies that would maintain American leverage while also permitting a fruitful relationship with Moscow. In this regard, Reagan's experience confirms that effective grand strategy often requires not simply vision and determination, but a willingness to learn and adapt as well.

It also demonstrates the crucial importance of timing and circumstance. Reagan's achievements would not have been possible in the mid-1970s, when Soviet power was in many ways on the ascent, when the old guard was firmly entrenched in Moscow, and when American foreign policy was crippled by the legacies of Watergate and Vietnam. Reagan had the good fortune to come along when the American psyche had begun to heal, when the various weak-nesses of the Soviet system were beginning to manifest themselves in earnest, and above all when an entirely different sort of leader was about to come to power in Moscow. To note all this is not to detract from Reagan's perfor-mance, for it took real acuity to perceive what was happening and real skill to exploit it. But it does remind us of something that Nixon and Kissinger knew all too well—that the permissiveness of the domestic and international envi-ronment does much to determine what any grand strategy can accomplish.

Finally, Reagan's record demonstrates that even successful grand strategies have their liabilities. One of Reagan's great strengths was his ability to gen-erate geopolitical pressure by bringing numerous anti-Soviet initiatives into alignment. Unfortunately, this single-minded determination to counter the Soviet threat also occasioned several less positive tendencies. It led the admin-istration to approve a level of defense spending that threw the economics of national security off kilter, to embrace morally and sometimes legally prob-lematic initiatives in the Third World, and arguably to do more to encour-age than restrain the threats that would preoccupy the next generation of American policy makers. If the transformation of U.S.-Soviet relations was the signal accomplishment of Reagan's grand strategy, these more troubling legacies represented the cost.

CHAPTER 4

The Dangers of Being Grand
George W. Bush and the Post-9/11 Era

Reagan's legacy loomed large for his successors, George W. Bush not least among them. During his run for the White House, the Texas governor invoked Reagan in reverential tones. The fortieth president, he declared, was

> a hero in the American story. A story in which a single individual can shape history. A story in which evil is real, but courage and decency triumph. We live in the nation President Reagan restored, and the world he helped to save. A world of nations reunited and tyrants humbled. A world of prisoners released and exiles come home. And today there is a prayer shared by free people everywhere: God bless you, Ronald Reagan.[1]

In Bush's telling, Reagan had dared to think big, to persevere in the face of crisis and danger, and the result had been to change human history. In this sense, Reagan's grand strategy was not just the key to the Cold War's end—it was a testament to what the clear-eyed, morally courageous statesman could accomplish with American power.

His admiration for Reagan notwithstanding, Bush did not initially seem destined to be a foreign-policy president. The 1990s had been a time when foreign policy was a secondary concern for most Americans, and Bush's early diplomatic forays left only an indistinct imprint. After the terrorist attacks of 9/11, however, Bush sought to write his own story in which courage and freedom triumphed. Along with a small group of advisers, the president crafted an extremely forward-leaning grand strategy for protecting the United States in a new era of danger. The goal of that strategy was not simply to destroy al-Qaeda and the Taliban, but to unleash America's overwhelming power so as to transform the larger threat environment the country now faced. The keystone of this program was the invasion of Iraq in 2003, an initiative designed to disrupt the potential nexus between terrorism and weapons of mass destruction (WMD), deter other hostile regimes from challenging U.S. interests, and address the root causes of terrorism by sparking a new age of freedom in the Middle East and beyond. This was America's next "great mission," Bush announced, and it would require bold, visionary action if it were to be accomplished.[2]

Bold actions were taken in the post-9/11 era, but success was often elusive. The Bush administration put American military power to highly efficient use in defeating the Taliban and scattering al-Qaeda in late 2001, and in destroying Saddam Hussein's regime in 2003. Yet it struggled to convert these initial victories into lasting strategic gains. Post-conflict stability in Afghanistan went wanting, and both the Taliban and al-Qaeda were soon resurgent. Meanwhile, the invasion of Iraq unleashed a torrent of violence and instability in that country, while incurring a host of generally unwelcome consequences in the Middle East and elsewhere. By the time Bush left office, the United States was also confronting a range of other security challenges, some of which had been exacerbated by the administration's own policies. Hopes for transformative grand strategic triumphs had long since faded; American power now seemed more beleaguered than at any time since the Cold War.

As these disappointing outcomes indicated, the Bush administration frequently struggled to turn its ambitious strategic ideas into policies that could stand the test of reality. In Iraq particularly, that failure flowed from severe deficiencies of planning, process, and execution, but it also flowed from the fact that Bush's grand strategy was conceptually flawed to begin with. After 9/11, the president and his advisers overestimated how much American power could achieve, and they underestimated the costs, risks, and uncertainties that inhered in their endeavors. The administration overreached, and it wound up with overstretch. At a time when American security seemed gravely imperiled and American influence was clearly unmatched, the Bush administration devised a grand strategy that was simply too grand.

George W. Bush became president a decade into the post–Cold War era, a period in which the United States seemed more powerful and safer than ever before. The collapse of the Soviet Union had left the United States with unchallenged global preeminence, and it removed the dominant security threat that had focused the country's attention for decades. To be sure, the international environment was far from entirely benign during the 1990s, as American officials faced issues ranging from humanitarian catastrophes and ethnic conflict to regional crises and nuclear proliferation. ("We have slain a large dragon," CIA Director James Woolsey liked to say, "but we now live in a jungle filled with a bewildering variety of poisonous snakes."[3]) Yet none of these challenges was remotely as dangerous as the Cold War–era Soviet Union, and the rapid spread of democracy and free-market economics created a sense that the world was remaking itself in America's image. The world had reached a "unipolar moment," argued neoconservative commentator Charles Krauthammer; America and its essential values reigned supreme.[4]

Precisely because the United States seemed so powerful, there was a pronounced ambivalence to American foreign policy during the 1990s. The Clinton administration grasped that America's dominant position was worth preserving and even improving, and many of the initiatives it pursued— from the expansion of NATO to the promotion of democracy and free markets—reflected these objectives. At the same time, however, the absence of any overriding security challenge meant that Americans were not eager to spend much blood or treasure abroad. The result was what one scholar calls a policy of "hegemony on the cheap."[5] Clinton was famously casualty averse even as he authorized a number of humanitarian interventions, and his administration generally sought to conduct policy in as cost-free a manner as possible. Democracy promotion was attempted largely through diplomatic and economic means, and after an initial misadventure in Somalia, the administration relied on cruise missiles and airpower when military force was required. "Right now the average American doesn't see our interests threatened to the point where we should sacrifice one American life," Clinton explained.[6]

The Clinton administration took an equally ambivalent attitude toward the idea of grand strategy itself. The president and several top aides believed that they needed to establish a new conceptual framework—a "new slogan," Clinton called it—that would guide policy and stabilize the public debate on America's global role. As Clinton told adviser and longtime friend Strobe Talbott, "You've still got to be able to crystallize complexity in a way people get right away." But in virtually the same breath, the president voiced deep skepticism about how useful grand strategy really was. He believed that strategic coherence "was largely imposed after the fact," and that successful leaders like Truman and Roosevelt had "just made it up as they went along."

In Clinton's eyes, grand strategy could actually cause more problems than it solved. "The Cold War was helpful as an organizing principle," he said, "but it had its dangers because every welt on your skin became cancer."[7]

This cognitive dissonance meant that there was always something conflicted about Clinton's approach to foreign policy. In September 1993, National Security Adviser Anthony Lake gave a major speech outlining the broad overall vision—and new slogan—that the president desired. "The successor to a doctrine of containment," Lake announced, "must be a strategy of enlargement—enlargement of the world's free community of market democracies." In an era of no existential threats and unmatched American power, the United States would ensure its future security by spreading its core values more widely than ever before.[8] Yet while the administration subsequently embraced the basic logic of enlargement, it was less diligent in doing the legwork necessary to translate that idea into a fully integrated and cohesive grand strategy. During the first term especially, the Clinton team was notorious for its disorganization, its inability to address key issues systematically, and its proclivity for ad hoc and crisis-driven decision making. "Clinton was not noted for his discipline," Lake later acknowledged, and the policy process could get "messy" in consequence.[9]

At a time of unassailable American preeminence, this modus operandi did not prevent Clinton from achieving a number of diplomatic successes. Among other things, his administration pushed the stabilizing influence of NATO into Eastern Europe; ended bloody wars in Bosnia and Kosovo; established a manageable if uncomfortable relationship with a rising China; and served as a strong supporter of expanded U.S. and global trade. It was a respectable list of accomplishments for an administration that focused primarily on domestic issues, and one that made the more strident contemporary critiques of Clinton's record seem overstated.

Yet if the Clinton years were not a "squandered presidency," they did show how a diffident attitude toward grand strategy could cause disorder and even incoherence in U.S. statecraft.[10] The president and his advisers continually had trouble setting and holding to a firm hierarchy of priorities, or recognizing that foreign policy was a discipline of trade-offs and limits. The administration averred that it had a fundamental interest in promoting liberalization and pro-Western elements in Russia, for instance, but its simultaneous pursuit of NATO expansion had the eventual effect of strengthening nationalist tendencies, weakening reformers, and humiliating the same Yeltsin government that Clinton sought to befriend.[11] Similarly, Clinton and his top aides frequently struggled to allocate their limited time and energy effectively. The president allowed himself and his secretaries of state to be pulled into immensely time-consuming and ultimately fruitless negotiations for Middle East peace, despite reasonable concerns about the opportunity cost involved. More broadly, in the absence of a more rigorous approach to grand strategy, there was a tendency for top-level involvement in foreign policy to be driven primarily by crises rather than long-term objectives. "Because I was interested in so much, I was insufficiently ruthless in setting priorities," Secretary of State Madeleine Albright later admitted.[12]

Clinton's undisciplined style also caused real difficulties when it came to the use of force. The administration stumbled badly in Somalia in 1993, embracing an expanded, riskier mission in that country while also withdrawing most U.S. troops and limiting the firepower available to those who remained. It was a classic ends-means mismatch engendered by presidential inattention and poor policy coordination, and it helped produce the "Blackhawk Down" disaster in October. Stung by the political fallout, Clinton reversed course dramatically, withdrawing from Somalia and discarding his broader humanitarian agenda so quickly and completely that the administration sat passive amid the Rwandan genocide several months later. (In a move that Lake thought "shameful," the White House and State Department even refused to call that genocide by its name, for fear that "if you used the word, then you're required to take action.") To its credit, the Clinton team subsequently recovered its footing, developing the airpower-only template that eventually worked well enough in Bosnia and Kosovo. Yet the same approach was badly insufficient for dealing with the rising threat of terrorism in the late 1990s, and despite the repeated urgings of mid-level officials, the president and his key aides never assembled an effective response to the danger. As Clinton's term came to a close, the dilemmas of post–Cold War military intervention continued to perplex the administration.[13]

Such perplexities endlessly annoyed the strategic studies community, which often alleged that American foreign policy lacked any direction whatsoever. The post–Cold War years had seen nothing but "ad hoc fits and starts," wrote one panel of experts in 1996. "It if continues, this drift will threaten our values, our fortunes, and indeed our lives."[14] For the most part, however, the broader electorate was not much concerned. As Clinton correctly understood, foreign policy was just not an important issue for most Americans in the decade after the Cold War. Polls taken in the late 1990s showed that only 2 to 3 percent of Americans saw foreign policy issues as the country's primary concern, and when respondents were asked to identify "two or three foreign policy problems facing the nation," the leading answer was "don't know." This apathy was reflected in the Congress, which slashed foreign aid and the State Department's budget as the decade went on. At a time when there seemed no overriding danger to national security, many citizens could afford to know little and care less about the broader world.[15]

George W. Bush's successful run for the presidency in 2000 was testimony to this fact. The Texas governor had famously flunked a televised pop quiz on world leaders in November 1999, and he gave relatively few major speeches on foreign policy during the campaign. Contrary to the contemporary caricature, his shallowness on the subject was not a function of subpar intelligence.[16] The problem was that Bush had virtually no direct experience with foreign policy, and unlike Reagan, he had not spent any real time formulating and refining his views on the subject prior to running for president. The candidate was learning on the fly, as he acknowledged at one campaign stop. "Nobody needs to tell me what I believe," Bush insisted. "But I do need somebody to tell me where Kosovo is."[17]

Insofar as the GOP featured a well-developed worldview in 1999–2000, it came not from Bush, but from a group of hawkish campaign advisers known as "the Vulcans." Led by Paul Wolfowitz and Condoleezza Rice, the Vulcans advocated unabashedly hegemonic statecraft. In 1992, when Wolfowitz was undersecretary of defense, his office had produced an eyebrow-raising document that called for a muscular—and essentially unilateral—approach to perpetuating America's post–Cold War dominance. The "Defense Planning Guidance" bluntly stated that the United States would not permit the rise of potential geopolitical competitors, and it advocated the unembarrassed use of American power to defeat emerging threats and shape the global environment. This "hard-hitting document" (in Wolfowitz's phrasing) quickly leaked and had to be rewritten, but the underlying ethos endured. During the 1990s, the Vulcans called for a major program of military modernization, deployment of missile defenses to protect against attacks by rogue states, a policy of "regime change" toward Iraq and possibly North Korea, and a stronger stance toward potential rivals like Russia and China. They were deeply skeptical of the United Nations, and disdained arms control and what Rice called "illusory 'norms' of international behavior." In essence, the Vulcans argued that the post–Cold War world was a very dangerous place, and that national security required the vigorous—and unfettered—employment of American might.[18]

Bush often spoke from the same script as the Vulcans during his presidential bid. The GOP nominee termed China a strategic "competitor" that bore careful watching, and he firmly supported missile defense. He disparaged Clinton-era agreements, such as the Comprehensive Test Ban Treaty, that provided "only words and false hopes and high intentions—with no guarantees whatsoever." He also pledged to tighten the screws on Saddam Hussein, and to assist the various exile groups that were seeking to overthrow him.[19] On many issues, then, Bush placed himself squarely in the company of those who called for a more robust and decisive use of American power. "This is still a world of terror and missiles and madmen," he warned; "a dangerous world still requires a sharpened sword."[20] Following the election, Vulcans like Wolfowitz and Rice secured key positions as deputy secretary of defense and national security adviser, and two similarly hard-line figures—Dick Cheney and Donald Rumsfeld—became vice president and secretary of defense. After 9/11, this group of officials would loom large in the shaping of a highly assertive grand strategy.

Early on, however, Bush's worldview was far from unambiguously hawkish. As a candidate, Bush showed a distinct aversion to "nation building," and he rejected the idea of promoting American values at the point of a gun: "I just don't think it's the role of the United States to walk into a country and say, 'We do it this way, so should you.'" At times, he even distanced himself from the more muscular themes that his closest counselors advocated. America's reputation "really depends upon how our nation conducts itself in foreign policy," he said in one debate. "If we're an arrogant nation, they'll resent us. If we're a humble nation but strong, they'll welcome us."[21] During the campaign, in fact, Bush called for only a $45 billion increase in defense spending over the next decade, less than half that advocated by his opponent and far below what the Joint Chiefs of Staff desired.[22] After the election, he gave the most prestigious appointment of all—secretary of state—to Colin Powell, a leading GOP moderate on foreign policy. If Bush seemed a card-carrying Vulcan in some instances, he looked the prudent, fiscally cautious conservative in others. When he took office in early 2001, it was not yet evident which tendency would win out.

The first eight months of his presidency did not substantially clarify things. On some issues, Bush hewed to a hawkish line. In April 2001, he announced that the United States intended to free itself from the strictures of the ABM Treaty, a pact that "prohibits us from exploring all options for defending against the threats that face us, our allies, and other countries."[23] The administration also flaunted its hostility to the Kyoto Protocol on global warming, killing the accord with a bluntness that even White House insiders later acknowledged was counterproductive.[24] By the summer of 2001, one observer noted that the "specter of unilateralism" had become the foremost concern of many U.S. allies.[25]

The hand-wringing was somewhat misplaced, though, for in other respects Bush's policies were far more understated. There was no real effort to achieve regime change in Iraq; the administration instead settled for an unsuccessful attempt to shore up the crumbling UN sanctions regime.[26] With respect to the military, Bush initially resolved that there would be "no new money for defense this year," reversing course and agreeing to a modest increase only to avert a potential revolt by congressional Republicans.[27] Most notably of all, when a U.S. spy plane was forced to land on Hainan Island after colliding with a Chinese fighter jet, Bush was restrained in his response. Many top advisers favored compelling Beijing to release the U.S. crew by threatening trade sanctions or other diplomatic measures, but Powell ultimately persuaded Bush to adopt less confrontational tactics. The State Department issued a carefully worded "non-apology" that nonetheless expressed regret over the incident, and the aircrew was released shortly thereafter. The *Weekly Standard* called the episode a "national humiliation," an overwrought reaction demonstrating mainly that Bush's early diplomacy managed to perplex neoconservatives and multilateralists alike.[28]

At the outset, then, it was hard to tell what kind of mark Bush would leave on foreign policy. And in fact, international issues were not a particularly important part of Bush's agenda through mid-2001. As was true throughout the 1990s, both the president and the public were more concerned with domestic issues such as education reform, tax cuts, and stem-cell research. Nearly eight months into Bush's term, it seemed improbable that his administration would soon author an immensely controversial grand strategy for dealing with a new era of danger.

Yet this was precisely what happened after 9/11. Following the attacks, the Bush administration launched a punishing military campaign against al-Qaeda and the Taliban. It simultaneously declared a broader "war on terror" and began to devise a grand strategy for that conflict. Within months, Bush was announcing his intention to preserve lasting American military hegemony, to strike preemptively—and unilaterally—against gathering threats, and to treat "rogue states" seeking weapons of mass destruction as no less a menace than terrorism. In accordance with those principles, he then proceeded to authorize an invasion of Iraq, a country that had nothing to do with 9/11, and to launch a campaign to democratize not just that nation but eventually the broader Middle East as well. In the space of eighteen months, the United States had embarked on a course of action that was breathtaking in its scope and ambition.

Strategic shocks can have a clarifying effect for policy makers, and this was certainly true of the Bush administration and 9/11. More pungently than almost anything imaginable, the attacks on the World Trade Center and the Pentagon demonstrated that the mere existence of American power did not guarantee American security. For a cost of some $500,000, nineteen men armed with box cutters had taken nearly three thousand lives and exposed the United States to a degree of destruction not seen in generations. The attacks constituted "the Pearl Harbor of the twenty-first century," Bush remarked; they showed that comparatively weak actors could perpetrate catastrophic levels of violence.[29] If al-Qaeda and other terrorist groups could mount similar strikes in the future, then the fundamentals of American life might be transformed. Intrusive security measures might be necessary; civil liberties and the openness of society would surely suffer. "What's at stake here," Rumsfeld pointed out, "is our way of life."[30]

Many years later, this statement may seem overly dramatic. At the time, however, it did not appear so far-fetched. The weeks after 9/11 saw the successful anthrax attacks of October 2001, as well as a scare in which it was initially believed that Bush and the White House staff had been exposed to botulinum toxin. Meanwhile, policy makers were bombarded with information suggesting that more terrorism was imminent. "Between 9/11 and mid-2003," Bush later reported, "the CIA reported to me an average of 400 specific threats each month."[31] It was all enough to make most top officials think that follow-on attacks were more a certainty than a likelihood. "It has been a month since the attack on the Pentagon," Rumsfeld wrote in October 2001. "More people are going to be killed if we don't produce some results fast." New terror attacks were "almost a certainty," Cheney said several months thereafter. "It's not a matter of if, but when."[32]

If 9/11 thus seemed to augur a future of persistent danger, it also showed how badly the country's previous security posture had failed. Since the mid-1990s, the threat from global terrorism—and from Osama bin Laden and al-Qaeda specifically—had been metastasizing. "Sooner or later," predicted one briefing paper, "bin Ladin will attack U.S. interests, perhaps using WMD."[33] Yet neither the Clinton nor the Bush administration had developed a sufficient response. Clinton's efforts were hampered by bureaucratic inertia and an unwillingness to bear the costs of anything more dramatic than one-off cruise missile strikes. For their part, Bush's advisers began to focus sustained, top-level attention on al-Qaeda only weeks before 9/11. After the attacks, it was painfully clear that the United States needed a more urgent and ruthless approach to dealing with rising threats. America was "at war with a new and different kind of enemy," Bush told advisers on September 12, and it had to start behaving as such.[34]

Indeed, 9/11 caused a profound transformation within Bush himself. The president had come to office as a domestically focused leader whose worldview was still taking shape. He emerged from the attacks with an intense focus on foreign policy and a penchant for seeing the world in starkly moralistic terms. The United States, he said on September 12, was locked in "a monumental struggle between good and evil."[35] Above all, Bush was driven by a relentless determination to take whatever steps were necessary to prevent anything like 9/11 from happening again. "The security of the American people," he later said, had become his "sacred duty."[36] In essence, Bush was now prepared to unleash American power, and this shift was evident in the changing bureaucratic balance within the administration. Prior to 9/11, Powell and the moderates had appeared to be winning several key policy debates; afterward, Bush's most hawkish aides—Cheney, Rumsfeld, Wolfowitz, and Rice—were indisputably ascendant. This small group of advisers quickly came to dominate the competition for the president's ear, and they formed a key base of support for the assertive policies to come.

The first manifestation of those policies came in Afghanistan. Following 9/11, the president resolved to strike al-Qaeda's leadership and infrastructure in that country, and to destroy the Taliban regime if it refused to break with bin Laden. "Let's hit them hard," he said. "We want to signal this is a change from the past."[37] Within days of 9/11, the State Department had isolated the enemy diplomatically by pressuring Pakistani president Pervez Musharraf to break with the Taliban and support the coming U.S. war effort.[38] For Rumsfeld's Pentagon, by contrast, dealing with remote and landlocked Afghanistan constituted a severe logistical challenge. Nonetheless, by early October the administration had begun to implement a creative plan of action that involved air strikes against the Taliban and al-Qaeda, targeted actions by CIA and special-forces operatives, and the use of money, airpower, and other support to empower the opposition Northern Alliance. This approach was meant to leverage unique, highly capable U.S. assets as well as the manpower and motivation of the Northern Alliance forces—in essence, to achieve maximum strategic impact at relatively minimal cost.[39]

Within weeks, the war plan proved its worth. The Northern Alliance, which had been near defeat in early September, now used U.S. support to reverse the military situation and put the Taliban and al-Qaeda to flight. By November, Kabul had fallen; by December, a new Afghan government was being installed. It was an amazingly efficient use of national power: by combining high-impact U.S. military capabilities with indigenous manpower, the Bush administration had destroyed al-Qaeda's sanctuary, killed hundreds of its operatives, and liberated the "graveyard of empires," all at virtually no cost in American lives. The post-9/11 era was off to a promising start.

Before the war in Afghanistan even began, however, the administration had already committed itself to something grander than a single campaign. A key national security directive made America's goal the "elimination of terrorism as a threat to our way of life," and in his landmark speech to Congress on September 20, Bush framed the issue in expansive terms.[40] "Our war on terror begins with al-Qaeda," he said, "but it does not end there. It will not end until every terrorist group of global reach has been found, stopped, and defeated." Bush further broadened the scope of the conflict by announcing that the United States would make no distinction between terrorists and the states that sponsored them, and he left no doubt that he viewed this incipient "war on terror" as a consuming global struggle and America's next call to greatness. "We have found our mission and our moment," he declared.

> Freedom and fear are at war. The advance of human freedom—the great achievement of our time, and the great hope of every time—now depends on us. Our nation—this generation—will lift a dark threat of violence from our people and our future. We will rally the world to this cause by our efforts, by our courage. We will not tire; we will not falter; and we will not fail.[41]

This broad definition of national purpose doubtlessly reflected the long-standing U.S. tendency to frame foreign policy crises in Manichean and universalistic terms.[42] It also stemmed from a concern that focusing only on America's immediate problem—al-Qaeda—would make it harder to line up international support. The need, Rice believed, was to "paint vividly an enemy against which the world could mobilize."[43] Most fundamentally, however, this encompassing "war on terror" flowed from the overarching strategic judgment that the United States had entered what Rumsfeld called a "new era of vulnerability," one in which a variety of enemies could exploit technological advances and the permeability of American society to attack the country in "novel and surprising ways." "There's always been terrorism," he explained, "but there's never really been worldwide terrorism at a time when the weapons have been as powerful as they are today, with chemical and biological and nuclear weapons spreading to countries that harbor terrorists." The United States was facing something bigger than a "one-country problem," and it would need to mount a broad, sustained response.[44]

It would also need a coherent grand strategy if it were to succeed. From Rice's perspective, 9/11 confirmed the importance of finding an "organizing principle" around which to center America's dealings with the world.[45] Similarly, Powell believed that good policy demanded "the establishment of priorities" that would be "unified by a strategy."[46] In the year following 9/11, the administration devoted itself to precisely this task, formulating a set of interlocking strategic concepts designed to orient American statecraft, and formalizing these ideas in the 2002 *National Security Strategy* (*NSS*) and other key speeches and documents. "We took as the model the historic NSC-68, Paul Nitze's seminal statement of U.S. objectives and strategy at the outset of the Cold War," Rice later wrote.[47] What emerged from this process was an extremely bold grand strategy aimed not simply at meeting the immediate threat, but also at fundamentally transforming the heightened threat environment that the country now faced.

At the core of this grand strategy was an appreciation of American power. "Today, the United States enjoys a position of unparalleled military strength and great economic and political influence," Bush wrote in his introduction to the 2002 *NSS*. No country could challenge American might; no economic or political model had proven more successful than the combination of "freedom, democracy, and free enterprise." This position of dominance had created a "time of opportunity for America," an opening in which the United States could shape the global environment to its lasting benefit. As the report stated, this would be the guiding goal of U.S. policy—to "translate this moment of influence into decades of peace, prosperity, and liberty."[48]

Doing so meant embracing an unapologetically hegemonic approach to global affairs. At the broadest level, the United States should keep its military so strong that no potential rival would even think of challenging for primacy. This idea had been central to the 1992 Defense Planning Guidance, and Bush firmly embraced the logic. In a speech at West Point in June 2002, he announced that "America has, and intends to keep, military strengths beyond challenge, thereby making the destabilizing arms races of other eras pointless, and limiting rivalries to trade and other pursuits of peace." In effect, the United States would act as a global military hegemon for the indefinite future, deterring a resurgence of great-power competition and preserving a stable, secure environment in which free institutions could flourish. The goal, according to the 2002 *NSS,* was "a balance of power that favors human freedom: conditions in which all nations and all societies can choose for themselves the rewards and challenges of political and economic liberty."[49] After shrinking during the 1990s, defense spending resumed a sharp upward climb during the Bush years, increasing by a real-dollar average of 7.4 percent between 2001 and 2009.[50]

From the outset, critics warned that a declared policy of perpetual hegemony might elicit the very international resistance it was meant to avoid. Yet top administration officials insisted that U.S. power would be viewed as largely benevolent, or at least benign, in nature. Multipolarity was "never a unifying idea, or a vision," Rice explained. "It was a necessary evil" that invited arms-racing and great-power rivalry. Moreover, to the extent that Washington used its military might to secure the global commons, defend its allies, and promote international prosperity, it would surely win the approbation of the world community. "Power in the service of freedom is to be welcomed," she averred.[51]

Having a world-dominant military was also essential if the United States was to defeat the major global threats to democracy, peace, and stability. After 9/11, it seemed unlikely that these virtues could thrive in an environment characterized by recurring, catastrophic terrorism. Nor, U.S. officials feared, could they be assured in a world where dangerous and sometimes unpredictable dictators armed themselves with nuclear, biological, and chemical weapons. And should these two threats—terrorism and WMD—somehow come together, the civilized world would be confronted with the worst scenario of all. "Mass civilian casualties is the specific objective of terrorists," the 2002 *NSS* stated, "and these losses would be exponentially more severe if terrorists acquired and used weapons of mass destruction."[52] By the time of his West Point speech, Bush was thus arguing that "the gravest danger to freedom lies at the perilous crossroads of radicalism and technology."[53] Dealing with this sinister "nexus," Powell subsequently explained, would be "the overriding security concern of our nation" for "years to come."[54]

As detailed in administration planning documents, Bush's grand strategy featured a three-pronged approach to dealing with these dangers.[55] First and most immediately, the United States would aggressively target those terrorist groups—particularly al-Qaeda—that posed major threats to American security. The goal was to "disrupt and destroy terrorist organizations of global reach," the 2002 *NSS* stated; the emphasis would be on "direct and continuous action using all the elements of national and international power."[56] In practice, this meant doing everything from gathering and sharing intelligence on terrorist groups, to waging diplomatic campaigns to deny them sanctuary and funding, to increasing homeland security efforts, to providing military and economic support to friendly partner nations. Above all, it entailed a willingness to use whatever level of force was deemed necessary to deal with the threat, from covert action to drone strikes to full-on, boots-on-the-ground military intervention. "This will not be an antiseptic, 'cruise missile war,'" Rumsfeld wrote. "There are causes so important that they require putting lives at risk—fighting terrorism is one."[57]

The short-term goal of all these initiatives was to keep al-Qaeda and similar organizations off balance so that they could not attack the United States.

"You cannot defend at every place at every time against every conceivable, imaginable, even unimaginable terrorist attack," Rumsfeld said in late 2001, so "the only way to deal with these terrorist threats is to go at them where they exist." Over the longer term, the idea was to make terrorism as unproductive and unrewarding as possible, and thereby encourage potential practitioners to think twice about its utility. Again, Rumsfeld laid out the logic. "We must put pressure on the terrorist networks and their supporters fast," he urged. "If we are to be successful in doing that, we must push them off balance, increase their costs and, over time, they will run out of money, be frightened, recruits will decline, defections will rise and their supporters will fall away."[58]

As the first prong of Bush's strategy began to produce results, the administration could increase its emphasis on the second prong: confronting state sponsors of terrorism, particularly those with known WMD ambitions. Countries like Libya, Iraq, Iran, and North Korea had long caused strategic problems for the United States, and after 9/11 the danger seemed much greater still. Al-Qaeda probably could not have conducted 9/11 without the protection of a government sponsor, and the power of this and other such organizations would certainly be magnified if they could draw on the resources and assistance of states. Moreover, state sponsorship offered a potential avenue for groups like al-Qaeda—which lacked advanced industrial capabilities of their own—to acquire WMD. As early as September 13, 2001, Wolfowitz had thus talked of "removing the sanctuaries, removing the support systems, ending states who sponsor terrorism."[59] Administration principals soon endorsed these basic objectives. "A key war aim," Rumsfeld wrote, "would be to persuade or compel States to stop supporting terrorism. The regimes of such States should see that it will be fatal to host terrorists who attack the U.S. as was done on September 11. If the war does not significantly change the world's political map, the U.S. will not achieve its aim."[60] A strategic guidance document prepared in the Pentagon formalized this idea: American forces would "disrupt, damage or destroy internal control mechanisms and the military capacity, including WMD, of regimes that continue to support terrorism."[61]

In some sense, this fear of state-sponsored WMD terrorism seemed overblown. Was there really much chance that Saddam or Kim Jong-Il would spend years developing these weapons, only to hand them over to uncontrollable extremists whose ultimate aims differed from their own? The answer was probably no, and administration officials never uncovered any solid evidence that such transfers had been attempted or even seriously considered. Yet in the months following 9/11, this was not much cause for comfort. For those in power, the anthrax attacks had made the prospect of WMD terrorism seem all too real. And because the potential consequences of such attacks were so grave, Bush and his top advisers were unwilling to accept *any* risk on this count. "As unfathomable as this was," Cheney had remarked on 9/11, "it could have been so much worse if they had weapons of mass destruction." It followed, as he said on a later occasion, that if there was even a "one percent chance" of al-Qaeda acquiring a nuclear weapon, "we have to treat it as a certainty in terms of our response."[62] Rice put it in similar terms. The "lesson of September 11," she said in early 2002, was to "take care of threats early."[63] When confronted with uncertainty, the administration would now err on the side of action rather than passivity.

What this meant in practice began to emerge in 2002. In his State of the Union address in January, Bush identified three states with known terrorist ties and WMD aspirations—Iraq, Iran, and North Korea—as an "Axis of Evil" that posed a "grave and growing danger." To deal with this threat, the president emphasized measures like missile defense and homeland security.[64] But in this and later speeches, he also argued that the United States had to be willing to move first. "Deterrence ... means nothing against shadowy terrorist networks with no nation or citizens to defend," he said at West Point in June. "Containment is not possible when unbalanced dictators with weapons of mass destruction can deliver those weapons on missiles or secretly provide them to terrorist allies." The war on terror would therefore not be "won on the defensive"; the United States might have to preemptively disarm its most dangerous adversaries. It would do so with international approval if possible, but it should not hesitate to strike alone if necessary. "In the world we have entered," Bush warned, "the only path to safety is the path of action."[65]

In asserting this doctrine of preemption, the administration actually engineered a subtle redefinition of the term. "Preemptive" action had traditionally entailed striking against a truly imminent threat, such as a hostile military buildup on one's borders. "Preventive" attacks aimed at avoiding longer-range threats by destroying a rising state's capabilities. From Bush's perspective, however, this distinction had become meaningless, because in an age of terrorism it might be impossible to know whether an attack was intended until it was too late to respond. It followed that America must "adapt the concept of imminent threat to the capabilities and objectives of today's adversaries," the 2002 *NSS* stated. If U.S. officials could not reliably know when or where an attack might come, they had no reasonable choice but to remove the capacity to attack altogether.[66]

When the Bush administration talked of unilateralism and preemption, of course, it was thinking primarily of Saddam's Iraq. There was no proof that

Saddam was directly linked to 9/11, and his ties to al-Qaeda were tenuous at best.[67] As early as late September 2001, however, Rumsfeld began reviewing and reformulating plans for an invasion of Iraq. In early 2002, Powell informed Congress that Bush favored "regime change," and that America "might have to do it alone."[68] By the fall of 2002, the administration was seeking to forge a domestic consensus for war by stressing (and sometimes exaggerating) seemingly persuasive intelligence on Saddam's WMD programs, and to build international support for the war by winning UN Security Council authorization. It succeeded politically but failed diplomatically, and the prospective invasion incited not just opposition but outrage among some of America's closest allies. Undeterred, the administration proceeded in precisely the preemptive and unilateral manner the 2002 *NSS* had prescribed. "The United Nations Security Council has not lived up to its responsibilities," Bush announced in March 2003, "so we will rise to ours."[69]

In retrospect, there were several interlocking reasons why the Bush administration was so fixated on toppling Saddam. In one sense, the rationale for confrontation predated 9/11. Key Pentagon officials—notably Wolfowitz and Rumsfeld—had long seen Saddam as a threat to Gulf stability, the security of Israel and other allies, and the free flow of oil supplies.[70] By the beginning of Bush's presidency, it was also obvious that the UN sanctions regime was breaking down, and it was almost universally suspected that Saddam was exploiting the absence of weapons inspectors to pursue his WMD programs. "Within a few years the U.S. will undoubtedly have to confront a Saddam armed with nuclear weapons," Rumsfeld predicted in mid-2001. When added to the substantial costs of containing Iraq militarily and diplomatically, all of this contributed to a widespread feeling that, as Rumsfeld put it, "If Saddam's regime were ousted, we would have a much-improved position in the region and elsewhere."[71] In fact, in the hours after 9/11, Rumsfeld was already wondering if the United States should "go massive," "sweep it all up," and "hit S.H." at the same time as bin Laden.[72]

There was not some precooked conspiracy to invade Iraq, however, because prior to 9/11 Bush had shown no inclination to pay the higher costs associated with forcible regime change.[73] Afterward, the situation changed completely. Saddam may not have been behind the attacks, but he had extensive ties to Middle Eastern terrorist groups, and no top policy maker doubted that at least some of his WMD programs were alive and well. Nor did they doubt that al-Qaeda was determined to acquire such weapons, even if it meant cooperating with otherwise distasteful partners.[74]

After 9/11, there was just no tolerance for the dangers that this confluence of activities seemed to present. As Lawrence Freedman writes, "worst-case analysis had suddenly gained a new credibility."[75] Determined not to be caught unawares again, Bush and his inner circle increasingly focused on what Saddam potentially *could* do with nuclear or other advanced weapons, and paid less attention to the probable *likelihood* of such actions. Cheney and top Pentagon officials warned that Saddam might use his advanced weapons to make another bid for regional hegemony, or perhaps distribute those weapons to terrorists as a way of gaining leverage on the United States.[76] Rice sketched similar scenarios, and argued that waiting for hard proof might mean waiting too long. The U.S. intelligence establishment had failed prior to 9/11; might it fail to predict an even more devastating attack in the future? The United States was not confronting Saddam "because you have some chain of evidence saying Iraq may have given a weapon to al-Qaeda," she explained in 2002. "But it is because Iraq is one of those places that is both hostile to us and, frankly, irresponsible and cruel enough to make this available."[77] In this dangerous new world, she argued, certainty was a luxury that Washington could no longer afford.

Bush's thinking evolved along the same lines. As one adviser put it, 9/11 predisposed him to "worry about the unthinkable—that the next attack could be with weapons of mass destruction supplied by Saddam Hussein."[78] Bush himself touched on this transformation in a later interview. After 9/11, he said, "Saddam Hussein's capacity to create harm . . . all his terrible features became much more threatening. Keeping Saddam in a box looked less and less feasible to me."[79] Following consultations with U.S. officials in early 2002, British foreign secretary Jack Straw captured the dynamic precisely:

> If 11 September had not happened, it is doubtful that the US would now be considering military action against Iraq. . . . Objectively, the threat from Iraq has not worsened as a result of 11 September. What has however changed is the tolerance of the international community (especially that of the US), the world having witnessed on September 11 just what determined evil people can these days perpetrate.[80]

Fundamentally, then, war with Iraq fit squarely within Bush's definition of preemption: in an atmosphere of great peril and imperfect information, the United States had to remove the threat before it fully matured.

The administration also expected that attacking Iraq would have positive ramifications reaching far beyond that country, particularly in the realms of deterrence and coercion. While top U.S. officials continually argued that tyrants like Saddam could not be reasoned with, they clearly hoped that removing this particular tyrant would have a sobering effect on other governments that might be tempted to develop WMD or cooperate with terrorists. "Disarming Saddam . . . is a very good demonstration," said Wolfowitz.[81] An internal administration document echoed this argument: "Regime change will remove a source of support for international terrorism, and will serve as an object lesson to other state supporters of terrorism."[82] Bush even made the same point publicly in early 2003: "Other regimes will be given a clear warning that support for terror will not be tolerated."[83] If the United States took down one rogue regime, in other words, then it might suddenly find the rest of them—Iran, Libya, North Korea, Syria—much easier to deal with. A policy of regime change in one or two places, Rumsfeld predicted, would "strengthen political and military efforts to change policies everywhere."[84]

Crucial to all this was maintaining momentum. It was not enough for the United States just to win in places like Afghanistan and Iraq. U.S. forces had to win quickly and decisively, so as to show that they could execute multiple missions in rapid succession and thereby create fear and uncertainty in the minds of potential enemies. As one Pentagon planning document put it, the military needed "creative, unconventional operational concepts designed to shock, overwhelm, intimidate, and demoralize the enemy and affect the calculations of other foreign states and entities."[85] Long, grinding campaigns were out of the question—they would consume American resources, undercut the crucial implied threat of follow-on actions, and thereby create windows of opportunity rather than vulnerability for other rogue states. If the United States became bogged down in places like Iraq or Afghanistan, the effect might be to encourage dangerous behavior rather than restrain it. "Momentum is crucial," Rumsfeld wrote in May 2002, "and it [is] important to pursue the campaign relentlessly."[86]

Finally, invading Iraq was central to the third and last prong of Bush's strategy—dealing with the root causes of the threats the United States now faced. Winning the war on terror ultimately meant addressing the conditions that bred terrorist acts, and after 9/11 there was a strong sense that fostering an "antiterrorist global environment" required addressing the sociopolitical pathologies caused by highly repressive, authoritarian governments.[87] As early as mid-2002, for instance, Wolfowitz was arguing that there was a correlation between the use of political violence at home and abroad: "Every regime that I know of that supports terrorism as a matter of national policy also terrorizes their own people."[88] For his part, Bush framed the issue as one of combating the feelings of hopelessness and impotence that caused radical acts. "Stable and free nations do not breed the ideologies of murder," he said in 2003. "They encourage the peaceful pursuit of a better life."[89] Similarly, U.S. officials linked the issues of authoritarianism and WMD, on grounds that democratic regimes would be less likely to pursue secret weapons programs or transfer the tools of destruction to terrorist groups. Given these considerations, there seemed a compelling strategic rationale for encouraging representative government abroad, particularly in the autocracy-laden Middle East. As Bush put it, the United States had "a responsibility to promote freedom that is as solemn as the responsibility to protect the American people, because the two go hand-in-hand."[90]

It was a striking reversal for an administration that had earlier criticized the idea of spreading democracy by force, and for a president who had called for humility in foreign policy. Driven by the imperatives of the war on terror, Bush had now come to see democracy promotion as critical to U.S. national security. Given a sense of moral purpose by 9/11, he evinced an unshakable certitude in the universality of American values. As he wrote in his introduction to the 2002 *NSS,* "These values of freedom are right and true for every person, in every society—and the duty of protecting these values against their enemies is the common calling of freedom-loving people across the globe and across the ages." The United States, that document proclaimed, would wage the war on terror "by encouraging free and open societies on every continent."[91] And it would do so as a matter of urgent priority in the Middle East—in Rice's phrasing, "that one vital region of the world where all the challenges of our time come together, perhaps in their most difficult forms."[92]

Iraq was to be the essential catalyst in this regard. Democracy promotion was never the *primary* reason for invading Iraq, but it did play an important *reinforcing* role in the decision. For Bush in particular, removing Saddam promised not simply to end a malignant despotism and permit the democratization of Iraq itself; it also had the potential to set off a broader regional domino effect. "Clearly there will be a strategic implication to a regime change in Iraq," the president predicted.[93] In this scenario, a vibrant Iraqi democracy would, by its very example, undermine illiberal governments in Iran and Syria. The ambition in the White House, one official later wrote, was that "with American troops so close, the Iranian people would be emboldened to rise against the mullahs."[94] Likewise, Iraqi democracy would lead Palestinians to demand greater accountability from their own leaders, isolating proponents of violence and restarting the moribund peace process with Israel.[95] A free Iraq might even spark political changes in Saudi Arabia—home to fifteen of the nineteen hijackers on 9/11—and the smaller Gulf states. "A new regime in Iraq," Bush promised, "would serve as a dramatic and inspiring example of freedom for other nations in the region."[96] A paper drafted in the Pentagon in 2003 was equally optimistic:

> It would be difficult to overstate the importance of Coalition success in Iraq. If Iraq, with its size, capabilities and resources, is able to move

to a path of representative democracy, the impact in the region and the world could be historic—with good effects on Iranians, Syrians, Palestinians and others. Iraq could conceivably become a model—an example that a moderate Muslim state can succeed in the battle against extremism taking place in the Muslim world.[97]

One U.S. official put it even more succinctly: "The road to the entire Middle East goes through Baghdad."[98]

As these comments indicate, the democracy promotion issue was not just moralistic window dressing. Rather, it constituted a key—if secondary—part of the strategic rationale for war, one that was reflected in top-level documents like the *NSS*, and one that was firmly supported by the president himself. Bush went to war primarily to remove a perceived threat to U.S. security, Rice later wrote, but he was also convinced that "democracy in the Arab heartland would in turn help democratize the Middle East and address the freedom gap that was the source of hopelessness and terrorism." Or as Cheney saw it, the president's goal was "democracy in Iraq and trying to transform the region."[99]

But how could such transformative objectives be reconciled with the strategic imperatives of speed and flexibility? After all, the buildup for the 1991 Gulf War—which aimed only at expelling Iraqi forces from Kuwait—had required six months to complete, and the total coalition force in the region had numbered nearly eight hundred thousand troops.[100] Saddam's military had been degraded significantly since then, but an exercise conducted in the late 1990s had indicated that the United States would need at least four hundred thousand troops just to stabilize Iraq after a regime collapse.[101] In early 2003, Army Chief of Staff Eric Shinseki also estimated that pacifying the country would require "something on the order of several hundred thousand soldiers," a prediction that was generally consonant with reconstruction scenarios in other post-conflict situations.[102] If these assessments were correct, then war with Iraq might well be a long and arduous endeavor, one that absorbed American power rather than augmenting it.

Rumsfeld was far more confident, however, and with Bush's approval he pressed U.S. Central Command (CENTCOM) head Tommy Franks to adopt a less ponderous approach to toppling Saddam. The resulting war plan envisioned using the precise, overwhelming application of U.S. military power to initiate something like immaculate regime change. American forces would exploit speed, surprise, and pinpoint firepower not just to defeat Saddam with far fewer troops than had been used in 1991, but essentially to decapitate the Baathist regime without destroying economic infrastructure or the lower-level governmental apparatus—the police, the ministries, even the regular army—that could provide postwar order. "We'll do it with great precision," Bush said privately in February 2003. "We can win without destruction."[103] Once this was done, the United States could install a transitional Iraqi leadership that would hold elections, shepherd a grateful citizenry to democracy, and allow American forces to withdraw expeditiously. As Franks and Rumsfeld envisioned it, all but 25,000–30,000 U.S. troops (out of an invasion force of roughly 150,000) would leave Iraq by August or September 2003.[104] In theory, the pieces all fit together. The United States could once again achieve maximum effect at minimal cost; it could catalyze Iraqi democratization without sacrificing strategic momentum.

To a remarkable degree, then, the disarming and dismantling of Saddam's regime was the linchpin of the grand strategy that emerged after 9/11. It was the key initiative that linked the administration's immediate objectives to its longer-term goals, and it was the action that most embodied the strategic concepts that had taken hold in Washington. Indeed, from Bush's perspective, confronting Iraq had the potential to serve a number of important aims. It would destroy one of the world's most threatening regimes, terminate a persistent problem in the U.S. security posture, deprive Middle Eastern terrorist groups of a sponsor and patron, and offer an unmistakable warning to other rogue states. Overthrowing Saddam might even open up the region to the liberalizing currents that, U.S. officials believed, offered the best long-term protection against violent extremism. In a single bold stroke, war with Saddam would radically improve the geopolitical landscape of the Middle East and beyond, opening the door to a new era of global freedom and U.S. influence.

Whether the administration could actually pull it off was another matter. In hindsight, one can see that the Bush grand strategy rested on a series of interrelated ideas and assumptions, many of which were quite optimistic. There was a nearly boundless faith in the efficacy of American military might, a conviction that taking on Saddam would further rather than impede the broader war on terror, and a belief that the United States could transform Iraq without becoming mired *in* Iraq. There was the general presumption that action—even dramatic and potentially disruptive action—was now less dangerous than inaction, and that the aggressive employment of America's power would not undercut the country's international prestige. Above all, there was a sense that the international order was highly malleable, and that the United States could therefore use its immense strength to effect rapid, dramatic change. As Rumsfeld put it, the post-9/11 era provided "the kind of opportunities that World War II offered, to refashion much of the world."[105]

The liabilities of this mind-set would become evident in due course. At the outset, though, the president and his advisers were buoyed by a sense of mission and purpose. "We have an opportunity to restructure the world toward freedom," the president told advisers, "and we have to get it right."[106] For her part, Rice was confident that the administration had finally crafted an enduring post–Cold War grand strategy for the United States. The White House, she argued in 2003, had forged a framework "as coherent as any since the end of World War II."[107] It was a bold claim that Rice made—and one that would be severely challenged by the trials of implementation.

This was certainly the case in Afghanistan. The initial U.S. campaign there had been a striking success, one that scattered al-Qaeda and severely disrupted its operations. It was not long, though, before the victory began to sour. Franks declined to insert a blocking force into the mountains near Tora Bora in December 2001, a decision that may have allowed bin Laden and hundreds of his followers to escape into Pakistan. From there, they would gradually rebuild a badly damaged al-Qaeda over the next several years, and coordinate high-profile attacks in Spain, England, and other countries. Meanwhile, post-Taliban stability in Afghanistan proved fleeting. The newly established Afghan government was far too weak to exert authority over most of the country, and by mid-2002 the Taliban was regrouping and a low-grade insurgency developing. Its growth was fueled by critical failures of governance, reconstruction, and security, as well as by the quasi-official tolerance (even support) of elements of the Pakistani government. By 2006–7, the Taliban was once again ascendant in large swaths of southern and eastern Afghanistan, and a rejuvenated al-Qaeda was acting as a strategic ally of the growing insurgency. By 2008–9, the country seemed to be drifting into chaos. No longer was Afghanistan an inspiring first victory in the war on terror. As one of Rice's top advisers put it, the U.S. mission was "nearing catastrophic failure."[108]

In fairness to the Bush administration, there was nothing easy about the challenges that the United States faced in Afghanistan from late 2001 onward. It would have been logistically difficult and militarily risky to insert several hundred (or more) troops into Tora Bora, and there was no guarantee that doing so would have finished off bin Laden and al-Qaeda.[109] Nor was stabilizing postwar Afghanistan a simple task. The country had been ravaged by decades of conflict, it was plagued by ethnic cleavages and appalling underdevelopment, and it had a complete lack of functioning government institutions in late 2001. As one U.S. Agency for International Development (USAID) official later said, "We found a nation without a viable security apparatus, without courts, without functioning ministries; in short, a place where all the basic trappings of a nation-state had been obliterated."[110] To make matters worse, Pakistan never really terminated its relationship with the Taliban after 9/11, continuing to treat that group as a strategic asset even as it otherwise supported the U.S. war effort. Looking back, Pentagon comptroller (and Afghanistan reconstruction coordinator) Dov Zakheim has argued that the United States could have forged a secure, pro-Western Afghanistan, but he also acknowledges that doing so would have required "constant monitoring, constant assistance, constant attention."[111]

The problem was that Afghanistan never received this level of attention or assistance from the United States. In principle, the administration certainly treated Afghan reconstruction as a top-tier strategic interest. Undersecretary of Defense for Policy Douglas Feith, a key adviser to Rumsfeld and Wolfowitz, thought it axiomatic that Washington "would have to help put a new Afghan government on a stable footing—not least in order to keep Afghanistan from reverting to its former status as a terrorist safe haven."[112] The logic of the 2002 *NSS* ran in the same direction: "Weak states, like Afghanistan, can pose as great a danger to our national interests as strong states."[113] And in early 2002, Bush invoked the Marshall Plan as a model for U.S. policy. "We will stay until the mission is done," he declared. "We know that true peace will only be achieved when we give the Afghan people the means to achieve their own aspirations." The United States must therefore be "relentless" in pursuing the remnants of al-Qaeda and the Taliban; it must also help Afghans develop a "stable government," economic infrastructure, and an "education system ... which works."[114]

In practice, however, the U.S. commitment was far more limited than such statements implied. In 2002, Rumsfeld persuaded Bush to leave just eight thousand U.S. troops (supplemented by four to five thousand NATO troops) in Afghanistan, a country roughly the size of Texas. The U.S. force was assigned with hunting al-Qaeda, while the NATO contingent was tasked with patrolling Kabul; neither group had the capabilities or the mandate to provide security outside the capital or Kandahar (home to a large American base).[115] U.S. reconstruction assistance was also minimal compared to the enormity of Afghanistan's needs. Between 2002 and 2009, the Afghan reconstruction and humanitarian budget averaged roughly $1.75 billion, far less per capita than the United States had spent in places like Bosnia, Kosovo, or East Timor during the 1990s. According to James Dobbins, a U.S. envoy to Afghanistan in 2001–2, "Afghanistan was the least resourced of any American nation-building enterprise in 60 years."[116] Resource levels subsequently crept upward, but under Bush they never approached the military and economic commitments made to Iraq.[117] In effect, the administration declared that stabilizing Afghanistan was a top strategic priority, and then proceeded to treat the country as a secondary or even tertiary issue.

This seemingly contradictory approach drew criticism at the time. During late 2001 and early 2002, State Department officials like Powell and Dobbins had warned that post-conflict stability was improbable without a robust international troop presence, and they predicted that a minimalist policy would invite renewed violence and upheaval. "The strategy has to be to take charge of the whole country by military force, police or other means," Powell believed. Similarly, Dobbins and Policy Planning Staff director Richard Haass favored sponsoring a several-fold enlargement of NATO forces in Afghanistan, so as to bring that contingent up to a total of between twenty thousand and forty thousand peacekeepers. These troops would provide order in the major cities and perhaps eventually elsewhere as well. In doing so, the thinking went, they would lay the foundations of stability on which the new Afghan government could build.[118]

These views received a hearing within the administration in the months after the Taliban fell, but the president was ultimately persuaded by a different set of calculations. He and Rumsfeld feared that using too many foreign troops risked antagonizing Afghan sensibilities and triggering a popular backlash, and they thought that a small force backed by ample firepower would be more than sufficient to deal with a weakened, seemingly defeated foe. "We had routed the Taliban" with a light force, Bush later wrote, "and it seemed that the enemy was on the run."[119] More broadly, there remained a strong suspicion of nation-building activities within the Pentagon, a hostility based partly on ideology and partly on the indisputable fact that such exercises were often long, costly, and frustrating. The Afghan government must not "be allowed to become dependent on U.S. forces to stay in power," Rumsfeld wrote.[120] Based on these considerations, it seemed logical that the foreign military footprint should remain as light as possible, that U.S. forces should rapidly train Afghans to provide their own security, and that Washington should encourage the United Nations and other countries to assume as much of the reconstruction burden as possible.

This minimalist policy was powerfully reinforced by a final factor—Iraq. "It is very important to keep our focus on this war in Afghanistan," Wolfowitz said in late 2001. "It's a classic military mistake to leave a partially defeated enemy on the battlefield."[121] Yet this was just what happened. Initial planning for war against Iraq began in late September 2001, and according to Feith, a key rationale for using a small force in Afghanistan was to preserve "ample additional capacity to do other missions—whether for the war on terrorism or for other purposes."[122] This emphasis on "momentum"—on striking enemies in rapid sequence—was ubiquitous in Pentagon thinking during this period, and it encouraged a desire to transition away from major commitments in Afghanistan as quickly as possible.[123] Rumsfeld and Franks began reassigning planners to focus on Iraq before the Taliban was even defeated, and some observers have since argued that the resulting distraction caused the failure to trap bin Laden.[124]

There is no hard proof of this particular assertion, but the specter of a showdown with Saddam loomed large in the resource decisions that followed. According to one analyst, during early 2002 Rumsfeld repeatedly "made it clear that he wanted U.S. forces out of Afghanistan as quickly as possible," so as to free up capacity for dealing with Iraq. Likewise, Deputy Secretary of State Richard Armitage later recalled that "once it became clear the Taliban was likely to fall, senior Pentagon officials wanted to turn to Iraq as quickly as possible."[125] Armitage and Powell apparently objected to shifting focus so quickly, arguing that the administration should "consolidate Afghanistan" and perhaps wait until Bush's second term to confront Saddam.[126] Yet Bush and his inner circle saw Iraq as an issue that was too urgent to wait, and the administration's gaze began to shift accordingly.

The effects of this change were not long to be felt. As early as late 2001 and early 2002, the administration began to divert key tools like special-forces operatives, CIA paramilitary assets, Predator drones, and Rivet Joint reconnaissance aircraft from Afghanistan to the Persian Gulf.[127] And once the Iraq War began, it became all the more difficult to find the resources necessary to address the gradually deteriorating situation in Afghanistan, because the "light footprint" approach was essentially locked in place. Afghanistan now had to compete with Iraq not just for badly stretched ground forces, but for reconstruction dollars as well. Moreover, with the attention of senior policy makers increasingly moving from the former country to the latter, the top-level involvement necessary to galvanize the bureaucracy also waned.[128] U.S. commanders began to call Afghanistan the "underresourced war," and the head of strategic plans and policy at the Pentagon acknowledged that "the priority now for resources is going towards Iraq, at this time." "There are some things we could do and … we would like to do," he added, but "we can't take those on now until the resource balance shifts."[129] By the time that the "resource balance" began to shift in 2008–9, Bush's presidency was virtually over.

Reasonable observers can debate the wisdom of prioritizing Iraq over Afghanistan, just as they can argue about the costs and benefits of nation building in such a devastated society. Less debatable is that the resource con-straints imposed on the U.S. mission in Afghanistan made the strategic goal of that mission—a secure, stable country that was no longer hospitable to al-Qaeda or the Taliban—exceedingly difficult if not impossible to achieve. This was not fully apparent at the outset, for key parts of the country—particularly the cities—remained calm, and the Afghan political process seemed to be delivering excellent results. Over time, however, it would become evident that America's capabilities had come out of alignment with its objectives in Afghanistan, and that the prospects for lasting stability had suffered considerably as a result.

This dynamic was visible at the regional and international level, where the persistent under-resourcing of Afghan reconstruction had counterpro-ductive effects. Pakistan might have played a spoiler's role in Afghanistan regardless of what the Bush administration did, for key players in the Mush-arraf government saw their country's vital interests at stake in preserving a friendly western neighbor. Yet based on what is known about decision making in Islamabad, Washington's minimalist approach exacerbated this tendency by reinforcing Pakistani desires to hedge against a potential U.S. withdrawal by maintaining close ties to the Taliban. As one Policy Planning Staff (PPS) official wrote after leaving government in 2007, the Pakistani defense and intelligence establishment maintained "these connections less out of ideological sympathy and more out of strategic calculation: as a hedge against abandonment by other allies—especially the United States."[130] Nor did Bush's policy produce the level of broader international support that U.S. officials had expected. There was initially much international enthusiasm for Afghan reconstruction, and early donors' conferences were promising. As Zakheim soon discovered, however, foreign governments proved less eager to give once they understood the limits of America's own commitment—and once the Iraq War began to poison the diplomatic climate.[131]

The consequences within Afghanistan were no less pernicious. In many ways, the light footprint was the original sin of postwar reconstruction. From the start, low troop levels ensured that there was a power vacuum in some areas outside the capital, and forced the United States to rely on brutal, self-interested warlords in others. "The central government is not extended outside of Kabul," noted one observer in 2003.[132] These developments steadily undermined the legitimacy of the new government, while fostering the grievances and insecurity—not to mention the booming opium trade—that soon facilitated that Taliban resurgence. Similarly, bureaucratic delays and insufficient resources impeded economic reconstruction projects, dissi-pating much of the popular optimism that had accompanied the Taliban's fall and Bush's "Marshall Plan" speech. As Zakheim later noted, critical projects "moved at a pace that made a snail's gait look like a greyhound's."[133] Even where reconstruction programs did proceed, a lack of security allowed the Taliban to target aid workers, government officials, and other key individuals. The emerging Afghan security forces could not fill the void, and by late 2004, large zones of southern and southeastern Afghanistan were "effectively out of bounds to the assistance community."[134]

Finally, the light footprint complicated U.S. dealings with the Afghan government itself. It caused President Hamid Karzai to doubt both the extent and duration of American support, and encouraged him—like the Pakistanis—to engage in hedging against potential abandonment. As time went on, Karzai proved especially reluctant to move forward on sensitive issues like countering corruption and promoting more responsive governance—both of which tasks were essential to discrediting the growing insurgency, but both of which were also likely to alienate powerful constituencies within Afghanistan. "Karzai worries endlessly about how firm our support is," noted U.S. ambassador Ronald Neumann. "Our tough message on the need for strong leadership will be much [more] effective if we do more to meet Karzai's urgent needs."[135]

In fact, force levels did gradually increase from 2003 onward, and by the close of 2007 there were some forty-one thousand U.S. and NATO troops in Afghanistan.[136] But by this time, the momentum had clearly passed to the enemy, and coalition forces could do little more than conduct a holding action as the situation on the ground steadily worsened. With the war in Iraq having reached its critical phase, the units necessary for anything more ambitious were just not available. "It is simply a matter of resources, of capacity," JCS Chairman Michael Mullen acknowledged in 2007. "In Afghanistan, we do what we can. In Iraq, we do what we must."[137] To compensate for these deficiencies in manpower, U.S. commanders often relied on the energetic use of firepower and airpower—tactics that led to increased civilian casualties and further alienated a population that had already grown disillusioned with a seemingly ineffectual international presence. By mid-2008, it had become obvious to Lieutenant General Douglas Lute, Bush's "war czar" for Iraq and Afghanistan, that the conflict "was really going bad on us."[138] It remained to be seen whether the incoming Obama administration could right the situation.

In Afghanistan, then, the administration never devised a coherent course of action that squared the resource levels it was willing to commit with the strategic ends it sought to achieve. This outcome showed that there was a certain cognitive dissonance in U.S. policy, in the sense that Rumsfeld and other top officials failed to reconcile their aversion to nation building, on the one hand, with the imperative of post-conflict stabilization, on the other. Yet it also hinted that the ends of American grand strategy might have been too ambitious from the outset. Bush's strategy hinged on the premise that the United States could successfully undertake multiple interventions at once (or at least in very close sequence)—or more specifically, that invading Iraq would not distort other aspects of the war on terror. If this was not the case—and the under-resourcing of the Afghan effort strongly implied that it was not—then perhaps the real problem was simply one of grand strategic overreach.

The gap between aspiration and achievement was even larger in Iraq. There as in Afghanistan, the war went supremely well at first. Since late 2001, Rumsfeld and Franks had assembled a war plan based on "surprise, speed, shock, and risk," one designed to use dominant technology and maneuver to eviscerate Iraqi resistance and achieve "decapitation of government" with a minimal commitment of forces.[139] Notwithstanding some slight delays, this was basically what happened in March and early April 2003, as a force of just under 150,000 U.S. ground troops (augmented by 20,000 British troops) caused the disintegration of Iraqi resistance and the demise of the regime within three weeks of the initial invasion. Coalition forces raced north from Kuwait; special-forces units secured oil fields and neutralized Saddam's Scud missiles; American airpower pounded Republican Guard formations along the approaches to Baghdad; and armored "thunder runs" into the capital sealed the outcome. It was an awesome display of U.S. military power, and one that seemed to vindicate the highest ambitions of the Bush grand strategy.[140]

Then everything fell apart. First to go was the central strategic rationale for the war, as Saddam's vaunted WMD stockpiles turned out not to exist. Next to unravel was Iraq itself. Contrary to Pentagon expectations, the toppling of Saddam's regime caused a full-scale collapse of public order, complete with looting, violence, and a general climate of anarchy. Chaos soon turned to insurgency, with the United States and the new Iraqi authorities facing off against several groups—radical Shiites, Sunni rejectionists, and al-Qaeda-linked foreign fighters—who waged war against the emerging order and against each other, as well. The security situation deteriorated even as the new democratic political process progressed, and by mid-2006 the country was teetering on the precipice. Sectarian conflict had taken on civil-war dimensions, terrorists and insurgents effectively controlled much of western and central Iraq, and U.S. forces seemed powerless to secure the country or even mitigate the bloodshed. "Here on the streets of Baghdad, it looks like hell," wrote one observer. "Corpses, coldly executed, are turning up by the minibus-load. Mortar shells are casually lobbed into rival neighborhoods. Car bombs are killing people wholesale, while assassins hunt them down one by one." Bush had set out to create a beacon of democracy in the Middle East; he touched off a ghastly inferno of violence instead.[141]

The war proved deeply counterproductive in other ways, as well. It inflamed sectarian tensions throughout the Middle East and caused massive refugee flows to Syria and Jordan. It generated a geopolitical windfall for Iran, which exploited the fall of Saddam's hostile, Sunni-dominated regime to achieve unprecedented influence in Baghdad and beyond.[142] Most troubling of all, the invasion served as a lifeline for a battered al-Qaeda, providing that organization with a new generation of recruits and a new battlefield in the heart of the Middle East. As National Intelligence Council Chairman Robert Hutchings put it in 2005, Iraq had become a "magnet for international terrorist activity," while bin Laden had positioned himself as the ideological leader of a diffuse but deadly network of al-Qaeda franchises spanning the region.[143] One intelligence assessment completed in 2006 concluded that "the Iraq war has made the overall terrorism problem worse" by fueling Muslim anger and allowing jihadists to develop new skills and tactics.[144] Another study compared terrorist violence before and after the invasion, finding that the rate of fatal jihadist attacks actually increased sevenfold in the three-plus years following March 2003.[145] "New jihadist networks and cells, sometimes united by little more than their anti-Western agendas, are increasingly likely to emerge," warned CIA Director Michael Hayden in 2006.[146]

The Iraq War not only reinvigorated the global jihad after Afghanistan; it also detracted from U.S. efforts to respond to this challenge. Feith and other Pentagon officials had initially hoped to launch a full-scale ideological counteroffensive against al-Qaeda, one aimed at identifying moderate Muslim leaders—from teachers to clerics to politicians—and using U.S. resources to amplify their collective voice. "Our goal," Feith said, is "to make terrorism like genocide, the slave trade or piracy—the kinds of activities that no one who aspires to respectability can condone, let alone support."[147] But Feith's plan encountered bureaucratic resistance even prior to 2003, and Iraq made it nearly impossible to implement. The war poisoned U.S. relations with many of the moderates Feith had sought to court. "Muslims do not 'hate our freedom,' but rather, they hate our policies," the Defense Science Board reported in 2004. As a result, "The United States today is without a working channel of communication to the world of Muslims and of Islam."[148] Moreover, as

Iraq consumed massive amounts of top-level time and attention, it naturally detracted from the effort to mount a comprehensive assault on al-Qaeda. "If there is a global war on terror, why do we not have National Security Council meetings on that subject?" Rumsfeld asked in 2006. "Instead, we have meeting, after meeting on Iraq."[149]

Meanwhile, the war's effect on the regional political atmosphere was ambiguous at best. The toppling of Saddam's regime and the subsequent holding of national elections did initially catalyze hopes for the reform in the Middle East. "When I saw the Iraqi people voting three weeks ago," said one Druze leader in Lebanon, "it was the start of a new Arab world."[150] By 2005–6, a series of events—the Cedar Revolution in Lebanon, the holding of elections in the Palestinian territories, the initiation of minor electoral reforms in Egypt and Kuwait—seemed to herald a wave of democratic change. The momentum did not last, though, in part because democratic elections sometimes brought about adverse results—such as the triumph of Hamas in the Palestinian polls—and in part because Iraq's descent into sectarian chaos had a chilling effect on political liberalization in the region. Washington no longer had the credibility to push reforms on its authoritarian allies; opponents of democracy had a ready-made argument for why hasty change should be avoided. As one Saudi saying had it, "Why start fires on the inside when there are fires on the outside?" After a promising start, one RAND Corporation report concluded, the war had "stalled or reversed the momentum of Arab political reform."[151]

These results were not what Bush had envisioned, but they were hugely expensive nonetheless—in terms of presidential prestige and credibility; in terms of America's international reputation; in terms of the nearly 4,500 U.S. military deaths incurred during the war; in terms of the immense stresses that the conflict imposed on the armed forces; and not least of all, in economic terms. In 2003, Budget Director Mitch Daniels predicted that the war would cost $50 billion to $60 billion. By the time Bush left office, the direct costs alone were estimated to be some $860 billion (much of it paid for with borrowed money), with the indirect costs perhaps totaling $2 trillion to $3 trillion or even higher. Calculating solely on the basis of direct costs in inflation-adjusted terms, the price was enough to make Iraq the second-most expensive war in American history.[152] It was a staggering bill for an operation that was supposed to be quick and decisive, and it raised the question of how an administration so concerned with grand strategy could have gotten its centerpiece so terribly wrong.

One overarching answer is that the Bush administration never summoned the basic policy competence to execute its grand strategy effectively.

From the start, the U.S. effort to democratize Iraq was riddled with misjudgments and errors. The trouble started with the war plan itself: Pentagon officials severely underestimated how badly Saddam's removal would destabilize Iraqi society, and they neglected to use enough troops to secure the country or grapple with the nascent insurgency. U.S. authorities in Baghdad then fueled that insurgency by disbanding the Iraqi army and aggressively de-Baathifying the Iraqi government, pursuing radical economic reforms that threw countless civilians out of work, and reneging on the original pledge of an early end to the occupation. These and other problems, in turn, were exacerbated by the administration's failure to recognize its initial missteps and adopt an adequately resourced counterinsurgency strategy for nearly four years after the invasion. Stephen Hadley (Rice's deputy and then successor at the NSC) gave the administration a "D-minus" for policy execution, while another adviser noted that "mistakes were made at virtually every turn."[153] These errors were all the more glaring because many of the problems the U.S.-led coalition eventually faced were eminently foreseeable—and were foreseen, by academics, intelligence officers, and military and State Department officials. Iraq, in other words, was the disaster that plenty of people saw coming.[154]

In retrospect, many of the mistakes that plagued U.S. policy can be traced to critical deficiencies of planning and process. While it is not true that the administration "failed to plan" for the postwar period, what planning did occur was superficial and inadequate. As early as mid-2002, British officials had worried that "there was little discussion in Washington of the aftermath after military action."[155] The situation did not greatly improve in the months that followed. Because Bush did not wish to create the impression that war was inevitable at just the time he was seeking to build political and diplomatic support for the administration's position, he did not authorize the creation of the Office for Reconstruction and Humanitarian Assistance (ORHA, the organization responsible for overseeing the initial postwar administration of Iraq) until January 2003. "At a moment when he was trying to reassure world leaders that he hoped to avoid war," Feith later wrote, Bush "didn't want to have to explain why the Pentagon was creating a new organization to run Iraq." "The benefits of getting a centralized planning effort under way were obvious," Feith added, "but the President had many interests to balance."[156]

While this delay may have made sense in political and diplomatic terms, its policy consequences were disastrous. Because ORHA came into existence just weeks before the war started, it had virtually no time to coordinate anything other than basic humanitarian aid. Several other groups—in the State Department, the Joint Staff, CENTCOM, and Rumsfeld's office—did their own planning, but in the absence of centralized direction these efforts remained diffuse, uncoordinated, and even contradictory in their assumptions and goals.[157] CENTCOM planners assumed that civilian agencies would take the lead following the invasion, and therefore devoted remarkably little attention to postwar scenarios. Meanwhile, Rumsfeld's office failed to prepare contingency plans in case the postwar situation did not unfold as smoothly as expected, and Rumsfeld—along with Cheney—sought to marginalize State Department officials who offered more pessimistic appraisals.[158] The upshot of all this was a thoroughly dysfunctional climate in which dissenting views were sidelined or ignored, and a severe preparation deficit that left U.S. forces and civilian officials hopelessly behind the curve in the crucial early period following the invasion. There loomed "serious planning gaps for post-conflict public security and humanitarian assistance," three State Department officials wrote just prior to the war.[159] In these circumstances, it is hardly surprising that the resulting improvisations often made matters worse.

Nor was U.S. policy well served by the administration's decision-making and management style. On one level, Bush's self-image as a "gut player," his reliance on a small group of similarly hawkish advisers, and his reflexive aversion to second-guessing meant that there was frequently an absence of checks (either bureaucratic or intellectual) on poorly informed decisions.[160] On another level, his detachment from the *details* of policy—combined with Rice's failure to make the interagency process run smoothly—ensured that confusion and ambiguity marred American efforts. It was surely notable, for instance, that L. Paul Bremer—the U.S. proconsul in Baghdad—made the fateful decision to disband the Baathist military without subjecting that decision to any meaningful interagency or NSC review. (Rice first read of the decision in the newspaper.)[161] Similarly, as the situation deteriorated in the months following the invasion there remained persistent uncertainty as to how quickly the United States would hand over sovereignty to Iraqi officials, and how much authority it would give them in the interim. American policy thus followed a kind of zigzag pattern that alienated potential Iraqi allies and created widespread doubts as to the basic intentions and competence of U.S. authorities. "The failure to fashion a deliberate, systematic approach" to the political transition, Rumsfeld later wrote, "was among the more consequential of the administration."[162] Or, as Zakheim later put it, "Real leadership is not only about setting directions. It also has to encompass a management style that can see efforts through to successful completion."[163]

The problems caused by the *lack* of such a management style were compounded by the overweening sense of confidence that Bush and his top advisers brought to the entire Iraq affair. After 9/11, many top officials—the president chief among them—were driven by a sense they had embarked on a grand, noble venture to defeat looming threats and make the world a fundamentally better place. "This is what I was put on earth for," Bush said.[164] This mind-set was only reinforced by the initial campaign in Afghanistan, a striking victory that seemed to show that freedom could be implanted even on inhospitable ground and that it was the administration—and not critics who had warned of a quagmire—that best understood the dynamics of the war on terror. By early 2003, the president and those closest to him were infused with moral certitude and an immense faith in their own abilities. This attitude was apparent in Rumsfeld's jaunty and self-assured dealings with the media, and no less in Bush's private meetings with foreign leaders. "The only thing that worries me about you is your optimism," Spanish prime minister José María Aznar warned Bush just weeks before the invasion. "I am an optimist," the president replied, "because I believe that I'm right."[165]

Yet excessive confidence can lead to arrogance—even dogmatism—and thereby make effective policy less likely. One could see this tendency when Rumsfeld and Wolfowitz reflexively dismissed Shinseki's prediction that pacifying Iraq would require several hundred thousand soldiers, despite the fact that Shinseki was presumably the expert on the subject.[166] One could see the same tendency when Pentagon and White House officials derided those regional specialists who warned that democratizing Iraq would be a long, costly business. Expertise "is not a guarantee that you will have the right strategy or policy," Feith explained. "You see, the great experts in certain areas sometimes get it fundamentally wrong."[167] And one could see this same pernicious tendency in the way that the administration compounded all of its initial errors by stubbornly refusing to admit that things were not going well, that the insurgency was growing and evolving, and that policy—particularly troop levels—needed to be adjusted accordingly. "You know, confidence is part of winning," said Wolfowitz in late 2003. "We need to project confidence. And we have every reason to project confidence, because we've done a fantastic job."[168] The result of this confidence was not success, however—it was to create a disconnect between policy and reality and to delay corrective action until the situation had nearly become irretrievable.

The Iraq War thus confirmed that the Bush administration struggled with the implementation of grand strategy—the translation of high-flown strategic concepts into workable policies on the ground. Yet as in Afghanistan, the war also revealed that those strategic concepts were flawed to begin with. For in the final analysis, Bush's approach to Iraq reflected a set of ideas and assumptions that went to the intellectual core of his grand strategy. To the extent that the war exposed the fallacy of those ideas, it laid bare the deficiencies of the overall grand strategy as well.

Consider, first, the belief that democratizing Iraq was something that could be accomplished with a minimal investment of time, resources, and bloodshed. This idea was not merely peripheral to Bush's grand strategy. Rather, it was the crucial intellectual link between the desire for transformative results and the imperative of winning quickly, and it was ubiquitous at the top levels of the administration in 2002–3. Cheney predicted that U.S. troops would be hailed as liberators rather than occupiers; Bush evinced confidence that removing a tyrant was all that was necessary to unleash "the unstoppable power of freedom."[169] The same optimism was evident in the projection of a top USAID official that rebuilding Iraq would cost American taxpayers only $1.7 billion, and no less in a Pentagon war plan that envisioned the prompt empowerment of an Iraqi government and the speedy withdrawal of nearly all U.S. troops.[170] "I can't tell you if the use of force in Iraq today would last five days, or five weeks, or five months," Rumsfeld predicted, "but it certainly isn't going to last any longer than that."[171] In effect, the president and his key advisers seemed to believe that democracy was the natural order of things, and that it would spring forth organically if the United States simply toppled Saddam and got the process moving.

As Steven Metz has observed, however, the trouble with this line of thinking was that it confused the *beginning* of democratization with the *accomplishment* of democratization.[172] The former task was something that could be accomplished through a rapid, low-cost invasion aimed at decapitating the regime. The latter was a process that, in most countries, had historically been long, bloody, and tumultuous. As the CIA reminded administration officials in August 2002, the transformation of Japan and Germany after World War II had required "a generational change reinforced by the continuing presence of U.S. troops" over many years.[173] To think that it would be otherwise in Iraq—where there was no real history of democratic rule, where there were profound sectarian divisions and countless scores to settle, and where there were numerous spoilers lurking both internally and externally—was to guarantee disappointment. As CIA Director George Tenet later put it, "We followed a policy built on hope rather than fact."[174]

The Iraq War also undermined a second and related tenet of Bush's grand strategy—its emphasis on remaking the strategic environment through the rapid, precise application of U.S. military power. The Bush strategy rested on the idea that the Pentagon could use relatively small, agile forces not just to defeat opponents, but to win so resoundingly as to dishearten other potential enemies, and so cleanly as to avoid the messiness associated with traditional military occupations. It was a concept that flowed naturally from Rumsfeld's preexisting desire to "transform" the American military, and one that seemed most powerfully vindicated by the initial U.S. triumphs in Afghanistan and Iraq. "By a combination of creative strategies and advanced technologies," Bush said in 2003, "we are redefining war on our terms."[175]

What Iraq showed was that this vision was not so much incorrect as incomplete. The U.S. military was certainly capable of breathtaking speed in taking down Saddam's regime—in this respect, its performance proved every bit as impressive as Rumsfeld had promised. But as events soon demonstrated, accomplishing the administration's strategic aims in Iraq required going beyond the initial military victory and reconstructing a society that had been traumatized by years of dictatorship, war, and sanctions. It was a task that required a set of doctrines and capabilities very different from those used to topple the Baathist government, and one that by its very nature could not be accomplished quickly and decisively. It entailed just the sort of heavy, long-term ground presence that Rumsfeld and Bush had hoped to avoid, and it could not easily be reconciled with the desire to maintain maximum strategic dexterity and momentum. There was, then, a crucial tension at the heart of the Bush grand strategy: the type of victory that the administration sought to achieve in Iraq was incompatible with the type of war it wanted to wage. The U.S. experience from 2003 onward represented a slow, painful adjustment to that basic contradiction.

Third, events in Iraq cast doubt on the risk calculus underlying the administration's grand strategy. In 2002–3, even the foremost advocates of war were not blind to the fact that invading Iraq was potentially a risky endeavor. In an October 2002 memorandum, Rumsfeld listed dozens of things that might go wrong: "The Arab street could erupt.... Another rogue state could take advantage of U.S. preoccupation.... Oil disruption could cause international shock waves.... U.S. could fail to find WMD on the ground in Iraq and be unpersuasive to the world.... U.S. could fail to manage post-Saddam Hussein Iraq successfully.... Recruiting and financing for terrorist networks could take a dramatic upward turn," and so on.[176] This "parade of horribles" memo was a fairly accurate prediction of what soon transpired, but at the time it had no significant impact on Rumsfeld's recommendations or U.S. decision making. For all of these risks had to be balanced against the perceived danger of leaving Saddam in power. And as Cheney put it quite clearly in August 2002, the presumption within the administration was that in a post-9/11 world, "the risks of inaction are far greater than the risk of action." Saddam, in other words, had to be removed at any cost.[177]

This was an understandable position to take after 9/11, but it was also a problematic one. As the events of 2002–3 so graphically illustrated, it encouraged an intense focus on removing low-probability dangers—such as the chance that Saddam might provide terrorists with WMD—through courses of action that were fraught with multiple dimensions of risk. It led policy makers to emphasize and even exaggerate worst-case scenarios for what might happen if Saddam remained in power, while generally embracing best-case scenarios for what would happen if he were removed.[178] (Rumsfeld's memo was the exception that proved the rule—the defense secretary enumerated many of the risks the United States might face in Iraq, but then proceeded as though those risks were unimportant.) In sum, it led to a loss of strategic proportionality—the careful calculation of how much risk decision makers should run in order to avoid risk.[179] After all, even in a post-9/11 world there was inevitably a point where the risks of action did outweigh the risks of inaction; the course of the Iraq War demonstrated that U.S. policy might well have passed that point.

Finally, the Iraq War undercut a fourth key assumption of the Bush grand strategy: that the world would welcome the energetic, even aggressive use of U.S. military power. Particularly after 9/11, officials like Bush, Cheney, and Rumsfeld showed little patience for the idea that the United States needed to calibrate its policies lest it alarm or offend international opinion. "The legitimacy of our actions does not depend on how many countries support us," Rumsfeld wrote. "More nearly the opposite is true: the legitimacy of other countries' opinions should be judged by their attitude toward this systematic, uncivilized assault on a free way of life."[180] In the Bush administration, the guiding ethos was that leadership would produce legitimacy. If the United States acted boldly and assertively to confront the dangers facing the civilized world, then other nations would rally to America's side.[181]

The effect of U.S. policy toward Iraq, however, was quite the opposite. As Feith acknowledged in an August 2002 memo, the doctrine of "anticipatory self-defense" was "unsettling to many people," for it "appears to introduce a certain instability and unpredictability into the international system."[182] Sure enough, the run-up to war produced a serious split with many of Washington's closest NATO allies, who worried that a U.S. invasion might be more destabilizing than the threat it was meant to remove. "What do we do," asked German foreign minister Joschka Fischer, "when … our most important partner is making decisions that we consider extremely dangerous?"[183] The war itself incited a violent backlash from those Iraqis and foreign fighters who took up arms to contest the intrusion of American military might into the heart of the Muslim Middle East. And in general, the episode created a widespread sense that it might actually be the Bush administration, with its massive military power and its doctrines of unilateralism and preemption, that represented the greatest menace to global security. As Rice later said, "There were times that it appeared that American power was seen to be more dangerous than, perhaps, Saddam Hussein."[184] In this sense, the lesson of Iraq was that when the United States used its power *too* assertively, it risked provoking a backlash that would ultimately leave it less respected and less influential in the world.

America's travails in Iraq were thus not simply a matter of deficient process, planning, and implementation, though these were all major problems. Rather, those travails inhered in the audacious concepts that drove Bush's statecraft. At a time of immense threats and tantalizing opportunities, well-meaning people devised a grand strategy that proved to be deeply flawed. For that strategy was based on an overly optimistic view of what American power could accomplish (and how quickly and cleanly it could accomplish it), and an insufficient regard for the risks and costs involved. As the course of the Iraq War demonstrated, this could be a very dangerous combination. Bush had started out hoping for a dramatic victory in Baghdad; by the end of 2006 he was staring at the possibility of a catastrophic failure instead.

If Bush could rightly be blamed for letting matters reach this point, he deserved the credit for what happened next. At a time when domestic opinion was turning sharply against the war, and when even Rice, Rumsfeld, and the JCS opposed any deeper U.S. commitment, the president chose to "surge" nearly thirty thousand additional troops into the battle. (He also fired Rumsfeld and selected a new general, David Petraeus, to command U.S. forces in Iraq.) This decision, which drew on several overlapping policy reviews conducted in 2006, was meant to give U.S. forces the manpower necessary to conduct a proper counterinsurgency strategy in Baghdad and parts of Anbar Province, thereby breaking the cycle of violence in key geographic areas.[185] At the same time, the administration quietly lowered its long-term ambitions in Iraq, shifting the emphasis from a fully functioning democracy to a government that was stable and "reasonably representative." Americans had to be "minimalists," Petraeus explained in early 2008. "We're not after the holy grail on Iraq; we're not after Jeffersonian democracy. We're after conditions that would allow our soldiers to disengage."[186] The language was uninspiring, but the significance was profound: the administration was narrowing the gap between resources and objectives, and thereby making it more likely that the former could produce the latter.

By the end of 2007, the surge had begun to have the desired effect. The infusion of U.S. troops was not, by itself, a silver bullet. But it did provide additional security where it was needed most, and it interacted synergistically with several other key trends—strategic overreach by al-Qaeda in Iraq, which through its brutality alienated many of its former Sunni allies; the resulting "Sunni Awakening" that began in Western Iraq and then spread throughout the country; the decision by Shiite leader Muqtada al-Sadr to stand down his forces—to cause a remarkable shift in the military situation. Civilian fatalities fell from over fifteen hundred per month in August 2006 to five hundred in December 2007, and declined further after that.[187] U.S. and Iraqi forces inflicted severe blows on insurgent and terrorist groups, and the number of enemy-initiated attacks dropped by roughly 70 percent from June 2007 to February 2008.[188] To be sure, Iraq was still a plenty deadly place. Yet minimal stability had been achieved, the political process had been given a chance to function, and by the end of Bush's presidency a timetable had been set for the eventual withdrawal of all U.S. troops.

"War," Georges Clemenceau once remarked, "is a series of catastrophes that results in a victory." When Bush left office—and for several years thereafter—it was not yet clear whether this aphorism would ultimately apply to Iraq. That country had been pulled back from the abyss, but it was still best described as a semi-stable semi-democracy, one that had been terribly scarred by sectarian violence, and one whose long-term trajectory remained uncertain. And regardless of the eventual outcome in Iraq, U.S. involvement in that country had proved far more costly, frustrating, and in many ways self-defeating than the Bush administration had predicted. The war exacted a heavy toll in lives, money, and reputation, and it exposed a number of key weaknesses in the administration's grand strategy. Not least of all, there was the question of opportunity cost—the extent to which the preoccupation with Iraq had distracted American policy makers not just from Afghanistan and al-Qaeda, but from a host of other international problems as well.

The Iraq War may have dominated U.S. foreign policy from 2003 onward, but the rest of the world did not stand still and wait for the dust to clear. By the end of Bush's presidency, the United States was facing a slew of new and old challenges, ranging from the continually festering Israeli-Palestinian conflict, to emerging nuclear threats from Iran and North Korea, to problems posed by global climate change, to the rise of a potential peer competitor in China. Meanwhile, there was a widespread sense—both at home and abroad—that the United States was in decline and that American hegemony was not what it had only recently been. A common critique of the Bush grand strategy was that it actually made all of these problems worse—that by embroiling the United States in a costly conflict in Iraq, it left the country ill-positioned to deal with other pressing matters and ultimately undercut the very global primacy it was meant to sustain.[189] From this perspective, Bush's grand strategy had provided *too much* focus, and it had thereby distorted, rather than rationalized, the use of American power.

Like many critiques of the Bush administration, this one can easily be taken too far. It is not evident that the United States could have resolved some of these problems—the Israeli-Palestinian dispute, for instance—even if it had given them infinite time and attention. (Those who believe otherwise would do well to study the experience of Bush's predecessor.) Nor was the rise of China something that was within Bush's power to stop, for that phenomenon had primarily to do with explosive economic growth and its logical geopolitical consequences. In these regards, a myopic grand strategy was hardly the chief culprit in the difficulties facing the United States. And in a broader sense, those difficulties were frequently exaggerated by domestic and international commentators alike. American power had certainly declined relative to that of potential competitors during the Bush years, but the United States still retained far more diplomatic, economic, military, and even ideological influence than any other nation in the world.[190]

One also has to keep in mind that the Iraq War did not prevent the Bush administration from doing a number of things very well. The president and his advisers developed tools like the Proliferation Security Initiative, which proved a valuable asset for combating the spread of WMD components. The administration extended timely diplomatic support to democratic activists in countries like Ukraine and Lebanon, and it concluded a series of important free-trade agreements with partners from Central America to South Korea. Perhaps most significantly of all, the Bush team conducted a successful diplomatic opening to India, a rising power in an increasingly crucial part of the world. That process culminated in a landmark bilateral agreement that effectively brought New Delhi out of the "nuclear ghetto," and it raised the prospect of closer strategic collaboration in years to come. In these and other cases, the charge that the Bush administration was completely consumed by Iraq does not ring true.

Finally, it has to be noted that the Iraq War did produce at least some of the positive spillover effects it was meant to generate. This was most notably the case in Libya, where months after the invasion the Qaddafi government agreed (among other things) to terminate its nuclear and chemical weapons programs. There were numerous motives behind this decision, which came as part of a negotiating process that had been in train for years before 9/11. Yet it seems that the Iraq War sent a powerful signal that reinforced

Qaddafi's motives for seeking an agreement and accelerated the timetable thereof. "U.S. credibility on the use of force was a factor," two scholars have written. The Bush administration sealed the deal by promising an expanded economic and diplomatic relationship, and pledging that the "regime change" option would be taken off the table if Qaddafi's WMD programs were scrapped.[191] The episode constituted an example of how invading Iraq could facilitate successful coercive diplomacy toward other rogue regimes, and it showed that in this case at least, the logic of Bush's grand strategy was valid.

Unfortunately, the administration could not replicate this achievement in dealing with the more important—and more problematic—cases of Iran and North Korea. Bush's grand strategy did not deter the two remaining members of the "Axis of Evil" from pursuing nuclear weapons. If anything, it seemed to have encouraged them to do so. When Bush left office, Iran was proceeding determinedly toward the uranium enrichment capability necessary to build a bomb, while North Korea had apparently constructed a small number of nuclear weapons and actually tested one in 2006.[192] It was proving "not only difficult, but possibly impossible" to "impose the leverage on Iran and/or North Korea required to cause them to discontinue their nuclear programs," Rumsfeld conceded just days before the 2006 test.[193] Bush had pledged that the United States would not allow the world's most dangerous regimes to develop the world's most dangerous weapons, yet in the end, he was unable to prevent this from happening.

Although neither Tehran nor Pyongyang had ever been easy to handle, there was real truth to the charge that the Bush administration worsened its own predicament in dealing with these two governments. In Iran's case, it initially seemed as though Bush might be on the verge of a major nonproliferation success. Iranian leaders had been pursuing a diplomatic dialogue with Washington since 9/11, and the shock of the rapid U.S. victory in Iraq moved representatives of the regime to propose comprehensive bilateral talks on everything from Tehran's nuclear program to its support for Hezbollah and Hamas. Unfortunately, Bush and his top advisers declined even to explore this overture, and they soon closed the diplomatic channel that had been opened after 9/11.[194]

This decision owed partly to skepticism regarding the authenticity of the Iranian offer, which went far beyond anything previously proposed by the key players in Tehran. Yet leading Iran experts have disputed this interpretation, and it is hard to see what would have been lost by at least seeking to draw Tehran out on the proposal. Fundamentally, it seems that the major obstacle to negotiation was a sense that the United States simply did not need to negotiate. It was apparent, NSC staffer Flynt Leverett later recalled, that "the Bush administration was not interested in a broader, strategic dialogue with Iran." Likewise, another administration insider later noted that Cheney and other hawks believed that the Iranian regime "was on the brink," and in the heady days after the triumph in Iraq they thought that the United States should seek regime change—or at least unilateral concessions—rather than a diplomatic give-and-take. As Cheney put it in another context, "We don't negotiate with evil, we defeat it."[195]

This approach fit nicely with the forward-leaning, pro-democracy themes of Bush's grand strategy, but it proved ill-suited to advancing U.S. interests. Hopes for a democratic revolution in Iran soon proved unfounded, and as the Iraq War turned into a quagmire, U.S. leverage vis-à-vis Tehran declined dramatically. In essence, the Bush administration had denied Iran any possibility of an improved bilateral relationship, but it had done so just as it began to lose the coercive strength that would make a harsher policy credible—and just as the Iraq War had also opened up major fissures between the United States and other members of the UN Security Council. In these circumstances, it is hardly surprising that the Iranian leadership subsequently resolved to move ahead with the uranium enrichment program. As Leverett writes, "Without the prospect of a strategic opening to the United States, Iran resumed converting raw uranium into gas in April 2005 … and began enriching small amounts of uranium to low levels" in August.[196] The administration eventually adapted by supporting multilateral negotiations with Tehran while also holding out the prospect of sanctions, but in the meantime the Iranian program had begun to show significant progress, and the likely parameters of any future agreement had shifted considerably.

U.S. policy toward North Korea proved equally problematic. Despite what is sometimes alleged, Bush's hard-line stance toward Pyongyang in 2001–2 did not precipitate the breakdown of the Agreed Framework negotiated during the 1990s, for Pyongyang had apparently been cheating on that accord for years.[197] Yet it is true that the administration's uncompromising approach, when combined with its simultaneous preoccupation with Iraq, left it no good response to what was essentially an effort at nuclear breakout by the North from late 2002 onward. After North Korea reactivated its plutonium reprocessing facility and withdrew from the nuclear Non-Proliferation Treaty, Bush refused to conduct bilateral negotiations with Pyongyang on grounds that doing so would mean yielding to nuclear blackmail. The president frequently framed this argument in moralistic terms, arguing that the despotic North Korean regime was unworthy of engagement. "I loathe Kim Jong Il," he said. "I've got a visceral reaction to this guy, because he's starving his people." "Either you believe in freedom … and worry about the human condition, or you don't," he commented at another point.[198] Similarly, administration hawks like Cheney and Rumsfeld believed that the North Korean regime was on the verge of collapse, and they favored increasing the pressure through economic isolation, coercive diplomacy, and possibly even the threat of military action.[199]

As with Iran, however, the North Korean regime was more resilient than U.S. officials had hoped. And with the United States obviously focusing its military energies on Iraq in late 2002 and early 2003, it was nearly impossible to send credible coercive signals to Pyongyang. There were some faint signs of progress in March and April, after the United States thrashed Saddam far more quickly than most observers had thought possible, but the momentum soon faded as American forces became bogged down in the growing insurgency. As NSC official Michael Green later wrote, North Korean intransigence was "almost certainly" influenced by "the deteriorating situation in Iraq, which undercut the indispensable coercive element in U.S. diplomacy."[200] Robert Joseph, a leading administration hard-liner on the issue, put it more bluntly: "If you are looking for the place where Iraq really distracted them, where we really paid the price, it was North Korea."[201] During Bush's second term, the administration entered into direct talks with Pyongyang within the framework of six-party negotiations involving a range of regional players, but by this time the North had effectively completed its nuclear breakout and reportedly assembled a small arsenal of bombs.[202]

There was thus good reason to think that Bush's grand strategy was counterproductive when it came to dealing with countries like Iran and North Korea. By including these regimes in the Axis of Evil, by shunning direct negotiations and semi-openly hoping for their overthrow, and above all by demonstrating that the United States would actually use force to take down Saddam's government, the Bush administration sent the unmistakable signal that *only* nuclear weapons could guarantee Iranian or North Korean security. (The National Intelligence Council had predicted as much in 2003, warning that after a U.S. invasion of Iraq, "States with developmental WMD programs would try to increase the secrecy and pace of those programs with the hope of developing deterrent capabilities before they could be preempted."[203]) Yet by committing U.S. military resources to what turned out to be a costly, draining war, the administration also lost the strength and the coercive credibility that were essential if such a confrontational policy was to have any chance of succeeding. Bush's policy deprived the United States of both the carrot and the stick, and the result was probably to encourage rogue-state proliferation rather than restrain it.

The Bush grand strategy also had unfortunate consequences with respect to the broader challenge of protecting U.S. primacy. To be sure, the Iraq War did not cause the growth of Chinese power, nor did it prevent the administration from establishing generally productive relations with Beijing on a wide range of issues. Yet if one of the administration's goals was to prevent the eventual rise of a peer challenger, then Iraq likely did more to undermine that objective than advance it. During 2001–2, key Pentagon officials like Andrew Marshall had argued that the United States needed to "begin shift of focus towards Asia" to deal with the prospect of an emergent China, but the United States soon found itself embroiled in the Middle East instead.[204] Chinese observers interpreted Washington's subsequent travails as proof that "America's sun is not bright," and as an opportunity to expand Beijing's diplomatic influence in East Asia while the United States was more distracted and unpopular than at any time since Vietnam. The events of 9/11 and their aftermath, notes a prominent China scholar, constituted a "strategic windfall" for Beijing.[205] From this perspective, Beijing's conspicuous effort to maintain good relations with the United States during the Bush years looks less like the product of savvy American diplomacy and more like a shrewd Chinese effort to keep a low profile while building economic, military, and diplomatic influence for the long term.[206]

And sure enough, the military balance in the Far East was shifting during Bush's tenure. By one measure, Chinese military spending increased by 189 percent in real terms during the first decade of the twenty-first century. The Chinese government invested heavily in anti-access / area denial capabilities such as cruise missiles, antiship ballistic missiles, antisatellite capabilities, modernized fighter-bombers and strike aircraft, and diesel-electric and nuclear submarines—precisely the weapons needed to hold U.S. forces at bay in a crisis over Taiwan or other regional contingencies.[207] In line with these acquisitions, the People's Republic was also developing strategic concepts meant to exploit American operational vulnerabilities and offset U.S. power projection capabilities in East Asia. According to a 2008 Defense Department report, "The PLA appears engaged in a sustained effort to develop the capability to interdict or attack, at long ranges, military forces—particularly air or maritime forces—that might deploy or operate within the Western Pacific."[208]

This buildup had begun well before Bush became president, and in a broad sense there was probably nothing his administration could have done to retard the general trend. Yet three leading observers have argued that the Iraq War "likely triggered a steady acceleration in the PRC's military budget increase" by stoking anxieties about potentially aggressive American behavior and providing a ready justification for ramped-up defense spending.[209] More concretely, U.S. military involvement in the Middle East made it far more difficult for the Pentagon to respond effectively. As one scholar wrote in 2007:

> Iraq has fundamentally reshaped the priorities for near-term technology development and strategic innovation and in doing so has disadvantaged the Pentagon's ability to maintain its lead over China. Rather than addressing critical needs in anti-submarine warfare (ASW) to respond to the frenetic pace of Chinese innovation and deployment, the Pentagon's attentions are focused on jamming garage door remote controls and cell phones that trigger buried artillery shells. Rather than invest in advanced fighter aircraft able to deploy far from China's sizable short-range ballistic missile arsenal, the Pentagon has had to bolt armor plates on its transport trucks.[210]

This diversion of resources did not cause any failures of deterrence during the Bush years, but it did mean that the U.S. military edge around Taiwan and elsewhere in East Asia had been significantly narrowed by the time he left office. "China is reshaping the military order in Asia," one Defense Department official warned in late 2008, "and it is doing so at our expense."[211]

The administration's grand strategy took a toll on U.S. power in other ways, as well. As noted above, the wars in Iraq and Afghanistan came at a massive financial cost, one that contributed—along with increased domestic expenditures and tax cuts—to an explosion of federal debt between 2001 and 2009. By the end of the Bush years, notes one historian, "U.S. financial strength and flexibility had been seriously eroded."[212] No less important was the damage to America's international prestige, an intangible but nonetheless critical component of overall national power. As Feith had written in 2002, "There is a price to be paid if U.S. actions are at odds with the civilized world's view of proper behavior in the world."[213] And then there was the psychological impact—not just on members of the armed forces, but on American society as a whole. Predictions of imminent decline were often exaggerated in 2008–9, but Bush's grand strategy had laid bare the limits of U.S. power and sapped the optimism that had characterized the post–Cold War era. It was hardly a coincidence that this period saw a marked rise in calls for overall geopolitical retrenchment. The Bush years had proved "exhausting" for many Americans, Rice later acknowledged; there was a widespread feeling that the country was simply "out of steam."[214]

In the end, Bush's grand strategy carried a fairly heavy price in the broader scheme of U.S. foreign policy. The administration had originally chosen to focus on Iraq not just because of the threat that Saddam seemed to pose, but because it expected that transforming that country would have positive strategic ramifications throughout the Middle East and beyond. When this high-risk endeavor went bad, however, it was largely the *negative* externalities that flowed far and wide. Bush had initially thought of the Iraq War as the keystone of an ambitious program for using and extending American primacy; it turned out to be more of a millstone instead.

When Bush left office in early 2009, there was a general domestic consensus that his grand strategy had failed. The president had been dogged by abysmal approval ratings for much of his second term, and allegations that he had overtaxed and squandered American power were ubiquitous. Some expert observers even argued that Bush's experience had shown that the entire concept of grand strategy was foolish. The president had articulated a bold, overarching vision of American policy, they pointed out. Did not the ensuing grief prove that such "grand theory" should be avoided altogether?[215]

Caution is surely necessary in issuing such sweeping judgments. It is not unusual for presidential reputations to improve as time passes and partisan controversies fade, and it is possible that Bush will benefit from such a reevaluation in the decades to come. After all, his administration was not without its accomplishments: the toppling of Saddam and the Taliban, the blows inflicted on al-Qaeda after 9/11, the dismantling of Libya's WMD capacity, the strategic opening to India, and others. Similarly, the president's more prosaic counterterrorism policies—intelligence sharing, increased funding for homeland security, emphasis on greater coordination between agencies at home and abroad, and other initiatives—probably contributed to the surprising avoidance of post-9/11 attacks on the United States, although the extent to which this is true cannot yet be ascertained.[216] Finally, depending on the future course of events in Iraq and the broader Middle East, the surge decision of 2006–7 may eventually come to be seen as an example of the courageous statesmanship to which Bush aspired.

Unfortunately, none of this is likely to obscure the generally disappointing trajectory of Bush-era grand strategy. Bush and his advisers crafted that grand strategy in the belief that the United States could wield its extraordinary power not simply to defeat the perpetrators of 9/11, but to achieve far-reaching changes in the global security environment. In the event, however, the performance never lived up to the promises. Bush's grand strategy lent itself not to the transformative outcomes the president had envisioned, but to a variety of pernicious consequences from Afghanistan to Iraq and beyond. By the time the president left office, the grand ambitions of 2001–2 were a distant memory. The administration was often struggling just to deal with the ramifications of its own actions and mistakes; American power seemed less imposing than at any time since the end of the Cold War.

The course of Bush's presidency therefore demonstrated two key points about the doing of American grand strategy. First, Bush's experience confirmed the truism that there is a long road between the articulation of a grand strategy and the successful implementation of that strategy. After 9/11, the Bush team had relatively little trouble formulating a broad, inspiring vision of where it wanted to go. Unfortunately, it could never actually get there. The administration encountered immense problems relating means to ends, overcoming unexpected obstacles, reconciling its various goals with one another, and otherwise turning its bold ideas into workable, day-to-day courses of action. These failures stemmed partly from inadequacies of planning and process in the execution of policy, and partly from deeply rooted conceptual flaws within the grand strategy itself. Either one of these shortcomings would have been highly problematic on its own; together, they made a strategy that Rice had touted as the most coherent since World War II seem anything *but* coherent in practice.

Second, while the Bush years did not necessarily discredit the idea of grand strategy writ large, they did show that a flawed or overambitious grand strategy could be quite dangerous. The Bush administration's basic problem was not an absence of big ideas or long-range thinking; the problem, rather, was that the ideas were simply too big from the start. Bush's grand strategy was too optimistic in its goals, too demanding in its requirements of American power, and too insensitive to essential issues like risk and cost. In these circumstances, grand strategy had fundamentally perverse effects: it led not to the rational and effective use of American power, but to the overextension, distortion, and even dissipation thereof. Even for the world's strongest nation, there was great peril in trying to be too grand.

Conclusion

Grappling with Grand Strategy

Grand strategy is an essentially optimistic undertaking. It rests on the idea that states can combine vision and rationality with power; it holds that leaders can salvage order from chaos and impose their own meaning on events. This is what Henry Kissinger meant when he wrote about rescuing "an element of choice from the pressure of circumstance."[1] As Kissinger understood, grand strategy involves more than matching means and ends, or overcoming one enemy or another. At its core, grand strategy is about asserting a degree of control and coherence in one's dealings with a very unruly world.

For precisely this reason, however, grand strategy is also an inherently fraught discipline. For in grappling with grand strategy, even capable leaders face a variety of potentially confounding factors: the limits of their own intelligence and foresight, the persistent complexity and volatility of world affairs, the actions of adversaries and even allies, the vagaries of bureaucracy and politics, and others. Throw in the pressure-cooker environment in which grand strategy usually has to be shaped and executed, and it is little wonder that the concept often meets with such skepticism. Grand strategy, writes one leading scholar and former policy maker, is but an "elusive holy grail."[2]

The foregoing chapters demonstrate both the promise and pitfalls of grand strategy. In one sense, they show that grand strategy is neither a chimera nor an elusive holy grail, but rather an immensely demanding task that talented policy makers have still sometimes managed to do quite well. One could certainly say this about the Truman and Reagan administrations, both of which were able to form keen strategic insights about the world they confronted, and then to translate those insights into policies that harnessed American power in support of great and worthy goals. In Truman's case, the result was to stabilize the Western world and give the United States lasting advantages in its struggle with the Soviet Union; in Reagan's case, the payoff was to help end the Cold War in a more decisive and peaceful manner than virtually anyone had thought possible. If these are not examples of successful grand strategy, then it is hard to think of anything that would be. And in a more limited sense, while the Nixon-Kissinger grand strategy could not ultimately meet the standards its creators imposed, it nonetheless demonstrated how creative long-range thinking and determined political leadership could deliver real benefits for a country in distress.

Yet if these cases testified to the potential of the grand strategic endeavor, they also underscored the inescapable difficulty thereof. For Truman and Reagan alike, grand strategy was a thoroughly messy and problematic affair. Both administrations had to learn and adapt in order to find the right mix of policies that would advance their grand strategic aims, and both administrations encountered serious trouble along the way. Truman and his advisers constantly labored to match means and ends, harmonize politics and policy, and contain Soviet influence without overheating the Cold War. In general, they succeeded more than they failed, but the failures still included an expanded Korean War, the beginnings of a quagmire in Southeast Asia, and other troubling legacies. More than three decades later, Reagan's intense focus on waging and ending the Cold War ultimately produced terrific results in U.S.-Soviet relations. But it also forced the United States to run great risks along the way, and it caused negative second-order consequences in the economic, moral, and geopolitical realms. Even where American grand strategy was largely effective, U.S. officials still struggled mightily with the challenges it posed.

And there were, of course, cases in which well-meaning and intelligent policy makers could not even manage this much. During the 1970s, Nixon and Kissinger eventually ran up against the limitations of their strategy and the difficulties of the environment they faced, and their heroic style of statecraft proved to be pernicious as well as productive. After 9/11, the Bush administration's foray into grand strategy was even more disappointing. It led not to the transformative triumphs the president and his advisers had envisioned, but to mismanaged wars in Iraq and Afghanistan, a crisis of America's international legitimacy, and a degree of strategic overstretch not seen since

Vietnam. In fact, the Bush years were in many ways a demonstration of how badly an overambitious grand strategy could backfire. The period showed, in pungent fashion, how flawed assumptions and incompetent implementation could shatter a grand design.

Taken together, these four cases illustrate the central dilemma of American grand strategy: the fact that it is an essential and potentially very rewarding undertaking, but one that is damned hard to get right. To the extent that these administrations—particularly Truman and Reagan, and to a lesser extent Nixon-Kissinger—succeeded in dealing with the challenges they confronted, it was largely because they were able to situate individual policies within relatively coherent and well-considered grand strategic frameworks. In these instances, grand strategy proved indispensable to organizing national goals and interests, bringing diverse initiatives into concert with one another, and generally providing a degree of order and direction to foreign policy. Much as Clausewitz argued that theory and planning could help military leaders overcome the pressures of crisis, grand strategy let American officials stay centered amid a cacophony of world events.

Yet if the cases surveyed here demonstrate enough success to conclude that grand strategy is both possible and useful, they reveal enough travail to be certain that it is a highly exacting proposition. In the more costly aspects of Truman and Reagan-era foreign policy, in the tribulations of Nixon and Kissinger, and most of all in the disappointments and failures of the Bush administration, one can see so many of the conceptual, bureaucratic, political, and geopolitical issues that frequently complicate the undertaking. The history of these administrations shows that even talented officials have struggled to balance commitments and capabilities, to manage the domestic and bureaucratic politics of foreign policy, to maintain the upper hand in competitive relationships, and to keep pace with the international changes occurring around them. Likewise, this history demonstrates that ambitious visions are worthless without competent implementation, and that there are sometimes just limits to what a creative grand strategy can accomplish in an adverse context. Good grand strategy may not be altogether illusory, then, but it can still prove frustratingly elusive. It is not necessarily a pipe dream, but it is by no means a panacea, either.

To some extent, grand strategy can even be a double-edged sword. The fact that grand strategy provides focus is usually a good thing, but the flip side of focus can be distortion or myopia. To put it another way, it is hard to see how grand strategy improved Truman's policy toward Indochina or Kissinger's approach to South Asia and Angola; the result, instead, was to *lessen* U.S. effectiveness in dealing with complicated local issues. In the same vein, Reagan's single-mindedness was both an asset and a liability for his statecraft, and Bush's overriding emphasis on Iraq almost certainly caused more problems than it solved. And as mentioned previously, this last case also underscores another potential drawback of grand strategy—that when it becomes unrealistic or grandiose in nature, it can end up having decidedly counterproductive effects.

Indeed, the more one studies grand strategy, the more one can see that the very concept is beset by a number of fundamental tensions—between the quest for coherence and the reality of complexity; between the need for foresight and the fact of uncertainty; between the steadiness and purpose that are necessary to plan ahead, and the agility that is required to adapt on the fly. One can see similar tensions between the opposing virtues of confidence and modesty that grand strategists must combine, and between the decisive authority that statesmen like Kissinger have sought to wield and the democratic accountability that the American system appropriately expects. One can even see tensions between the audacity that is required to think in big, bold strokes, and the "small ball" technical competence that is needed to turn these ideas into reality.

The list could easily go on, but the underlying point remains: these are the sort of tensions that can probably never be resolved entirely, so the best one can do is to mitigate them to the extent feasible. No administration will ever achieve flawless strategic vision or seamless coherence of policy, especially on anything like a day-to-day basis. The real question is whether American leaders can achieve enough vision and enough coherence—enough of the time—so that the United States can protect its vital interests and accomplish its basic purposes. Grand strategy, in this sense, can never be a game of perfect; it can only be a game of good enough.

Looking to the future, there is little reason to think that grand strategy will become any easier or, for that matter, any less consequential. The United States now confronts an increasingly fluid and multidimensional international environment. There is no longer any overarching threat to focus American energies, but rather a variety of lesser but still worrying challenges—international terrorism, the rise of China, nuclear proliferation, and many others—that compete for attention and resources. Those resources, in turn, seem far scarcer than they did just a decade ago. These factors will both demand and complicate the doing of grand strategy; the fact that this task will have to be performed in a highly polarized political climate will only add to the challenge. The United States will certainly need a coherent grand strategy in the coming years, but whether it can produce and sustain one remains to be seen.

What can be said is that grand strategy will have to be approached with a mixture of discipline, flexibility, and humility. American officials will need the discipline to work through problems systematically, to understand the limits and possibilities of U.S. power, and to keep an eye on the long term in dealing with the immediate. They will need the flexibility to change tack when policy proves flawed or rigid. Not least of all, they will need the humility to understand the limits of the grand strategic endeavor and thus to keep their intellectual balance when things go awry. Cultivating these qualities will not allow American officials to wholly transcend the tensions within grand strategy, but it may, perhaps, lessen the unhappy effects.

What follows are ten basic suggestions for how American leaders might approach this challenge.[3] These suggestions are not intended to provide detailed answers to specific policy issues, or even to advocate any particular grand strategy. (The debate on these subjects is already quite lively.) Rather, they are meant simply as an intellectual took kit for the aspiring grand strategist, as a set of essential guidelines for thinking about the endeavor and the dilemmas it entails.

1. *There is no good alternative to grand strategy.* Even as grand strategy has often seemed all the rage in recent years, a number of prominent observers have suggested that the concept is an anachronism. In an era in which there is no overriding threat around which to organize American policy, they contend that grand strategy has become a quixotic and even pernicious pursuit. "Given the divisions and uncertainties of the contemporary environment," notes former PPS director Stephen Krasner, "it is impossible to frame a successful grand strategy."[4] Proponents of this idea often cite the Bush years as evidence of their claims. Bush's search for "grand theory" proved "fruitless, overrated, and even dangerous in the complex world of the 21st century," write James Goldgeier and Derek Chollet; future administrations should avoid this quest altogether.[5] Because Goldgeier, Chollet, and Krasner each have high-level policy-making experience, their skepticism on this count is all the more striking.[6]

And in some ways, the argument that these and other critics make seems appealing. The difficulties and drawbacks of grand strategy are undeniable, and there is no question that Bush's particular grand strategy had numerous perverse effects. Moreover, the past few years have been replete with events that have challenged long-standing assumptions, upended existing policies, and sent strategic planners back to the drawing board—the Iraq War, the Arab Spring, the global financial and economic crisis, and others. Against the backdrop of all this upheaval, the bearish view of grand strategy seems plausible enough.

Upon closer analysis, however, this view becomes less persuasive. For start-ers, the failures of the Bush administration do not necessarily discredit grand strategy writ large; they simply show that Bush's own grand strategy was not a good one. More importantly, the premise upon which many of these critiques are based—that the security environment is infinitely more complex now than it was during the Cold War—is debatable. Admittedly, the Soviet threat did concentrate the attention of U.S. policy makers, and it provided a "north star" of sorts in debates on grand strategy. But it most certainly did not exempt American officials from having to deal with complexity, unpredictability, or nasty strategic shocks. Such developments were really the norm rather than the exception during the Cold War, from the end of the U.S. atomic monop-oly and the fall of Nationalist China in 1949, to the emergence of the Third World during the 1950s and 1960s, to the collapse of détente in the mid- and late 1970s, and so on. As one recent article puts it, "Complexity, or the perception of complexity, is the timeless companion of the national security strategist."[7] Grand strategy may be hard today, but it was never easy in the past.

Indeed, while no one should minimize the challenges of doing grand strat-egy in the contemporary security environment, it is difficult to see how deliberately *avoiding* grand strategy offers a superior alternative. The Clinton years showed some of the drawbacks inherent in a diffident approach to grand strategy, from ends-means gaps to rapid policy reversals to difficulties in main-taining a clear hierarchy of priorities. More broadly, the "strategic nihilism" that some observers urge is a counsel of despair rather than a constructive course of action.[8] Refusing to do grand strategy will not allow the United States to escape the dilemmas that make that task so difficult; it will only exacerbate the confusion and contradictions within American policy. And the more daunting the conditions, the *higher* the premium one should place on the intellectual legwork associated with grand strategy: setting priorities, thinking systematically about means and ends, and establishing general strategic ideas that can serve as conceptual anchors amid the geopolitical storms.

Obviously, none of this will remove the need for recalibration and even improvisation as time goes on. But it can increase the odds that these adjust-ments will be made intelligently, in ways that are more congruent than not with long-term national interests. As Dwight Eisenhower liked to say, "The plans are nothing, but the planning is everything."[9] Ike was right. Policy makers would be wise to be skeptical about grand strategy, but they would be foolish to dispense with it altogether.

2. *Start with first principles.* Grand strategy can only be valuable, however, if policy makers are willing to begin with the basics. It is a truism that

grand strategy is about setting priorities and limits, balancing means and ends, and generally asking the fundamental questions about a country's role in the world. In practice, however, this can prove surprisingly hard to do. Precisely because the United States is able to do so much in the world, there is a near-constant temptation for it to do more—to accumulate new commitments and responsibilities, to label additional interests as "vital" to the nation's well-being. In these circumstances, it is easy for obligations to outrun capabilities, or for hierarchies of interest and threat to become blurred or collapse altogether.[10] This may be an unavoidable problem of superpowerdom, and it is one that is compounded by the environment in which U.S. policy is made. Because American officials are usually pressed for time and buffeted by numerous competing demands, there are fewer opportunities than one would like for asking the truly searching questions. Policy acquires a momentum of its own; muddling through becomes the default option.

This tendency is understandable, but it is also problematic. The United States now finds itself in a position where prioritization and reassessment are not luxuries but necessities. As Leslie Gelb has written, American leaders "must either choose or lose."[11] The past decade has shown that even "hyperpowers" have to deal with resource constraints, and in light of current fiscal and political realities, it seems likely that spending on national security programs will contract in the coming years. Over the longer term, the United States may well face something like a zero-sum competition between rising expenditures at home (particularly on mandatory entitlement programs) and strategic commitments abroad.[12] Finally, U.S. leaders will have to deal with all of these constraints at a time when the country faces a dizzying array of global issues, and when the demands on American power seem as great as ever before. The question, then, is not *whether* big decisions and hard choices are coming; it is *how well* those choices will end up being made.

If American grand strategy is to be effective, U.S. officials will have to go back to first principles and confront some of the most difficult questions about the country's global role. What is the nature of the international system in the twenty-first century, and in what direction is that system evolving? Do national security and global stability require a strategy of American primacy, or can a more austere approach like "offshore balancing" do the job?[13] Which commitments are truly vital and what threats are really most menacing, and what can this tell us about how—or even whether—to respond to emerging challenges and opportunities? What tools and institutions are serving the purposes for which they were designed, and which ones need to be modified or simply junked? What part should nontraditional security issues play in the country's strategic posture? What is the proper balance between domestic and foreign commitments in the years and decades to come?[14] Answering these questions will not be easy or painless, but avoiding them would be far worse. After all, these issues will inevitably have to be addressed in one way or another; surely it is preferable that they be tackled as deliberately and systematically as possible.

3. *Invest in planning.* In practice, this means that future administrations will have to invest in planning. The idea of strategic planning has taken a beating in recent years, with some observers describing it as a lost art and others arguing that the world is just too stubbornly unpredictable for planning to be of much use.[15] Yet if grand strategy is to have any value, planning—the effort to look beyond the current crisis and think rigorously about the future—will be extremely important. In one sense, the sort of fundamental questions that grand strategy must address cannot usually be answered intelligently through mere intuition or instinct, but rather demand a more thorough, searching form of analysis.[16] In another sense, while planning cannot eliminate uncertainty or the need for judgment calls, it can provide a better conceptual foundation for dealing with that uncertainty and making those judgment calls more effectively. It can do so by giving leaders a firmer sense of the essential goals and interests that transcend any given crisis, and by forcing them to think about different scenarios and eventualities before they actually occur. Planning, like grand strategy as a whole, can help policy makers maintain their equilibrium in a constantly shifting world.

Yet for planning to be effective, planners have to be put in a position to succeed. Presidents and their top advisers need to make clear that strategic planning is a priority, and they need to open bureaucratic windows in which planners—whether at the State Department, the Pentagon, or the NSC—can interact meaningfully with the day-to-day policy process. To put it bluntly, they will have to give strategic planning "teeth" by endowing planners with the prestige, resources, and bureaucratic stature that they need to actually budge the interagency machinery.[17] Most of all, there is no substitute for doing these things at the very outset of a new administration, that fleeting period when concepts have not yet congealed and top officials have not yet been sucked into what Kissinger called "foreign policy by momentum."[18] As former PPS director Richard Haass notes, "Policy planners have a structural advantage at such times because all new administrations feel a certain pressure to invent. Further along in any administration new ideas gain less traction. . . . Absent intervening events that create windows for rethinking, changing policies in an administration tends to be like steering a supertanker: difficult, slow, and sure to meet resistance."[19] Once one falls behind the geopolitical and bureaucratic curve, getting back in front can be exceedingly challenging.

The precise manner of avoiding this fate will vary by administration, but a modest recommendation would be that new presidents should make the prompt completion of the *National Security Strategy* a top priority. The *NSS* is a much-derided document, in part because administrations never seem to release them as frequently or as soon as the law technically mandates, and in part because the report often bears the scars of writing-by-committee.[20] Yet if the process of drafting the *NSS* is given real weight at the outset of an administration, it can still have a salutary impact. The writing of the *NSS* is essentially an administration-wide exercise in grand strategy and policy planning. It represents a chance for incoming officials to think through the most basic strategic issues, to establish hierarchies of goals and threats, and to consider how all the various pieces fit together. Just as important, it offers an opportunity to begin building internal consensus on these concepts. Not all of the resulting insights will make it into print (the *NSS* remains a public document), and the drafting process will not always be an attractive one.[21] But as an opening move toward doing planning seriously, the work of pulling the *NSS* together can nonetheless be quite valuable.

4. *Think of grand strategy as a process, not a blueprint.* None of this is to say that grand strategy should be thought of as some immutable blueprint from which policy must never deviate. In public parlance, grand strategy is too often associated with the promulgation of official "doctrines," pronouncements that lay down—in advance—what the American response will be to a specified action or set of circumstances.[22] (The Truman Doctrine, for instance, announced that it would be U.S. policy "to support free peoples who are resisting attempted subjugation by armed minorities or outside pressures" in the context of the emerging Cold War. More recently, those calling for an "Obama Doctrine" were usually seeking some equally explicit statement of American policy toward the Arab Spring or humanitarian intervention more broadly.[23]) Doctrines have their uses, for they signal resolve and provide both international and domestic audiences with an easily understandable expression of U.S. goals. Grand strategy, however, should be something different.

Because foreign policy deals with a dynamic world, flexibility and recalibration are essential to any good grand strategy. If a grand strategy is soundly conceived, then the overall goals or guiding principles may remain the same over a period of years or even decades. But the precise combination of policies used to pursue those goals will undoubtedly shift as conditions change and rivals react. As we have seen, the "golden age" of American grand strategy was characterized by near-continual reassessments of what mix of means and commitments was required to contain Soviet power, even as that overarching objective stayed unchanged. The Reagan years saw a similar process of adaptation, as the president learned from his early experiences and moved to a less confrontational posture from late 1983 onward, all while remaining within the general strategic framework he had laid out from the beginning. In both of these cases, grand strategy was "emergent" as well as "deliberate": it required a firm sense of purpose and priorities, but significant tactical dexterity as well.[24]

The same holds true today. "Real strategy," note two observers, "is made in real time."[25] Grand strategy should start with systematic planning, the setting of goals and priorities, and the outlining of a realistic course of action for realizing those objectives. Yet regardless of how well this initial planning is done, the subsequent progression of events will inevitably require the road map to be revised, the assumptions reconsidered, and new routes plotted for getting from here to there. Surprises and friction may be unwelcome, but they are unavoidable in foreign affairs. High officials are perpetually confronted with scenarios they have not expected, and even the most meticulous contingency preparations cannot possibly anticipate everything that might go wrong. Accordingly, leaders need a core set of principles and objectives, but they also need to avoid wedding themselves so tightly to a single course of action that change becomes unthinkable and contrary indicators are ignored. For the real test of a grand strategy often lies in how effectively its authors can adapt when things do not proceed precisely according to design.

Grand strategy, then, should not be seen as something fixed or finite. Rather, it is properly viewed as an iterative, continuous *process*—one that involves seeking out and interpreting feedback, dealing with surprises, and correcting course where necessary, all while keeping the ultimate objective in view. Planning and reassessment are constants, and the work of the grand strategist is rarely done. Former NSC and PPS official Andrew Erdmann puts it best: grand strategy is the "never-ending race."[26]

5. *Emphasize the "how" as well as the "what."* As much of the foregoing analysis indicates, conception and implementation are both vital aspects of grand strategy, and neither one is worth much without the other. Accordingly, grand strategy requires vision and planning, but it also demands basic, day-to-day policy competence. To borrow a famous juxtaposition, policy makers have to be "foxes" as well as "hedgehogs."[27] They need to know (as hedgehogs do) the one "big thing" that tells them where they want to go and what their overriding priorities should be, but they also need to know (like foxes)

the many "little things" that are necessary to turn big ideas into workable policies on the ground. In fact, having either foxes or hedgehogs dominate the policy process is a sure recipe for trouble. Foxes need hedgehogs to give them direction and purpose, but hedgehogs need foxes to keep their grand schemes tethered to reality. The Truman and Reagan administrations mostly managed to maintain this essential balance; the Bush administration, unfortunately, did not.

Presidents thus need to cultivate an environment that emphasizes planning and vision, but one that pays due heed to the exigencies of competent execution as well. This does not mean that the chief executive needs to micromanage policy down to the tactical level; this is what foxes are for. But it does mean that the president should shape the overall process so that implementation does not become the poor cousin of conception. Presidents need to appoint advisers who collectively represent a mixture of strategic big-think on the one hand, and tactical and administrative aptitude on the other. They also need to establish a climate that is receptive to expert advice rather than openly contemptuous of it.

Above all, presidents must "own" the implementation of their grand strategy no less than the concepts underlying it. They need to ask hard questions about the plans that are presented to them; they need to press their advisers to ensure that alternatives have been considered and contingency plans devised. In short, they need to invest themselves in the "how" of their grand strategy as well as the "what." This is the unglamorous side of grand strategy, but there is no evading the task. As one Bush-era official later acknowledged, "Even the best policy goals are not likely to be fulfilled without equally good plans for implementing them."[28]

It may even be useful to reconceptualize the relationship between planning and implementation. These two tasks should not be seen as fully distinct or sequential parts of the policy process; rather, they should form two interrelated aspects of a continuing, reciprocal dialogue. Planning works best when it is informed by operators' input on what can work and what will not. Similarly, operations should be tailored so that the characteristics of a given initiative (whether diplomatic, military, or other) do not undercut broader strategic goals and plans. Accordingly, planners and operators need to be brought together at every stage of the process. Bringing operators into the planning stages of grand strategy can help sensitize planners to the nearer-term requirements of good policy; bringing planners into operations can provide a longer-range perspective that is sometimes missing from the management of day-to-day affairs. None of this will eliminate the difficulties inherent in the relationship between vision and competence, planning and implementation—but it might ease, if only by a degree, the bureaucratic disconnects that often exacerbate these problems.[29]

6. *Embrace the democratic messiness of grand strategy.* The question of whether democracies can conduct a policy that blends thoughtfulness, strategic consistency, and tactical agility has long perplexed observers of the American system. Nearly two centuries ago, Alexis de Tocqueville argued that

> foreign politics demand scarcely any of those qualities which are peculiar to a democracy; they require, on the contrary, the perfect use of almost all those in which it is deficient. . . . A democracy can only with great difficulty regulate the details of an important undertaking, persevere in a fixed design, and work out its execution in spite of serious obstacles. It cannot combine its measures with secrecy or await their consequences with patience.[30]

More recently, this critique has been echoed by some of America's most influential policy makers. During the late 1940s, George Kennan continually lamented the inefficiencies of democratic foreign policy; a generation later, Nixon and Kissinger sought to address the problem by making foreign policy less democratic. "Most foreign policy setbacks are inflicted by foreigners," Kissinger explained. "Ours instead are being inflicted by ourselves."[31]

Kennan, Kissinger, and their intellectual brethren were certainly right in arguing that the vicissitudes of democracy can have pernicious effects on policy. Moreover, the present political climate often seems downright hostile to reasoned strategic debate. But just as there is no good alternative to grand strategy, there is really no good substitute for embracing this messiness and making the best of it. It has yet to be shown that authoritarian regimes are any better at grand strategy than democracies, because arbitrary rule and personalistic decision making bring about pathologies all their own.[32] More to the point for American purposes, the experiences of those who have sought to address the problem by dramatically centralizing power in the White House—Nixon and Kissinger foremost among them—have usually ended in grief.[33]

This hardly means that there is no place for secrecy or decisive executive action in foreign policy, for U.S. laws and the American political tradition provide room for both. Nor does it mean abandoning presidential leadership and doing a least-common-denominator policy. What it means is that there is a crucial political aspect to grand strategy, one that requires as much attention as the geopolitical aspects. Making any grand strategy work requires building consensus both within and outside an administration.

Within the executive branch, presidents would be well advised to involve the key bureaucratic players early enough in the planning process so that they do not feel that they are being confronted with a fait accompli or otherwise incentivized to obstructionism.[34] Outside the executive branch, there is no substitute for persistent efforts to explain an administration's grand strategy once it is formulated, and for early, real, and regular consultation with the congressional leaders whose cooperation will be necessary to turn ideas into action. (This latter task was one at which the Truman administration particularly excelled with its courtship of leading Republicans like Arthur Vandenberg during the late 1940s.) All this, in turn, will unavoidably entail bargaining, compromise, and the frustration that comes with them. This is never going to be a pretty or an entirely satisfying process, but there is no good way around it.

7. *Don't treat bureaucracy as the enemy of policy.* A corollary to the preceding point is that policy and bureaucracy need not be mortal foes. To be sure, there is frequently a tension between strategic coherence and bureaucratic procedure, and the temptation to centralize authority has long been a strong one. During their time in power, Nixon and Kissinger often treated statecraft as a zero-sum struggle between creative leaders and benighted civil servants. After 9/11, the top level of the Bush administration also eschewed a deliberate decision-making style and input from various sectors of the bureaucracy. The goal, in both cases, was to streamline the process, bypass centers of potential resistance, and ultimately make policy more responsive to guidance from the top.[35]

Such an approach has its advantages. Only presidents can make the really tough decisions that cause a grand strategy to rise or fall, and it is eminently reasonable for them to seek as much latitude as possible in making these choices. As the Nixon-Kissinger era demonstrated, dramatically narrowing the decision-making process can permit greater flexibility and decisiveness, and it can empower individual leaders to act on those bold, creative ideas that might otherwise be ensnared in cumbersome interagency procedures. In periods of crisis, when threats loom large and time runs short, this style can be all the more appealing.

Yet as the preceding chapters also show, trying to make and sustain grand strategy in this fashion can be a very dangerous game. A centralized style can easily lead to confusion or even obstructionism by officials who feel shut out of the loop, thereby undercutting the very unity of action it is meant to produce. Additionally, a restricted decision-making process places extraordinary demands on the intelligence and judgment of those few individuals at the top. It increases the dangers of groupthink, limits the extent to which flawed assumptions can be probed or exposed, and generally discourages top officials from exploiting the full range of bureaucratic expertise that would otherwise be available to them. One could see many of these unfortunate tendencies during the Nixon-Kissinger and Bush years, as the decision-making and management styles employed by these administrations eventually proved counterproductive.

Conversely, for all its inefficiencies, a rigorous and inclusive process can bring important benefits. It can help puncture bad ideas before they make it into policy, and it can minimize the ambiguity and confusion that often result from a closed, secretive approach. It can provide mechanisms for systematic planning and reassessment, for mediating intramural disputes, and for obtaining buy-in from various governmental constituencies. Not least of all, it can help ensure that the intellectual burdens of dealing with a vast, complicated world are shared rather than concentrated. A deliberate process need not be the enemy of good policy; it can actually be an important ally.[36]

Presidents and their top aides should thus invest their energies in making the interagency process work, rather than getting around it or making it irrelevant. Presidents have every right to expect that policy will reflect their preferences, and given the intricacies of the federal bureaucracy it is crucial that they appoint a strong national security adviser who can adjudicate disagreements and encourage faithful implementation. But they would also do well to emphasize procedures that elicit a diverse range of viewpoints, foster a sense of participation among the relevant stakeholders, and generally maximize rather than minimize the scope of knowledge that can be brought to bear on immensely difficult problems. After all, even Kissinger eventually found that the world was too much for a single statesman to manage.

8. *Look backward as well as forward.* Grand strategy is obviously a forward-looking discipline: it involves setting long-term goals and crafting ideas that will carry policy ahead in the years to come. Yet as Peter Feaver has pointed out, it is also a backward-looking discipline, one that is informed as much by insights from the past as predictions about the future.[37] Truman's grand strategy, for instance, was unmistakably influenced by the experience of World War II. It aimed to prevent Stalin from accomplishing what the Axis powers had nearly done—dominating Eurasia—without starting another world war in the process. More than three decades later, Reagan's grand strategy was shaped by judgments about the apparent shortcomings of détente, as well as by his own sense of the longer-running historical trends at play. Similarly, George W. Bush's grand strategy stemmed from the conviction that the

United States must never allow another 9/11, and it focused on dealing (in a highly expansive way) with the conditions that had seemingly left the country so vulnerable on that day. In this sense, the past is always present in the shaping of grand strategy.

Grand strategy is about looking backward in other ways, as well. It is impossible to understand which way the world is moving without understanding how things came to be as they are, just as it is impossible to comprehend our own country's position in the world without comprehending how we arrived at this point. Moreover, grand strategy is a discipline that necessarily involves as much reassessment as it does forecasting. Setting out on a long-term journey requires a degree of self-confidence that one is ultimately headed in the right direction, but the only way to test that belief is to evaluate (and reevaluate) whether one's policies are producing the desired short- and medium-term results. In a way, then, grand strategy depends on the rigorous study of the recent past to determine what mix of perseverance and flexibility constitutes the proper way forward. "Second-guessing" need not be a pejorative in this regard; it is, rather, an indispensable element of the overall process.

What this suggests is that leaders need to foster an atmosphere in which reassessment and self-scrutiny can occur.[38] What it also suggests is that aspiring grand strategists should be sensitive to history. They need to understand how much the study of the past can tell them about the world they are dealing with, as well as their own efforts to deal with it. They need to see that history can provide the valuable, longer-term viewpoint that is often missing from hectic policy debates. And they need to be aware that the lack of such perspective can prove quite costly. For while an ability to look backward and engage in critical reassessment will hardly ensure success when it comes to grand strategy, an *inability* to do so will definitely heighten the chances of failure.

9. *Power must be conserved as well as exploited.* As Liddell Hart observed long ago, grand strategy is about being both effective and efficient in the use of power. Grand strategy involves using the full range of a country's capabilities so as to defeat enemies and accomplish essential national objectives, but it also involves conserving and protecting the underlying sources of that power. Accordingly, good grand strategists have to understand that power is simultaneously multidimensional and finite. It is multidimensional in the sense that countries—particularly the United States—possess a wide range of tools that they can use to achieve desired goals. But it is finite in the sense that there are never enough resources to go around, that overstretch continually lurks,

and that statesmen thus have to be highly judicious in how they define and pursue those goals in the first place. From the Truman presidency to the Bush years, one can readily see the relevance of this insight in each of the cases studied here.

Understanding the dual nature of power is no less important today. From the rise of China to the threats posed by international terrorism and nuclear proliferation, so many of the challenges the United States confronts cannot be addressed solely through one form of action or another. Rather, they require American policy makers to synergistically combine a range of tools: military might, multilateral diplomacy, economic and ideological influence, and others. If the United States is to be effective on the world stage, it will have to leverage the full breadth of its considerable national strength.

Yet U.S. officials will also have to be more attentive to the requisites of preserving that strength over the long run. The future of American primacy now appears far less assured than it did a decade ago, and the Iraq War has demonstrated precisely how draining the incautious use of national power can be. Sustaining U.S. influence in decades to come will certainly require a more robust economic performance, but it will also demand that American strategists employ the country's capabilities as discerningly as possible. One recent essay puts it aptly: "Good grand strategy must strike the correct balance between maintaining the United States' role as a global leader, while ensuring that U.S. leadership does not face strategic exhaustion."[39]

There is no surefire mechanism for striking this balance, but a good place to start would be recognizing that the need for balance exists. The United States simply cannot do everything well, nor can it ever achieve absolute security in an insecure world. Trade-offs will have to be made, and a certain level of danger will have to be tolerated. Going forward, American grand strategists should therefore place a premium on prudence and proportion. They will need to focus on defining goals that can be achieved at a cost commensurate to the benefit, and on avoiding those high-risk initiatives where failure is potentially catastrophic. Above all, they will need to pay constant attention to the imperative of getting the resource balance right—of maintaining the proper equilibrium not just between various U.S. commitments abroad, but between those commitments and the country's economic and domestic interests as well. To do otherwise is to risk geopolitical exhaustion and political disillusion, neither of which will be conducive to good policy over the long run.

10. *Keep expectations realistic.* All of these suggestions point to a final issue—the need to limit one's expectations as to what grand strategy can accomplish.

George Kennan, who is often thought of as America's archetypal grand strategist, was fond of discussing the limitations of that concept—and of human foresight more broadly—in his famous talks at the National War College during the late 1940s. As he put it in his valedictory lecture prior to leaving the Policy Planning Staff at the end of 1949:

> It is simply not given to human beings to know the totality of truth. Similarly, no one can see in its totality anything so fundamental and so unlimited in all its implications as the development of our people in their relation to their world environment. . . . I sometimes like to think of the substance of human knowledge as a sort of sphere, and at the center of that sphere there must lie a core which is absolute truth. We keep charging into that sphere from various angles, knowing that we are always going to be deflected at tangents, like moths off the light bulb, before we get to the center.[40]

When it comes to thinking about grand strategy as an endeavor, the same basic point still holds. Too often, grand strategy is thought of as a grandiose, transformative project to remake the global order, or as a panacea that will wipe away the complexity of world affairs. Both of these aspirations are simply begging for disappointment. In view of its current economic troubles and the experience of the last decade, the United States will probably not be able to undertake any grand transformative schemes in the near future. Nor can any amount of strategizing allow American policy to transcend the uncertainties and challenges of a changing global order. At best, grand strategy can provide an intellectual reference point for dealing with those challenges, and a process by which dedicated policy makers can seek to bring their day-to-day actions into better alignment with their country's enduring interests. Achieving this would be good enough; expecting more would probably be unrealistic.

NOTES

Introduction

1. Carl von Clausewitz, *On War,* ed. and trans. Michael Howard and Peter Paret (Princeton, NJ: Princeton University Press, 1984), 132.

2. On the difficulty of defining strategy and grand strategy, see Williamson Murray and Mark Grimsley, "Introduction: On Strategy," in *The Making of Strategy: Rulers, States, and War,* ed. Alvin H. Bernstein, MacGregor Knox, and Williamson Murray (New York: Cambridge University Press, 1994), 1–2; Timothy Andrews Sayle, "Defining and Teaching Grand Strategy," Foreign Policy Research Institute *Telegram,* no. 4, January 2011.

3. German military writers apparently used the term during the eighteenth century, but more narrowly, to refer to military training, tactics, and operations. Peter Trubowitz, *Politics and Strategy: Partisan Ambition and American Statecraft* (Princeton, NJ: Princeton University Press, 2011), 2.

4. Quoted in Paul Kennedy, "Grand Strategy in War and Peace: Toward a Broader Definition," in *Grand Strategies in War and Peace,* ed. Paul Kennedy (New Haven, CT: Yale University Press, 1991), 1.

5. J. F. C. Fuller, *The Generalship of Ulysses S. Grant* (New York: Dodd, Mead and Co., 1929), 4–5; also Hew Strachan, "The War Experienced: Command, Strategy, and Tactics, 1914–18," in *A Companion to World War I,* ed. John Horne (Oxford: John Wiley & Sons, 2010), 35–40.

6. Edward Mead Earle, introduction in *Makers of Modern Strategy: Military Thought from Hitler to Machiavelli,* ed. Edward Mead Earle (Princeton, NJ: Princeton University Press, 1943), viii–x.

7. B. H. Liddell Hart, *Strategy* (New York: Praeger, 1957), 336; also 366–372.

8. See, on these points, Sayle, "Defining and Teaching"; Robert Art, *A Grand Strategy for America* (Ithaca, NY: Cornell University Press, 2003); Kennedy, "Grand Strategy"; John Lewis Gaddis, *Strategies of Containment: A Critical Appraisal of American National Security Policy during the Cold War* (New York: Oxford University Press, 2005); John Lewis Gaddis, "What Is Grand Strategy?" Karl von der Hayden Distinguished Lecture, Duke University, February 26, 2009; Colin Dueck, *Reluctant Crusaders: Power, Culture, and Change in American Grand Strategy* (Princeton, NJ: Princeton University Press, 2008), 9–10; Williamson Murray, "Thoughts on Grand Strategy," in *The Shaping of Grand Strategy: Policy, Diplomacy, and War,* ed. Williamson Murray, Richard Hart Sinnreich, and James Lacey (New York: Cambridge University Press, 2011), 8; Edward Luttwak, *The Grand Strategy of the Byzantine Empire* (Cambridge, MA: Harvard University Press, 2009), 409; Walter McDougall, "Can the United States Do Grand Strategy?" *Orbis* 54, no. 2 (Spring 2010): 165–184; John M. Collins, *Grand Strategy: Principles and Practices* (Annapolis: Naval Institute Press, 1973).

9. Colin Gray, *The Strategy Bridge: Theory and Practice* (New York: Oxford University Press, 2010), 17.

10. This definition builds on those used by Barry Posen, *The Sources of Military Doctrine: France, Britain, and Germany between the World Wars* (Ithaca, NY: Cornell University Press, 1984), 13; Dueck, *Reluctant Crusaders,* 9–12; Hal Brands, *From Berlin to Baghdad: America's Search for Purpose in the Post–Cold War World* (Lexington: University Press of Kentucky, 2008), passim.

11. Dean Acheson, *Present at the Creation: My Years in the State Department* (New York: W. W. Norton, 1987), 214; also Daniel W. Drezner, ed., *Avoiding Trivia: The Role of Strategic Planning in American Foreign Policy* (Washington, DC: Brookings Institution Press, 2009).

12. The classic treatment is Paul Kennedy, *The Rise and Fall of the Great Powers* (New York: Random House, 1987).

13. Gaddis, *Strategies.*

14. Clausewitz, *On War,* 77. On the competitive nature of grand strategy, see Thomas Mahnken, ed., *Competitive Strategies for the 21st Century: Theory, History, and Practice* (Stanford, CA: Stanford University Press, 2012).

15. Edward Luttwak, *Strategy: The Logic of War and Peace* (Cambridge, MA: Harvard University Press, 1987).

16. In the United States, the demand for a public articulation of grand strategy became particularly pronounced after the end of the Cold War led to some confusion—both within and outside government—as to the central purpose of American policy. See Brands, *Berlin to Baghdad,* chaps. 2–3; also Derek Chollet and James Goldgeier, *America between the Wars: From 11/9 to 9/11: The Misunderstood Years between the Fall of the Berlin Wall and the Start of the War on Terror* (New York: Public Affairs, 2008).

17. Luttwak may put it a bit too strongly in saying that "all states have a grand strategy, whether they know it or not," but he is correct that grand strategic decision making is unavoidable. Luttwak, *Grand Strategy of the Byzantine Empire,* 409.

18. The reference is to Trotsky's (perhaps apocryphal) insight about war. See Michael Walzer, *Just and Unjust Wars: A Moral Argument with Historical Illustrations* (New York: Basic Books, 2006), 29.

19. Murray, "Thoughts," 3–4.

20. Quoted in Martin Samuels, *Command or Control? Command, Training and Tactics in the British and German Armies, 1888–1918* (London: Frank Cass, 1995), 14.

21. Strobe Talbott, *The Russia Hand: A Memoir of Presidential Diplomacy* (New York: Random House, 2002), 133–134.

22. See, on these issues, Melvyn Leffler, *A Preponderance of Power: National Security, the Truman Administration, and the Cold War* (Stanford, CA: Stanford University Press, 1992); Aaron Friedberg, *The Weary Titan: Britain and the Experience of Relative Decline, 1895–1905* (Princeton, NJ: Princeton University Press, 1989).

23. Brands, *Berlin to Baghdad,* esp. 336–340. The term "theateritis" is widely attributed to George Marshall, though it may trace back to Hap Arnold. Forrest Pogue, *George C. Marshall: Organizer of Victory, 1943–1945* (New York: Viking Press, 1973), 335.

24. Gaddis, "What Is Grand Strategy?"

25. The point about military strategy and violence is made in Richard K. Betts, "Is Strategy an Illusion?" *International Security (IS)* 25, no. 2 (Fall 2000): 5.

26. The phrase is from Stephen Krasner, "An Orienting Principle for Foreign Policy: The Deficiencies of 'Grand Strategy,'" *Policy Review,* no. 163 (October 2010): 5.

27. "Background Briefing," August 14, 1970, in *Foreign Relations of the United States, 1969–1976,* vol. 1 (Washington, DC: Government Printing Office, 2003), Document no. 69. Hereafter, documents from this series are cited as *FRUS* followed by year, volume, and document or page number.

28. Clausewitz, *On War,* 578.

29. Allan R. Millett and Williamson Murray, "Lessons of War," *National Interest,* Winter 1988/89; also Millett and Murray, eds., *Military Effectiveness,* 3 vols. (London: Allen & Unwin, 1988).

30. David D'Lugo and Ronald Rogowski, "The Anglo-German Naval Race and Comparative Constitutional 'Fitness,'" in *The Domestic Bases of Grand Strategy,* ed. Richard Rosecrance and Arthur Stein (Ithaca, NY: Cornell University Press, 1993), 65–94; also Paul Kennedy, *The Rise of the Anglo-German Antagonism: 1860–1914* (London: Allen & Unwin, 1980).

31. Jack Snyder, *The Ideology of the Offensive: Military Decision Making and the Disasters of 1914* (Ithaca, NY: Cornell University Press, 1984), 108–116; Manfred Jonas, *The United States and Germany: A Diplomatic History* (Ithaca, NY: Cornell University Press, 1985), 113–124.

32. Thomas Nichols, "Carter and the Soviets: The Origins of the U.S. Return to a Strategy of Confrontation," *Diplomacy & Statecraft (D&S)* 13, no. 2 (June 2002): 21–42; also Vladislav Zubok, *A Failed Empire: The Soviet Union in the Cold War from Stalin to Gorbachev* (Chapel Hill: University of North Carolina Press, 2007), 247–264.

33. Vietnam is the classic example. See Leslie Gelb and Richard Betts, *The Irony of Vietnam: The System Worked* (Washington, DC: Brookings Institution Press, 1979); George Herring, *America's Longest War: The United States and Vietnam, 1950–1975* (New York: Alfred A. Knopf, 1986).

34. See, for instance, Herbert Simon, *Models of Bounded Rationality,* vol. 1 (Cambridge, MA: MIT Press, 1984).

35. On the role of ideology, misperception, and other cognitive biases, see Robert Jervis, *Perception and Misperception in International Politics* (Princeton, NJ: Princeton University Press, 1976); also Michael Hunt, *Ideology and U.S. Foreign Policy* (New Haven, CT: Yale University Press, 1987).

36. Memorandum of Conversation with the Business Council, December 1, 1971, *FRUS 1969–1976,* vol. 1, Document no. 101.

37. Deborah Welch Larson, *Origins of Containment: A Psychological Explanation* (Princeton, NJ: Princeton University Press, 1985), 129.

38. Quoted in Amy Zegart, "Why the Best Is Not Yet to Come in Policy Planning," in Drezner, *Avoiding Trivia,* 119. Classic discussions of bureaucratic politics and American foreign policy included Morton H. Halperin and Arnold Kanter, *Readings in American Foreign Policy: A Bureaucratic Perspective* (Boston: Little, Brown, 1973); Graham Allison, *Essence of Decision: Explaining the Cuban Missile Crisis* (Boston: Little, Brown, 1971).

39. Walter Russell Mead, *Special Providence: American Foreign Policy and How It Changed the World* (New York: Alfred A. Knopf, 2001).

40. See Peter Trubowitz, *Defining the National Interest: Conflict and Change in American Foreign Policy* (Chicago: University of Chicago Press, 1998).

41. As this statement implies, I do not intend to re-litigate the debate about whether public opinion is well or poorly informed, or whether democracy is a net positive or negative in foreign policy. (In the aggregate, I think that democracies are probably superior to the competition.) Rather, I am simply noting that democratic politics have the potential to encourage suboptimal grand strategic decisions. For careful consideration of these issues, see Miroslav Nincic, *Democracy and Foreign Policy: The Fallacy of Political Realism* (New York: Columbia University Press, 1994); Ole Holsti, *Public Opinion and American Foreign Policy* (Ann Arbor: University of Michigan Press, 2004).

42. Clausewitz, *On War,* 119.

43. A. J. P. Taylor, *The Origins of the Second World War* (New York: Atheneum, 1983), 72.

44. Edward Luttwak, *Strategy and History: Collected Essays,* vol. 2 (New Brunswick, NJ: Transaction Publishers, 1985), xi–xii.

45. McDougall, "Can the United States Do Grand Strategy?" 167.

46. Steve Yetiv, *The Absence of Grand Strategy: The United States in the Persian Gulf, 1972–2005* (Baltimore: Johns Hopkins University Press, 2008), 197. Other studies that question the feasibility of grand strategy to one degree or another include Brands, *Berlin to Baghdad;* Melvyn P. Leffler and Jeffrey W. Legro, "Conclusion: Strategy in a Murky World," in *In Uncertain Times: American Foreign Policy after the Berlin Wall and 9/11,* ed. Melvyn Leffler and Jeffrey W. Legro (Ithaca, NY: Cornell University Press, 2011); Marc Trachtenberg, "Making Grand Strategy: The Early Cold War Experience in Retrospect," *SAIS Review* 19, no. 1 (February 1999): 33–40; Betts, "Is Strategy an Illusion?"

47. Policy Review Committee Meeting, March 24, 1977, box 24, Subject File (SF), Zbigniew Brzezinski Donated Materials, Jimmy Carter Presidential Library (JCL).

48. Quoted in Leslie H. Gelb, *Power Rules: How Common Sense Can Rescue American Foreign Policy* (New York: HarperCollins, 2009), 103.

49. Talbott, *Russia Hand,* 133.

50. Throughout this book, the presidencies of Nixon and Ford are treated as a single unit.

Chapter 1

1. Clark Clifford Oral History, April 13, 1971, Harry S. Truman Presidential Library (HSTL), 81.

2. Leslie H. Gelb, *Power Rules: How Common Sense Can Rescue American Foreign Policy* (New York: HarperCollins, 2009), 103. See also Mr. Y [Wayne Porter and Mark Mykleby], "A National Strategic Narrative," Woodrow Wilson Center, Washington, DC, 2011; Thomas Friedman, "Rethinking Foreign Affairs," *New York Times (NYT),* February 7, 1992; Thomas Mann, "What Bush Can Learn from Truman," *NYT,* October 6, 2002; Jim Lacey, "Finding X: The Quest to Outline the U.S.'s Future Grand Strategy," *National Review Online,* May 11, 2011.

3. Melvyn Leffler, *A Preponderance of Power: National Security, the Truman Administration, and the Cold War* (Stanford, CA: Stanford University Press, 1992), passim. Leffler's book is now the standard work on the period and has influenced my own interpretation in important ways. A more critical take is Arnold Offner, *Another Such Victory: President Truman and the Cold War* (Stanford, CA: Stanford University Press, 2002).

4. "Organization Meeting on Russia," June 12, 1946, box 298, George F. Kennan Papers (GFKP), Seeley Mudd Manuscript Library (SMML), Princeton University.

5. G. John Ikenberry, *After Victory: Institutions, Strategic Restraint, and the Rebuilding of Order after Major Wars* (Princeton, NJ: Princeton University Press, 2001), 167–168; Paul Kennedy, *The Rise and Fall of the Great Powers* (New York: Random House, 1987), 357–358.

6. George Herring, *From Colony to Superpower: U.S. Foreign Relations since 1776* (New York: Oxford University Press, 2008), 598.

7. Report by the Joint Strategic Survey Committee, April 29, 1947, *FRUS 1947,* 1:739. See also Melvyn Leffler, "The American Conception of National Security and the Beginnings of the Cold War, 1945–48," *American Historical Review* 89, no. 2 (April 1984): esp. 350–359.

8. Thomas Paterson, *On Every Front: The Making and Unmaking of the Cold War* (New York: W. W. Norton, 1992), 15.

9. OSS, "Problems and Objectives of United States Policy," April 12, 1945, Declassified Documents Reference System (DDRS); William Curti Wohlforth, *The Elusive Balance: Power and Perceptions during the Cold War* (Ithaca, NY: Cornell University Press, 1993), 121–122.

10. Wilson Miscamble, *From Roosevelt to Truman: Potsdam, Hiroshima, and the Cold War* (New York: Cambridge University Press, 2007), 34–86.

11. Quoted in Randall Bennett Woods, *A Changing of the Guard: Anglo-American Relations, 1941–1946* (Chapel Hill: University of North Carolina Press, 1990), 286; also Miscamble, *Roosevelt to Truman,* chaps. 2–7.

12. Robert H. Ferrell, ed., *Off the Record: The Private Papers of Harry S. Truman* (Columbia: University of Missouri Press, 1997), 80. For an account that stresses the insecurities of both sides, see Melvyn Leffler, *For the Soul of Mankind: The United States, the Soviet Union, and the Cold War* (New York: Hill & Wang, 2007), 11–83.

13. Moscow to State, February 22, 1946, *FRUS 1946,* 6:696–709.

14. X [George F. Kennan], "The Sources of Soviet Conduct," *Foreign Affairs* 25, no. 4 (July 1947): esp. 576–582.

15. Henry Kissinger, *White House Years* (Boston: Little, Brown, 1979), 135.

16. X, "Sources," 576, 580–582; Dean Acheson, *Present at the Creation: My Years in the State Department* (New York: W. W. Norton, 1987), 151; Kennan to Lippmann (unsent), April 6, 1948, box 299, GFKP, SMML.

17. Quoted in Leffler, *Preponderance,* 124; also Offner, *Another Such Victory,* chaps. 6–7.

18. "Special Message to the Congress on Greece and Turkey," March 12, 1947, American Presidency Project (APP), University of California–Santa Barbara.

19. Harry S. Truman, *Years of Trial and Hope* (Garden City, NY: Doubleday, 1956), 124–128.

20. Robert A. Lovett Oral History, July 7, 1971, 20, HSTL; also Michael Hogan, *A Cross of Iron: Harry S. Truman and the Origins of the National Security State, 1945–1954* (New York: Cambridge University Press, 1998), esp. 69–81.

21. Forrestal Diary, April 26, 1947, box 146, Forrestal Papers, SMML; Wilson Miscamble, *George F. Kennan and the Making of American Foreign Policy, 1947–1950* (Princeton, NJ: Princeton University Press, 1992), 4–6; Acheson, *Present,* 157–163.

22. Cabinet Meeting, March 7, 1947, box 1, Matthew Connelly Papers, HSTL; also Meeting of the Secretaries of State, War, and Navy, February 26, 1947, *FRUS 1947,* 5:57.

23. George F. Kennan, *Memoirs, 1925–1950* (Boston: Little, Brown, 1967), 327; Kennan, "Measures Short of War (Diplomatic)," National War College (NWC) Lecture, September 16, 1946, box 298, GFKP, SMML.

24. See JCS 1769/1, "United States Assistance to Other Countries from the Standpoint of National Security," April 29, 1947, *FRUS 1947,* 1:736–740.

25. Forrestal Diary, May 21, 1948, box 147, Forrestal Papers, SMML.

26. Kennan, "Planning of Foreign Policy," NWC Lecture, June 18, 1947, box 298, GFKP, SMML.

27. Offner, *Another Such Victory,* 214.

28. PPS 1, "Policy with Respect to American Aid to Western Europe," May 23, 1947, box 7, Bohlen Papers, RG 59, NARA; also Kennan, "Problems of U.S. Foreign Policy after Moscow," NWC Lecture, May 6, 1947, box 298, GFKP, SMML.

29. Kennan, "Russia's National Objectives," NWC Lecture, April 10, 1947, box 298, GFKP, SMML; Report by the Joint Strategic Survey Committee, April 29, 1947, *FRUS 1947,* 1:736–740. The role of Germany in the Marshall Plan is covered in greater detail in Carolyn Eisenberg, *Drawing the Line: The American Decision to Divide Germany, 1944–1949* (New York: Cambridge University Press, 1996), 282–287, 320–321; Melvyn Leffler, "The United States and the Strategic Dimensions of the Marshall Plan," *Diplomatic History (DH)* 12, no. 3 (July 1988): 277–306.

30. PPS 1, "Policy with Respect to American Aid to Western Europe."

31. The quotes are from Truman, "Address before the Rio de Janeiro Inter-American Conference for the Maintenance of Continental Peace and Security," September 2, 1947, APP; MemCon, April 3, 1949, box 12, Lot 53D444, RG 59, NARA; Kennan, "Where Are We Today?" NWC Lecture, December 21, 1948, box 299, GFKP, SMML. See also PPS 13, "Resume of World Situation," November 6, 1947, *State Department Policy Planning Staff Papers* (New York: Garland, 1983), 1:129–136, hereafter *PPSP;* Robert McMahon, *Dean Acheson and the Creation of an American World Order* (Washington, DC: Potomac Books, 2009), 96.

32. See Walter Hixson, *George F. Kennan: Cold War Iconoclast* (New York: Columbia University Press, 1989), esp. chap. 3.

33. Kennan to Lippmann (unsent), April 6, 1948, box 299, GFKP, SMML; Marshall to Lovett, April 23, 1948, *FRUS 1948,* 3:103; John Lewis Gaddis, *Strategies of Containment: A Critical Appraisal of American National Security Policy during the Cold War* (New York: Oxford University Press, 2005), 59–61.

34. CIA, "Review of the World Situation as It Relates to the Security of the United States," September 26, 1947, box 176, NSC Files, HSTL; also CIA, "Review of the World Situation as It Relates to the Security of the United States," April 8, 1948, ibid.

35. Forrestal Diary, April 28, 1947, box 146, Forrestal Papers, SMML; Forrestal to Gurney, December 8, 1947, in *The Forrestal Diaries,* ed. Walter Millis (New York: Viking, 1951), 350–351; also CIA, "Threats to the Security of the United States," September 28, 1948, CIA FOIA.

36. Quoted in James Chace, *Acheson: The Secretary of State Who Created the American World* (New York: Simon & Schuster, 2007), 174.

37. Kennan to Lyons, October 13, 1947, box 33, PPS Records, RG 59, NARA; PPS 13, "Resume of World Situation"; also John Lamberton Harper, *American Visions of Europe: Franklin D. Roosevelt, George F. Kennan, and Dean G. Acheson* (New York: Cambridge University Press, 1996), chap. 5. Even in the 1950s, Dwight Eisenhower hoped that growing Western European strength and assertiveness would allow the United States to withdraw its troops from the continent. Marc Trachtenberg, *A Constructed Peace: The Making of the European Settlement, 1945–1963* (Princeton, NJ: Princeton University Press, 1999), 147–156.

38. Ikenberry, *After Victory,* 201.

39. MemCon, January 21, 1948, box 9, Bohlen Records, RG 59, NARA; George Marshall, "The Problems of European Revival and German and Austrian Peace Settlements," *Department of State Bulletin (DOSB)*, November 30, 1947, 1024–1025.

40. Kennan, "Planning of Foreign Policy"; also John Lewis Gaddis, *The Long Peace: Inquiries into the History of the Cold War* (New York: Oxford University Press, 1987), esp. 57–61.

41. PPS 13, "Resume of World Situation"; Marshall in Forrestal Diary, November 7, 1947, box 147, Forrestal Papers, SMML. Kennan also discussed the importance of the Middle East in PPS 13, but he placed less emphasis on this region because Great Britain still bore primary responsibility for Western security interests there.

42. Kennan to Marshall, November 4, 1947, box 13, PPS Records, RG 59, NARA; "The Situation in China and U.S. Policy," November 3, 1947, box 13, ibid.; Kennan to Carter, February 10, 1948, box 13, ibid.; Miscamble, *George F. Kennan,* 218–223.

43. Kennan, "Problems of Far Eastern Policy," January 14, 1948, box 299, GFKP, SMML; "Conversation between General of the Army MacArthur and Mr. George F. Kennan," March 5, 1948, *FRUS 1948,* 6:699–700; PPS 23, "Review of Current Trends in U.S. Foreign Policy," February 24, 1948, *PPSP,* 2:123. See also Michael Schaller, "Securing the Great Crescent: Occupied Japan and the Origins of Containment in Southeast Asia," *Journal of American History (JAH)* 69, no. 2 (September 1982): esp. 396–397.

44. Kennan, "Russia's National Objectives," April 10, 1947, box 298, GFKP, SMML.

45. See, for instance, Michael J. Hogan, *The Marshall Plan: America, Britain, and the Reconstruction of Western Europe, 1947–1952* (New York: Cambridge University Press, 1989), esp. 431–444; Arthur J. Alexander, *The Arc of Japan's Economic Development* (New York: Routledge, 2008), 87–90.

46. On pressures to avoid major rearmament costs, see Hogan, *Cross of Iron,* chap. 3, quoted at 87.

47. Quote from William Hitchcock, *France Restored: Cold War Diplomacy and the Quest for Leadership in Europe* (Chapel Hill: University of North Carolina Press, 1998), 94; also John Young, *Britain, France, and the Unity of Europe, 1945–1951* (Leicester: Leicester University Press, 1984), 77–85.

48. "Summary of State Department's Proposed Positions Papers for London Meeting of CFM," undated, box 141, President's Secretary's Files (PSF), HSTL; Lovett in Leffler, "Strategic Dimensions."

49. See "GFK Notes for Secy. Marshall," July 21, 1947, box 33, PPS Records, RG 59, NARA.

50. Marshall to the Embassy in France, February 24, 1948, *FRUS 1948,* 6:736; also Vojtech Mastny, *The Cold War and Soviet Insecurity: The Stalin Years* (New York: Oxford University Press, 1998), 30–34, 41–43.

51. Herring, *Colony to Superpower,* 616; John Lewis Gaddis, *George F. Kennan: An American Life* (New York: Penguin, 2011), 293–295; Miscamble, *George F. Kennan,* 88–99.

52. Quoted in Ferrell, *Off the Record,* 148–149; "Meeting of the Secretary of Defense and the Service Chiefs with the Secretary of State 1045 Hours," October 10, 1948, box 147, Forrestal Papers, SMML. On U.S. perceptions of Soviet motives, see "Berlin Matter: Meeting of Ministers," September 21, 1948, box 5, Bohlen Papers, RG 59, NARA; CIA 8–48, "Review of the World Situation as It Relates to the Security of the United States," August 19, 1948, box 177, NSC, HSTL; Greg Behrman, *The Most Noble Adventure: The Marshall Plan and the Time When America Helped Save Europe* (New York: Simon & Schuster, 2007), 206.

53. Jessup, "The United States Goal in Tomorrow's World," *DOSB,* February 27, 1949, 246; also Lovett's comments in "Minutes of the Second Meeting of the Washington Exploratory Talks on Security," July 6, 1948, *FRUS 1948,* 3:152–155; Harriman to Marshall and Forrestal, June 14, 1948, box 272, Harriman Papers, Library of Congress (LC); PPS 27/1, "Western Union and Related Problems," April 6, 1948, *PPSP,* 2:165–174.

54. Initially, the alliance was known simply as the North Atlantic Treaty. "NATO" came into common usage during the early 1950s, following the outbreak of the Korean War.

55. Quoted in "Address on the Occasion of the Signing of the North Atlantic Treaty," April 4, 1949, APP; also MemCon, April 3, 1949, box 12, Lot 53D444, RG 59, NARA; Ikenberry, *After Victory,* 194–199.

56. Bohlen's quotes in "Notes for Off-the Record Remarks," undated, box 8, Bohlen Records, RG 59, NARA. See also Harriman to Marshall and Forrestal, June 14, 1948, box 272, Harriman Papers, LC; Timothy Ireland, *Creating the Entangling Alliance: The Origins of the North Atlantic Treaty Organization* (Westport, CT: Greenwood Press, 1981).

57. It is notable that Kennan, probably the strongest proponent of the third-force concept, opposed NATO and spent much of 1948 seeking to undermine the idea. Hickerson, conversely, became one of NATO's strongest supporters. The evolution of American thinking on European defense arrangements is covered in Lawrence S. Kaplan, *NATO 1948: The Birth of the Transatlantic Alliance* (New York: Rowman & Littlefield, 2007), chaps. 1–4; also Secretary of State to British Ambassador, January 20, 1948, *FRUS 1948,* 3:8–9; PPS 43, "Considerations Affecting the Conclusion of a North Atlantic Security Pact," November 24, 1948, *FRUS 1948,* 3:283–289.

58. "Memorandum," November 11, 1948, box 272, Harriman Papers, LOC.

59. Quoted in Memorandum for the President, November 26, 1948, box 186, NSC, HSTL; PPS 23, "Review of Current Trends in U.S. Foreign Policy," February

24, 1948, *PPSP,* 2:122–123; also Shu Guang Zhang, *Deterrence and Strategic Culture: Chinese-American Confrontations, 1949–1958* (Ithaca, NY: Cornell University Press, 1992), 40.

60. John Lewis Gaddis, "The Strategic Perspective: The Rise and Fall of the 'Defensive Perimeter' Concept, 1947–1951," in *Uncertain Years: Chinese-American Relations, 1947–1950,* ed. Dorothy Borg and Waldo Heinrichs (New York: Columbia University Press, 1980), 61–75, esp. 63.

61. Quoted in Gordon Chang, *Friends and Enemies: The United States, China, and the Soviet Union, 1948–1972* (Stanford, CA: Stanford University Press, 1990), 48; also NSC 34/2, February 28, 1949, *FRUS 1949,* 9: esp. 494–495; PPS 39, "To Define United States Policy toward China," September 7, 1948, *FRUS 1948,* 8:146–155; Michael Hunt, *Crises in U.S. Foreign Policy: An International History Reader* (New Haven, CT: Yale University Press, 1996), 172–173.

62. Chen Jian, "The Myth of America's 'Lost Chance' in China: A Chinese Perspective in Light of New Evidence," *DH* 21, no. 1 (Winter 1997): 77–86; John Lewis Gaddis, *We Now Know: Rethinking Cold War History* (New York: Oxford University Press, 1998), 64.

63. Quotes from Acheson to Hanoi, May 20, 1949, *FRUS 1949,* 7:29; Offner, *Another Such Victory,* 307, 345. Similarly, in 1951 Truman declared that the United States could not abandon the Korean peninsula lest its allies be "murdered by a bunch of Chinese bandits." MemCon, January 29, 1951, box 142, PSF, HSTL.

64. Acheson quoted in Warren Cohen, *America's Response to China: A History of Sino-American Relations* (New York: Columbia University Press, 2000), 166; This paragraph and the preceding one draw on Cohen's work, ibid., 164–169; William Leary and William Stueck, "The Chennault Plan to Save China: U.S. Containment in Asia and the Origins of the CIA's Aerial Empire," *DH* 8, no. 4 (Fall 1984): 349–364; Clark to Acheson, August 9, 1949, *FRUS 1949,* 8:477–488; Acheson to Strong, August 24, 1949, ibid., 503; Robert Beisner, *Dean Acheson: A Life in the Cold War* (New York: Oxford University Press, 2006), 187–189; Robert Edwin Herzstein, *Henry R. Luce, Time, and the American Crusade in Asia* (New York: Cambridge University Press, 2005), chaps. 5–6.

65. Quoted in Forrestal Diary, January 16, 1948, box 147, Forrestal Papers, SMML; also CIA, "The Current Situation in the Mediterranean and the Near East," October 11, 1947, CIA FOIA; ORE 25–48, "The Break-Up of the Colonial Empires and Its Implications for U.S. Security," September 3, 1948, CIA FOIA; Kennan, "Comments on the General Trend of U.S. Foreign Policy," August 20, 1948, box 163, GFKP, SMML; PPS 25, "French North Africa," March 22, 1948, *PPSP,* 2:142–149.

66. PPS 51, "United States Policy toward Southeast Asia," May 19, 1949, *PPSP,* 3: esp. 38; CIA, "Strategic Importance of Japan," May 24, 1948, CIA FOIA; see also "Record of Round-Table Discussion by Twenty-Five Far East Experts with the Department of State on 'American Policy toward China,'" October 6–8, 1949, box 151, PSF, HSTL.

67. George Herring, *America's Longest War: The United States and Vietnam, 1950–1975* (New York: Alfred A. Knopf, 1986), 16.

68. PPS 51, "United States Policy toward Southeast Asia," 38–40, 52; "Problem Paper Prepared by a Working Group in the Department of State," February 1, 1950,

FRUS 1950, 6:711–714; also Memorandum by the Assistant Secretary of State to Rusk, January 5, 1950, *FRUS 1950,* 6:690; Truman to Acheson, May 1, 1950, *FRUS 1950,* 6:791.

69. Butterworth to Lovett, October 1, 1947, *FRUS 1947,* 6:820–821; also William Stueck, *The Road to Confrontation: American Policy toward China and Korea, 1947–1950* (Chapel Hill: University of North Carolina Press, 1981), esp. 75–88.

70. Quoted in NSC 8, "Report by the National Security Council on the Position of the United States with Respect to Korea," April 2, 1948, *FRUS 1948,* 6:1166–1167; Simei Qing, *From Allies to Enemies: Visions of Modernity, Identity, and U.S.-China Diplomacy, 1945–1960* (Cambridge, MA: Harvard University Press, 2007), 104.

71. There was an extended debate over what to do about Taiwan in 1949–50. In brief, Acheson and Truman were willing to use diplomatic or covert means to keep the island out of Mao's hands if such methods held any promise of being successful, but until the Korean War broke out in June 1950, they refused to commit U.S. military forces to defend Taiwan.

72. Acheson to Jessup, July 18, 1949, box 5, Bohlen Records, RG 59, NARA.

73. See Michael Schaller, *The American Occupation of Japan: The Origins of the Cold War in Asia* (New York: Oxford University Press, 1985), 241–245.

74. In this sense, Acheson's speech, which placed South Korea outside the defensive perimeter, was a technically accurate—if somewhat misleading—statement of policy.

75. MemCon, April 3, 1949, box 12, Lot 53D444, RG 59, NARA.

76. PPS 59, "U.S. Policy toward the Soviet Satellites in Eastern Europe," August 25, 1949, *FRUS 1949,* 5:21–25, quoted at 21; Record of the 36th Meeting of the PPS, March 1, 1949, ibid., 9–10; also Scott Lucas and Kaeten Mistry, "Illusions of Coherence: George F. Kennan, U.S. Strategy and Political Warfare in the Early Cold War, 1946–1950," *DH* 33, no. 1 (January 2009): 56–61.

77. Beisner, *Dean Acheson,* 161–162; also CIA 3–49, "Review of the World Situation," March 16, 1949, box 178, NSC, HSTL.

78. Forrestal Diary, February 12, 1948, box 147, Forrestal Papers, SMML; Trachtenberg, *Constructed Peace,* 87–90.

79. David Alan Rosenberg, "American Atomic Strategy and the Hydrogen Bomb Decision," *JAH* 66, no. 1 (June 1979): esp. 64–73, quoted at 72.

80. Quoted in MemCon, April 3, 1949, box 12, Lot 53D444, RG 59, NARA; Col. R. B. Landry to General Spatz, January 27, 1948, box 28, Carl Spaatz Papers, LC.

81. Quotes from PPS 33, "Factors Affecting the Nature of the U.S. Defense Arrangements in the Light of Soviet Policies," June 23, 1948, *PPSP,* 2:289; Acheson to Acting Secretary, May 9, 1950, *FRUS 1950,* 3:1015.

82. Forrestal to Walter G. Andrews, December 13, 1948, in Millis, *Forrestal Diaries,* 536; also Truman to Edwin Nourse, March 25, 1948, box 1, Keyserling Papers, HSTL.

83. Quoted in NSC 35, "Existing International Commitments Involving the Possible Use of Armed Forces," November 17, 1948, box 177, NSC, HSTL; Acheson, *Present,* 735. See also Forrestal to Truman, December 1, 1948, box 21, Leahy Papers, RG 218, NARA. The figure is from Allan R. Millett and Peter Maslowski, *For the Common Defense: A Military History of the United States of America* (New York: Free Press, 1984), 481.

84. Joseph Marion Jones, *The Fifteen Weeks, February 21–June 5, 1947* (New York: Harcourt, Brace & World, 1964), 151.

85. Marc Selverstone, *Constructing the Monolith: The United States, Great Britain, and International Communism, 1945–1950* (Cambridge, MA: Harvard University Press, 2009), 88–89.

86. USDEL to Webb, May 11, 1950, *FRUS 1950,* 3:1038; McMahon, *Dean Acheson,* 110–111; Guangqio Xu, *Congress and the U.S.-China Relationship, 1949–1979* (Akron, OH: University of Akron Press, 2007), chap. 1.

87. "Current Soviet Intentions," February 28, 1950, box 14, Lot 58D776, RG 59, NARA.

88. ORE 32–50, "The Effect of the Soviet Possession of Atomic Bombs on the Security of the United States," June 9, 1950, National Security Archive (NSA), Washington, DC.

89. This was a danger identified by the drafters of NSC-68. See NSC-68, "United States Objectives and Programs for National Security," April 12, 1950, PSF, HSTL.

90. See Kennan's comments in "Minutes of the 148th Meeting of the PPS," October 11, 1949, *FRUS 1949,* 1:402. These issues are discussed in greater detail in Trachtenberg, *Constructed Peace,* 96–99; and Trachtenberg, "A 'Wasting Asset': American Strategy and the Shifting Nuclear Balance, 1949–1954," *IS* 13, no. 1 (Winter 1988–89): esp. 11–12, 16–18, 21–23.

91. See Statement Appended to the Report of the General Advisory Committee, October 30, 1949, *FRUS 1949,* 1:571.

92. Eban Ayers Diary, February 4, 1950, in Eban Ayers and Robert Ferrell, *Truman in the White House: The Diary of Eban A. Ayers* (Columbia: University of Missouri Press, 1991), 340–341.

93. The change argument is represented in Gaddis, *Strategies,* chaps. 2–4. The continuity thesis is in Leffler, *Preponderance,* 355–360.

94. NSC-68, "United States Objectives and Programs for National Security."

95. Ibid.

96. Ibid.

97. Bohlen to Nitze, April 5, 1950, box 6, Bohlen Records, RG 59, NARA.

98. Gaddis, *Strategies,* 110; also Paul Nitze Oral History Interview, various dates, 232, 244–245, Oral Histories, HSTL.

99. "Statement by the President on the Situation in Korea," June 27, 1950, APP. On changing power dynamics and Stalin's policy, see Kathryn Weathersby, "'Should We Fear This?' Stalin and the Danger of War with America," Cold War International History Project (CWIHP) Working Paper No. 39 (Washington, DC: Woodrow Wilson Center, 2002), esp. 9–11; Odd Arne Westad, *The Global Cold War: Third-World Interventions and the Making of Our Times* (New York: Cambridge University Press, 2006), 66.

100. Paris to Acheson, June 26, 1950, *FRUS 1950,* 7:174–175; Memorandum of Conversation, June 25, 1950, ibid., 158; also Acheson to Moscow, June 26, 1950, ibid., 176–177; "Intelligence Estimate Prepared by the Estimates Group," Office of Intelligence Research, Department of State, June 25, 1950, ibid., 148–154.

101. NSC 73/4, "The Position and Actions of the United States with Respect to Possible Further Soviet Moves in the Light of the Korean Situation," August 25,

1950, box 180, NSC, HSTL; also Memorandum for the President, October 2, 1950, box 187, NSC, HSTL; Beisner, *Dean Acheson,* 335–337, 352–355, also chaps. 21–22.

102. Acheson and Johnson to Truman, September 8, 1950, *FRUS 1950,* 3:273; also Paper Prepared by the JCS, undated (September 1950), *FRUS 1950,* 3:291–292; Philip Jessup to James Lay, October 9, 1950, box 181, NSC, HSTL.

103. Memorandum for the President, August 25, 1950, box 187, NSC, HSTL; also "Extracts of Views of the Joint Chiefs of Staff with Respect to Western Policy toward Germany," June 1950, box 180, NSC, HSTL; MemCon between Acheson, Marshall, Harriman, Nitze, and other officials, October 5, 1950, box 14, Lot 53D444, RG 59, NARA.

104. Robert D. Schulzinger, *A Time for War: The United States and Vietnam, 1941–1975* (New York: Oxford University Press, 1997), 48; also James Webb to James Lay, March 15, 1951, box 182, NSC, HSTL.

105. Second Meeting between President Truman and Prime Minister Attlee, December 5, 1950, box 1, Omar Bradley Papers, RG 218, NARA.

106. Rusk to Acheson, August 24, 1950, box 5, Conference Files, RG 59, NARA.

107. NSC, "The Position and Actions of the United States with Respect to Possible Further Soviet Moves in the Light of the Korean Situation," August 25, 1950, *FRUS 1950,* 1:385.

108. Memorandum for the President, October 2, 1950, box 187, NSC, HSTL. The figures are from Hogan, *Cross of Iron,* 311.

109. Meeting of the NSC in the Cabinet Room at the White House, June 28, 1950, box 13, Lot 53D444, RG 59, NARA. For concerns that the United States might lose a global war in 1950–51, see Trachtenberg, "'Wasting Asset,'" 21–26.

110. Kirk to Acheson, July 27, 1950, *FRUS 1950,* 7:485; also Memorandum for the President, July 27, 1950, box 136, Nitze Papers, LC; JCS to Johnson, July 10, 1950, *FRUS 1950,* 7:346.

111. Quoted in Kirk to Acheson, July 27, 1950, *FRUS 1950,* 7:483; also Draft Memorandum Prepared by the PPS, July 22, 1950, *FRUS 1950,* 7:449–454; Butler Draft Memorandum, July 25, 1950, ibid., 469–473; MemCon, June 30, 1950, ibid., 258–259; Memorandum by the Director of the Office of Chinese Affairs, October 4, 1950, ibid., 864–865; Kennan to Acheson, August 8, 1950, *FRUS 1950,* 1: esp. 361–363; Rosemary Foot, *The Wrong War: American Policy and the Dimensions of the Korean Conflict, 1950–1953* (Ithaca, NY: Cornell University Press, 1985), 81–93.

112. Meeting of the President with Congressional Leaders in the Cabinet Room, December 13, 1950, box 142, PSF, HSTL.

113. Acheson, *Present,* 468.

114. Beisner, *Dean Acheson,* 399.

115. "Notes on the Wake Island Meeting," October 14, 1950, box 306, Harriman Papers, LC; also "Memorandum of Conversation" with MacArthur, undated, ibid.; CIA Situation Summary, September 22, 1950, box 211, Intelligence File, HSTL; CIA, "Threat of Soviet Intervention in Korea," October 12, 1950, box 304, Harriman Papers, LC; CIA, "General Soviet and Chinese Communist Intentions and Capabilities in the Far East," October 12, 1950, ibid.

116. Allison to Nitze, July 24, 1950, *FRUS 1950,* 7:460–461; also Draft Memorandum Prepared in the Department of Defense, July 31, 1950, *FRUS 1950,* 7:506;

James Matray, "Truman's Plan for Victory: National Self-Determination and the Thirty-Eighth Parallel in Korea," *JAH* 66, no. 2 (September 1979): 314–333.

117. Allison's Memorandum of Conversation between Acheson and Kenneth Younger, October 4, 1950, *FRUS 1950,* 7:868.

118. Draft Memorandum Prepared by the PPS, July 22, 1950, *FRUS 1950,* 7:452.

119. "Threats to Democracy and Its Way of Life," April 22, 1950, in *DOSB,* May 1, 1950, 675; also Nancy Bernhard, "Clearer Than Truth: Public Affairs Television and the State Department's Domestic Information Campaign, 1947–1952," *DH* 21, no. 4 (Fall 1997): 561–564.

120. Beisner, *Dean Acheson,* 251.

121. Ibid., 416.

122. "Statement by General of the Army Omar N. Bradley, Chairman of the Joint Chiefs of Staff before the Senate Armed Services and Foreign Relations Committee," undated (May 15, 1951), box 4, Bradley Papers, RG 218, NARA; Foot, *Wrong War,* 105–129.

123. Memorandum for the President, November 28, 1950, box 187, NSC, PSF, HSTL.

124. Memorandum for the President, December 15, 1950, box 136, Nitze Papers, LC.

125. Eisenhower to Harriman, December 14, 1951, box 278, Harriman Papers, LC; Millett and Maslowski, *Common Defense,* 496; Herring, *Colony to Superpower,* 646; Trachtenberg, *Constructed Peace,* chap. 4.

126. MemCon, January 8, 1952, box 99, PSF, HSTL.

127. James Webb to James Lay, March 15, 1951, box 182, NSC, HSTL; Mark Lawrence, *The Vietnam War: A Concise International History* (New York: Oxford University Press, 2010), 40.

128. Peter Hahn, *The United States, Great Britain, and Egypt, 1945–1956: Strategy and Diplomacy in the Early Cold War* (Chapel Hill: University of North Carolina Press, 1991), 93–154, quoted at 111; James A. Bill, *The Eagle and the Lion: The Tragedy of American-Iranian Relations* (New Haven, CT: Yale University Press, 1988), 57–86.

129. Millett and Maslowski, *Common Defense,* 491; "Estimated U.S. and Soviet/Russian Nuclear Stockpiles, 1945–94," *Bulletin of the Atomic Scientists,* December 1994, 59; Hogan, *Cross of Iron,* 324; also Annual Report of General Dwight D. Eisenhower, April 2, 1952, box 278, Harriman Papers, LC.

130. Memorandum for the President, October 11, 1951, box 136, Nitze Papers, LC.

131. Annual Report of General Dwight D. Eisenhower, April 2, 1952, box 278, Harriman Papers, LC; also Eisenhower to Harriman, December 14, 1951, ibid.; and Eisenhower's comments in Trachtenberg, *Constructed Peace,* 173.

132. MemCon between Truman and Pleven, January 29, 1951, box 142, PSF, HSTL.

133. Alonzo Hamby, *Man of the People: A Life of Harry S. Truman* (New York: Oxford University Press, 1995), 574; Foot, *Wrong War,* 150–198.

134. Ogburn to Rusk, August 18, 1950, *FRUS 1950,* 6:863; also Allison to Acheson, February 11, 1952, *FRUS 1952–1954,* vol. 13, pt. 1: 28–34; NIE [National Intelligence Estimate] 35/2, "Probable Developments in Indochina through Mid-1953," August 29, 1952, ibid., esp. 243–244.

135. Nitze in NSC 141, "Reexamination of United States Programs for National Security," January 19, 1953, box 136, Nitze Papers, LC; Acheson quoted in Memorandum of Dinner Meeting on SS *Williamsburg,* January 5, 1952, box 15, Conference Files, RG 59, NARA; also Nitze to Acheson, January 12, 1953, *FRUS 1952–1954,* vol. 2, pt. 1: 202–205.

136. NIE-17, "Probable Soviet Reactions to a Remilitarization of Western Germany," December 27, 1950, CIA FOIA; also Memorandum for the President, January 25, 1951, box 187, NSC, HSTL.

137. Trachtenberg, "'Wasting Asset,'" 47–49.

138. Geoffrey Roberts, *Stalin's Wars: From World War to Cold War, 1939–1953* (New Haven, CT: Yale University Press, 2006), 361–362; Yoram Gorlizki and Oleg Mhlevniuk, *Cold Peace: Stalin and the Soviet Ruling Circle, 1945–1953* (New York: Oxford University Press, 2004), 98–100.

139. "Meeting of President Truman and President Auriol," March 29, 1952, box 142, PSF, HSTL.

140. Aaron Friedberg, *In the Shadow of the Garrison State: America's Anti-statism and Its Cold War Grand Strategy* (Princeton, NJ: Princeton University Press, 2000), 70–71, 117–123, quoted at 123.

141. There was no "clearly delineated doctrine or strategy of containment" in the late 1940s, writes Wilson Miscamble; Truman-era policy did not "[conform] to any overarching strategy." Miscamble, *George F. Kennan,* 347, xiv; also Robert Jervis, "The Impact of the Korean War on the Cold War," *Journal of Conflict Resolution* 24, no. 4 (December 1980): 563–592. In fairness to Miscamble, scholars like Leffler may somewhat overestimate the degree of continuity that characterized U.S. policy from 1946 onward. On this point, see Lynn Eden, "The End of U.S. Cold War History?" *International Security* 18, no. 1 (Summer 1993): esp. 195.

142. "Comments on the General Trend of U.S. Foreign Policy," August 20, 1948, box 163, GFKP, SMML.

Chapter 2

1. Henry Kissinger, *American Foreign Policy* (New York: W. W. Norton, 1977), 96.

2. Henry Kissinger, *The Necessity for Choice: Prospects of American Foreign Policy* (New York: Harper & Brothers, 1961), 8. On Nixon and the "big play," see William Safire, *Before the Fall: An Inside View of the Pre-Watergate White House* (New Brunswick, NJ: Transaction Publishers, 2005), 97–106.

3. MemCon between Kissinger and *Time* Editorial Board, November 11, 1974, box 26, Henry A. Kissinger (HAK) Records, RG 59, NARA.

4. Henry Kissinger, *A World Restored: Metternich, Castlereagh, and the Problems of Peace, 1812–1822* (Boston: Houghton Mifflin, 1957), 329.

5. The phrase "new equilibrium" is Kissinger's. See Henry Kissinger, *White House Years* (Boston: Little, Brown, 1979), 65.

6. Ibid., 54–70. Good biographies of Kissinger include Walter Isaacson, *Kissinger: A Biography* (New York: Simon & Schuster, 1992); Jeremi Suri, *Henry Kissinger and the American Century* (Cambridge, MA: Harvard University Press, 2007).

7. "Transcript of a Speech Given by Richard Nixon at the Bohemian Grove," July 29, 1967, box 1, White House Special Files, Nixon Presidential Materials (NPM). On Nixon, see Melvin Small, *The Presidency of Richard Nixon* (Lawrence: University Press of Kansas, 2003); Robert Dallek, *Nixon and Kissinger: Partners in Power* (New York: HarperCollins, 2007).

8. Joan Hoff, *Nixon Reconsidered* (New York: Basic Books, 1994), 155. A good overview of the relationship, although one that is perhaps overly sympathetic to Kissinger, is Suri, *Henry Kissinger and the American Century,* 200–211.

9. Kissinger to Nixon, April 10, 1970, *FRUS 1969–1976,* 2: Doc. 317. Kissinger was summarizing (with apparent approval) a memorandum prepared by another adviser. For additional illustrations of these tendencies, see Telephone Conversation between Nixon and Kissinger, November 13, 1972, Editorial Note, *FRUS 1969–1976,* 2: Doc. 347; Editorial Note on Kissinger's Meeting with Nixon, December 12, 1971, *FRUS 1969–1976,* 11: Doc. 283; Editorial Note on Meeting between Nixon and Kissinger, December 12, 1971, ibid., Doc. 281.

10. Nixon to Haldeman, December 4, 1970, Donated Nixon Documents, NPM.

11. Peter W. Rodman Oral History, May 22, 1994, Foreign Affairs Oral History Collection (FAOHC), LC.

12. David Greenberg, "Nixon as Statesman: The Failed Campaign," in *Nixon in the World: American Foreign Relations, 1969–1977,* ed. Fredrik Logevall and Andrew Preston (New York: Oxford University Press, 2008), 48.

13. MemCon between Nixon and Zhou, February 23, 1972, NSA.

14. Nixon to Haldeman, December 4, 1970, Donated Nixon Documents, NPM.

15. Kissinger, *White House Years,* 38, 130, 54.

16. Ibid., 55.

17. Kissinger, "The White Revolutionary: Reflections on Bismarck," *Daedalus* 97, no. 3 (Summer 1968): 910. See also Kissinger, *World Restored,* 213.

18. Kissinger, *Does America Need a Foreign Policy?* (New York: Simon & Schuster, 2001), 285; Kissinger, "White Revolutionary," 910, passim.

19. Kissinger, "Domestic Structure and Foreign Policy," *Daedalus* 95, no. 2 (Spring 1966): 511.

20. Kissinger, *Years of Renewal* (New York: Simon & Schuster, 1999), 1065; also Kissinger, "Reflections on American Diplomacy," *Foreign Affairs* 35, no. 1 (October 1956): 53.

21. Dallek, *Nixon and Kissinger,* 133; bombing statistics in George Herring, *From Colony to Superpower: U.S. Foreign Relations since 1776* (New York: Oxford University Press, 2008), 762.

22. Kissinger, *White House Years,* 226–227.

23. Robert Collins, "The Economic Crisis of 1968 and the Waning of the 'American Century,'" *American Historical Review* 101, no. 2 (April 1996): 396–422, quoted at 416.

24. Kissinger to Nixon, undated (late 1969), *FRUS 1969–1976,* 1: Doc. 39.

25. Kissinger Background Briefing, February 16, 1970, *FRUS 1969–1976,* 1: Doc. 58; also "Transcript of a Speech Given by Richard Nixon at the Bohemian Grove."

26. MemCon between Kissinger and Harvard Fellows, December 7, 1971, NSA. See also MemCon between Kissinger and French Officials, August 4, 1969, NSA.

27. Quoted in Jeffrey Kimball, *Nixon's Vietnam War* (Lawrence: University Press of Kansas, 1998), 51.

28. Kissinger, *White House Years,* 1049.

29. "Transcript of a Speech Given by Richard Nixon at the Bohemian Grove."

30. "Essay by Henry A. Kissinger," *FRUS 1969–1976,* 1: Doc. 4.

31. Editorial Note on a Conversation between Nixon and Kissinger, October 12, 1970, *FRUS 1969–1976,* 1: Doc. 75; also MemCon between Nixon and Elliot Richardson, February 15, 1973, box 1, MemCons, NSA Files, Gerald Ford Library (GFL).

32. "Address by Richard Nixon at the Air Force Academy," June 4, 1969, *FRUS 1969–1976,* 1: Doc. 27.

33. Editorial Note on Nixon's Acceptance Speech at the Republican Convention, August 8, 1968, *FRUS 1969–1976,* 1: Doc. 6; also "Radio Address on Foreign Policy," November 4, 1972, APP.

34. "Essay by Henry A. Kissinger."

35. Kissinger Background Briefing, December 18, 1969, *FRUS 1969–1976,* 1: Doc. 47. See also MemCon between Kissinger and French Officials, August 4, 1969, NSA.

36. "Essay by Henry A. Kissinger"; Kissinger Background Briefing, December 18, 1969, *FRUS 1969–1976,* 1: Doc. 47.

37. Kissinger Background Briefing, August 14, 1970, *FRUS 1969–1976,* 1: Doc. 69.

38. MemCon between Kissinger and Harvard Fellows, December 7, 1971, NSA.

39. Kissinger, *White House Years,* 126–127; Interagency Working Group, "How the Soviets View the Strategic Balance," May 1969, box 2, Lot 72D504, RG 59, NARA.

40. Background Briefing by Kissinger, August 14, 1970, *FRUS 1969–1976,* 1: Doc. 69.

41. Nixon to Laird, February 4, 1969, *FRUS 1969–1976,* 12: Doc. 10.

42. Kissinger, *White House Years,* 128.

43. The phrase was Kissinger's. See "Essay by Henry A. Kissinger," *FRUS 1969–1976,* 1: Doc. 4.

44. MemCon between Nixon and Brezhnev, May 23, 1972, in Department of State, *Soviet-American Relations: The Detente Years, 1969–1972* (Washington, DC: Government Printing Office, 2007), Doc. 352. This collection is cited subsequently as *FRUS: SAR.*

45. Kissinger to Walsh, February 21, 1969, *FRUS 1969–1976,* 12: Doc. 20.

46. Nixon to Laird [drafted by Kissinger], February 4, 1969, *FRUS 1969–1976,* 12: Doc. 10; Kissinger to Nixon, February 18, 1969, *FRUS 1969–1976,* 12: Doc. 17. This emphasis on carefully doling out rewards and punishments helps explain why the Nixon administration, despite its own move toward negotiations with the Soviets, was comparatively reluctant to see its allies do likewise. Kissinger and Nixon were particularly skeptical about *Ostpolitik,* West German chancellor Willy Brandt's policy of reaching out to the East to expand ties and reduce tensions between the two German states. They feared that West German eagerness might produce a race to win favor in Moscow, thereby weakening NATO and allowing the Soviets to play Bonn and Washington off one another. "Brandt is sincere," Kissinger told Acheson, "but there are a lot of sincere fools in the world." TelCon between Acheson and Kissinger, December 9, 1970, box 8, HAK TelCons, NSC, NPM. See also NSC Minutes, October 14, 1970, box H-109, NSC Institutional Files, NPM; Gottfried

Nidhart, "U.S. Détente and West German Ostpolitik: Parallels and Frictions," in *The Strained Alliance: U.S.-European Relations from Nixon to Carter*, ed. Matthias Schulz and Thomas A. Schwartz (New York: Cambridge University Press, 2010), 26–30.

47. MemCon between Kissinger and Zhou, June 21, 1972, NSA.

48. "Radio Address on Foreign Policy," November 4, 1972, APP. On "self-containment," see Olav Njølstad, "The Collapse of Superpower Détente, 1975–1980," in *Cambridge History of the Cold War*, ed. Melvyn Leffler and Odd Arne Westad, vol. 3 (New York: Cambridge University Press, 2010), 135–155.

49. Richard Nixon, "Asia after Viet Nam," *Foreign Affairs (FA)* 46, no. 1 (October 1967): 121.

50. MemCon between Boris Davidov and William Stearman, August 18, 1969, NSA.

51. A good account is William Burr, "Sino-American Relations, 1969: The Sino-Soviet Border War and Steps toward Rapprochement," *Cold War History (CWH)* 1, no. 3 (April 2001): 73–112; see also the chronology in Rodman to Kissinger, October 13, 1971, box 13, HAK Administrative and Staff Files, NSC, NPM.

52. Kissinger to Nixon, September 29, 1969, NSA.

53. Quoted in "President Nixon's Comments to Chiefs of Mission, Bangkok," July 30, 1969, box 8, Marshall Green Papers, Hoover; also SRG Meeting, November 20, 1969, box H-111, NSC Institutional Files, NPM.

54. MemCon between Nixon and Edward Heath, December 20, 1971, box 1025, Presidential/HAK MemCons, NPM.

55. Editorial Note, Record of a Conversation between Nixon and Kissinger, February 14, 1972, *FRUS 1969–1976,* 1: Doc. 105.

56. Quoted in Evelyn Goh, "Nixon, Kissinger, and the 'Soviet Card' in the U.S. Opening to China, 1971–1974," *DH* 29, no. 3 (June 2005): 475. See also Excerpts from Kissinger Background Briefing, "U.S. Relations with PRC and USSR," undated, box 16, HAK Administrative and Staff Files, NSC, NPM; Burr, "Sino-American Relations, 1969," 14–17.

57. MemCon between Nixon and U.S. officials in Bangkok, July 29, 1969, *FRUS 1969–1976,* 1: Doc. 31.

58. MemCon between Nixon and Zhou, February 21, 1972, NSA.

59. Kissinger to Nixon, February 5, 1972, box 13, HAK Administrative and Staff Files, NSC, NPM; MemCon between Kissinger and Business Council, December 1, 1971, *FRUS 1969–1976,* 1: Doc. 101; MemCon between Kissinger and Moshe Dayan, March 29, 1974, box 7, HAK Records, RG 59, NARA; MemCon between Ford and Kissinger, January 30, 1975, box 9, MemCons, NSA Files, GFL.

60. Kissinger Background Briefing, "U.S. Relations with PRC and USSR," undated, box 16, HAK Administrative and Staff Files, NSC, NPM.

61. "President Nixon's Comments to Chiefs of Mission," July 30, 1969, box 17, William Bundy Papers, SMML.

62. MemCon between Kissinger and Schumann, August 4, 1969, NSA; also MemCon between Kissinger and Lee Kwan Yew, December 13, 1968, box 2, HAK Administrative and Staff Files, NSC, NPM; Nixon, "Address to the Nation on the War in Vietnam," November 3, 1969, APP.

63. Notes of NSC Meeting, January 25, 1969, *FRUS 1969–1976,* 6: Doc. 10; also Editorial Note, *FRUS 1969–1976,* 6: Doc. 68; Kissinger to Nixon, December 20,

1968, box 2, HAK Administrative and Staff Files, NSC, NPM; Kissinger to Nixon, January 2, 1969, ibid.; Dale Van Atta, *With Honor: Melvin Laird in War, Peace, and Politics* (Madison: University of Wisconsin Press, 2008), 160–162, 176, 183–184.

64. Kissinger was particularly skeptical about Vietnamization. See Editorial Note, *FRUS 1969–1976,* 1: Doc. 36.

65. MemCon between Kissinger and Dobrynin, October 1, 1969, NSA; also MemCon between Nixon, Kissinger, and Dobrynin, October 20, 1969, box 489, NSC, NPM; Kissinger, *White House Years,* 1190; Jussi Hanhimaki, *The Flawed Architect: Henry Kissinger and American Foreign Policy* (New York: Oxford University Press, 2004), 216–217. On Nixon's skepticism, see "President Nixon's Comments to Chiefs of Mission," July 30, 1969, box 17, Bundy Papers, SMML.

66. See H. R. Haldeman with Joseph Dimona, *The Ends of Power* (New York: Times Books, 1978), 83.

67. Kissinger to Nixon, March 16, 1969, *FRUS 1969–1976,* 6: Doc. 40; NSC Meeting, January 25, 1969, *FRUS 1969–1976,* 6: Doc. 10.

68. Kissinger to Bunker, May 7, 1972, *FRUS 1969–1976,* 8: Doc. 128. These initiatives are described in greater detail in Kimball, *Nixon's Vietnam War;* Larry Berman, *No Peace, No Honor: Nixon, Kissinger, and Betrayal in Vietnam* (New York: Touchstone, 2002); Pierre Asselin, *A Bitter Peace: Washington, Hanoi, and the Making of the Paris Agreement* (Chapel Hill: University of North Carolina Press, 2002); and Scott D. Sagan and Jeremi Suri, "The Madman Nuclear Alert: Secrecy, Signaling, and Safety in October 1969," *International Security* 27, no. 4 (Spring 2003): 150–183. Kissinger did show some hesitation in endorsing the invasion of Cambodia in 1970, because he feared that it might lead to massive antiwar protests and cause members of his staff to resign (both of which did happen). Yet he ultimately supported this and other escalations, which were quite consonant with his general views on the need to make U.S. military power more usable.

69. Isaacson, *Kissinger,* 246.

70. Kissinger, *The Troubled Partnership: A Re-appraisal of the Atlantic Alliance* (New York: McGraw-Hill, 1965), 232–233; "Essay by Henry A. Kissinger."

71. Richard Nixon, untitled notes, July 7, 1968, box 1, Richard Nixon Papers, Hoover.

72. Editorial Note, *FRUS 1969–1976,* 1: Doc. 29. Jeffrey Kimball has argued that Nixon never intended his Guam speech to be a global statement of U.S. policy. This is true in a narrow sense, as Nixon's remarks were geared primarily toward East Asia. Yet the Nixon Doctrine was fully consistent with the broader ideas that both Nixon and Kissinger had been expressing for some time, and also with the general policy—encouraging greater self-reliance and initiative by allies—that they subsequently pursued in places from Brazil to Southeast Asia. And as Kimball himself notes, "There is little doubt that President Nixon wanted 'no more Vietnams.'" See Jeffrey Kimball, "The Nixon Doctrine: A Saga of Misunderstanding," *Presidential Studies Quarterly* 36, no. 1 (March 2006): 59–74, quoted at 72.

73. William Bundy, *A Tangled Web: The Making of Foreign Policy in the Nixon Presidency* (New York: Farrar, Straus and Giroux, 1998), 140–144; Nixon, "Asia after Viet Nam," 120–121.

74. Marc Trachtenberg, "The French Factor in U.S. Foreign Policy during the Nixon-Pompidou Period, 1969–1974," *Journal of Cold War Studies (JCWS)* 13, no. 1 (Winter 2011): 4–59, esp. 4–8.

75. Harold James, *International Monetary Cooperation since Bretton Woods* (New York: Oxford University Press, 1996), 243; also Francis Gavin, *Gold, Dollars, and Power: The Politics of International Monetary Relations* (Chapel Hill: University of North Carolina Press, 2004), 188–198.

76. The souring of U.S. relations with Western Europe and Japan during the early 1970s reflected other factors as well. The Japanese were worried by the prospect of a Sino-American partnership, and no less by the fact that the administration's emphasis on secrecy ensured that they received virtually no advance warning of this rapprochement. The French, in turn, were concerned that Washington and Moscow would seek to arrange global affairs without input from middle powers like Paris. On these issues, see Trachtenberg, "French Factor"; Michael Schaller, *Altered States: The United States and Japan since the Occupation* (New York: Oxford University Press, 1997), 210–244.

77. On these various initiatives, see NSDM 92, November 7, 1970, box H-208, NSC Institutional Files, NPM; Odd Arne Westad, *The Global Cold War: Third-World Interventions and the Making of Our Times* (New York: Cambridge University Press, 2006), 200–201, 211–212; Marshall Green to Kissinger, June 27, 1969, box 2, Green Papers, Hoover; MemCon between Nixon and Suharto, May 28, 1970, NSA; Canberra to State, June 17, 1972, box 954, VIP Visits, NSC, NPM; Matias Spektor, *Kissinger e o Brazil* (Rio de Janeiro: Zahar, 2009).

78. Quoted in MemCon between Médici and Kissinger, December 8, 1971, box 911, VIP Visits, NSC Files, NPM.

79. Kissinger Background Briefing, February 16, 1970, *FRUS 1969–1976,* 1: Doc. 58.

80. See Hal Brands, "Rethinking Nonproliferation: LBJ, the Gilpatric Committee, and U.S. National Security Policy," *JCWS* 8, no. 2 (Spring 2006): 83–113; Brands, "Progress Unseen: U.S. Arms Control Policy and the Origins of Détente," *DH* 30, no. 2 (April 2006): esp. 262–273.

81. Francis Gavin, *Nuclear Statecraft: History and Strategy in America's Atomic Age* (Ithaca, NY: Cornell University Press, 2012), 116–118.

82. Winston Lord to Dr. Kissinger, "Issues Raised by the Nixon Doctrine for Asia," January 23, 1970, NSA.

83. MemCon between Kissinger and Ambassador Jacques Kosciusko-Morizet, April 13, 1973, NSA; also Gavin, *Nuclear Statecraft,* 117–118; Trachtenberg, "French Factor," 6–8.

84. Editorial Note on a Conversation between Kissinger and Nixon, December 9, 1971, *FRUS 1969–1976,* 11: Doc. 256. See also Editorial Note on Nixon's Meeting with the Republican Leadership, April 20, 1971, *FRUS 1969–1976,* 1: Doc. 88.

85. "Address to the Nation on the Situation in Southeast Asia," April 30, 1970, APP.

86. These themes are developed in John Lewis Gaddis, *Strategies of Containment: A Critical Appraisal of American National Security Policy during the Cold War*

(New York: Oxford University Press, 2005), 299–301. Gaddis applies this idea primarily to the administration's efforts in Vietnam, but I believe it had a broader global relevance.

87. Quoted in NSC Meeting, November 5, 1970, box H-029, NSC Institutional File, NPM. On the other cases, see Kissinger, *American Foreign Policy*, 321; MemCon between Ford, Kissinger, and Scowcroft, August 15, 1974, box 5, Mem-Cons, NSA File, GFL; MemCon between Ford, Kissinger, and Scowcroft, July 17, 1975, box 13, MemCons, NSA File, GFL; NSC Meeting Minutes, May 13, 1975, NSC Meetings File, GFL.

88. Dacca to State, March 28, 1971, NSA.

89. Editorial Note on a Conversation between Kissinger and Nixon, December 9, 1971, *FRUS 1969–1976*, 11: Doc. 256. See also Robert McMahon, "The Danger of Geopolitical Fantasies: Nixon, Kissinger, and the South Asia Crisis of 1971," in Logevall and Preston, *Nixon in the World*, 263–265.

90. Note on Kissinger's Meeting with Nixon, December 12, 1971, *FRUS 1969–1976*, 11: Doc. 283. U.S. officials later claimed that their actions had deterred an Indian invasion of West Pakistan, but such an invasion was probably never intended. See Bundy, *Tangled Web*, 282; Vojtech Mastny, "The Soviet Union's Partnership with India," *JCWS* 12, no. 3 (Summer 2010): 70.

91. MemCon between Nixon, Kissinger, and other officials, October 17, 1973, box 2, MemCons, NSA, GFL.

92. MemCon between Kissinger and Golda Meir, May 7, 1974, box 7, HAK Records, RG 59, NARA; Francis Gavin, "Nuclear Nixon: Ironies, Puzzles, and the Triumph of Realpolitik," in Logevall and Preston, *Nixon in the World*, 127.

93. Quoted in Kissinger, *White House Years*, 1474; "Third Annual Report to the Congress on United States Foreign Policy," February 9, 1972, APP. These reports were issued in Nixon's name, but prepared by Kissinger and his staff.

94. Thomas Alan Schwartz, "'Henry … Winning an Election Is Terribly Important': Partisan Politics in the History of U.S. Foreign Relations," *DH* 33, no. 2 (April 2009): 173.

95. Herring, *Colony to Superpower*, 765.

96. Quote from MemCon between Kissinger and the Business Council, December 1, 1971, *FRUS 1969–1976*, 1: Doc. 101; also Kissinger Background Briefing, August 14, 1970, *FRUS 1969–1976*, 1: Doc. 69; Jeremi Suri, *Power and Protest: Global Revolution and the Rise of Détente* (Cambridge, MA: Harvard University Press, 2003), chap. 6.

97. "Transcript of a Speech Given by Richard Nixon at the Bohemian Grove"; "Essay by Henry A. Kissinger."

98. MemCon between Kissinger and Congressmen, January 28, 1975, box 22, HAK Records, RG 59, NARA.

99. MemCon between Kissinger and Stanford Faculty and Students, May 6, 1970, *FRUS 1969–1976*, 1: Doc. 65.

100. David Rothkopf, *Running the World: The Inside Story of the National Security Council* (New York: Public Affairs, 2005), 112; Richard Nixon, *RN: The Memoirs of Richard Nixon* (New York: Grosset & Dunlap, 1978), 770.

101. "Inaugural Address," January 20, 1969, APP; also Kissinger, *American Foreign Policy*, 122.

102. "Address at the Commemorative Session of the North Atlantic Council," April 10, 1969, *FRUS 1969–1976*, 1: Doc. 18.

103. MemCon between U.S., German, French, and British Officials, September 5, 1975, box 23, HAK Records, RG 59, NARA.

104. Haig to Rodman, August 30, 1970, box 14, HAK Office Files, NSC, NPM, cited in Dan Caldwell, "The Legitimation of the Nixon-Kissinger Grand Design and Grand Strategy," *DH* 33, no. 4 (August 2009): 651.

105. See Barbara Keys, "Congress, Kissinger, and the Origins of Human Rights Diplomacy," *DH* 34, no. 5 (November 2010): esp. 824, 840–850.

106. Asaf Siniver, *Nixon, Kissinger, and U.S. Foreign Policy Making: The Machinery of Crisis* (New York: Cambridge University Press, 2008), 63–64. The phrase "palace coup" comes from Bundy, *Tangled Web,* 54–55.

107. Theodore Eliot to John Irwin, October 28, 1970, box 1, Lot 74D164, RG 59, NARA; also Memorandum for the Under Secretary, December 9, 1970, box 1, Lot 74D164, RG 59, NARA.

108. Dallek, *Nixon and Kissinger,* 250.

109. Kissinger, "Reflections," 37.

110. Nixon is quoted in MemCon with the CENTO Foreign Ministers, May 22, 1974, box 4, MemCons, NSA File, GFL; Robert Mason, *Richard Nixon and the Quest for a New Majority* (Chapel Hill: University of North Carolina Press, 2004), 160.

111. Yang Kuisong, "The Sino-Soviet Border Clash of 1969: From Zhenbao Island to Sino-American *Rapprochement,*" *CWH* 1, no. 1 (August 2000): 43–46; also Yafeng Xia, "China's Elite Politics and Sino-American Rapprochement, January 1969–February 1972," *JCWS* 8, no. 4 (Fall 2006): 3–28.

112. Quotes from MemCon between Zhou and Kissinger, July 9, 1971, NSA; MemCon between Nixon, Kissinger, and Zhou, February 21, 1972, NSA. On these issues, see also Kissinger to Nixon, July 14, 1971, NSA; Kissinger, *White House Years,* esp. 1089–1090; Margaret Macmillan, *Nixon and Mao: The Week That Changed the World* (New York: Random House, 2007).

113. See MemCon between Mao, Kissinger, and Zhou, February 17, 1973, box 6, President's Personal File, NPM; Yang Kuisong and Xia Yafeng, "Vacillating between Revolution and Détente: Mao's Changing Psyche and Policy toward the United States, 1969–1976," *DH* 34, no. 2 (April 2010): 408.

114. Dobrynin to Soviet Foreign Ministry, July 17, 1971, *FRUS: SAR,* Doc. 177. See also Vladislav Zubok, "The Soviet Union and Détente of the 1970s," *CWH* 8, no. 4 (November 2008): 435–436; Hanhimaki, *Flawed Architect,* 152.

115. Dobrynin to Soviet Foreign Ministry, March 8, 1972, *FRUS: SAR,* Doc. 267.

116. *DOSB,* June 26, 1972, 898–899.

117. "Fourth Annual Report to the Congress on United States Foreign Policy," May 3, 1973, APP.

118. SALT II was eventually completed during the Carter years, but because of the Soviet invasion of Afghanistan it was never ratified.

119. MemCon between Brezhnev, Ford, and other officials, November 24, 1974, box 1, Vladivostok Summit, Kissinger Reports on USSR, China, and Middle East Discussions, GFL; Anatoly Dobrynin, *In Confidence: Moscow's Ambassador to America's Six Cold War Presidents* (New York: Times Books, 1995), 301.

120. See Piero Gleijeses, *Conflicting Missions: Havana, Washington, and Africa, 1959–1976* (Chapel Hill: University of North Carolina Press, 2002), esp. chaps. 12–15; Vladislav Zubok, *A Failed Empire: The Soviet Union in the Cold War from Stalin to Gorbachev* (Chapel Hill: University of North Carolina Press, 2007), 238.

121. Peter Rodman, *More Precious Than Peace: The Cold War and the Struggle for the Third World* (New York: Scribner, 1994), 154; also Raymond Garthoff, *Détente and Confrontation: Soviet-American Relations from Nixon to Reagan* (Washington, DC: Brookings Institution Press, 1994), esp. 42–53.

122. Odd Arne Westad, "Moscow and the Angolan Crisis, 1974–1976: A New Pattern of Intervention," Cold War International History Project *Bulletin 8–9* (Winter 1996/97): 21; also Westad, *Global Cold War,* chaps. 6–8.

123. Vorontsov to Foreign Ministry, December 5, 1971, *FRUS: SAR,* Doc. 228.

124. Dobrynin to Foreign Ministry, May 5, 1972, *FRUS: SAR,* Doc. 322.

125. Julian Zelizer, "Détente and Domestic Politics," *DH* 33, no. 4 (September 2009): 653–671; Anna Kasten Nelson, "Senator Henry Jackson and the Demise of Détente," in *The Policy Makers: Shaping American Foreign Policy from 1947 to the Present,* ed. Anna Kasten Nelson (New York: Rowman & Littlefield, 2009), 91–98.

126. MemCon between Kissinger and Rabin, October 13, 1974, box 22, HAK Records, RG 59, NARA; Robert David Johnson, *Congress and the Cold War* (New York: Cambridge University Press, 2006), chaps. 5–6.

127. Colby quoted in NSC Meeting Notes, September 14, 1974, NSC Meetings File, GFL; statistics from Millett and Maslowski, *Common Defense,* 569.

128. MemCon, NSC Meeting on Defense Strategy, August 13, 1971, *FRUS 1969–1976,* 1: Doc. 96.

129. TelCon between Kissinger and Ted Koppel, January 15, 1975, NSA; also "Secretary's Meeting with Princeton Summer Interns," August 14, 1974, box 5, Secretary's Staff Meetings, HAK Records, RG 59, NARA.

130. MemCon between Kissinger, Scowcroft, and Ford, December 18, 1975, box 17, MemCons, NSA File, GFL. See also Robert David Johnson, "The Unintended Consequences of Congressional Reform: The Clark and Tunney Amendments and U.S. Policy toward Angola," *DH* 27, no. 2 (April 2003): 215–243; Kissinger, *Years of Renewal,* chaps. 15–17.

131. Sarah B. Snyder, "Through the Looking Glass: The Helsinki Final Act and the 1976 Election for President," *D&S* 21, no. 1 (March 2010): 91.

132. Quoted in MemCon between Kissinger and Media Representatives, August 15, 1975, box 23, HAK Records, RG 59, NARA; also Angela Romano, "Détente, Entente, or Linkage? The Helsinki Conference on Security and Cooperation in Europe in U.S. Relations with the Soviet Union," *DH* 33, no. 4 (September 2009): 714; Hanhimaki, "'They Can Write It in Swahili': Kissinger, the Soviets, and the Helsinki Accords, 1973–5," *Journal of Transatlantic Studies* 1, no. 1 (2003): 37–55.

133. Winston Lord, head of Policy Planning at the State Department under Kissinger, reports that Kissinger seriously considered resigning after losing his NSC job. But the episode "was pretty ridiculous because Kissinger was still dominant and was still the Secretary of State. The more we tried to construct a suitable letter of resignation, the more we had trouble in explaining why Kissinger was quitting." Winston Lord Oral History Interview, September 17, 1999, FAOHC, LC.

134. Njølstad, "Collapse of Superpower Détente," 140; MemCon between Ford, Kissinger, and Scowcroft, August 7, 1975, box 14, MemCons, NSA File, GFL; MemCon between Kissinger, Ford, and Scowcroft, September 12, 1975, box 15, MemCons, NSA File, GFL; MemCon between Ford and Gromyko, October 1, 1976, box 21, MemCons, NSA File, GFL.

135. MemCon between Kissinger and Meir, May 2, 1974, box 7, HAK Records, RG 59, NARA.

136. The point is nicely made in Noam Kochavi, "Insights Abandoned, Flexibility Lost: Kissinger, Soviet Jewish Immigration, and the Demise of Détente," *DH* 29, no. 3 (June 2005): 503–530.

137. Lodge to Nixon, February 12, 1969, *FRUS 1969–1976,* 6: Doc. 20; also Bundy to Rogers, January 24, 1969, box 3, NSC Meeting Files, Lot 71D175, RG 59, NARA; Editorial Note on Kissinger's Memo to Nixon, September 10, 1969, *FRUS 1969–1976,* 1: Doc. 36.

138. Asselin, *Bitter Peace,* 180.

139. Qiang Zhai, *China and the Vietnam Wars, 1950–1975* (Chapel Hill: University of North Carolina Press, 2000), 204–205; Lorenz Luthi, "Beyond Betrayal: Beijing, Moscow, and the Paris Negotiations, 1971–1973," *JCWS* 11, no. 1 (Winter 2009): 71, 76, 93, 104. See also Stephen J. Morris, "The Soviet-Chinese-Vietnamese Triangle in the 1970s: The View from Moscow," CWIHP Working Paper No. 25 (Washington, DC: Wilson Center, April 1999), 12–14, 16–17.

140. MemCon between Kissinger and Dobrynin, April 15, 1969, *FRUS 1969–1976,* 6: Doc. 60.

141. Odd Arne Westad, Chen Jian, Stein Tonnesson, Nguyen Vu Tungand, and James G. Hershberg, "77 Conversations between Chinese and Foreign Leaders on the Wars in Indochina, 1964–1977," CWIHP Working Paper No. 22 (Washington, DC: Wilson Center, May 1998), 179–180, 183; also Chris Connolly, "The American Factor: Sino-American Rapprochement and Chinese Attitudes to the Vietnam War, 1968–72," *CWH* 5, no. 4 (November 2005): 513.

142. Luthi, "Beyond Betrayal," 60, 62, 73.

143. Henry Kissinger, *Ending the Vietnam War: A History of America's Involvement in and Extrication from the Vietnam War* (New York: Simon & Schuster, 2003), 239; Connolly, "American Factor," 520; also Ilya Gaiduk, *The Soviet Union and the Vietnam War* (Chicago: Ivan R. Dee, 1996), 239–241; Zhai, *China and the Vietnam Wars,* 203; Ramesh Takur and Carlyle Thayer, *Soviet Relations with India and Vietnam* (New York: Palgrave Macmillan, 1992), 117.

144. Nixon, *RN,* 458; Lawrence, *Vietnam War,* 147.

145. MemCon between Kissinger, Haig, and Nixon, September 29, 1972, *FRUS 1969–1972,* 8: Doc. 271; also Ken Hughes, "Fatal Politics: Nixon's Political Timetable for Withdrawing from Vietnam" *DH* 34, no. 3 (June 2010): 497–506, esp. 498.

146. Editorial Note on Nixon's Meeting with the Australian Prime Minister, April 1, 1969, *FRUS 1969–1976,* 1: Doc. 17; MemCon between Kissinger and Lee Kuan Yew, April 11, 1973, box 1027, Presidential HAK MemCons, NSC, NPM; Kissinger, *Ending the Vietnam War,* 560.

147. Ben Kiernan, *The Pol Pot Regime: Race, Power, and Genocide in Cambodia under the Khmer Rouge* (New Haven, CT: Yale University Press, 2008), 16–25, quoted at 16. See also Kenton J. Clymer, *The United States and Cambodia, 1969–2000* (New York: Routledge, 2004), chaps. 1–3.

148. Conversation between Nixon and Kissinger, Conversation 760–6, August 3, 1972, Oval Office Series, NPM.

149. The comments are written on Briefing Book for Kissinger's July 1971 trip to China, box 850, NSC, NPM. The relevant portions are reproduced in Jeffrey

Kimball, *The Vietnam War Files: Uncovering the Secret History of Nixon-Era Strategy* (Lawrence: University Press of Kansas, 2004), 187. See also MemCons between Kissinger and Zhou, July 9 and 10, 1971, and July 20, 1972, NSA.

150. Dallek, *Nixon and Kissinger,* 453.

151. Kissinger recognized as much at the time. See his comments in NSC Meeting Minutes, April 9, 1975, NSC Meeting Files, GFL; also Notes of Cabinet Meeting, April 16, 1975, box 4, James Connor Files, GFL.

152. Editorial Note on a Meeting in May 1972, *FRUS 1969–1976,* 14: Doc. 195.

153. Kissinger, "Reflections," 56; also Kissinger, *White House Years,* 39.

154. Kissinger to Nixon, October 20, 1969, *FRUS 1969–1976,* 1: Doc. 41.

155. Editorial Note on Conversation between Nixon and Kissinger, December 12, 1971, *FRUS 1969–1976,* 11: Doc. 281; Garthoff, *Détente and Confrontation,* 309–310.

156. As evidence, consider the fact that the administration scored two of its greatest achievements—the summits in Beijing and Moscow in the first half of 1972—just months after the war.

157. Editorial Note on Conversation between Nixon and Kissinger, December 12, 1971, *FRUS 1969–1976,* 11: Doc. 281.

158. Gleijeses, *Conflicting Missions;* Garthoff, *Détente and Confrontation,* 556–593; Hanhimaki, *Flawed Architect,* 403–412.

159. MemCon between Ford, Kissinger, and Scowcroft, August 17, 1974, box 5, MemCons, NSA File, GFL; Douglas Little, *American Orientalism: The United States and the Middle East since 1945* (Chapel Hill: University of North Carolina Press, 2008), 145.

160. Jakarta to State, December 6, 1975, NSA; also Secretary's Staff Meeting, June 17, 1976, NSA; Brad Simpson, "'Illegally and Beautifully': The United States, the Indonesian Invasion of East Timor and the International Community, 1974–76," *CWH* 5, no. 3 (August 2005): 281–315, esp. 303.

161. Memorandum of Conversation, December 8, 1971, box 911, VIP Visits, NSC, NPM.

162. Quoted in "Conversation between President Richard Nixon and Secretary of State William Rogers," December 7, 1971, NSA. See also Canberra to Department of State, June 17, 1972, box 954, VIP Visits, NSC, NPM; MemCon between Nixon and Médici, December 9, 1971, NSA; Hal Brands, *Latin America's Cold War* (Cambridge, MA: Harvard University Press, 2010), 158.

163. Kissinger to Nixon, November 5, 1970, box H-029, Meetings File, NSC Institutional Files, NPM. See also NSC Meeting, November 5, 1970, ibid.

164. Quoted in Canberra to State, June 17, 1972, box 954, VIP Visits, NSC, NPM. On these subjects, see Tanya Harmer, "The Rules of the Game: Allende's Chile, the United States, and Cuba, 1970–1973" (PhD dissertation, London School of Economics, 2008), 170–174; TelCon between Nixon and Kissinger, September 16, 1973, NSA; Jonathan Haslam, *The Nixon Administration and the Death of Allende's Chile: A Case of Assisted Suicide* (London: Verso, 2005).

165. MemCom between Kissinger and Pinochet, June 8, 1976, NSA; also Hal Brands, "Third World Politics in an Age of Global Turmoil: The Latin American Challenge to U.S. and Western Hegemony, 1965–1975," *DH* 32, no. 1 (January 2008): 131–132.

166. MemCon between Kissinger and César Augusto Guzzetti, June 10, 1976, NSA; INR, "Argentina: Six Months of Military Government," September 30, 1976, box 4, Patricia Derian Papers, Duke University; John Dinges, *The Condor Years: How Pinochet and His Allies Brought Terrorism to Three Continents* (New York: New Press, 2004).

167. MemCon between Kissinger, Fraser, and Others, December 17, 1974, box 22, HAK Records, RG 59, NARA. The growth of the human rights movement is covered in Kathryn Sikkink, *Mixed Signals: U.S. Human Rights Policy and Latin America* (Ithaca, NY: Cornell University Press, 2004), chap. 3.

168. Brands, *Latin America's Cold War,* 176.

169. Secretary's Staff Meeting, October 22, 1974, box 5, Secretary's Staff Meetings, HAK Records, RG 59, NARA. Kissinger's views on the role of moral issues in foreign policy is nicely spelled out in the speeches reproduced in Kissinger, *American Foreign Policy.*

170. MemCon between Kissinger and Carvajal, September 29, 1975, NSA.

171. Keys, "Congress, Kissinger," 838.

172. Ibid., esp. 838–851.

173. On Soviet intentions, see Zubok, *Failed Empire,* 239–240.

174. MemCon between Kissinger and the WSAG, October 13, 1973, box 2, MemCons, NSA File, GFL. See also MemCon between Kissinger and Huang Zhen, October 25, 1973, NSA.

175. MemCon between Kissinger and Golda Meir, May 4, 1974, box 7, HAK Records, RG 59, NARA; also MemCon between Kissinger and Golda Meir, May 2, 1974, ibid.

176. Salim Yaqub, "The Weight of Conquest: Henry Kissinger and the Arab-Israeli Conflict," in Logevall and Preston, *Nixon in the World,* 227–248.

177. MemCon between Kissinger and Meir, May 2, 1974, box 7, HAK Records, RG 59, NARA.

178. MemCon between Kissinger, Fraser, and Others, December 17, 1974, NSA.

179. Quoted in MemCon between Ford, Kissinger, and Scowcroft, August 17, 1974, box 5, NSA File, MemCons, GFL; also Daniel Sargent, "The United States and Globalization in the 1970s," in *The Shock of the Global: The 1970s in Perspective,* ed. Niall Ferguson et al. (Cambridge, MA: Harvard University Press, 2010), 49–50; Andrew Scott Cooper, "Showdown at Doha: The Secret Oil Deal That Helped Sink the Shah of Iran," *Middle East Journal* 62, no. 4 (Autumn 2008): 575–576.

180. Cooper, "Showdown," quoted at 575, also 578–591; F. Gregory Gause, *The International Relations of the Persian Gulf* (New York: Cambridge University Press, 2010), 32, 38–40.

181. See "Foreword by Anatoly Dobrynin," *FRUS: SAR,* xxi.

182. Marshall Green, one of the few State Department officials to work closely with Kissinger during his time as national security adviser, has since criticized Kissinger's reliance on secrecy but acknowledges that it paid dividends in this case. Marshall Green to William Bundy, January 18, 1992, box 17, Bundy Papers, SMML.

183. Kissinger, *Years of Renewal,* 1060; Suri, *Henry Kissinger,* chap. 6.

184. Editorial Note, *FRUS 1969–1976,* 2: Doc. 347.

185. "Secretary's Meeting with Princeton Summer Interns," August 14, 1974, box 5, Secretary's Staff Meetings, HAK Records, RG 59, NARA; Peter W. Rodman

Oral History, May 22, 1994, FAOHC, LC; Hannah Gurman, "The Other Plumbers Unit: The Dissent Channel of the U.S. State Department," *DH* 35, no. 2 (April 2011): 330–332.

186. Elmo Zumwalt, *On Watch: A Memoir* (New York: Quadrangle, 1976), 375–376, quoted in Van Atta, *With Honor,* 303–304. On these issues, see also Gurman, "The Other Plumbers Unit," 330; Kissinger, *Years of Renewal,* 178–180; Stansfield Turner, *Burn before Reading: Presidents, CIA Directors, and Secret Intelligence* (New York: Hyperion, 2005), 128; Robert Jervis, "Why Intelligence and Policymakers Clash," *Political Science Quarterly (PSQ)* 125, no. 2 (2010): 197; Van Atta, *With Honor,* 224.

187. Dallek, *Nixon and Kissinger,* 119–121; Bundy, *Tangled Web,* 147–148; Siniver, *Nixon, Kissinger, and U.S. Foreign Policy Making,* 71–114; Marshall Green to William Bundy, March 27, 1991, box 17, Bundy Papers, SMML. See also SNIE 14.3–1-70, "North Vietnamese Intentions in Indochina," June 26, 1970, box 18, ibid.

188. See Dacca to State, March 28, 1971, NSA; Samuel Hoskinson to Kissinger, March 28, 1971, NSA; Dacca to State, April 6, 1971; Siniver, *Nixon, Kissinger, and U.S. Foreign Policy Making,* 148–184.

189. Garthoff, *Détente and Confrontation,* 181–185; Gerard Smith, *Double Talk: The Story of SALT I* (Lanham, MD: University Press of America, 1980), 228–229.

190. MemCon between Ford and Kissinger, February 25, 1976, box 18, MemCons, NSA File, GFL; also MemCon between Ford, Kissinger, and Scowcroft, August 7, 1975, box 14, MemCons, NSA File, GFL.

191. Bush's Summary of Meeting, December 10, 1971, NSA; also Barbara Keys, "Henry Kissinger: The Emotional Statesman," *DH* 35, no. 4 (September 2011): 587–609.

192. William Schaufele, Samuel Lewis, John Armitage, and William Luers to Kissinger, April 30, 1976, box 1, HAK Records, RG 59, NARA.

193. Hanhimaki, *Flawed Architect,* 450.

194. See Gaddis Smith, *Morality, Reason, and Power: American Diplomacy in the Carter Years* (New York: Farrar, Straus and Giroux, 1986), chaps. 1–2; Johnson, *Congress and the Cold War,* chap. 6.

195. Editorial Note on Meeting between Nixon and Kissinger, December 12, 1971, *FRUS 1969–1976,* 11: Doc. 281.

196. This point is sometimes lost of the more vocal critics of Nixon and Kissinger. While recent scholarship has often focused on the failures of their statecraft and the unattractive personal qualities that influenced their actions, the two men must nonetheless be credited for achieving as much as they did at a very difficult time.

197. Kissinger, *Crisis: The Anatomy of Two Major Foreign Policy Crises* (New York: Simon & Schuster, 2003), 143.

Chapter 3

1. Quoted in Paul Lettow, *Ronald Reagan and His Quest to Abolish Nuclear Weapons* (New York: Random House, 2005), 33; and "'State of the Union' Speech," March 13, 1980, in *Reagan, in His Own Hand: The Writings of Ronald Reagan That Reveal His Revolutionary Vision for America,* ed. Kiron Skinner, Annelise Anderson, and Martin Anderson (New York: Free Press, 2001), 472.

2. As a representative sampling of these perspectives, see John Lewis Gaddis, *Strategies of Containment: A Critical Appraisal of American National Security Policy during the Cold War* (New York: Oxford University Press, 2005), 342–379; Peter Schweizer, *Victory: The Reagan Administration's Secret Strategy That Hastened the Collapse of the Soviet Union* (New York: Atlantic Monthly Press, 1994); Steven F. Hayward, *The Age of Reagan: The Conservative Counterrevolution* (New York: Random House, 2009); Lettow, *Ronald Reagan;* John Arquilla, *The Reagan Imprint: Ideas in American Foreign Policy from the Collapse of Communism to the War on Terror* (Chicago: Ivan R. Dee, 2006); Beth A. Fischer, *The Reagan Reversal: Foreign Policy and the End of the Cold War* (Columbia: University of Missouri Press, 1997); James Mann, *The Rebellion of Ronald Reagan: A History of the End of the Cold War* (New York: Viking, 2009); James Graham Wilson, "How Grand Was Reagan's Strategy, 1976–1984?" *D&S* 18, no. 4 (Fall 2007): 773–803; Raymond Garthoff, *The Great Transition: American-Soviet Relations and the End of the Cold War* (Washington, DC: Brookings Institution Press, 1994); Frances FitzGerald, *Way Out There in the Blue: Reagan, Star Wars, and the End of the Cold War* (New York: Simon & Schuster, 2000); John Prados, *How the Cold War Ended: Debating and Doing History* (Washington, DC: Potomac Books, 2011); Edmund Morris, *Dutch: A Memoir of Ronald Reagan* (New York: Random House, 1999).

3. Prados, *How the Cold War Ended,* 178–179.

4. The "reversal" thesis is argued in Fischer, *Reagan Reversal.*

5. As foregoing paragraphs indicate, this chapter presents what might be termed a "moderate revisionist" appraisal of Reagan's statecraft. It departs from the assessments of critics like Raymond Garthoff, John Prados, and James Graham Wilson in depicting Reagan as a purposeful leader whose grand strategy ultimately made a significant contribution to the end of the Cold War. But it also contests the more laudatory claims of hagiographers like Peter Schweitzer (and, to a lesser extent, scholars like John Lewis Gaddis) in drawing attention to the limits and liabilities of Reagan's policies, and also to the degree of adaptation involved in his statecraft.

6. NIE, "Soviet Goals and Expectations in the Global Power Arena," July 7, 1981, NSA; also Robert Gates, *From the Shadows: The Ultimate Insider's Story of Five Presidents and How They Won the Cold War* (New York: Simon & Schuster, 1996), 170–174; Gerhard Wettig, "The Last Soviet Offensive of the Cold War: Emergence and Development of the Campaign against NATO Euromissiles, 1979–1983," *CWH* 9, no. 1 (February 2009): 82–83.

7. Anatoly Dobrynin, *In Confidence: Moscow's Ambassador to America's Six Cold War Presidents* (New York: Times Books, 1995), 408.

8. Yuri Andropov, Speech at the Political Consultative Committing Meeting in Prague, January 4–5, 1983, in *A Cardboard Castle? An Inside History of the Warsaw Pact, 1955–1991,* ed. Vojtech Mastny and Malcolm Byrne (Budapest: Central European University Press, 2005), 472; also Wettig, "Last Soviet Offensive," 83–84, 86–87; Hal Brands, *Latin America's Cold War* (Cambridge, MA: Harvard University Press, 2010), 196.

9. Raymond Garthoff, *Détente and Confrontation: Soviet-American Relations from Nixon to Reagan* (Washington, DC: Brookings Institution, 1994), 1068.

10. Quotes from Morris, *Dutch,* 414; Paul Nitze, "Reagan as Foreign Policy Strategist," in *Foreign Policy in the Reagan Presidency: Nine Intimate Perspectives,* ed. Kenneth W. Thompson (Lanham, MD: University Press of America, 1993), 145.

11. Interview with Dr. George A. Keyworth, September 28, 1987, Oral Histories, Ronald Reagan Presidential Library (RRL).

12. Quoted in Skinner, Anderson, and Anderson, *Reagan, in His Own Hand,* 139.

13. George Shultz Oral History, December 18, 2002, Presidential Oral History Project, Miller Center, University of Virginia.

14. See, for instance, "Excepts from Remarks by the Hon. Ronald Reagan, Bonds for Israel Dinner," April 10, 1978, box 3, Ronald Reagan Subject Collection (RRSC), Hoover; Reagan, "Republican Associates Luncheon at Biltmore Bowl," October 25, 1962, box 2, ibid.

15. "'State of the Union' Speech," March 13, 1980, in Skinner, Anderson, and Anderson, *Reagan, in His Own Hand,* 476–477; Lettow, *Ronald Reagan,* 33.

16. Reagan, "World Challenges, 1979," January 12, 1979, box 3, RRSC, Hoover.

17. "Text of Governor Ronald Reagan's Nation-Wide Television Address," March 31, 1976, box 1, RRSC, Hoover; see also "Foreign Affairs, the Need for Leadership," Reagan Address to Conservative Political Action Conference Banquet, March 17, 1978, box 3, ibid.; "Address by the Honorable Ronald Reagan to the Los Angeles World Affairs Council, December 14, 1978," THCR 2/2/1/27, Thatcher MSS, Margaret Thatcher Foundation Archive.

18. The quotes are from Reagan, "Reprint of a Radio Program entitled 'Rostow IV,'" undated, box 168, Committee on the Present Danger Papers, Hoover; Reagan, "World Challenges, 1979." See also Reagan, "Neutron Bomb," undated (1978), box 2, Ronald Reagan Radio Commentary (RRRC), Hoover. For the contrary view, see Robert Jervis, "Why Nuclear Superiority Doesn't Matter," *PSQ* 94, no. 4 (Winter 1979–80): 617–633.

19. Quoted in "The Russian Wheat Deal," October 1975, in Skinner, Anderson, and Anderson, *Reagan, in His Own Hand,* 31, 30; also Ronald Reagan, *An American Life* (New York: Simon & Schuster, 1990), 267.

20. "Viewpoint with Ronald Reagan: Communism, the Disease," undated (1975), box 1, RRRC, Hoover; "Détente: Viewpoint with Ronald Reagan," early 1975, ibid.; "Bukovsky," June 29, 1979, in Skinner, Anderson, and Anderson, *Reagan, in His Own Hand,* 149–150.

21. "Reagan's Foreign Policy Views: West Should Bolster Defenses," 1975, RRSC, box 2, Hoover; also Reagan, "Reprint of a Radio Program entitled 'Rostow V.'"

22. "Russian Wheat Deal," in Skinner, Anderson, and Anderson, *Reagan, in His Own Hand,* 30.

23. See "Strategy I" and "Strategy II," May 4, 1977, ibid., 110–113, quoted at 113; "Statement by Ronald Reagan," March 4, 1976, box 1, RRSC, Hoover.

24. Reagan to Edward Langley, January 15, 1980, box 3, RRSC, Hoover; William LeoGrande, *Our Own Backyard: The United States in Central America, 1977–1992* (Chapel Hill: University of North Carolina Press, 1996), 145; also "Foreign Policy Statement, with Emphasis on U.S.-Soviet Relations for Governor Reagan, Prepared by Prof. Richard Pipes," June 12, 1980, Fred Iklé Papers, Hoover.

25. Quoted in "Bukovsky," June 29, 1979, in Skinner, Anderson, and Anderson, *Reagan, in His Own Hand,* 149–150; and "Korea," August 15, 1977, ibid., 42. On export controls, see "Soviet Trade," July 9, 1979, ibid., 73–74; also Douglas Brinkley, ed. *The Reagan Diaries* (New York: HarperCollins, 2007), 2.

26. Reagan, "Soviet Workers," undated (1976–77), box 8, RRSC, Hoover; also "Détente: Viewpoint with Ronald Reagan," 1975, box 1, RRRC, Hoover.

27. Lettow, *Ronald Reagan,* 23; "Defense IV," September–October 1979, box 2, RRRC, Hoover.

28. MemCon, "President's Working Lunch with Agostino Cardinal Casaroli," December 15, 1981, box 49, SF, NSC Executive Secretariat File (ESF), RRL.

29. "Are Liberals Really Liberal?" circa 1963, in Skinner, Anderson, and Anderson, *Reagan, in His Own Hand,* 442.

30. MemCon, "President's Working Lunch with Agostino Cardinal Casaroli."

31. Richard Pipes, *Vixi: Memoirs of a Non-Belonger* (New Haven, CT: Yale University Press, 2003), 153; Melvyn Leffler, *For the Soul of Mankind: The United States, the Soviet Union, and the Cold War* (New York: Hill & Wang, 2007), 348–350.

32. Jack F. Matlock, *Reagan and Gorbachev: How the Cold War Ended* (New York: Random House, 2004), 103.

33. Reagan to John Koehler, July 9, 1981, in Kiron Skinner, Annelise Anderson, and Martin Anderson, eds., *Reagan: A Life in Letters* (New York: Free Press, 2003), 375.

34. Reagan's style was born of a determination that "no one would have a special claim on him," Kissinger later wrote. "Reagan was the quintessential loner." Kissinger, *Diplomacy* (New York: Simon & Schuster, 2011), 766. Reagan's operating style is also discussed in Richard V. Allen Oral History, May 28, 2002, Miller Center.

35. Jesus Velasco, *Neoconservatives in U.S. Foreign Policy under Ronald Reagan and George W. Bush* (Baltimore: Johns Hopkins University Press, 2010), 144.

36. NSDD 56, September 15, 1982, box 3, NSDD File, NSC ESF, RRL; National Security Planning Group (NSPG) Meeting, January 13, 1983, box 91306, NSC ESF, RRL; Wettig, "Last Soviet Offensive," 87–88.

37. "Address at Commencement Exercises at Eureka College in Illinois," May 9, 1982, APP; also Reagan's comments in NSC Meeting, April 16, 1982, box 91284, NSC Meetings, NSC ESF, RRL.

38. See Douglas W. Skinner, *Airland Battle Doctrine* (Alexandria, VA: Center for Naval Analyses, 1988).

39. Maritime Strategy Presentation, November 4, 1982, in John B. Hattendorf and Peter Swartz, *U.S. Naval Strategy in the 1980s: Selected Documents* (Newport, RI: Naval War College, 2008), quoted at 35.

40. NSC Meeting, April 16, 1982, box 91284, NSC Meetings, NSC ESF, RRL.

41. Reagan, *American Life,* 238. For the percentage, see Stephen Kotkin, *Armageddon Averted: The Soviet Collapse, 1970–2000* (New York: Oxford University Press, 2000), 61.

42. Quotes from Reagan, *American Life,* 238; Arquilla, *Reagan Imprint,* 39–40; Richard Halloran, "Pentagon Draws Up First Strategy for Fighting a Long Nuclear War," *NYT,* May 30, 1982; Weinberger to Reagan, "MX Missile Deployment," Fall 1982, box III: 3, Weinberger Papers, LC.

43. "Address to the Nation on Defense and National Security," March 23, 1983, APP.

44. MemCon, Meeting with British Prime Minister Margaret Thatcher, December 28, 1984, box 90902, European and Soviet Affairs Directorate, NSC, RRL.

45. MemCon between U.S. and Soviet Officials, October 12, 1986, NSA; also Lettow, *Ronald Reagan,* 98, 117–119.

46. MemCon, Meeting with British Prime Minister Margaret Thatcher, December 28, 1984, box 90902, European and Soviet Affairs Directorate, NSC, RRL. See also Margaret Thatcher, *The Downing Street Years* (New York: HarperCollins, 1993), 467; "Bud McFarlane," Interview with Hedrick Smith, March 20, 1986, box 48, Smith Papers, LC.

47. NSC Meeting, February 6, 1981, box 91282, NSC ESF, RRL; also MemCon between Reagan and Roberto Viola, March 17, 1981, box 48, SF, NSC ESF, RRL. For Casey's views, see NSC Meeting, April 16, 1982, box 91284, NSC ESF, RRL.

48. NSC Meeting, February 6, 1981, box 91282, NSC ESF, RRL; also Kathryn Sikkink, *Mixed Signals: U.S. Human Rights Policy and Latin America* (Ithaca, NY: Cornell University Press, 2004), chap. 7; Comptroller General, "U.S. Military Aid to El Salvador and Honduras," August 22, 1985, box 2, Oliver North Files, RRL.

49. Reagan to Edward Langley, January 15, 1980, box 3, RRSC, Hoover; LeoGrande, *Our Own Backyard,* 145.

50. "Reuters News Dispatch," March 18, 1981, box 46, Richard Allen Papers, Hoover; also NSC Meeting, November 3, 1982, box 91305, NSC ESF, RRL; "Remarks of William J. Casey before Los Angeles World Affairs Council," September 27, 1984, CIA FOIA. The best study of the Reagan Doctrine is James Scott, *Deciding to Intervene: The Reagan Doctrine and American Foreign Policy* (Durham, NC: Duke University Press, 1996).

51. "Response to NSSD 11–82: U.S. Relations with the USSR," late 1982, box 91278, NSDDs, NSC ESF, RRL.

52. Quoted in "Remarks at the Annual Convention of the Congressional Medal of Honor Society in New York City," December 12, 1983, APP; also Colin Dueck, *Hard Line: The Republican Party and U.S. Foreign Policy since World War II* (Princeton, NJ: Princeton University Press, 2010), 215–216.

53. "The President's News Conference," June 16, 1981, APP; "Response to NSSD 11–82: U.S. Relations with the USSR."

54. Brinkley, *Reagan Diaries,* 30.

55. Quotes from NSC Meeting, December 21, 1981, box 91283, NSC Meetings, NSC ESF, RRL; NSDD 54, September 2, 1982, box 1, NSDD File, RRL. For the warning to Brezhnev, see Reagan to Brezhnev, April 3, 1981, box 38, Head of State File (HOS), NSC ESF, RRL. On covert support and sanctions, see State to Bonn, Paris, and London, January 2, 1982, DDRS; Reagan to Jaruzelski, December 23, 1981, box 91283, NSC ESF, RRL; Prados, *How the Cold War Ended,* 155–156.

56. NSC Meeting, May 24, 1982, box 91284, NSC ESF, RRL; also NSC Meeting, December 21, 1981, box 91283, NSC ESF, RRL.

57. Kenneth Aaron Rodman, *Sanctions beyond Borders: Multinational Corporations and U.S. Economic Statecraft* (New York: Rowman & Littlefield, 2001), 80–81; Schweizer, *Victory,* 72–74.

58. In April 1982, the National Intelligence Council had reported that Soviet hard currency earnings represented a point of particular vulnerability vis-à-vis the West. See "The Soviet Bloc Financial Problem as a Source of Western Influence," April 1982, NSA.

59. The quote is from National Intelligence Council, "The Soviet Bloc Financial Problem as a Source of Western Influence," April 1982, NSA. The pipeline controversy and the struggle to achieve a unified NATO position can be seen in

Reagan to Thatcher, January 13, 1982, box 35, HOS, NSC ESF, RRL; USDEL Secretary Aircraft to SecState, January 29, 1982, ibid.; Haig to Reagan, January 29, 1982, ibid.; Meeting in the Cabinet Room, March 25, 1982, box 91283, NSC Meetings, NSC ESF, RRL; State to Bonn, August 11, 1982, DDRS; NSC Meeting, November 9, 1982, box 91284, NSC Meetings, NSC ESF, RRL; McFarlane, "East-West Economic Relations," undated, box 20, Country File, NSC ESF, RRL. On the NATO counterespionage operation, see Thomas Reed, *At the Abyss: An Insider's History of the Cold War* (New York: Random House Digital, 2005), 269–270.

60. Reed, *At the Abyss,* 267–269, quoted at 269; also Arquilla, *Reagan Imprint,* 43; Dueck, *Hard Line,* 212; Schweizer, *Victory,* 31–32, 92–99, 141–143, 202–205, 232–234.

61. "Memorandum for the Secretary," October 27, 1981, in *Historic Documents of 1981* (Washington, DC: CQ Press, 1982), 780–783; Daniel Tauber, "A Conversation with Elliott Abrams," *Jerusalem Post,* August 23, 2012; Sarah Snyder, *Human Rights Activism and the End of the Cold War: A Transnational History of the Helsinki Network* (New York: Cambridge University Press, 2011), 140–159.

62. "Remarks at the Annual Convention of the National Association of Evangelicals in Orlando, Florida," March 8, 1983, APP; "Address at Commencement Exercises at the University of Notre Dame," May 17, 1981, APP.

63. Quotes from "Address to Members of the British Parliament," June 8, 1982, APP; "Response to NSSD 11–82: U.S. Relations with the USSR"; also John Lewis Gaddis, *The Cold War* (London: Allen Lane, 2005), 222–225.

64. Clark to Reagan, January 10, 1983, box 91306, NSC ESF, RRL.

65. Douglas Selvage, "The Politics of the Lesser Evil: The West, the Polish Crisis, and the CSCE Review Conference in Madrid, 1981–1983," in *The Crisis of Détente in Europe: From Helsinki to Gorbachev, 1975–1985,* ed. Leopoldo Nuti (New York: Routledge, 2009), 46; Brinkley, *Reagan Diaries,* 142; Pipes, *Vixi,* 193. Casey's views are discussed in Odd Arne Westad, *The Global Cold War: Third-World Interventions and the Making of Our Times* (New York: Cambridge University Press, 2006), 354.

66. Matlock, *Reagan and Gorbachev,* 61.

67. NSC Meeting, November 30, 1983, box 91303, NSC ESF, RRL.

68. "Remarks to Members of the National Press Club on Arms Reduction and Nuclear Weapons," November 18, 1981, APP; also NSPG Meeting, January 13, 1983, box 91306, NSC ESF, RRL; NSDD 56, September 15, 1982, box 3, NSDD File, NSC ESF, RRL.

69. Perle's view is discussed in Prados, *How the Cold War Ended,* 50. The administration's maximalist stance was best indicated when Reagan, at the urging of Perle and Weinberger, disavowed a potential compromise on INF in 1982 (the famous "Walk in the Woods" agreement). On this episode, see MemCon, July 16, 1982, box 3, William Clark Files, RRL; Rostow to Reagan, July 30, 1982, ibid.; Memorandum for the President, August 5, 1982, ibid. As it turned out, the Soviet government also repudiated this potential compromise.

70. "Congressional Meeting on Nuclear Freeze," April 12, 1983, box 1, Meeting File, Presidential Handwriting File, RRL.

71. "Text of President Reagan's Handwritten Message to President Brezhnev," April 1981, box 38, HOS, RRL. As Reagan privately acknowledged, this grain embargo decision also had to do with a desire to aid farmers (a key Republican

voting bloc) in the United States. Because of the embargo, he said, "Our agriculture here was in a tailspin." NSC Meeting, October 16, 1981, box 91282, NSC ESF, RRL.

72. Quoted in NSDD 75, "U.S. Relations with the USSR," January 17, 1983, box 91287, NSDD File, NSC ESF, RRL; "Radio Address to the Nation on East-West Trade Relations and the Soviet Pipeline Sanctions," November 13, 1982, APP. On the possibility of a summit, see Matlock, *Reagan and Gorbachev,* 66; Brinkley, *Reagan Diaries,* 220.

73. NSDD-32, "U.S. National Security Strategy," May 20, 1982, box 1, NSDD File, ESF, RRL. NSDD-32 drew on a longer study completed in April 1982. That document laid out many of the specific initiatives that characterized U.S. policy toward the Soviet Union. At an NSC meeting, Reagan termed this study "one of the most significant and meaningful statements of U.S. national strategy." See "U.S. National Security Strategy," April 1982, box 4, Related Documents, Records Declassified and Released by the National Security Council, RRL; NSC Meeting, April 27, 1982, box 91284, NSC ESF, RRL.

74. NSDD-75, "U.S. Relations with the USSR." There has now emerged evidence that Reagan was directly involved in the crafting of NSDD-75. In particular, he intervened to strike a controversial passage (dealing with economic warfare) that he feared would leak and thereby prejudice the chances for negotiation. Reagan told the NSC "that nothing should be in the paper that we don't want to tell the Russians; we know what our policy is if the situation calls for its implementation … He did not want to compromise our chance of exercising quiet diplomacy." NSC Meeting, December 16, 1982, box 91285, NSC ESF, RRL; also Pipes, *Vixi,* 201.

75. "Address to the Nation and Other Countries on United States-Soviet Relations," January 16, 1984, APP. For Soviet views, see Robert Patman, "Reagan, Gorbachev, and the Emergence of the 'New Political Thinking,'" *Review of International Studies* 25, no. 4 (October 1999): 591–599; Westad, *Global Cold War,* 336–337; Vojtech Mastny, "How Able Was 'Able Archer'? Nuclear Trigger and Intelligence in Perspective," *JCWS* 11, no. 1 (Winter 2009): 115–116.

76. Herbert Meyer to DCI, "What Should We Do about the Russians?" June 28, 1984, CIA FOIA; National Intelligence Council, "Dimensions of Civil Unrest in the Soviet Union," April 1983, NSA; NIE, "Domestic Stresses on the Soviet System," November 1985, CIA FOIA; also Stephen Brooks and William Wohlforth, "Power, Globalization, and the End of the Cold War: Reevaluating a Landmark Case for Ideas," *IS* 25, no. 3 (Winter 2000/2001): 13–28.

77. The liabilities of U.S. intervention are discussed at greater length later in this chapter.

78. This is not to say that U.S. policy in Central America was as successful as Reagan had hoped—the Salvadoran and Nicaraguan conflicts dragged on until after he left office—but simply to note that American intervention helped arrest the erosion of Washington's position in the region. The most comprehensive study of these conflicts is LeoGrande, *Our Own Backyard,* esp. 582–583. LeoGrande is highly critical of U.S. policy but nonetheless acknowledges that it was central to preserving the Salvadoran regime and keeping the Nicaraguan government under pressure.

79. The best account is Steve Coll, *Ghost Wars: The Secret History of the CIA, Afghanistan, and bin Laden, from the Soviet Invasion to September 10, 2001* (New York: Penguin, 2004), esp. 55–90; also Scott, *Deciding to Intervene,* 40–81, 221.

80. For these and similar quotes, see Patman, "'New Political Thinking,'" 588–589. See also William Curti Wohlforth, *The Elusive Balance: Power and Perceptions during the Cold War* (Ithaca, NY: Cornell University Press, 1993), 240–241.

81. In 1986, Reagan asked Gorbachev why the Soviets were not purchasing more U.S. grain under the terms of a bilateral agreement concluded in the early 1980s. Gorbachev replied that "all the money the Russians had hoped to spend on grain was in America and Saudi Arabia as a result of lower oil prices." MemCon, Meeting between U.S. and Soviet Officials in Reykjavík, October 12, 1986, NSA. For an account that strongly implies that U.S.-Saudi collusion was responsible for this effect, see Schweizer, *Victory.* For a contrary viewpoint, see Dick Combs, *Inside the Soviet Alternate Universe: The Cold War's End and the Soviet Union's Fall Reappraised* (University Park: Penn State Press, 2008), 230–231.

82. On Solidarity and the economic issues, see Prados, *How the Cold War Ended,* 156–158; Gates, *From the Shadows,* 237–238; Garthoff, *Great Transition,* 31–32; Arquilla, *Reagan Imprint,* 43.

83. See Randall Stone, *Satellites and Commissars: Strategy and Conflict in the Politics of Soviet-Bloc Trade* (Princeton, NJ: Princeton University Press, 1996), 42–43.

84. Dobrynin, *In Confidence,* 527.

85. See BDM Corporation, *Soviet Intentions, 1965–1985,* vols. 1–2, EBB 285, NSA.

86. Mikhail Gorbachev, *Memoirs* (New York: Doubleday, 1995), 444.

87. Quoted in Patman, "'New Political Thinking,'" 596–597. Soviet views of SDI are also evident in Dobrynin, *In Confidence,* 528; Gorbachev, *Memoirs,* 455; Pavel Palazchenko, *My Years with Gorbachev and Shevardnadze: The Memoir of a Soviet Interpreter* (University Park: Pennsylvania State University Press, 1997), 41; Peter J. Westwick, "'Space-Strike Weapons' and the Soviet Response to SDI," *DH* 32, no. 5 (November 2008): 955–979.

88. William Odom, "Dilemmas and Directions in Soviet Force Development Policy," February 28, 1985, box 29, Odom Papers, LC.

89. Andropov's Speech at the Political Consultative Committing Meeting in Prague, January 4–5, 1983, in Mastny and Byrne, *Cardboard Castle,* 472–479.

90. Quoted in Andrei Gromyko, *Memoirs* (New York: Doubleday, 1989); also NIE, "Domestic Stresses on the Soviet System," November 1985, CIA FOIA.

91. Quoted in Small Group Meeting, November 19, 1983, box 34, Matlock Files, RRL; Jack F. Matlock, *Autopsy on an Empire: The American Ambassador's Account of the Collapse of the Soviet Union* (New York: Random House, 1995), 78; also Garthoff, *Great Transition,* 132–133.

92. "Interview with Representatives of Western European Publications," May 21, 1982, APP.

93. Quoted in Andrei Grachev, *Gorbachev's Gamble: Soviet Foreign Policy and the End of the Cold War* (Cambridge: Polity Press, 2008), 21; Vladislav Zubok, *A Failed Empire: The Soviet Union in the Cold War from Stalin to Gorbachev* (Chapel Hill: University of North Carolina Press, 2007), 275.

94. Dobrynin, *In Confidence,* 527.

95. Transcript of Interview with Charles Hill, July 20, 1989, 7, box 2, Don Oberdorfer Papers, SMML.

96. "Reuters News Dispatch," March 18, 1981, box 46, Allen Papers, Hoover; for "shovels" and loose talk about war, see Robert Scheer, *With Enough Shovels: Reagan, Bush, and Nuclear War* (New York: Vintage Books, 1983).

97. George Herring, *From Colony to Superpower: U.S. Foreign Relations since 1776* (New York: Oxford University Press, 2008), 866.

98. The quotes are from "Address to the Nation on the Soviet Attack on a Korean Civilian Airliner," September 5, 1983, APP; Mann, *Rebellion,* 73.

99. Quoted in MemCon, "U.S.-Soviet Relations," October 11, 1983, box 2, Matlock Files, RRL; Garthoff, *Great Transition,* 135–136. On the false alarms, see Zubok, *Failed Empire,* 274.

100. In particular, Reagan chose not to participate personally in the exercise. See David Hoffman, *The Dead Hand: The Untold Story of the Cold War Arms Race and Its Dangerous Legacy* (New York: Doubleday, 2009), 94–95; also Mastny, "How Able Was 'Able Archer?'"; Leffler, *Soul of Mankind,* 356–358.

101. Reagan, *American Life,* 585–586, 588; Brinkley, *Reagan Diaries,* 199.

102. Brinkley, *Reagan Diaries,* 199; Matlock, *Reagan and Gorbachev,* 76.

103. Quoted in "A Public Affairs Program to Support the Administration's Nuclear Policy," attached to Bremer to Clark, May 5, 1982, box 69, SF, NSC ESF, RRL; also McFarlane to James Baker, August 27, 1982, box 70, ibid.; "A Public Affairs Campaign to Support and Follow Up President Reagan's Trip to Europe June 2–11," undated, box 90100, Sven Kraemer Files, RRL.

104. "Address to the Nation and Other Countries on United States–Soviet Relations," January 16, 1984, APP; Hayward, *Conservative Counterrevolution,* 336–337.

105. Reagan to Chernenko, April 16, 1984, in Skinner, Anderson, and Anderson, *Reagan: A Life in Letters,* 743; MemCon, "The President's Meeting with Foreign Minister Andrei A. Gromyko of the Soviet Union," September 28, 1984, box 47, Matlock Files, RRL.

106. Gates, *From the Shadows,* 400. See also Brinkley, *Reagan Diaries,* 277.

107. "Points to Make: U.S.-Soviet Relations," September 29, 1984, box 59, Matlock Files, RRL.

108. George Shultz, *Turmoil and Triumph: My Years as Secretary of State* (New York: Scribner, 1993), 478. The importance of the succession is conveyed in NSDD 75, "U.S. Relations with the USSR."

109. Gorbachev in MemCon, May 30, 1988, Morning Session, Fritz Ermath Files, RRL; Reagan in Prados, *How the Cold War Ended,* 84.

110. Anatoly Chernyaev, *My Six Years with Gorbachev* (University Park: Pennsylvania State University Press, 1993), 46.

111. Archie Brown, *The Gorbachev Factor* (New York: Oxford University Press, 1996), 221, 227, 234, 249–250; Archie Brown, *Seven Years That Changed the World: Perestroika in Perspective* (New York: Oxford University Press, 2007), 242–243.

112. Gorbachev, *Memoirs,* 401; Chernyaev, *My Six Years,* 46.

113. Brown, *Gorbachev Factor,* 226–227; also Patman, "'New Political Thinking,'" 597.

114. Chernyaev, *My Six Years,* 83–84.

115. Quotes from Peter Rodman, *Presidential Command: Power, Leadership, and the Making of Foreign Policy from Richard Nixon to George W. Bush* (New York: Random House, 2009), 155.

116. Quoted in NIE, "Domestic Stresses on the Soviet System," November 1985, CIA FOIA. These issues are covered in William Jackson, "Soviet Reassessment of Ronald Reagan, 1985–1988," *PSQ* 113, no. 4 (Winter 1998–1999): 618–622; Geir Lundestad, "'Imperial Overstretch,' Mikhail Gorbachev, and the End of the Cold War," *CWH* 1, no. 1 (September 2000): 7.

117. Jackson, "Soviet Reassessment," 621–622, 629–630; Dobrynin, *In Confidence,* 570; also Gorbachev's comments in "Conference at the CC CPSU on Preparation for the XXVII Congress of the CPSU," November 28, 1985, NSA.

118. Quoted in Gorbachev to Reagan, December 24, 1985, box 214, Donald Regan Papers, LC; Svetlana Savranskaya, "Gorbachev and the Third World," in *The End of the Cold War and the Third World,* ed. Artemy Kalinovsky and Sergey Radchenko (New York: Taylor & Francis, 2011), 29–30. On these various issues, see also Gorbachev to Reagan, June 10, 1985, NSA; Westad, *Global Cold War,* 370; Brands, *Latin America's Cold War,* 216–217.

119. Quoted in Politburo Meeting, February 26, 1987, NSA. Very similar quotes by other Soviet officials can be found in Zubok, *Failed Empire,* 316; Matlock, *Autopsy,* 68.

120. There is evidence to support both arguments. See Zubok, *Failed Empire,* 280–302; and alternatively, Brooks and Wohlforth, "Power, Globalization, and the End of the Cold War"; Wohlforth, "Realism and the End of the Cold War," *IS* 19, no. 3 (Winter 1994–95): 91–129. A retrospective analysis by Chernyaev indicates that necessity and sincerity were both at work. See Chernyaev, "Gorbachev's Foreign Policy: The Concept," in *Turning Points in Ending the Cold War,* ed. Kiron Skinner (Stanford, CA: Hoover Institution Press, 2008), 111–113, 116.

121. The quotes are from "Gorbachev," assessment composed by Reagan on October 13, 1985, box 215, Regan Papers, LC; MemCon, "Summary of President's NATO Consultations: Special Session of the North Atlantic Council," November 21, 1985, Robert Linhard Files, OA 92178, RRL. See also Shultz to Reagan, March 25, 1985, box 39, HOS, NSC ESF, RRL; Shultz, *Turmoil and Triumph,* 531.

122. "Record of a Meeting Held at the White House on Thursday 26 February (1981)," PREM 19/600 f291, Thatcher MSS.

123. Shultz, "Managing the U.S.-Soviet Relationship over the Long Term," October 18, 1984, box 128, Charles Hill Papers, Hoover; Shultz to Reagan, May 21, 1983, box 91278, NSDD File, NSC ESF, RRL; Matlock, *Reagan and Gorbachev,* 84–85.

124. Shultz, "Managing the U.S.-Soviet Relationship."

125. Reagan, "Gorbachev."

126. Shultz, *Turmoil and Triumph,* 1004; also Reagan's comments in "Remarks on Soviet–United States Relations at the Town Hall of California Meeting in Los Angeles," August 26, 1987, APP. As James Mann has illustrated, this was one of the key motivations behind Reagan's famous speech in Berlin in 1987—to indicate to Gorbachev that ending the division of Europe was essential to easing East-West tensions. Mann, *Rebellion,* esp. 218.

127. MemCon, Meeting with British Prime Minister Margaret Thatcher, December 28, 1984, box 90902, European and Soviet Affairs Directorate, NSC File, RRL.

128. Reagan, *American Life,* 637; also Reagan, "Gorbachev"; MemCon, "Summary of President's NATO Consultations: Special Session of the North Atlantic Council," November 21, 1985, OA 92178, Linhard Files, RRL; NSC Meeting, September 20, 1985, box 91303, NSC ESF, RRL.

129. Reagan, "Gorbachev." On human rights and SDI, see MemCon, "Third Private Meeting," November 20, 1985, box 92151, Rodman Files, RRL; MemCon, "Second Private Meeting," November 19, 1985, NSA; MemCon, "Third Plenary Meeting," November 20, 1985, NSA.

130. MemCon, Meeting between U.S. and Soviet Officials in Reykjavík, October 12, 1986, NSA; also "First Private Meeting," November 19, 1985, NSA; Reagan to Gorbachev, March 11, 1985, NSA.

131. See particularly "Remarks to the World Affairs Council of Western Massachusetts in Springfield," April 21, 1988, APP, a speech given when Reagan needed conservative support to ensure smooth ratification of the INF Treaty. The need to appease conservatives may also have figured in Reagan's decision to disown the unratified (but still observed) SALT II treaty in 1986.

132. The meeting did produce agreements on several other bilateral issues, such as people-to-people exchanges, cooperation on scientific research, and the opening of new consulates in New York and Kiev.

133. Hayward, *Conservative Counterrevolution,* 460–461; Reagan to George Murphy, December 19, 1985, in Skinner, Anderson, and Anderson, *Reagan: A Life in Letters,* 415–416; also "Debriefing of President," November 19, 1985, box 215, Regan Papers, LC.

134. Quoted in Dobrynin, *In Confidence,* 592–593; Gorbachev to Reagan, April 2, 1986, box 214, Regan Papers, LC; "Joint Soviet–United States Statement on the Summit Meeting in Geneva," November 21, 1985, APP.

135. Chernyaev, *My Six Years,* 83–84; Zubok, *Failed Empire,* 288.

136. The logic of this particular offer, which Reagan had broached before Reykjavík, was to allay Soviet concerns that SDI might enable a successful U.S. first strike against the Soviet Union (conducted on the assumption that American missile defense systems could blunt Moscow's response). With this concern in mind, Reagan proposed that strategic missile defenses would not be deployed until offensive ballistic missiles had been eliminated.

137. The negotiations can be followed in MemCon, "First Meeting," October 11, 1986, NSA; MemCon between U.S. and Soviet Officials, October 11, 1986, NSA; and various MemCons between U.S. and Soviet Officials, October 12, 1986, NSA; "Final Proposal," October 12, 1986, box 215, Regan Papers, LC; Reagan, *American Life,* 675–679; Shultz, *Triumph and Turmoil,* 757–773.

138. See William Cockell to Join Poindexter, October 24, 1986, DDRS; Thatcher, *Downing Street Years,* 470–472.

139. "Remarks at a Meeting with Officials of the State Department and the U.S. Arms Control and Disarmament Agency on the Meetings in Iceland with Soviet General Secretary Gorbachev," October 14, 1986, APP.

140. Quoted in "Session of the Politburo of the CC CPSU," October 14, 1986, NSA; Dobrynin, *In Confidence,* 610.

141. NSPG Meeting, April 16, 1986, box 91308, NSDD File, NSC ESF, RRL; also Memorandum for the Record, NSPG Meeting, June 6, 1986, box III: 2, Weinberger Papers, LC.

142. Quoted in Brown, *Seven Years,* 85. As this comment shows, the NATO INF deployment was important in two respects. First, it redressed the imbalance of strategic power in Europe and established that Moscow would only become more vulnerable if the competition continued. But second, it also meant that Soviet INF cuts would no longer be *unilateral.* The United States and its allies would also be reducing their missile forces, a formula that was more palatable to Soviet military leaders.

143. Gorbachev to Reagan, June 19, 1986, box 214, Regan Papers, LC.

144. Poindexter to Reagan, undated, box 91639, Alton Keel Files, RRL; Mem-Con, "First Meeting," October 11, 1986, NSA; MemCon, Meeting between U.S. and Soviet Officials, October 11, 1986, NSA; Shultz, *Turmoil and Triumph,* 764–768.

145. Gorbachev quoted in Politburo Meeting, February 26, 1987, NSA; Shultz in Lettow, *Ronald Reagan,* 234.

146. Quote from Notes of Shultz-Gorbachev Meeting on April 14, 1987, box 5, Don Oberdorfer Papers, SMML; also Shultz, *Turmoil and Triumph,* 1006; William Odom, *The Collapse of the Soviet Military* (New Haven, CT: Yale University Press, 1998), 134; Reagan to Mrs. William Loeb, December 18, 1987, in Skinner, Anderson, and Anderson, *Reagan: A Life in Letters,* 384.

147. Reagan, "Gorbachev."

148. Gorbachev, *Memoirs,* 443, 445, 450; Chernyaev, *My Six Years,* 142–143; Mann, *Rebellion,* 238–240, 273–278.

149. Gorbachev to Reagan, December 14, 1985, box 214, Regan Papers, LC.

150. MemCon, "Working Luncheon with General Secretary Mikhail Gorbachev," December 10, 1987, NSA. See also Artemy Kalinovsky, *A Long Goodbye: The Soviet Withdrawal from Afghanistan* (Cambridge, MA: Harvard University Press, 2011), chap. 4, esp. 119.

151. See Scott, *Deciding to Intervene,* 60–63.

152. NSDD 288, "My Objectives at the Summit," November 10, 1987, box 2, NSDD File, RRL; see also "Talking Points for President's Meeting with Gorbachev, December 9—Regional Issues," undated (December 1987), box 2, Howard Baker Papers, RRL; Reagan, "Address to the People of Western Europe on Soviet–United States Relations," November 4, 1987, APP; Reagan to Gorbachev, undated (1985–86), box 41, HOS, NSC ESF, RRL.

153. Grachev, *Gorbachev's Gamble,* 111–112. The linkage between U.S.-Soviet relations and Moscow's Third World policies is confirmed in Savranskaya, "Gorbachev and the Third World," 30; Westad, *Global Cold War,* 371; Mark Kramer, "The Decline in Soviet Arms Transfers to the Third World, 1986–1991: Political, Economic, and Military Dimensions," in Kalinovsky and Radchenko, *End of the Cold War and the Third World,* 47; and particularly Georgi I. Mirski, "Soviet-American Relations in the Third World," in Skinner, *Turning Points,* 172–173, 179–180.

154. Quotes from Leffler, *Soul of Mankind,* 409–410.

155. Chernyaev Diary, April 1, 1988, EBB 250, NSA; also Shultz, *Turmoil and Triumph,* 1094; Scott, *Deciding to Intervene,* 79.

156. Snyder, *Human Rights Activism,* 159–165, quoted at 159. On Gorbachev's irritation, see also MemCon, "Working Luncheon with General Secretary Mikhail Gorbachev," December 10, 1987, NSA.

157. Lisa Jameson to various officials, November 12, 1987, DDRS; Shultz to Reagan, undated, box 2, Howard Baker Papers, RRL; Paul Schott Stevens to various officials, November 25, 1987, box 991, William Graham Files, RRL; MemCon, Third Private Meeting, November 20, 1985, box 92151, Rodman Files, RRL; Mem-Con, "President's First One-on-One Meeting with General Secretary Gorbachev," May 29, 1988, NSC System File Folder 8791367, RRL.

158. Quoted in NSDD 288, November 10, 1987, box 2, NSDD File, RRL; Reagan, *American Life,* 645. See also Garthoff, *Great Transition,* 268; MemCon, Meeting between U.S. and Soviet Officials, October 12, 1986, NSA.

159. Reagan, "Gorbachev."

160. MemCon, Meeting between U.S. and Soviet Officials at Reykjavík, October 12, 1986, NSA.

161. MemCon between U.S. and Soviet Officials, May 29, 1988, NSA.

162. Shultz, *Turmoil and Triumph*, 888, 892.

163. Brown, *Gorbachev Factor*, 81, 137, 163–164.

164. Quoted in Vienna to State, June 20, 1988, DDRS; also Zubok, *Failed Empire*, 298; Snyder, *Human Rights Activism*, 158–173, 197.

165. Quoted in Matlock, *Reagan and Gorbachev*, 251; also Chernyaev, "Gorbachev's Foreign Policy," 125; Mirski, "Soviet-American Relations," 172–173.

166. Quotes from Shultz, *Turmoil and Triumph*, 894; Office of Soviet Analysis, "Where Is the USSR Headed?" undated (1988), CIA FOIA. Statistics from Sarah Snyder, "Principles Overwhelming Tanks: Human Rights and the End of the Cold War," in *The Human Rights Revolution: An International History*, ed. Akira Iriye, Petra Goedde, and William Hitchcock (New York: Oxford University Press, 2012), 270–273.

167. MemCon, March 11, 1988, RAC box 1, Lisa Jameson Files, RRL.

168. For U.S. appraisals of Soviet reform, see Reagan to George Murphy, July 8, 1988, in Skinner, Anderson, and Anderson, *Reagan: A Life in Letters*, 387; also Reagan, *American Life*, 686, 702–703; Matlock, *Autopsy*, 121–123; MemCon, "The President's Private Meeting with Gorbachev," December 7, 1988, NSA. Reagan's emphasis on human rights at the Moscow summit is evident in MemCon, "President's Second One-on-One Meeting with General Secretary Gorbachev," May 31, 1988, NSC System File Folder 8791367, RRL.

169. This episode and its significance are discussed in Mann, *Rebellion*, 304–306.

170. Gorbachev, *Memoirs*, 457.

171. As Reagan put it at the Governor's Island summit in December 1988, "We were all on Gorbachev's side concerning the reforms he was trying to make in the Soviet system." MemCon, "The President's Private Meeting with Gorbachev," December 7, 1988, NSA. The irony, of course, is that Gorbachev's reforms were actually destroying the foundations of the Soviet state. He did not realize this, of course, and at present there is little evidence to suggest that Reagan foresaw the long-term result, either. The president did realize, however, that the liberalization of the Soviet Union would likely be beneficial for the United States.

172. Matlock, *Autopsy*, 142; Odom, *Collapse*, 119–122; CIA, "Soviet National Security Policy: Responses to the Changing Military and Economic Environment," June 1988, NSA.

173. See "The Gorbachev Visit; Excerpts from Speech to U.N. on Major Soviet Military Cuts," *NYT*, December 8, 1988; Gorbachev, *Memoirs*, 460.

174. Quotes from Odom, *Collapse*, 136; MemCon, "The President's Private Meeting with Gorbachev," December 7, 1988, NSA.

175. George W. Breslauer and Richard Ned Lebow, "Leadership and the End of the Cold War: A Counterfactual Thought Experiment," in *Ending the Cold War: Interpretations, Causation, and the Study of International Relations*, ed. Richard K. Hermann and Richard Ned Lebow (New York: Palgrave Macmillan, 2004), 184.

176. NSC Meeting, March 19, 1981, box 91282, NSC ESF, RRL.

177. Fareed Zakaria, "The Reagan Strategy of Containment," *PSQ* 105, no. 3 (Autumn 1990): 380.

178. MemCon, "Meeting with Prime Minister Margaret Thatcher of the United Kingdom of Great Britain and Northern Ireland," November 16, 1988, DDRS; Garthoff, *Great Transition,* 505–506.

179. "Remarks at the Annual Dinner of the Conservative Political Action Conference," March 1, 1985, APP.

180. The quote on El Salvador is from National Foreign Assessment Center, "El Salvador: The Significance of Popular Support," February 27, 1981, NSA. On these issues, see LeoGrande, *Our Own Backyard,* passim, esp. 582–583. For contra atrocities against literacy volunteers, see Ernesto Vallecillo to Carlos Carrión, undated (probably May 1980), CNA D35G1 0004, Instituto de Historia de Nicaragua y Centroamérica; "Los problemas de seguridad de la Cruzada Nacional de Alfabeticazión y medidas que convendría tomar," May 7, 1980, ibid.

181. Reagan probably did know of lesser—but still illegal—violations of the congressional ban on aid. LeoGrande, *Our Own Backyard,* 502–503.

182. NSPG Meeting, June 25, 1984, NSA.

183. Reagan obliquely acknowledged as much in his "Address to the Nation on the Iran Arms and Contra Aid Controversy," March 4, 1987, APP; also Shultz Oral History, Miller Center.

184. Reagan's hopes for progress on START are evident in NSDD 250, "Post-Reykjavik Follow-Up," November 3, 1986, box 91287, NSDD File, NSC ESF RRL.

185. Quotes from Shultz to Reagan, November 29, 1982, DDRS; Arquilla, *Reagan Imprint,* 95.

186. Quoted in William Webster Oral History Interview, August 21, 2002, Miller Center; Gates, *From the Shadows,* 561. See also John Prados, "Notes on the CIA's Secret War in Afghanistan," *JAH* 89, no. 2 (September 2002): 466–471.

187. The quotes are from Shultz, *Turmoil and Triumph,* 1100, 1089; also Kalinovsky, *Long Goodbye,* 128–132.

188. Indeed, had Reagan not done so well in managing the Cold War, issues like terrorism and nuclear proliferation would have remained second-tier national security threats.

Chapter 4

1. George W. Bush, "A Distinctly American Internationalism," November 19, 1999, https://www.mtholyoke.edu/acad/intrel/bush/wspeech.htm.

2. Quoted in Bush's introduction to the *National Security Strategy of the United States of America, September 2002,* available at http://georgewbush-whitehouse.archives.gov/nsc/nss/2002/ (hereafter *NSS* 2002).

3. Quoted in Douglas Jehl, "C.I.A. Nominee Wary of Budget Cuts," *NYT,* February 3, 1993.

4. Charles Krauthammer, "The Unipolar Moment," *FA* 70, no. 1 (Winter 1990/1991): 23–33.

5. Colin Dueck, *Reluctant Crusaders: Power, Culture, and Change in American Grand Strategy* (Princeton, NJ: Princeton University Press, 2008), 114–146.

6. Hal Brands, *From Berlin to Baghdad: America's Search for Purpose in the Post–Cold War World* (Lexington: University Press of Kentucky, 2008), 134; also Jeremi Suri, "American Grand Strategy from the Cold War's End to 9/11," *Orbis* 53, no. 4 (August 2009): 611–627.

7. Strobe Talbott, *The Russia Hand: A Memoir of Presidential Diplomacy* (New York: Random House, 2002), 133–134.

8. Anthony Lake, "From Containment to Enlargement," September 21, 1993, http://www.mtholyoke.edu/acad/intrel/lakedoc.html.

9. John P. Burke, *Honest Broker? The National Security Advisor and Presidential Decision Making* (College Station: Texas A&M University Press, 2009), 346–350, quoted at 346.

10. See Richard Haass, "The Squandered Presidency: Demanding More from the Commander in Chief," *FA* 79, no. 3 (May/June 2000): 136–140.

11. On U.S.-Russian relations and the tensions caused by NATO expansion, see Jeffrey Mankoff, *Russian Foreign Policy: The Return of Great Power Politics* (Lanham, MD: Rowman & Littlefield, 2011), 154–159; Brands, *Berlin to Baghdad,* 204–216.

12. Madeleine Albright, *Madam Secretary: A Memoir* (New York: Miramax Books, 2003), 507. For concerns about the opportunity cost of pursuing Middle East peace, see Albright's comments in Thomas Lippman, "Albright Pessimistic as Mideast Trip Ends," *Washington Post (WP)*, September 16, 1997.

13. On these subjects see David Halberstam, *War in a Time of Peace: Bush, Clinton, and the Generals* (New York: Simon & Schuster, 2002); National Commission on Terrorist Attacks upon the United States, *The 9/11 Commission Report,* available at http://www.9–11commission.gov/report/911Report.pdf. Lake quoted in John Darnton, "Revisiting Rwanda's Horrors with an Ex-National Security Adviser," *NYT,* December 20, 2004.

14. Brands, *Berlin to Baghdad,* 195.

15. Stephen M. Walt, "Two Cheers for Clinton's Foreign Policy," *FA* 79, no. 2 (March–April 2000), 65; James Lindsay, "The New Apathy," *FA* 79, no. 5 (September–October 2000): 3–4.

16. Robert Maranto and Richard Redding, "Bush's Brain (No, Not Karl Rove): How Bush's Psyche Shaped His Decision-Making," in *Judging Bush,* ed. Robert Maranto, Tom Lansford, and Jeremy Johnson (Stanford, CA: Stanford University Press, 2009), 23–24.

17. Quoted in Tucker Carlson, "Devil May Care," *Talk Magazine,* September 1999, 108.

18. Quotes from Wolfowitz to Cheney, May 5, 1992, EBB 245, NSA; and Condoleezza Rice, "Promoting the National Interest," *FA* 79, no. 2 (April–May 2000): 48. On the Vulcans, see James Mann, *Rise of the Vulcans: The History of Bush's War Cabinet* (New York: Viking, 2004); Ivo Daalder and James Lindsay, *America Unbound: The Bush Revolution in Foreign Policy* (Hoboken, NJ: John Wiley & Sons, 2005), esp. 36–43. The key tenets of the Defense Planning Guidance can be pieced together from "Excerpts from Pentagon's Plan," *NYT,* March 8, 1992; and "FY 94–99 Defense Planning Guidance Sections for Comment," February 18, 1992, EBB 245, NSA.

19. See Bush, "Distinctly American Internationalism"; Colin Dueck, *Hard Line: The Republican Party and U.S. Foreign Policy since World War II* (Princeton, NJ: Princeton

University Press, 2010), 268–269; Transcript of Second Presidential Debate, October 11, 2000, Federal News Service (FNS) transcript.

20. "Remarks by Governor George W. Bush," Cedar Rapids, Iowa, June 12, 1999, http://www.gwu.edu/~action/bushannc.html.

21. Commission on Presidential Debates, "October 11, 2000 Debate Transcript," http://www.debates.org/index.php?page=october-11-2000-debate-transcript.

22. Roberto Suro, "Gore, Bush Defense Plans Short of Military Demands," *WP*, October 28, 2000.

23. "Remarks at the National Defense University," May 1, 2001, APP.

24. Condoleezza Rice, *No Higher Honor: A Memoir of My Years in Washington* (New York: Crown, 2011), 41–42.

25. Pascal Boniface, "The Specter of Unilateralism," *Washington Quarterly* (*WQ*) 24, no. 3 (Summer 2001): 155–162.

26. F. Gregory Gause, *The International Relations of the Persian Gulf* (New York: Cambridge University Press, 2010), 188–189.

27. Paul Krugman, "Guns and Bitterness," *NYT*, February 4, 2001.

28. Jane Perlez and David Sanger, "Bush Aides Saying Some Hope Is Seen to End Standoff," *NYT*, April 6, 2001; Daalder and Lindsay, *America Unbound*, 66–69.

29. Quoted in Bob Woodward, *Bush at War* (New York: Simon & Schuster, 2002), 37. On the cost of the attacks, see Kevin McGrath, *Confronting al Qaeda: New Strategies to Combat Terrorism* (Annapolis: Naval Institute Press, 2011), 80.

30. Department of Defense News Briefing, September 25, 2001, NSA.

31. George W. Bush, *Decision Points* (New York: Crown, 2010), 151–153, 157–158.

32. Quoted in Rumsfeld to Myers and Pace, October 10, 2001, Rumsfeld Papers (RP), www.rumsfeld.com; "Expect New Strikes at U.S., Veep Warns," *New York Daily News,* May 20, 2002.

33. *9/11 Commission Report,* quoted at 112.

34. See *9/11 Commission Report,* quoted at 330; also chaps. 4, 6, and 8.

35. Woodward, *Bush at War,* 45.

36. Bob Woodward, *Plan of Attack* (New York: Simon & Schuster, 2004), 27.

37. Daalder and Lindsay, *Bush Unbound,* 103–104.

38. See Islamabad to State, September 13, 2001, EBB 325, NSA; State to Islamabad, September 14, 2001, EBB 343, NSA; and Islamabad to State, September 14, 2001, EBB 325, NSA.

39. See Douglas Feith, *War and Decision: Inside the Pentagon at the Dawn of the War on Terrorism* (New York: HarperCollins, 2008), 50–138; also Stephen Biddle, "Afghanistan and the Future of Warfare," *FA* 82, no. 2 (March–April 2003): 31–46.

40. *9/11 Commission Report,* 330–331.

41. "Address to the Nation," September 20, 2001, APP.

42. See Melvyn Leffler, "9/11 and American Foreign Policy," *DH* 29, no. 3 (June 2005): esp. 396, 406.

43. Rice, *No Higher Honor,* 98.

44. Quotes from Donald Rumsfeld, "Beyond This War on Terrorism," *WP*, November 1, 2001; James Dao, "Defense Secretary Warns of Unconventional Attacks," *NYT*, October 1, 2001; also Department of Defense News Briefing, September 20, 2001, NSA.

45. Elisabeth Bumiller and David Sanger, "Threat of Terrorism Is Shaping the Focus of Bush Presidency," *NYT,* September 11, 2002.

46. "Remarks by Secretary of State Colin Powell to the George Washington University Elliott School of International Affairs Re: U.S. Foreign Policy and National Security Strategy," September 5, 2003, FNS.

47. Rice, *No Higher Honor,* 153. For a revealing account of how the 2002 *NSS* was drafted, see Richard Haass, *War of Necessity, War of Choice: A Memoir of Two Iraq Wars* (New York: Simon & Schuster, 2009), 200–201, 221–222.

48. *NSS* 2002.

49. Quotes from "Commencement Address at the United States Military Academy at West Point," June 1, 2002, APP; *NSS* 2002.

50. "Background Paper on SIPRI Military Expenditure Data, 2010," Stockholm International Peace Research Institute, April 11, 2011, http://www.sipri.org/research/armaments/milex/factsheet2010.

51. "Condoleezza Rice Delivers Remarks," June 26, 2003, Federal Document Clearing House (FDCH) transcripts; also Rice, "A Balance of Power that Favors Freedom," October 1, 2002, FDCH.

52. *NSS* 2002; also NSPD 17, "National Strategy to Combat Weapons of Mass Destruction," December 2002, http://www.fas.org/irp/offdocs/nspd/nspd-17.html.

53. "Commencement Address at the United States Military Academy at West Point."

54. Colin Powell, "The Administration's Position with Regard to Iraq," September 19, 2002, State Department FOIA Electronic Reading Room.

55. The concept of a three-pronged approach is discussed most explicitly in the "National Military Strategic Plan for the War on Terror," a still-classified document whose contents have been discussed in media reports. The three stages described in those reports broadly correspond to those described in this chapter. See Eric Schmitt, "Pentagon Draws Up a 20–30-Year Antiterror Plan," *NYT,* January 17, 2003.

56. *NSS* 2002.

57. "Major Directional Decisions—9/11/01 et seq.," compiled May 10, 2002, in Rumsfeld to Cheney, September 3, 2002, RP.

58. Quoted from "Rumsfeld and Myers Briefing on Enduring Freedom," October 7, 2001, NSA; Rumsfeld to Myers and Pace, October 10, 2001, RP. See also Rumsfeld, "What Are We Fighting? Is It a Global War on Terror?" June 18, 2004, DOD FOIA.

59. "DoD News Briefing—Deputy Secretary Wolfowitz," September 13, 2001, NSA.

60. Rumsfeld to Bush, September 30, 2001, RP.

61. "Campaign against Terrorism: Strategic Guidance for the U.S. Department of Defense," October 2, 2001, RP.

62. Cheney quoted in Glenn Kessler, "U.S. Decision on Iraq Has Puzzling Past," *WP,* January 12, 2003; Ron Suskind, *The One Percent Doctrine: Deep Inside America's Pursuit of Its Enemies since 9/11* (New York: Simon & Schuster, 2006), 62.

63. Brands, *Berlin to Baghdad,* 314.

64. "State of the Union Address," January 29, 2002, APP.

65. "Commencement Address at the United States Military Academy at West Point." See also "Richard Cheney Delivers Remarks to the International Democratic Union Party Leaders Meeting," June 10, 2002, FDCH.

66. *NSS* 2002.

67. See, for instance, Senate Select Committee on Intelligence, *Report on the U.S. Intelligence Community's Prewar Intelligence Assessments on Iraq* (Washington, DC: Government Printing Office, 2004), 343–347; *9/11 Commission Report,* 334–335.

68. For Powell, see Todd Purdum, "U.S. Weighs Tackling Iraq on Its Own, Powell Says," *NYT,* February 7, 2002.

69. "Address to the Nation on Iraq," March 17, 2003, APP.

70. See the open letter from the Project for the New American Century to Clinton, January 26, 1998, http://www.newamericancentury.org/iraqclintonletter. htm.

71. Quotes from Rumsfeld to Rice, July 27, 2001, EBB 326, NSA. See also J. L. Jones to Chairman, Joint Chiefs of Staff, August 31, 2001, DOD FOIA.

72. Stephen Cambone Notes, September 11, 2001, EBB 326, NSA.

73. See Gause, *International Relations,* 184–240, esp. 186–190.

74. On these issues, see Kevin Woods and James Lacey, *Iraqi Perspectives Project: Saddam and Terrorism: Emerging Insights from Captured Iraqi Documents* (Alexandria, VA: Institute for Defense Analyses, 2007); *The Commission on the Intelligence Capabilities of the United States regarding Weapons of Mass Destruction: Report to the President of the United States* (Washington, DC: Government Printing Office, 2005); Carla Anne Robbins and Jeanne Cummings, "How Bush Decided That Hussein Must Be Ousted from atop Iraq," *Wall Street Journal,* June 14, 2002.

75. Lawrence Freedman, "War in Iraq: Selling the Threat," *Survival* 46, no. 2 (Summer 2004): 16.

76. See Kessler, "U.S. Decision on Iraq Has Puzzling Past"; Feith, *War and Decision,* 215, 514–515.

77. Robbins and Cummings, "How Bush Decided."

78. Gause, *International Relations,* 193.

79. Woodward, *Plan of Attack,* 27.

80. Jack Straw to Tony Blair, April 2002, http://web.archive.org/web/ 20100723165758/http://www.michaelsmithwriter.com/memo_six.html. See also P. F. Ricketts to Secretary of State, March 22, 2002, EBB 300, NSA.

81. Wolfowitz in Gordon, "Serving Notice of a New U.S., Poised to Hit First and Alone," *NYT,* January 27, 2003.

82. "Presentation—the Case for Action," September 12, 2002, EBB 254, NSA.

83. "Full Text: George Bush's Speech to the American Enterprise Institute," *Guardian,* February 27, 2003.

84. Rumsfeld to Bush, September 30, 2001, RP.

85. "Campaign against Terrorism: Strategic Guidance for the U.S. Department of Defense," October 2, 2001, RP.

86. "Major Directional Decisions—9/11/01 et seq.," May 10, 2002, in Rumsfeld to Cheney, September 3, 2002, RP.

87. The phrase is from an official describing the *National Military Strategic Plan for the War on Terrorism,* quoted in Schmitt, "Pentagon Draws Up a 20–30-Year Antiterror Plan."

88. State Department, "Wolfowitz Says Coalition Must Keep Pressure on al-Qaida; Terrorists Continue Efforts to Regroup, He Says," July 10, 2002, Lexis-Nexis.

89. "George Bush's Speech to the American Enterprise Institute."

90. Benjamin Miller, "Explaining Changes in U.S. Grand Strategy: 9/11, the Rise of Offensive Liberalism, and the War in Iraq," *Security Studies* 19, no. 1 (March 2010): 49.

91. *NSS* 2002.

92. "Remarks as Prepared for Delivery by National Security Advisor Condoleezza Rice," FNS, August 7, 2003.

93. Woodward, *Plan of Attack,* 162.

94. David Frum, *The Right Man: The Surprise Presidency of George W. Bush* (New York: Random House, 2003), 196.

95. See the comments of Undersecretary of Defense Douglas Feith in "Hearing of the Senate Foreign Relations Committee," September 26, 2002, FNS; also "George Bush's Speech to the American Enterprise Institute."

96. "George Bush's Speech to the American Enterprise Institute."

97. "Principles for Iraq—Policy Guidelines," May 13, 2003, RP.

98. Miller, "Explaining Changes," 59.

99. Quotes from Rice, *No Higher Honor,* 187; Woodward, *Plan of Attack,* 284.

100. The statistic is from Lawrence Freedman and Efraim Karsh, *The Gulf Conflict, 1990–1991: Diplomacy and War in the New World Order* (Princeton, NJ: Princeton University Press, 1993), 409.

101. Barbara Slavin and Dave Moniz, "War in Iraq's Aftermath Hits Troops Hard," *USA Today,* July 21, 2003; "Desert Crossing Seminar: After Action Report," June 28–30, 1999, EBB 207, NSA.

102. Quoted in "The Fiscal Year 2004 Defense Budget," Hearing of the Senate Armed Services Committee, February 25, 2003, FNS. See also Thom Shanker, "New Strategy Vindicates Ex-Army Chief Shinseki," *NYT,* January 12, 2007.

103. Bush-Aznar MemCon, February 22, 2003, http://www.nybooks.com/articles/archives/2007/nov/08/the-moment-has-come-to-get-rid-of-saddam/?pagination=false. On the U.S. war plan, see Rumsfeld Notes for Briefing with Franks, November 27, 2001, EBB 326, NSA; Thomas Ricks, *Fiasco: The American Military Adventure in Iraq* (New York: Penguin, 2006), chap. 5; Michael Gordon and Bernard Trainor, *Cobra Two: The Inside Story of the Invasion and Occupation of Iraq* (New York: Pantheon, 2006), chaps. 1–8.

104. See Terry Anderson, *Bush's Wars* (New York: Oxford University Press, 2011), 141; Special Inspector General for Iraq Reconstruction, *Hard Lessons: The Iraq Reconstruction Experience* (Washington, DC: Government Printing Office, 2008), 11–12, 42, 72.

105. "Secretary Rumsfeld Interview with the New York Times," October 12, 2001, http://www.defense.gov/transcripts/transcript.aspx?transcriptid=2097.

106. Quoted in Robert Jervis, "Understanding the Bush Doctrine," *PSQ* 118, no. 3 (Fall 2003): 368.

107. "Dr. Condoleezza Rice Delivers Remarks at Los Angeles Town Hall Breakfast," FDCH, July 12, 2003.

108. State Department Counselor Eliot Cohen, paraphrased in Rice, *No Higher Honor,* 636. On the Taliban resurgence, see Seth Jones, "The Rise of Afghanistan's Insurgency: State Failure and Jihad," *IS* 32, no. 4 (Spring 2008): 7–40.

109. The difficulties are discussed in Feith,*War and Decision,* 135–137. For a contrary view, see Peter Bergen, *The Longest War: The Enduring Conflict between America and al-Qaeda* (New York: Free Press, 2011), 81–85.

110. James Kunder, Deputy Assistant USAID Administrator for Asia and the Near East, "United States Policy in Afghanistan," FDCH Congressional Testimony, October 16, 2003.

111. Dov Zakheim, *A Vulcan's Tale: How the Bush Administration Mismanaged the Reconstruction of Afghanistan* (Washington, DC: Brookings Institution Press, 2011), 181.

112. Feith,*War and Decision,* 102.

113. *NSS* 2002.

114. "Remarks at the Virginia Military Institute in Lexington, Virginia," April 17, 2002, APP.

115. Troop levels are discussed in Seth Jones, *In the Graveyard of Empires: America's War in Afghanistan* (New York: W. W. Norton, 2009), 109–115.

116. Quoted in National Public Radio Transcript, "U.S. Troops in Afghanistan Being Cut," January 16, 2006, Lexis-Nexis. For the numbers and comparisons, see Bergen, *Longest War,* 180; Ahmed Rashid, *Descent into Chaos: The U.S. and the Disaster in Pakistan, Afghanistan, and Central Asia* (New York: Penguin, 2008), 189; Daalder and Lindsay, *America Unbound,* 112.

117. As of 2007, there were a total of forty-one thousand U.S. and NATO troops in Afghanistan. David Sanger, *The Inheritance: The World Obama Confronts and the Challenges to American Power* (New York: Harmony Books, 2009), 146. The number grew significantly after Barack Obama took office.

118. Quote and troop levels from David Rohde and David Sanger, "How a 'Good War' in Afghanistan Went Bad," *NYT,* August 12, 2007. See also James Dobbins, *After the Taliban: Nation-Building in Afghanistan* (Washington, DC: Potomac Books, 2008), 127–130; Jones, *Graveyard,* 109–114.

119. Bush, *Decision Points,* 207. On the fear of replicating the Soviet experience in Afghanistan, see Rumsfeld to Bush, August 20, 2002, RP; Donald Rumsfeld, *Known and Unknown* (New York: Penguin, 2011), 367–368; Michael Gordon and Eric Schmitt, "A War on a Small Scale, Possibly Long and Risky," *NYT,* September 29, 2001.

120. Rumsfeld, *Known and Unknown,* 407; also Zakheim, *Vulcan's Tale,* 129; Dobbins, *After the Taliban,* 124–125, 130.

121. "DoD News Briefing—Deputy Secretary Wolfowitz and Rear Adm. Stufflebeem," December 10, 2001, http://www.defense.gov/transcripts/transcript.aspx?transcriptid=2628.

122. Feith,*War and Decision,* 123, 218–219.

123. These broad themes are evident in Rumsfeld to Myers and Pace, October 10, 2001, RP; "Campaign against Terrorism: Strategic Guidance for the U.S. Department of Defense," October 2, 2001, RP; "Major Directional Decisions—9/11/01 et seq.," May 10, 2002, in Rumsfeld to Cheney, September 3, 2002, RP; Rumsfeld, *Known and Unknown,* 399.

124. The reassignments are discussed in Jones, *Graveyard,* 126.

125. Ibid., 112, 125–128.

126. Feith,*War and Decision,* 246.

127. Rohde and Sanger, "How a 'Good War' in Afghanistan Went Bad"; Jones, *Graveyard,* 127–129.

128. On this point, see Zakheim, *Vulcan's Tale,* 170–171; also Dobbins, *After the Taliban,* 134–135.

129. Quoted in Senate Armed Services Committee, "Hearing to Receive Testimony on the Strategy in Afghanistan and the Recent Reports by the Afghanistan Study Group and the Atlantic Council of the United States—Morning Session," February 14, 2008 (Washington, DC: Government Printing Office, 2008), 30; and Steven Simon, "The Iraq War and the War on Terror: The Global Jihad after Iraq," in *Balance Sheet: The Iraq War and U.S. National Security,* ed. John S. Duffield and Peter Dombrowski (Stanford, CA: Stanford University Press, 2009), 35.

130. Daniel Markey, "A False Choice in Pakistan," *FA* 86, no. 4 (July–August 2008): 92.

131. Zakheim, *Vulcan's Tale,* 211, 219–220; Rashid, *Descent,* 137–138; Jones, *Graveyard,* 128.

132. Quoted in "25 June 2003 Luncheon Meeting with President Musharraf at the Vice President's Residence," DOD FOIA; also Rashid, *Descent,* 125–144; Bergen, *Longest War,* 180–182.

133. Zakheim, *Vulcan's Tale,* 266–268.

134. Quote from Government Accountability Office, "Afghanistan Reconstruction: Despite Some Progress, Deteriorating Security and Other Obstacles Continue to Threaten Achievement of U.S. Goals," GAO 05–742, July 2005, 55.

135. Neumann to State, September 19, 2006. This cable was part of a large document release in late 2010 and can be accessed at www.cablegatesearch.net.

136. Sanger, *Inheritance,* 146.

137. Julian E. Barnes, "U.S. Calls Iraq the Priority," *Los Angeles Times,* December 12, 2007.

138. Bergen, *Longest War,* 194.

139. "Rumsfeld Notes for Briefing with Franks," November 27, 2001, EBB 326, NSA.

140. Because of discrepancies in counting methods, estimates of troop levels vary considerably. A good guide is Amy Belasco, "Troop Levels in the Afghan and Iraq Wars, FY2001–FY2012: Costs and Other Potential Issues (Washington, DC: Congressional Research Service, July 2009), esp. 35, 64–66. On the course of the war, see Williamson Murray and Robert H. Scales, *The Iraq War: A Military History* (Cambridge, MA: Harvard University Press, 2003).

141. Quoted in Charles J. Hanley, "Has Civil War Begun? As Experts Weigh What's Happening in Iraq, Baghdadis Just Know Things Are Getting Worse," *Houston Chronicle,* March 16, 2006. See also Anderson, *Bush's Wars,* 196–199.

142. See Gause, *International Relations,* 168, 171–174; Frederic Wehrey, Dalia Dassa Kaye, Jessica Watkins, Jeffrey Martin, and Robert A. Guffey, *The Iraq Effect: The Middle East after the Iraq War* (Santa Monica, CA: RAND Corporation, 2010), passim, esp. xi–xiii, 21–28, 79–83, 95–101.

143. Quoted in Dana Priest, "Iraq New Terror Breeding Ground," *WP,* January 14, 2005.

144. The quote is from an intelligence official familiar with the document, cited in Mark Mazzetti, "Spy Agencies Say Iraq War Worsens Terrorism Threat," *NYT,* September 24, 2006.

145. Bergen, *Longest War,* 172.

146. Quoted in Mazzetti, "Spy Agencies"; also National Intelligence Council, "Trends in Global Terrorism: Implications for the United States," April 2006, www.dni.gov/nic/special_global_terrorism.html.

147. "Foreign Press Center Briefing with Douglas Feith, Undersecretary of Defense for Policy," October 8, 2002, FNS; also Feith, *War and Decision,* 140, 169–177.

148. *Report of the Defense Science Board Task Force on Strategic Communication* (Washington, DC: Office of the Under Secretary of Defense for Acquisition, Technology, and Logistics, 2004), 40–41.

149. Rumsfeld to Hadley, February 6, 2006, RP.

150. F. Gregory Gause, "The Iraq War and American National Security Interests in the Middle East," in Duffield and Dombrowski, *Balance Sheet,* 76.

151. Quotes in Wehrey et al., *Iraq Effect,* xv, 7.

152. The figures are from Elisabeth Bumiller, "The Cost: White House Cuts Estimate of Cost of War with Iraq," *NYT,* December 31, 2002; James Glanz, "The Economic Cost of War," *NYT,* February 28, 2009; "U.S. CBO Estimates $2.4 Trillion Long-Term War Costs," Reuters, October 24, 2007; Linda Bilmes and Joseph Stiglitz, *The Three Trillion Dollar War: The True Cost of the Iraq Conflict* (New York: W. W. Norton, 2008); Mike Dorning, "Iraq War Lives on as Second-Costliest U.S. Conflict Fuels Debt," *Business Week,* January 3, 2012.

153. Quoted in Bob Woodward, "Secret Reports Dispute White House Optimism," *WP,* October 1, 2006; Larry Diamond, *Squandered Victory: The American Occupation and the Bungled Effort to Bring Democracy to Iraq* (New York: Times Books, 2005), 279. See also Daniel Byman, "An Autopsy of the Iraq Debacle: Policy Failure or Bridge Too Far?" *Security Studies* 17, no. 4 (2008): 599–643, esp. 619–633; Nora Bensahel et al., *After Saddam: Prewar Planning and the Occupation of Iraq* (Santa Monica, CA: RAND Corporation, 2008), passim.

154. See James Fallows, *Blind into Baghdad: America's War in Iraq* (New York: Random House, 2006), 43–106.

155. Matthew Rycroft to David Manning, July 23, 2002, EBB 328, NSA.

156. Feith, *War and Decision,* 317.

157. See Special Inspector General, *Hard Lessons,* 13, 31–32; Bensahel et al., *After Saddam,* xvii–xx; 9, 50–66; Fallows, *Blind into Baghdad,* 61–69.

158. See George Packer, *The Assassin's Gate: America in Iraq* (New York: Farrar, Straus and Giroux, 2005), 124–125; Bensahel et al., *After Saddam,* esp. xx–xxi.

159. Lorne Craner, Arthur Dewey, and Paul Simons to Under Secretary Dobriansky, February 7, 2003, EBB 163, NSA.

160. On this dynamic, see Gideon Rose, *How Wars End: Why We Always Fight the Last Battle* (New York: Simon & Schuster, 2011), 263–265.

161. Rice, *No Higher Honor,* 238.

162. Rumsfeld, *Known and Unknown,* 487; also Byman, "Autopsy," 629–630; James Dobbins, Seth Jones, Benjamin Runkle, and Siddharth Mohandas, *Occupying Iraq: A History of the Coalition Provisional Authority* (Santa Monica, CA: RAND Corporation, 2009), xix–xxi, xxxv–xxxvi, 31, 40, 294.

163. Zakheim, *Vulcan's Tale,* 295.

164. Quoted in Dan Caldwell, *Vortex of Conflict: U.S. Policy toward Afghanistan, Pakistan, and Iraq* (Stanford, CA: Stanford University Press, 2011), 87.

165. Bush-Aznar MemCon, February 22, 2003.

166. See Shanker, "New Strategy Vindicates Ex-Army Chief Shinseki."

167. Quoted in Paul Pillar, *Intelligence and U.S. Foreign Policy: Iraq, 9/11, and Misguided Reform* (New York: Columbia University Press, 2011), 54; also Packer, *Assassin's Gate,* 124–125.

168. Quoted in Deputy Secretary of Defense Paul Wolfowitz, "Testimony as Delivered to the Senate Armed Services Committee: Helping Win the War on Terror," September 9, 2003, http://www.defense.gov/speeches/speech.aspx?speechid=527.

169. See Bush-Aznar MemCon, February 22, 2003; "Vice President Dick Cheney Discusses a Possible War with Iraq," March 16, 2003, NBC News Transcripts, Lexis-Nexis. To their credit, State Department and CIA officials warned—correctly—that democratizing Iraq would not be so easy. See Haass, *War of Necessity,* 255, 279–294.

170. The $1.7 billion figure comes from Special Inspector General, *Hard Lessons,* 51.

171. "Secretary of Defense Donald Rumsfeld Radio Town Hall Meeting on Infinity CBS Radio Connect," November 14, 2002, FNS.

172. Steven Metz, *Iraq and the Evolution of American Strategy* (Washington, DC: Potomac Books, 2008), 98.

173. CIA, "The Postwar Occupations of Germany and Japan: Implications for Iraq," August 7, 2002, EBB 328, NSA.

174. George Tenet, *At the Center of the Storm: My Years at the CIA* (New York: HarperCollins, 2007), 493.

175. "Remarks to Employees at the Boeing F-18 Production Facility in St. Louis, Missouri," April 16, 2003, APP.

176. Rumsfeld, "Iraq: An Illustrative List of Potential Problems to Be Considered and Addressed," October 15, 2002, RP.

177. "Remarks by Vice President Cheney at the Opening Session of the 103rd National Convention of the Veterans of Foreign Wars," August 26, 2002, FNS.

178. See Ricks, *Fiasco,* 58–84.

179. On this point, see Metz, *Iraq,* 86.

180. Rumsfeld to Bush and others, September 19, 2001, RP.

181. Woodward, *Bush at War,* 42.

182. The memo is reproduced in Feith, *War and Decision,* 295–298, quoted at 296.

183. Quoted in Robert Kagan, "America's Crisis of Legitimacy," *FA* 83, no. 2 (March–April 2004): 69.

184. Quoted in Mike Allen and Susan Glasser, "Bush Urges an Alliance against Terror," *WP,* June 1, 2003.

185. On the origins of the surge, see Thomas Ricks, *The Gamble: General David Petraeus and the American Military Adventure in Iraq, 2006–2008* (New York: Penguin, 2009); Steven Metz, *Decisionmaking in Operation Iraqi Freedom: The Strategic Shift of 2007* (Carlisle Barracks, PA: Strategic Studies Institute, 2010); also Peter Feaver, "The Right to Be Right: Civil Military Relations and the Iraq Surge Decision," *IS* 35, no. 4 (Spring 2011): 87–125. Different observers give different estimates of the total number of surge troops. The range comes largely from differences in whether one counts only combat troops or whether one includes support troops as well. The number cited above includes the latter, and is drawn from Belasco, "Troop Levels," 35.

See also Brookings Institution, *Iraq Index: Tracking Variables of Reconstruction and Security in Post-Saddam Iraq,* September 27, 2007, www.brookings.edu/iraqindex.

186. Quoted in Fred W. Baker III, "Petraeus, Crocker Finish Marathon of Testimony," American Forces Press Service, April 9, 2008, http://www.defense.gov/news/newsarticle.aspx?id=49522. See also Ricks, *Gamble,* 163–165.

187. Stephen Biddle, Jeffrey Friedman, and Jacob Shapiro, "Testing the Surge: Why Did Violence Decline in Iraq in 2007?" *IS* 37, no. 1 (Summer 2012): 1–34, esp. 1.

188. Government Accountability Office, *Security, Stabilizing, and Rebuilding Iraq: Progress Report: Some Gains Made, Updated Strategy Needed* (Washington, DC: GAO, 2008), executive summary.

189. Sanger, *Inheritance.*

190. See Robert Lieber, "Staying Power and the American Future: Problems of Primacy, Policy, and Grand Strategy," *Journal of Strategic Studies* 34, no. 3 (Fall 2011): 509–530.

191. Bruce Jentleson and Christopher Whytock, "Who 'Won' Libya? The Force-Diplomacy Debate and Its Implications for Theory and Policy," *IS* 30, no. 3 (Winter 2005–06): 62–77, quoted at 75.

192. On the North Korean arsenal, see Bruce Bechtol Jr., *Defiant Failed State: The North Korean Threat to International Security* (Washington, DC: Potomac Books, 2010), 95–96.

193. Rumsfeld to Bush, Cheney, and Hadley, October 5, 2006, DOD FOIA.

194. See Donette Murray, *U.S. Foreign Policy and Iran: American-Iranian Relations since the Islamic Revolution* (New York: Routledge, 2010), 120–122; Trita Parsi, *Treacherous Alliance: The Secret Dealings of Israel, Iran, and the United States* (New Haven, CT: Yale University Press, 2007), 240–244, 253.

195. Quoted in Flynt Leverett, *Dealing with Tehran: Assessing U.S. Diplomatic Options toward Iran* (New York: Century Foundation, 2006), 12; Sanger, *Inheritance,* 49, 302; see also Murray, *U.S. Foreign Policy and Iran,* 126–128; Ray Takeyh, *Hidden Iran: Power and Paradox in the Islamic Republic* (New York: Times Books, 2006), 127–129; Parsi, *Treacherous Alliance,* 240–244.

196. Leverett, *Dealing,* 13.

197. On this point, see Joel S. Wit, Daniel Poneman, and Robert L. Gallucci, *Going Critical: The First North Korean Nuclear Crisis* (Washington, DC: Brookings Institution Press, 2005), 372. In fairness, the United States had also failed to live up to its commitments under the accord.

198. Quoted in Brands, *Berlin to Baghdad,* 304; Mike Chinoy, *Meltdown: The Inside Story of the North Korean Nuclear Crisis* (New York: St. Martin's Press, 2008), 95. The administration did reluctantly agree to multilateral talks involving China and then several other regional players.

199. Chinoy, *Meltdown,* 95, 138–139, 158–159, 178–180, 197; Rumsfeld, *Known and Unknown,* 642.

200. Michael Green, "The Iraq War and Asia: Assessing the Legacy," *WQ* 31, no. 2 (2008): 192.

201. Sanger, *Inheritance,* 283.

202. Chinoy, *Meltdown,* chaps. 13–18.

203. National Intelligence Council (NIC), "Regional Consequences of Regime Change in Iraq," ICA-2003–03, January 2003, reproduced in Senate Select Committee

on Intelligence, *Report on Prewar Intelligence Assessments about Postwar Iraq* (Washington, DC: Government Printing Office, 2007). The quote is from p. 7 of the NIC estimate.

204. See Marshall to Rumsfeld, May 2, 2002, RP; also Khalilzad to Rumsfeld, January 2, 2001, RP.

205. Quoted in Peter Hays Gries, "China Eyes the Hegemon," *Orbis* 116, no. 3 (Summer 2005): 406; John W. Garver, "Is China Playing a Dual Game in Iran?" *WQ* 34, no. 1 (Winter 2011): 79.

206. On this point, see Aaron Friedberg, *A Contest for Supremacy: China, America, and the Struggle for Mastery in Asia* (New York: W. W. Norton, 2011).

207. See the Pentagon's annual reports to Congress on Chinese military power, http://www.defense.gov/pubs/china.html. The figure is from "Background Paper on SIPRI Military Expenditure Data, 2010," 2.

208. Quoted in Office of the Secretary of Defense, *Military Power of the People's Republic of China: 2008* (Washington, DC: Department of Defense, 2008), 23.

209. Kurt M. Campbell, Nirav Patel, and Richard Weitz, *The Ripple Effect: China's Responses to the Iraq War* (Washington. DC: Center for a New American Security, 2008), 25. As evidence, the authors cite statistics showing that the Chinese buildup slowed somewhat in 2003 (the last year for which planning would have been completed prior to the invasion of Iraq) and then accelerated again after that.

210. Christopher Twomey, "Missing Strategic Opportunity in U.S. China Policy since 9/11: Grasping Tactical Success," *Asian Survey* 47, no. 4 (July/August 2007): 550.

211. Quoted in Jonathan Holslag, *Trapped Giant: China's Military Rise* (London: International Institute for Strategic Studies, 2010), 7.

212. Melvyn Leffler, "9/11 in Retrospect: George W. Bush's Grand Strategy, Reconsidered" *FA* 90, no. 5 (September/October 2011): 38.

213. Feith, *War and Decision,* 297.

214. Rice, *No Higher Honor,* 734.

215. Derek Chollet and James Goldgeier, "Good Riddance to the Bush Doctrine," *WP,* July 13, 2008.

216. The difficulty of determining why another major attack did not occur on Bush's watch is discussed in Dallas Boyd, Lewis Dunn, and James Scouras, "Why Has the United States Not Been Attacked Again?" *WQ* 32, no. 3 (June 2009): 3–19. See also Bergen, *Longest War,* 244–246. It is also worth noting that Bush invested heavily in drone warfare and other technologies put to good use by the Obama administration.

Conclusion

1. Henry Kissinger, *White House Years* (Boston: Little, Brown, 1979), 54.

2. Stephen Krasner, "An Orienting Principle for Foreign Policy: The Deficiencies of 'Grand Strategy,'" *Policy Review,* no. 163 (October 2010): 4. Two other observers have mocked grand strategy as "grand flattery," the idea being that policy makers flatter themselves to think that they are capable of imposing order on a disorderly world. Thomas Meany and Stephen Wertheim, "Grand Flattery: The Yale Grand Strategy Seminar," *Nation,* May 28, 2012, 27–31.

3. These suggestions are distilled from the analysis in the foregoing chapters, as well as from a broader analytical engagement with the dilemmas of grand strategy.

4. Krasner, "Orienting Principle," 9.

5. Derek Chollet and James Goldgeier, "Good Riddance to the Bush Doctrine," *WP,* July 13, 2008. See also Fareed Zakaria, "Stop Searching for an Obama Doctrine," *WP,* July 6, 2011. For earlier skepticism regarding grand strategy, see Robert Jervis, "U.S. Grand Strategy: Mission Impossible," *Naval War College Review* 51, no. 5 (Summer 1998): 22–36; and Sandy Berger's comments in R. W. Apple, "A Domestic Sort with Global Worries," *NYT,* August 25, 1999.

6. Goldgeier worked for the State Department and National Security Council during the mid-1990s. Chollet has now held several national security positions at the NSC, State Department, and Pentagon.

7. See Michael J. Gallagher, Joshua A. Geltzer, and Sebastian L. V. Gorka, "The Complexity Trap," *Parameters* 42, no. 1 (Spring 2012): 9.

8. The phrase is taken from Richard K. Betts, "Is Strategy an Illusion?" *IS* 25, no. 2 (Fall 2000): 16. A critique of grand strategy that flirts with strategic nihilism is Meany and Wertheim, "Grand Flattery."

9. Quoted in Robert Bowie and Richard Immerman, *Waging Peace: How Eisenhower Shaped an Enduring Cold War Strategy* (New York: Oxford University Press, 2000), vii.

10. As noted in the previous chapter, this was a problem that the Clinton administration ran into in dealing with an uncertain international environment during the 1990s. "We do have a set of priorities that have been established by Presidential Decision Directive that basically looks at the world and says that there are 10 or 15 things that matter most to American security," CIA Director Tenet told the Senate Select Committee on Intelligence in 1997. Tenet (and presumably Clinton) neglected to consider that having fifteen top priorities was probably equivalent to having zero top priorities. See Brands, *Berlin to Baghdad,* 202.

11. Leslie H. Gelb, *Power Rules: How Common Sense Can Rescue American Foreign Policy* (New York: HarperCollins, 2009), 243.

12. See Stephan B. Seabrook, "Federal Spending, National Priorities, and Grand Strategy," RAND Corporation Working Paper, April 2012. This will particularly be the case if federal revenues do not increase markedly.

13. On the case for offshore balancing, see Christopher Layne, *The Peace of Illusions: American Grand Strategy from 1940 to the Present* (Ithaca, NY: Cornell University Press, 2006), chap. 8. For a full-throated defense of primacy, see Robert Kagan, *The World America Made* (New York: Alfred A. Knopf, 2012).

14. This issue is stressed in Adam Grissom, "What Is Grand Strategy? Reframing the Debate on American Ends, Ways, and Means," RAND Corporation Working Paper, April 2012.

15. See Aaron L. Friedberg, "Strengthening U.S. Strategic Planning," *WQ* 31, no. 1 (2007): 47–60; also Richard Danzig, *Driving in the Dark: Ten Propositions about Prediction and National Security* (Washington, DC: Center for a New American Security, 2011).

16. There are certainly exceptions to this rule, but even policy makers who were renowned for their intuition and instinct—Reagan, for instance, or Kissinger—had

spent years refining their ideas on foreign policy. In a way, they had engaged in something of a personal planning process before coming to power.

17. There are, of course, various ways of approaching this challenge. What is most important is that presidents and cabinet-level officials are aware of the need to integrate planning and policy in some systematic form, and that they are willing to spend bureaucratic capital to make it happen. For one useful discussion of this issue, see Bruce Jentleson and Andrew Bennett, "Policy Planning: Oxymoron or Sine Qua Non for U.S. Foreign Policy?" in *Good Judgment in Foreign Policy: Theory and Application,* ed. Stanley Allen Renshon and Deborah Welch Larson (New York: Rowman & Littlefield, 2003), 219–246.

18. Kissinger, *White House Years,* 48.

19. Richard Haass, "Planning for Policy Planning," in *Avoiding Trivia: The Role of Strategic Planning in American Foreign Policy,* ed. Daniel W. Drezner (Washington, DC: Brookings Institution Press, 2009), 26.

20. For criticism of the *NSS,* see Stephen Walt, "Snoozing through the National Security Strategy," *ForeignPolicy.com,* May 28, 2010 (accessed September 15, 2012); Barry Watts, *Why Strategy? The Case for Taking It Seriously and Doing It Well* (Washington, DC: Center for Strategic and Budgetary Assessments, 2007).

21. The Reagan administration did prepare what was essentially a classified version of its *National Security Strategy,* but it seems to have been the historical exception rather than the rule in this regard. Prior to 1986 (when the Goldwater-Nichols Act was passed), presidential administrations had periodically prepared similar reports: NSC-68 in 1950, for instance, or the annual reports on foreign policy prepared by Kissinger's staff between 1970 and 1973. These reports were not, however, mandated by law.

22. See Zakaria, "Stop Searching for an Obama Doctrine."

23. See Thom Shanker and Helene Cooper, "Doctrine for Libya: Not Carved in Stone," *NYT,* March 29, 2011; Brad Knickerbocker, "With Libya, Is 'Obama Doctrine' on War Emerging?" *Christian Science Monitor,* March 19, 2011.

24. On emergent and deliberate strategy, see Henry Mintzberg, *Tracking Strategies: Toward a General Theory* (New York: Oxford University Press, 2007).

25. See Sarah Kaplan and Eric Beinhocker, "The Real Value of Strategic Planning," *Sloan Management Review* 44, no. 2 (Winter 2003): 72.

26. Andrew P. N. Erdmann, "Foreign Policy Planning through a Private Sector Lens," in Drezner, *Avoiding Trivia,* 159–151, quoted at 151.

27. Isaiah Berlin, *The Hedgehog and the Fox: An Essay on Tolstoy's View of History* (Chicago: Ivan R. Dee, 1993).

28. Dov Zakheim, *A Vulcan's Tale: How the Bush Administration Mismanaged the Reconstruction of Afghanistan* (Washington, DC: Brookings Institution Press, 2011), 294. Also useful on this subject is Clark Murdock and Kevin Kallmyer, "Applied Grand Strategy: Making Tough Choices in an Era of Limits and Constraint," *Orbis* 55, no. 4 (Fall 2011): 541–557.

29. On this general idea, see Erdmann, "Foreign Policy Planning," esp. 151.

30. Quoted in Miroslav Nincic, *Democracy and Foreign Policy: The Fallacy of Political Realism* (New York: Columbia University Press, 1994), 3.

31. MemCon between Kissinger, Dean Rusk, Cyrus Vance, McGeorge Bundy, et al., March 31, 1975, box 22, HAK Records, RG 59, NARA.

32. See John Lewis Gaddis, *We Now Know: Rethinking Cold War History* (New York: Oxford University Press, 1998), esp. 288–291.

33. One could make the same point about the Bush administration and the Iraq War. The administration's exaggeration of the intelligence regarding Saddam's WMD played well in the run-up to war, but when the weapons turned out to be nonexistent, the result was a severe erosion of Bush's credibility.

34. For more on this, see point no. 7, below.

35. See chaps. 3 and 5. On the Bush years, see also Steven Metz, *Decision-Making in Operation Iraqi Freedom: Removing Saddam Hussein by Force* (Carlisle Barracks, PA: Strategic Studies Institute, 2010), esp. 7–8, 17–19.

36. The literature on these subjects is immense. As one perspective, see Meena Bose, *Shaping and Signaling Presidential Policy* (College Station: Texas A&M University Press, 1998).

37. Peter Feaver, "Debating American Grand Strategy after Major War," *Orbis* 53, no. 4 (Fall 2009): 549; also Feaver, "8 Myths about American Grand Strategy," November 23, 2011, http://shadow.foreignpolicy.com/posts/2011/11/23/8_myths_about_american_grand_strategy. This idea is further developed in Hal Brands and Peter Feaver, "Common Fallacies and Uncommon Fixes in the American Grand Strategy Debate," RAND Corporation Working Paper, September 2012.

38. Motivated by all that had gone wrong during its first term, the Bush administration sought to establish just such a "second-guessing" capability during its second. Among the responsibilities of the Strategic Planning and Institutional Reform cell were "retrospective studies" and "internal critiques" of existing policy lines. See Peter Feaver and William Inboden, "A Strategic Planning Cell on National Security at the White House," in Drezner, *Avoiding Trivia,* 98–109.

39. Murdock and Kallmyer, "Applied Grand Strategy," 551.

40. George Kennan, "Where Do We Stand?" NWC Lecture, December 21, 1949, box 299, GFKP, SMML.

INDEX

Able Archer crisis, 104, 124
ABM (antiballistic missile) system, 69
ABM Treaty, 79, 80, 150
Acheson, Dean: on China and Southeast
Asia, 37–38, 40–41, 44; on defensive
perimeter concept, 36, 41, 47; on grand
strategy, 4, 46, 54; and Indochina, 39–40,
44, 55; and Korean War, 48, 49, 51, 52;
and Middle East, 53, 55; on military
budget in late 1940s, 43; on NATO, 42;
and peace treaty with Japan, 52; and
South Korea, 40, 216n74; and Taiwan,
40–41, 48, 216n71; on Truman's containment policy, 17; as undersecretary of
state after World War II, 24; and West
Germany, 43, 52; on World War II's
impact, 19
Adams, John Quincy, 15
Afghanistan: and al-Qaeda, 145, 153–54,
165, 166, 169; bin Laden's escape from,
165; Carter's policy on, 106; casualties
from U.S. war against, 153; CIA in, 113;
goal of U.S. invasion of, 153, 169; Gorbachev's plan for coalition government
in, 141–42; initial victory of U.S. in, 153,
176, 178; new government in, following fall of Taliban, 153, 165, 167, 169,
170; Northern Alliance in, 153; Reagan's
policy on, 106, 113, 120, 130, 134, 135,
141–42; Soviet invasion of, 105, 106,
117, 120, 122, 128, 129, 130; Soviet
withdrawal from, 126, 127, 134, 135,
141–42; and Taliban, 142, 145, 151, 153,
165–69; U.S. and NATO peacekeep-
ing troops in, 166–70; U.S. support for
mujahideen in, 106, 113, 120, 134, 135,
141–42; U.S. war against and minimalist postwar reconstruction of, 153–54,
165–71, 187, 191
Agriculture Department, U.S., 83
Albright, Madeleine, 148
Allende, Salvador, 75, 91–92

al-Qaeda: in Afghanistan, 145, 153–54,
165, 166, 169; in Iraq, 171, 181; and
Iraq War, 172; 9/11 attacks by, 157; U.S.
attention to, before 9/11, 152, 188; U.S.
war on terror against, 151, 152, 156–60,
172, 173
al-Sadr, Muqtada, 181
Andropov, Yuri, 105, 120–23, 125, 126
Angola, 75, 81, 82, 85, 90–91, 135, 192
anthrax attacks, 152, 158
Arab oil embargo, 95
Arabs. *See* Middle East
Arab Spring, 194, 198
Argentina, 98, 113
Armitage, Richard, 168
arms control: Bush and his campaign
advisers ("the Vulcans") on, 149–50;
and Comprehensive Test Ban Treaty,
149; and Gorbachev, 126–33; Reagan's
policy on, 108, 111, 117, 122, 125–33;
and West Germany, 133. *See also* nuclear
weapons
Arnold, Henry (Hap), 208n23
Asia. *See* Southeast Asia; *and specific countries*
atomic bombs. *See* nuclear weapons
Australia, 52
Austria, 33
Aznar, José María, 176

Berlin airlift, 34, 41
bin Laden, Osama, 152, 159, 165
Bismarck, Otto von, 63
"Blackhawk Down" disaster, 148
Bohlen, Charles, 35, 47, 50
Bosnia, 147, 148, 166
botulinum toxin scare, 152
Bradley, Omar, 47, 51–52
Brandt, Willy, 222n46
Brazil, 65, 73, 74, 91, 93
Bremer, L. Paul, 175
Breslauer, George W., 138
Bretton Woods system, 64

weapons of mass destruction (WMD): authoritarianism linked with, 161–62; consequences of Iraq War for development of, 185; and Iran, 157, 158; and Iraq, 145, 157–60, 171, 178, 179, 259n33; and Libya, 157, 182–83, 188; and North Korea, 157, 158; Proliferation Security Initiative against, 182; and terrorism generally, 145, 152, 156, 157–58. *See also* nuclear weapons
wedge strategy, 37–38, 44
Weinberger, Caspar, 110–12, 117, 123, 126, 131, 237n69
Western Europe: Communist parties in, 25, 32; Marshall Plan for, 18, 26–29, 31–36, 39, 41, 43, 57; recovery of, from postwar devastation, 54; and third-force concept, 29, 34, 214n57. *See also* NATO; *and specific countries*
West Germany: and arms control, 133; economy of, 65; formation of, 35; military vulnerability of, in late 1940s, 43; *Ostpolitik* of, 222n46; and Pershing IIs, 124, 125; and Reagan's policy on Soviet Union, 116–17; rearmament of, 48, 52, 55–56; rehabilitation of, 35, 54,

57; Truman's policy on, 18, 43. *See also* Germany
Wilson, James Graham, 233n5
WMD. *See* weapons of mass destruction (WMD)
Wolfowitz, Paul: on Afghanistan war, 167; as Bush's adviser, 149, 150, 153; and confronting state sponsors of terrorism, 157; on defense planning, 149; and Iraq War, 176; on Saddam Hussein, 159, 160; on terrorism, 161
Woolsey, James, 146
World War I, 9
World War II, 18–20

Yeltsin, Boris, 147
Yetiv, Steve, 14
Yom Kippur War, 75–76, 81, 82, 93–95, 96, 100
Yugoslavia, 34, 37, 41, 52

Zakheim, Dov, 166, 169, 170, 175
Zhou Enlai, 63, 71, 79–80, 87
Zia-ul-Haq, Muhammad, 141
Zumwalt, Elmo, 97